Intercultural Communication

An advanced resource book for students

Third edition

Adrian Holliday, John Kullman and Martin Hyde

Routledge
Taylor & Francis Group

LONDON AND NEW YORK

Third edition published 2017
by Routledge
2 Park Square, Milton Park, Abingdon, Oxon OX14 4RN

and by Routledge
711 Third Avenue, New York, NY 10017

Routledge is an imprint of the Taylor & Francis Group, an informa business

First edition published 2004 by Routledge
Second edition published 2010 by Routledge

British Library Cataloguing-in-Publication Data
A catalogue record for this book is available from the British Library

Library of Congress Cataloging-in-Publication Data
Names: Holliday, Adrian, author. | Hyde, Martin, 1960- author. | Kullman, John, 1957– author.
Title: Intercultural communication : an advanced resource book for students / Adrian Holliday, Martin Hyde and John Kullman.
Description: Third Edition. | Milton Park, Abingdon, Oxon ; New York, NY : Routledge, [2016] | Includes bibliographical references and index.
Identifiers: LCCN 2016015799 | ISBN 9781138183629 (hardback) | ISBN 9781138183636 (pbk.) | ISBN 9781315460659 (ebook)
Subjects: LCSH: Intercultural communication.
Classification: LCC P94.6 .H64 2016 | DDC 302.2–dc23
LC record available at https://lccn.loc.gov/2016015799

ISBN: 978-1-138-18362-9 (hbk)
ISBN: 978-1-138-18363-6 (pbk)
ISBN: 978-1-315-46065-9 (ebk)

Typeset in Akzidenz Grotesk, Minion and Novarese
by Keystroke, Neville Lodge, Tettenhall, Wolverhampton

Extra resources on this subject can be found at http://www.routledgetextbooks.com/textbooks/languageandcommunication

INTERCULTURAL COMMUNICATION

Routledge Applied Linguistics is a series of comprehensive textbooks, providing students and researchers with the support they need for advanced study in the core areas of English language and Applied Linguistics.

Each book in the series guides readers through three main sections, enabling them to explore and develop major themes within the discipline.

* Section A, Introduction, establishes the key terms and concepts and extends readers' techniques of analysis through practical application.
* Section B, Extension, brings together influential articles, sets them in context, and discusses their contribution to the field.
* Section C, Exploration, builds on knowledge gained in the first two sections, setting thoughtful tasks around further illustrative material. This enables readers to engage more actively with the subject matter and encourages them to develop their own research responses.

Throughout the book, topics are revisited, extended, interwoven and deconstructed, with the reader's understanding strengthened by tasks and follow-up questions.

This highly-successful text introduces and explores the dynamic area of intercultural communication, and the updated third edition features:

* new readings by Prue Holmes, Fred Dervin, Lei Guo and Summer Harlow, Miriam Sobré-Denton and Nilaniana Bardham, which reflect the most recent developments in the field
* refreshed and expanded examples and exercises including new material on the world of business, radicalisation and cultural fundamentalism
* extended discussion of topics which include cutting-edge material on cosmopolitanism, immigrants' intercultural communication and cultural travel
* revised further reading.

Written by experienced teachers and researchers in the field, *Intercultural Communication, Third Edition* provides an essential textbook for advanced students studying this topic.

Adrian Holliday is Professor of Applied Linguistics at Canterbury Christ Church University, UK. **John Kullman** is a Principal Lecturer in the Department of English and Language Studies at Canterbury Christ Church University, UK. **Martin Hyde** is Director of Operations for Student Recruitment and Events at PlattForm Education UK.

ROUTLEDGE APPLIED LINGUISTICS

SERIES EDITORS

The late **Christopher N. Candlin** was Series Editor of the *Routledge Applied Linguistics* series for over 15 years. He was a Senior Research Professor Emeritus in the Department of Linguistics at Macquarie University, Australia and Professor of Applied Linguistics at the Open University, UK. In his lifetime, he wrote or edited over 150 publications. From 1996 to 2002 he was President of the International Association of Applied Linguistics (AILA), and he also acted as a consultant in more than 35 countries and as external faculty assessor in 36 universities worldwide. He was made Officer of the Order of Australia in 2015 for his services to Higher Education.

Ronald Carter is Research Professor of Modern English Language at the University of Nottingham, UK. He has published extensively in the fields of applied linguistics, corpus linguistics and literature and language in education and is the author, co-author and editor of over 40 books and one hundred articles in these fields. Professor Carter is a fellow of the British Academy of Social Sciences and has been a chair of BAAL (British Association for Applied Linguistics). He was awarded an MBE in 2009 for services to education and in 2013 received an honorary doctorate (DUniv) from the Open University for his contributions to the field of applied linguistics. He has edited five series in English Language and Applied Linguistics for Routledge.

TITLES IN THE SERIES

Intercultural Communication: An advanced resource book for students, 3rd edition
Adrian Holliday, John Kullman and Martin Hyde

Pragmatics: An advanced resource book for students
Dawn Archer, Karin Aijmer and Anne Wichmann

Research Methods for Applied Language Studies: An advanced resource book for students
Keith Richards, Steven John Ross and Paul Seedhouse

Language and Interaction: An advanced resource book
Richard F. Young

Literacy: An advanced resource book for students
Brian V. Street and Adam Lefstein

Bilingualism: An advanced resource book
Ng Bee Chin and Gillian Wigglesworth

Language Testing and Assessment: An advanced resource book
Glenn Fulcher and Fred Davidson

Translation: An advanced resource book, 2nd edition (forthcoming)
Basil A. Hatim and Jeremy Munday

We would like to dedicate this volume to the memory of Chris Candlin for a lifetime of inspiration.

Contents

Contents cross-referenced

othering

*create vt for each persons
point in each theme
→ microsoft pwrpt shared?*

create vt for each persons

*○ individuals do pieces of
each theme*

this week ←

next week 10

4/1

next week 11

4/11

checkpoint for readings

presentation due: 4/27 (T)

Illustrations

FIGURES

TABLES

Series editors' preface

The Routledge Applied Linguistics series provides a comprehensive guide to a number of key areas in the field of applied linguistics. Applied linguistics is a rich, vibrant, diverse and essentially interdisciplinary field. It is now more important than ever that books in the field provide up-to-date maps of what is an ever-changing territory.

The books in this series are designed to give key insights into core areas of applied linguistics. The design of the books ensures, through key readings, that the history and development of a subject is recognized while, through key questions and tasks, integrating understandings of the topics, concepts and practices that make up its essentially interdisciplinary fabric. The pedagogic structure of each book ensures that readers are given opportunities to think, discuss, engage in tasks, draw on their own experience, reflect, research and to read and critically re-read key documents. Each book has three main sections, each made up of approximately ten units.

A: An **Introduction** section: in which the key terms and concepts which map the field of the subject are introduced, including introductory activities and reflective tasks, designed to establish key understandings, terminology, techniques of analysis and the skills appropriate to the theme and the discipline.

B: An **Extension** section: in which selected core readings are introduced (usually edited from the original) from existing key books and articles, together with annotations and commentary, where appropriate. Each reading is introduced, annotated and commented on in the context of the whole book, and research/follow-up questions and tasks are added to enable fuller understanding of both theory and practice. In some cases, readings are short and synoptic and incorporated within a more general exposition.

C: An **Exploration** section: in which further samples and illustrative materials are provided with an emphasis, where appropriate, on more open-ended, student-centred activities and tasks designed to support readers and users in undertaking their own locally relevant research projects. Tasks are designed for work in groups or for individuals working on their own. They can be readily included in award courses in applied linguistics or as topics for personal study and research.

The target audience for the series is upper undergraduates and postgraduates on language, applied linguistics and communication studies programmes as well as teachers and researchers in professional development and distance learning programmes. High-quality applied research resources are also much needed for teachers of EFL/ESL and foreign language students at higher education colleges and universities worldwide. The books in the Routledge Applied Linguistics series are aimed at the individual reader, the student in a group and at teachers building courses and seminar programmes.

We hope that the books in this series meet these needs and continue to provide support over many years.

THE EDITORS

The late Professor Christopher N. Candlin and Professor Ronald Carter are the series editors. Both have extensive experience of publishing titles in the fields relevant to this series. Between them they have written and edited over one hundred books and two hundred academic papers in the broad field of applied linguistics. Chris Candlin was president of AILA (International Association for Applied Linguistics) from 1996 to 2002 and Ron Carter was chair of BAAL (British Association for Applied Linguistics) from 2003 to 2006.

Professor Christopher N. Candlin   Professor Ronald Carter
Formerly at the Department of Linguistics School of English Studies
Macquarie University   University of Nottingham

and

Faculty of Education and Language Studies
The Open University

Acknowledgements

The editors and publishers wish to thank the following for permission to use copyright material.

John Wiley & Sons Inc for material from R. Scollon and S. Wong Scollon, 'Discourse and intercultural communication' in D. Schiffrin, D. Tannen and H. E. Hamilton (eds) (2001) *The Handbook of Discourse Analysis*; C. Roberts and S. Sarangi (2005) 'Theme-oriented discourse: analysis of medical encounters', *Medical Education* 39, pp. 632–40 and S. Rich and S. Troudi (2006) 'Hard times: Arab TESOL students' experiences of racialization and Othering in the United Kingdom', *TESOL Quarterly* 40/3, pp. 615–24

Cambridge University Press for material from Yoshio Sugimoto (1997) *An Introduction to Japanese Society*

Marshall Cavendish for material from Lee Su Kim (2011) *A Nyonya in Texas: Insights of a Straits Chinese Woman in the Lone Star State*

McGraw Hill for material from Teun A. van Dijk (2000) 'New(s) racism: a discourse analytical approach' in Simon Cottle (ed.) (2000) *Ethnic Minorities and the Media*, Chapter 2

Palgrave Macmillan for material from G. Moloney 'Social representations and the politically satirical cartoon: the construction and reproduction of the refugee and asylum-seeker identity' in G. Moloney and I. Walker (eds) (2007) *Social Representations and Identity: Content, Process and Power*; and Broelman and Nicholson for the accompanying cartoons

Sage Publications for material from U. Hannerz (1999) 'Reflections of varieties of culturespeak' in C. Mallinson and Z. W. Brewster (2005) '"Blacks and bubbas": stereotypes, ideology, and categorization processes in restaurant servers' discourse', *Discourse and Society* 16/6, pp. 787–807

Taylor and Francis Group Ltd. for material from J. N. Martin and T. K. Nakayama, 'Thinking dialectically about culture and communication' in M. K. Asante, Y. Miike and J. Yin (eds) (2008) *The Global Intercultural Communication Reader*; G. Matthews (2000) *Global Culture/Individual Identity: Searching for Home in the*

Cultural Supermarket; R. Dyer (1997) *White;* V. Burr (1996) *An Introduction to Social Constructionism*; S. E. Hampson 'The social psychology of personality' in C. Cooper and V. Varma (eds) (1997) *Processes in Individual Differences*, pp. 77–81; M. Sobré-Denton & N. Bardhan (2013) *Cultivating Cosmopolitanism for Intercultural Communication*; J. Verschueren (2008) 'Intercultural communication and the challenges of migration', *Language and Intercultural Communication* 8/1, pp. 21–35; M. Cooke (1997) 'Listen to the image speak', *Cultural Values*, 1/1, pp. 102–6; G. Shuck (2006) 'Racializing the nonnative English speaker', *Journal of Language Identity and Education* 5/4, pp. 259–76; T. Beaven (2007) 'A life in the sun: accounts of new lives abroad as intercultual narratives', *Language and Intercultural Communication*, 17/3, pp. 188–202; P. Holmes (2015) '"The cultural stuff around how to talk to people": immigrants' intercultural communication during a pre-employment work-placement', *Language and Intercultural Communication* 15/1, pp. 109–24; L. Guo and S. Harlow (2014) 'User-generated racism: an analysis of stereotypes of African Americans, Latinos, and Asians in YouTube videos', *Howard Journal of Communications* 25, pp. 281–302; F. Dervin (2014) 'Exploring "new" interculturality online', *Language and Intercultural Communication* 14/2, pp. 191–206; and A. Holliday (2016) 'Difference and awareness in cultural travel: negotiating blocks and threads', *Language and Intercultural Communication* 16/3, pp. 318–31.

University of Texas Press for material from J. R. Ribeyro (1972) 'Alienation' in *Palabra del Mudo*, trans. D. Douglas (1993) in *Marginal Voices*

Westview Press, a member of Perseus Books, LLC, for material from Harry C. Triandis (1995) *Individualism and Collectivism*, pp. 1–2, 4–5. Copyright © 1995 by Westview Press, a member of Perseus Books Group

Yale University Press for material from B. Kumaravadivelu (2008) *Cultural Globalization in Language Education*

While the publishers have made every effort to contact copyright holders of material used in this volume, they would be grateful to hear from any that they were unable to contact.

How to use this book

This third edition has the same structure and basic content as the first and second editions, but has been updated throughout and new material has been added with particular reference to recent theoretical perspectives. Section A has been updated throughout to accommodate new thinking. In Section B there are new texts published since the last edition.

The book is divided into three parts:

- *Section A. Defining concepts*, which aims to present concepts which will be the basis for study throughout the book
- *Section B. Extension*, which will develop and continue to explore these concepts in dialogue with a series of readings
- *Section C. Exploration*, which will realise the discussions of the first two parts within a series of research tasks, and which will establish a methodology for addressing intercultural communication.

Each part will also be divided into three *themes*:

- *Theme 1: Identity* deals with the way in which we all bring with us our own discourses and feelings of culture and negotiate these in communication.
- *Theme 2: Othering*, deals with a major hindrance to communication in the way in which we over-generalise, stereotype and reduce the people we communicate with to something different or less than they are.
- *Theme 3, Representation*, looks at the way in which culture is communicated in society, through the media, professional discourses and everyday language. It focuses on how we need critically to recognise and address the ways in which these representations influence our own perceptions if we are to communicate effectively.

It is a tenet of the book that the disciplines that are presented in the following Section A and applied to research tasks in Section C are usable in all intercultural communication contexts, and as it is argued, all communication is intercultural, and that this book is ultimately about developing skilled communication strategies and principles in a globalising world. Furthermore, the book is not based upon the principle that cultural differences exist as real and tangible entities, but are intersubjective and negotiated processes (admittedly affected by power structures).

There is therefore no attempt to offer a manual of prescribed cultural differences or exotic examples of cultural behaviours. The book therefore follows the principle that intercultural issues are universal to the extent that the details of particular cases have underlying features that can be generalised to other events and places.

For this reason, in this third edition, Section A has been edited throughout and the examples used have been stripped of reference to particular countries and nationalities. This follows the practice in Holliday (2011, 2013). Furthermore, references to Middle Eastern settings in the previous two editions have now become dated in a rapidly changing world. To make such references would indeed to be to enter into the process of Othering, decried as a major problem in intercultural communication in the world today. Section B has also been brought up-to-date with new thinking, with five new texts, and rewritten and extended commentaries throughout. Section C has also been updated and edited throughout to further make the book more relevant to those in the field of business studies and with their eye on the corporate world, also with further emphasis on language, radicalisation and cultural fundamentalism.

SECTION A
Introduction: Defining concepts

Each unit in Section A will comprise the presentation of an *experience* or situation in the form of an example, and a *deconstruction* of this example through which basic concepts will be introduced. By deconstruction we mean 'taking apart' to enable greater insight and analysis. This is an essential skill which will prepare readers to be able to look at their own interaction with others analytically and with fresh eyes in order to solve the puzzle of what is going on. It is particularly important, where we feel that much intercultural communication is marred by prejudice, to be able to take apart and undo this prejudice. The concepts introduced in Section A can then be responded to in the rest of the book. The emphasis is not only on people with different nationalities, but also with other senses of belonging, whether community, class, occupational, gender, and so on. There will then be a final section in each unit that focuses on what is needed for successful communication. This will take the form of *disciplines* about what to be aware of in the process of intercultural communication, which will then be collected together at the end of each theme.

These disciplines will not be based on what a person from culture X is like and therefore how we should communicate with them. There is enough published along these lines, which we consider to be largely essentialist and reductive. By essentialist we mean, presuming that there is a universal essence, homogeneity and unity in a particular culture. By reductive we mean reducing cultural behaviour down to a simple causal factor. The disciplines will thus be basic principles about understandings which need to be achieved in order to interact with different individuals in different contexts. This order of example, deconstruction and disciplines, binds the book together; and our belief is that intercultural communication should grow from an understanding of people, culture and society generally. The deconstruction of the examples will attempt an understanding, and observations about communication will grow from them. Each unit will also finish with a task which will help you to link the examples and concepts it provides with your own experience.

The examples in each unit are reconstructed from actual experience. They have been edited, sometimes mixed together, the characters, genders, nationalities changed, with fictitious names and situations, so that no-one can be recognised, and also to bring out the issues we have found important. The approach in this part of the book is therefore novelistic. The deconstruction of what happens in each example is subjective. We do not however feel that the subjectivity is problematic.

As in more formal qualitative research, each instance speaks for itself, its value being in the resonance or dissonance each example creates – in the degree to which the reader can say 'this makes sense to me; I can recognise this type of thing from my own experience', or 'this makes no sense; I need to think about this more'.

The examples are all about particular people in particular situations. They have been taken from a range of nationalities and social groupings. However, really, it does not matter which nationality or group they come from, as the aim is not to describe what someone from a particular culture is like and then suggest how to communicate with them. Each example shows one or two people struggling with their differences, perceived or real, sometimes succeeding, sometimes failing, sometimes understanding, sometimes falling into an essentialist trap. If the balance is more on the side of people failing, followed with discussion on how they went wrong, this is because in the majority of cases we do indeed get things seriously wrong, and this is something which needs to be dealt with. It needs to be realised that the reason for failure is essentialism.

Section A introduces a non-essentialist view of culture which is then followed up in the rest of the book. It focuses on the complexity of culture as a fluid, creative social force which binds different groupings and aspects of behaviour in different ways, both constructing and constructed by people in a piecemeal fashion to produce myriad combinations and configurations.

The difference between 'non-essentialism' and 'essentialism', which are terms used by social scientists in their discussion about the nature of culture (Dobbin 1994; Jensen 2006; Keesing 1994), is described in Table A0.1.1. There is a movement in the table from very definite statements about cultures as physical places on the left of the table to far more hesitancy about cultural tendencies on the right. Even there, on the right of the table, though, there needs to be caution. The statements are what could be said by some people and not statements of how things are in particular locations.

We realise that the essentialist–non-essentialist distinction, like all other dichotomies, is harsh and ignorant of the fact that in reality views range between the two extremes. Nevertheless, essentialism in the way we see people and culture is the same essentialism which drives sexism and racism. The equivalent condition, culturism, or sometimes referred to as culturalism (e.g. Dervin 2011: 38), similarly reduces and Others the individual and underlies many of the problems in the world today. By Othering we mean imagining someone as alien and different to 'us' in such a way that 'they' are excluded from 'our' 'normal', 'superior' and 'civilised' group. Indeed, it is by imagining a foreign Other in this way that 'our' group can become more confident and exclusive. Essentialism therefore needs to be defined strongly, recognised and fought against wherever it is found. This particular definition of essentialism might be different to that of others. As with racism and sexism, the concept needs to be discussed and continuously revisited.

Table A0.1.1   Essentialism vs non-essentialism

	Essentialist view of culture	How people talk about it	Non-essentialist view of culture	How people talk about it
Nature	**i** 'A culture' has a physical entity, as though it is a place, which people can visit. It is homogeneous in that perceived traits are spread evenly, giving the sense of a simple society	'I visited three cultures while on holiday. They were Spain Morocco and Tunisia.'	**ii** Culture is a social force which is evident where it is significant. Society is complex, with characteristics which are difficult to pin down.	'There was something culturally different about each of the countries I visited.'
Place	**iii** It is associated with a country and a language, which has an onionskin relationship with larger continental, religious, ethnic or racial cultures, and smaller sub-cultures.	'Japanese culture', 'European culture', 'Hindu culture', 'Black culture', 'Japanese secondary school culture'	**iv** It is associated with a value, and can relate equally to any type or size of group for any period of time, and can be characterised by a discourse as much as by a language.	'There is a more homogenous culture of food in Japan than in Britain.' Schools in France have a more evident culture of sport than schools in Japan.'
Relation	**v** The world is divided into mutually exclusive national cultures. People in one culture are essentially different from people in another.	'When crossing from Japanese culture to Chinese culture . . .', 'People from Egypt cannot . . . when they arrive in French culture'	**vi** Cultures can flow, change, intermingle, cut across and through each other, regardless of national frontiers, and have blurred boundaries.	'There is more of a culture of . . . in Egypt than in India', 'Schools throughout the world have a lot of cultural similarities'.
Membership	**vii** People belong exclusively to one national culture and one language.	'No matter how long she lives in Italy, she belongs to Austrian culture', 'Which culture do you originally come from?' 'One can never totally learn a 2nd culture.'	**viii** People can belong to and move through a complex multiplicity of cultures both within and across societies.	'I feel most Malaysian when I travel abroad to places where that is meaningful. A sense of history from my family and upbringing comes into play when I listen to Mexican music, speak the language and think of global politics.

Table A0.1.1   continued

	Essentialist view of culture	How people talk about it	Non-essentialist view of culture	How people talk about it
Behaviour	**ix** 'A culture' behaves like a single-minded person with a specific, exclusive personality. People's behaviour is defined and constrained by the culture *in* which they live.	'German culture believes that . . .', 'In Middle Eastern culture there is no concept of . . .', 'In French culture, people . . .', 'She belongs to Norwegian culture, therefore she . . .'	**x** People are influenced by or make use of a multiplicity of cultural forms.	'At the moment the strongest cultural force in my life comes from the international women's group to which I belong, through conferences, journals and email contact. These are the people to whom I feel culturally closest. The people I find most culturally strange are my children's friends and the village where I was a child. My Mexican-ness enriches my perceptions of and participation in Malaysian society, and vice versa.'
Communication	**xi** To communicate with someone who is foreign or different we must first understand the details, or stereotype of their culture.	'When you want to greet a Swedish businessman, you need to know that in Swedish culture . . .'	**xii** To communicate with anyone who belongs to a group with whom we are unfamiliar, we have to understand the complexity of who she is.	'What you have to understand about her is that she does not conform to the stereotype of North African women that we see in the media, which she considers false and ignorant. In reality she is different to what we expected.'

It is perhaps noticeable that the entries on the right hand side of the table (for non-essentialism) represent more complex and perhaps obscure ideas than those on the left hand side. In this sense, essentialism is the 'easy' answer for culture, which has become popular, useable and marketable in such as management studies and foreign language education where people are looking for simple formulae for communicating with clients, students and colleagues from 'other places and backgrounds'. For this reason, the tone of this book is to go against these 'easy' answers, to struggle with dominant discourses, and to problematise what is normally thought.

The final row in the table addresses the final question posed by this book, developing strategies for intercultural communication. Again, whereas the essentialist side provides an answer, the non-essentialist side poses more of a problem which is complex and requires an understanding of things which are not at all clear and different to what we imagine. Thus, the angle on communication within the theme of *identity* will be how identity is constructed and how individuals define their own identities. Within the theme of *Othering*, the focus will be how to avoid the trap of over-generalisation and reduction when describing and interacting with others. Within the theme of *representation* the emphasis will be on deconstructing the imposed images of people from the media and popular discourse.

The purpose of this book is to engage in a dialogue with the reader. We do not believe there is only one route to achieving successful intercultural communication. You will therefore encounter different perspectives, possibly contradictory, within the book.

Theme 1
Identity

This theme will explore how people construct their own identities.

UNIT A1.1   PEOPLE LIKE ME

'This is whom I want to be represented by'

Experience

This unit explores the complexity of people's cultural identity in terms of how they want to represent themselves. Consider this example:

Example A1.1.1 Being represented

Parisa had been coming to international conventions on food processing for several years. She had made several good friends; but there was a gnawing problem which always came back unresolved. She was the only person at the convention who came from her country; and no matter how friendly and sincere, she knew that her colleagues saw her in a particular way which just wasn't her at all. It was from their passing comments, their casual, unguarded turns of phrase, in which they seemed to show surprise when she was creative, assertive or articulate, as though she *ought* to be somehow unable to be good at all the things she did. One of her colleagues did not actually say 'well done!' but certainly implied it in her tone of voice. She also felt isolated as the only person from her particular background at these conventions. There was nobody else to represent who she was. It also hurt her when someone said that because they thought of her as being 'like them' really, that she was 'not a real' representative of her 'culture'. This seemed like a no-win situation. If her behaviour was 'recognised', she was not real; and if she was considered 'real', she wasn't supposed to behave like that. She didn't mind them thinking that she was like them, but certainly not at the expense of not being a person on her own terms.

Then something happened which both confirmed her fears and gave her support. She invited three of her colleagues to see a film that was directed by someone from her country which was showing at the local university. They came willingly – very interested. When she asked one of them what she found so fascinating, she replied that she was particularly impressed by the female characters who portrayed such strong women. Indeed, a woman played a major executive role in a film crew. She hired and fired people and drove around in a jeep. Parisa's colleague said that she had no idea such women existed in her country, and that she always thought 'their women' were supposed to be subservient. Parisa was also pleased because the women in the film, while being very independent, were at the same time certainly 'real' in that they wore traditional clothes, and the woman who drove the jeep wore the black headscarf and long coat that she imagined fitted the 'stereotype'.

Shortly after this, another person from her country arrived at the convention. Parisa was very pleased that he was educated, worldly, urbane, well-dressed and also extremely articulate. This was no more or less than *she* would expect of her countrymen; but she was pleased because here was further evidence for her other colleagues of the sort of people she belonged to. Moreover, it was very clear that he had tremendous respect for her as an equal, an academic and a professional. Parisa wondered though if they considered *him* a 'real' representative of their 'culture'. After all, he wore a smart suit and didn't have a beard.

Afterwards though, she thought more about this. Why shouldn't he have a beard? She was worried that not having a beard meant that after all he was leaving his culture, and that the people at the conference would think that he was 'modern' because he didn't have a beard and was therefore 'like them'? No, the point she wanted to make was quite different to that. She, and all her countrypeople could be modern or not, whether they fitted the stereotype of 'traditional' appearance or not. Him not having a beard simply illustrated the possibility of this diversity to her colleagues at the conference.

Deconstruction

Apart from the problem of being stereotyped and Othered, perhaps on the basis of the popular media images, which may depict women from her part of the world as lacking in power, Parisa's predicament in Example A1.1.1 is that she lacks other images on the basis of which the people around her can judge who she is. Although her colleagues have got to know her and see her as their friend, they lack real knowledge of what sort of group she belongs to in order to place her. In this sense, they are also in a predicament, and indeed vulnerable to the stereotypes with which they are presented from other sources. Two concepts which need to be focused on are:

- The multi-facetedness of other people and societies
- The way people talk.

Multi-facetedness

At one level, one might say that Parisa wants to be associated with a certain type of person from her country – educated, worldly, a working woman in the same way as her new male colleague is a working man – which she does not perceive as conforming to the popular stereotype. However, at another level it is more complex than this. Her society, like all others, is complex and multi-faceted; and in order for anyone to show who they really are, this complexity has to be visible. The film that her friends saw showed this complexity, as often art forms are able to do more than any other media form. The woman, in black traditional clothes, driving a jeep, being her own person, educated and a working woman, yet wearing the expected traditional clothing, hiring and firing extras for the film she is involved in making, begins successfully to show the layers and depths of a complex society in which identity is multi-faceted and shifting.

Another element in Parisa's quest to be recognised is her desire to be associated with other people like herself. Again, at one level she wants to be associated with people like her in that they are middle class etc.; but at a deeper level, they should represent the same many-faceted complexity as she sees in herself. Thus, the new male colleague is also different to what she imagines her other colleagues would expect – not conforming to the stereotype, while at the same time being what *she* would expect of a man from her country in his civility, good manners, worldliness, and, moreover, respect towards her and the qualities she wishes to be noticed for by others.

The way which these elements contribute to a person's recognition of where she comes from is depicted in Figure A1.1.1. As well as evidence of complexity, layers and facets, there is the unexpected juxtaposed against what is expected. The unexpected is inevitable where any society must always be far more than any outsider can imagine.

The principle of discovery is also implicit in *thick description* – seeing the complexity of a social event by looking at it from different aspects. The figure shows that the

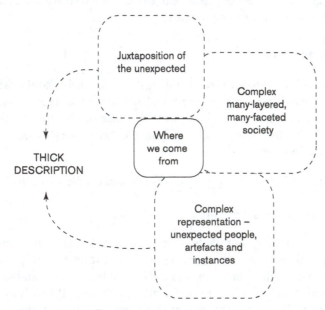

Figure A1.1.1 Elements of where we come from

knowledge derived from understanding the juxtaposition of unexpectedness (for example, the woman in the film), complexity (for example, the layers in the film), and encounters with people, artefacts and instances (for example, Parisa's new colleague, the film, how the new colleague treats Parisa) results in thick description. Thick description as a term comes from anthropology and qualitative research and involves two elements:

- deriving meaning from a broad view of social phenomena which pieces together different, interconnected perspectives
- exploration, in which sense is made from an ongoing emergence of social phenomena, which may not immediately seem to connect, and which may indeed be unexpected.

Parisa is particularly troubled by the knowledge that her colleagues feel she is not a 'real' representative of her country because she appears to be 'like them'. She also suspects that her new compatriot colleague will also be seen as not being 'real'. The fact that her colleagues think of her in this way derives from an essentialist perception that her particular 'national culture' is so different from their own (Table A0.1.1, cell v) that it would not be possible to share features. This way of thinking creates a marked 'us'-'them' attitude that: if Parisa in any way behaves like 'us', she must have become like 'us' and left the essentialist attributes of 'them' behind. Hence, if women from her country are 'subservient', they cannot be 'creative, assertive or articulate'.

The non-essentialist view, in contrast, has no difficulty with the notion that cultural attributes can flow between societies (cell vi). Parisa desperately needs her colleagues to understand that her society is sufficiently complex and big to include the cultural attributes which they consider exclusive to them, but which are in fact normal for many people who come from her country.

The way people talk

It is not only this essentialist view that disturbs Parisa. It is also the fact that she gleans it from 'passing comments', 'the casual, unguarded turns of phrase', through which her colleagues seem to show surprise when she is creative, assertive or articulate – 'no matter how friendly and sincere' her colleagues seem. There are several implications here:

- This thinking is deep in everyday discourse; and people are probably unaware of it.
- They do not see it as derogatory.

In both cases the passing comments are in conflict, in Parisa's view, with apparent friendliness. This is especially worrying because it implies a deep seated, tacit essentialism that is hidden between the lines in people's attitudes and socialisation – an issue which will be taken up in Theme B, Othering. If this is the case, her colleagues are in effect aware that they are being profoundly patronising and think it appropriate to comment on, perhaps praising, unexpected 'achievement' for someone from 'her culture' – rather as they would a child who achieves above their years – 'well done!'.

Communication

There are important implications here with regard to communication. We have seen how Parisa feels, not only about direct communication but also about asides and tones of voice. Parisa *may* be more sensitive than many, but this one instance – as in the case of any qualitative analysis – illuminates a particular predicament which makes one see intercultural communication in a certain way. It becomes clear that Parisa's colleagues feel confident to communicate with her on the basis of established stereotypes. This strategy is prescriptive and indeed essentialist in that it tends to define the person before understanding the person. Rather than being a matter of prescribed information, the non-essentialist strategy implies a moral imperative to do with how we approach and learn about a person as a human being (Table A0.1.1, cell xii). There are several disciplines that might be observed here:

1. Respond to people according to how you find them rather than according to what you have heard about them.
2. Avoid easy answers about how people are. Bracket – put aside simplistic notions about what is 'real' or 'unreal' in your perception of 'another culture'.
3. Appreciate that every society is as complex and culturally varied as your own.
4. Learn to build up thick descriptions of what happens between you and others – to work out how to communicate as you go along.

Task A1.1.1 Thinking about Parisa

➤ Think of a situation you have been in which is like the Parisa example and describe it in similar detail.

➤ Explain how you can better understand one or more people in the situation with the help of Figure A1.1.1 and the disciplines listed above.

➤ What can you learn from this about intercultural communication?

UNIT A1.2   ARTEFACTS OF CULTURE

Telling cultural stories, closing ranks

Experience

This unit continues to unravel the complexities of cultural identity by looking at what might lie behind what people *say* about their culture.

Example A1.2.1 Teachers

Janet got to know Zhang and Ming when they were doing their masters course together. She found that Zhang talked a lot both in class and at other times about The Code of Civility and how it was the basis of his culture. They soon got into an ongoing discussion about what teachers and students could be expected to do in university English classes in his country. He said that because of The Code of Civility, just as it was impolite for children to question their parents, it was impolite for students to question their teachers. This meant that all sorts of things which were recommended on their course, like discovery learning and classroom discussions, were culturally inappropriate in their culture.

As the masters course progressed, Janet noticed that Zhang was getting increasingly unhappy. She asked Ming, who came from the same country, what Zhang's problem was. He explained that some people found it more difficult than others to cope with being in a foreign environment. She had noticed that Zhang was very silent when there was a class discussion; and she asked Ming if this was to do with The Code of Civility. Ming said that this was certainly a factor, as it was indeed quite influential; but when Janet told him what Zhang had told her about students having to obey their teachers, Ming said that this was not strictly true – that he knew lots of teachers who were prepared to be engaged in discussion by their students, that students were certainly not always prepared to submit to teachers who would not listen to them, and that many parents did not approve of the sort of authority that Zhang was talking about. Janet told him that this shocked her because it was not just from Zhang that she had heard about this. There were so many books she had read and quite a lot of articles which reported how cultures in their part of the world were bound by The Code of Civility. There were also two other people on the course who said that all the people they had met from those cultures said the same thing. Ming said that there were different ways of looking at this. On the one hand, it could not be denied that The Code of Civility had been a very powerful influence for thousands of years. On the other hand, not everyone had to be bound by this influence; and different people could be influenced in different ways.

Janet then read an article that had quite a different approach to the others she had read. It argued that people tended to exaggerate aspects of their own cultural identity when they were faced with difficult pressures when travelling abroad. When she put this idea to Ming, he said that there was no need to read too much into Zhang's statements about The Code of Civility. He thought it was really far simpler than that. He had encountered people from Janet's country living in his town who said all sorts of things about *their* culture that certainly did not seem to hold true when he came here. Surely was it not the case that *all* people drew more heavily on certain cultural resources when they felt culturally threatened by strange behaviour. So does that mean that The Code of Civility is a 'cultural resource' she wondered.

Deconstruction

In this example we see someone trying to make sense of conflicting messages about people from another country. The first impression that Zhang presents her with tends towards the essentialist view – that his 'culture' is characterised by The Code of Civility, which in turn determines the behaviour of parents, children, teachers and students who come from that culture. The conflicting impression that Ming presents is more non-essentialist – that what Zhang says is not necessarily true, that the influence of The Code of Civility is far from straightforward. If we assume that Janet has read Unit A1.1 and learnt that the essentialist view denies the complexity of one's identity and society, Zhang's point of view becomes even more puzzling for her. What, therefore, are the reasons for Zhang's essentialist point of view? Ming and Janet herself have already gone some way in answering this question. The following disciplines underpin this understanding (the numbering follows on from the previous unit):

5. When people are in a difficult, strange environment, they can close ranks and exaggerate specific aspects of their cultural identity.
6. Different cultural resources can be drawn upon and invoked at different times depending on the circumstances.

In both cases, because of the strength of statement, there can be an *appearance* of essentialist national culture. We shall now look in more detail at these phenomena, and at a related third:

7. What people say about their cultural identity should be read as the image they wish to project at a particular time rather than as evidence of an essentialist national culture.

Closing ranks

Zhang's exaggeration, according to Ming, of the influence of The Code of Civility represents a closing of ranks in the face of a cultural threat. Adrian Holliday remembers an example of this where young Englishmen encountered culture shock while living in Iran in the 1970s. They took a deep interest in military music from the Coldstream Guards, which they would never have been interested in at home, because of its nationalistic reference. An inverse of this may be where people in strange environments also construct essentialist descriptions of 'local people' – for example, as 'subservient', 'hierarchical', 'corrupt', inhibited by extended families and arranged marriages, lacking in individualism, unable to make decisions, and so on. Such descriptions are more likely to be people's constructions of the opposite of what they consider themselves to be than grounded in the behaviour they observe around them.

The threat that gives rise to such exaggeration could be from other national, international or global quarters resulting in a sense of invading a person's sense of identity. As teachers, Zhang and other teachers who have told Janet and others about how they are bound by The Code of Civility, may be reacting to the pedagogies they are being taught on their course which they find too difficult to deal with.

Cultural resources

The Code of Civility for Zhang thus became a convenient cultural resource around which to marshal his threatened professional identity. Just as we can define the foreign Other as opposite to ourselves, the particular resources which are chosen may well be the ones which are most opposite to the cultural features of the threat. The exaggeration of particular cultural resources may also serve other purposes, for example the phenomenon of image building that can be seen in commercial settings, as discussed by Moeran (1996) with regard to the very strong description of Japaneseness that has been used to promote a marketable exoticness.

Cultural resources can be found on the left side of Holliday's grammar of culture (adapted from Holliday 2011: 131; 2013), which is presented in Figure A1.2.1. (See also the discussion with reference to the grammar of culture in Holliday's text (B3.6.2).) The grammar is intended to be a loose arrangement of factors that do not so much explain the workings of the intercultural, as help us to understand how things relate. It indicates that cultural resources are within the broad domain of the particular social and political structures within which we are brought up. It is therefore clear that different cultural resources can be used by a particular person in particular settings depending on what is going on. Towards the centre of the grammar are personal cultural trajectories through life that will be different for each person and will lead them to draw on different resources at different times. Indeed, it is these individual trajectories that provide the basis for individuals to negotiate the structures of their societies. The arrows at the top and bottom of the grammar indicate that there are possibilities for innovation as well as forces of conformity.

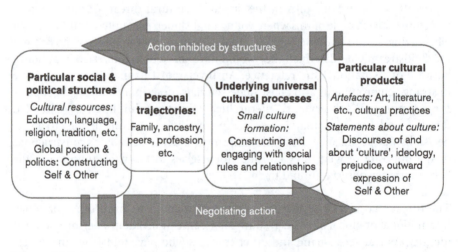

Figure A1.2.1 Grammar of culture

There are therefore a range of possible resources, perhaps the most obvious of which might be:

- Ceremonies and festivals: for example, national, religious, family, age group, sports, community, etc.
- Clothing – to do with look, fashion, religion, etc.
- Etiquette – to do with eating, greeting, addressing, clothing, etc.
- Family – to do with relations, loyalties, who lives with whom, etc.
- Fine arts, literature, music – the big C cultural products that we feel represent our civilisation.
- Food – cuisine, ingredients, eating traditions and rituals, etiquette, etc.
- Ideology – the big systems of ideas, values, principles, behaviour, and so on, that can be promoted by particular political or religious groups.
- Language – to do with ideals, what we think of standards and aesthetics of expression – particular ways of saying things that we consider to hold cultural significance.
- Personality – to do with what sorts of people we think we are.

Although ideology is an item in the alphabetical list, it is a force that will govern all the other items in that the sense that we make of them will almost always be ideological. 'Particular' is the key word here because this is *by no means* a set of universals. Every person who reads this would use different resources to deal with different scenarios that they encounter, and because of this they might appear quite culturally different in each set of circumstances that drive them to draw on these resources. Examples of such scenarios, and the particular resources a person may draw on to counter what they do not like, to reassure themselves or to strengthen their sense of identity are in Table A1.2.2.

One may think that the 'you' in each of the cases in Table A1.2.1 is being deceitful or duplicitous, playing with or selecting what they like from their culture in this way. This would be an essentialist view. The non-essentialist view would be that culture is a shifting reality anyway, and people make of it what they need to as they live their identities in different circumstances. This view of culture as a shifting reality can be compared with the discussion in Hannerz (1999) in Text B0.1.1, where there is a reference to people being 'more or less Confucian', and to the multiplicity of cultural identity reported by Baumann (1996) in Text B0.1.2.

Artefacts of culture

There are dangers with the non-essentialist view just as there are with the essentialist view. It would be a grave mistake for the essentialist to think Ming was not a 'real' representative of his country because he did not conform to The Code of Civility. In the same way it would also be a grave mistake to think that Zhang was not to be

Table A1.2.1   Employing cultural resources

Scenario	Resources	How you present yourself and 'your culture'
You find the politics of the society or of a particular social group 'distasteful'	A particular aspect of personality, literature and ideology	Left-wing activist
You find a moral code that you encounter 'strange'	Religious beliefs, clothing and etiquette	Religious with particular dress codes
People you meet do not understand who you are because they have no knowledge of where you come from	Ceremonies, festivals and family values	Defined by ceremonies, festivals and family values
You cannot identify with aspects of big C culture that you encounter	Fine arts, cuisine and music	Defined by fine arts, cuisine and music

taken seriously because he was being 'naïve' about the role of The Code of Civility. Even though it might be the case that Zhang's statements about how The Code of Civility determines the behaviour of teachers and students might be considered essentialist, these statements are still extremely meaningful to him, just as the behaviour of all the people mentioned in this unit would be extremely real to them. In each case, these are constituents of how individuals need to work their own personal identities. If we as communicators are to take people from other backgrounds seriously, we should take every aspect of what they do and say seriously. In this sense, every instance of behaviour becomes an artefact of who people are. In other words, what they say tells us something about how they wish to present themselves.

Thus, what *can* be said about Zhang is that what he chooses to say about The Code of Civility is part and parcel of his cultural identity. The *way* he talks about The Code of Civility is an artefact of what *he* believes about The Code of Civility; and this in itself may indeed be cultural. Indeed, if more and more people from a particular country were heard to talk about The Code of Civility in this way, one may conclude that 'there is a tendency for some people from that country to say that The Code of Civility influences every part of their lives'. Such *statements about culture*, as projected constructs rather than descriptions of what people actually do, are referred to at the bottom right of the grammar of culture in Figure A1.2.1.

Table A1.2.2 demonstrates this. On the left, essentialist descriptions are based on prescription, while on the right, non-essentialist descriptions are very cautious and qualified, based on what can be observed. Indeed, the non-essentialist descriptions should also be *ephemeral* – that is, perhaps true at a particular time, but changing.

Table A1.2.2 What people say

Essentialist description based on stereotypes	Non-essentialist description based on observation
In national culture A people's behaviour is determined by The Code of Civility	Some people from country A feel it important to say that their behaviour is determined by The Code of Civility. Others say that this is an overgeneralisation.
In national culture B students are silent and passive in the classroom	Some people from country B prefer to remain silent when in language classrooms in country C
In national culture D young people liked military music	Some young people from country D found military music comforting while living abroad

In some cases, the inaccuracy of the statements on the left of the table will seem glaringly untrue to people who know the country in question. The third case in the table relates to my British friends in Iran listening to military music. Anyone from Britain at that time would know how untrue the generalisation on the left of the final row is. In other cases, however, the essentialist statements on the left of the table might be harder to shake. It might be the case that these statements are indeed generally believed to be the case. Kumaravadivelu (2012: 23) makes the point that a lot of people marginalise themselves by buying into the stereotypes that are imposed upon them by others. He also refers to this process as self-Othering; and this can be a widespread phenomenon where the stereotype becomes the dominant discourse.

Communication

The lessons to be learnt about communication from Example A1.2.1 build on those in the previous unit. Janet has indeed learnt some of the lessons from Unit A1.1 and listens carefully to Zhang and Ming and places what she learns against what she has heard from other people about things related to The Code of Civility – thus creating her own thick description. Taking a non-essentialist line, she sees Ming, despite his doubts about The Code of Civility, as just as 'real' a representative of his country as Zhang. If she believes Ming's doubts about The Code of Civility, how should she therefore respond to Zhang? The answer may be that she should follow these disciplines (the numbering of which follows on from earlier in the unit):

8. While respecting whatever people say about their own cultural background, take what they say as evidence of what they wish to project rather than as information about where they come from.

9. Take what people say about their own cultural background as a personal observation which should not be generalised to other people who come from the same background.

Notice here that the reference is to cultural background rather than 'culture'. In the non-essentialist mode, 'culture' as a concept that is too easily associated with national culture needs to be problematised.

 Task A1.2.1 Thinking about Zhang and Ming

➤ Think of a situation you have been in which is like the Zhang and Ming example and describe it in similar detail.

➤ Explain how you can better understand one or more people in the situation with the help of the explanations in the Deconstruction section, Table A1.2.2 and the disciplines listed above.

➤ Use Table A0.1.1, and the resources listed earlier, and describe what sorts of cultural resources were being used by one of the participants and why.

➤ Think about when you and others make statements about 'my culture'. How far are these really descriptions of what people actually do? How far do they relate to assertions about Self and Other, as referred in the bottom left and right of the grammar of culture in Figure A1.2.1.

UNIT A1.3   IDENTITY CARD

'I am who I can make myself and make others accept me to be.'

Experience

This unit explores the principle that while one person may be exchanging information with another person, they are both, be it intentionally or unintentionally, also sending messages about their cultural identity – about how they want the other person to see them. The example is different to those in previous units in that it does not concern people from different societies. It is about people in the same society, but from very different cultural groups. This is to illustrate the non-essentialist point that cultural difference by no means has to be connected with national difference (Table A0.1.1, cells vi, viii). Also, by looking at a small culture, rather than at culture that is associated with nation, it is easier to see the details of cultural formation. See the discussion of small cultures in Holliday (2013) and in Holliday (2005) and (2016) in Texts B0.2.2 and B3.6.2. Consider this event:

Example A1.3.1 Girl on the bus

A public bus in South East England was mainly occupied by school children returning home to the villages after attending school in the city. Several of the other passengers were annoyed by what they considered noisy bad language from some of the children. The most vociferous and extreme swearing was from a group of girls. The bus stopped and a further schoolgirl got on. She joined the group, one of whom shouted, 'hello you big fat tart', to which the new girl loudly retorted, 'fuck off bitch'. This exchange seemed to serve as a greeting as the two did not appear in any way genuinely angry with each other. The volume of their utterances was also noticeably loud enough for all the bus occupants to hear – in other words it was unnecessarily loud for communication to occur just between themselves. The first interactant then admired a new item of jewellery her friend had around her neck: 'where did you get that you dirty slag?' to which she was answered: 'none of your business you fucking nosy cow!'

After this, the first interactant's attention became fixed upon a school boy, who was smaller than the girls, sitting several seats away. 'Darren! – Oi Darren! Fucking listen to me! Darren – Are you a poof Darren?' The girls laughed and the boy looked embarrassed and at a loss as to how to reply. 'No I'm not' he finally protested, and looked out of the window, no doubt hoping the girls' attention would wander to someone else. Then another girl's voice: 'Darren, Michaela says you're a poof'. Darren's bus journey was going to be a longer one than he might have hoped!

Deconstruction

In this example we see a group of schoolgirls asserting their cultural identity to the outside world who are represented by the culturally different Other people on the bus, who are in turn shocked and perhaps disgusted by their explicit display. In many ways, the girls are doing the same as Parisa in Unit A1.1 and Zhang in Unit A1.2, but whereas they were pulling elements from their distant homes to reinforce identity in the face of strangers, these girls are on their home ground, and we see the details of actual small cultural formation – still, though, in the face of strangers. There are several related concepts at work:

- The multiplicity of identities.
- The creation of an identity card.
- The marking out of territory.

Cultural identity and multiplicity

The two girls derive and achieve an identity by signalling belongingness to the particular small culture of swearing girls on the bus. Belongingness among the members of any group partly involves the learning and use of particular discourses. It is a person's familiarity and ease of use of these discourses that demonstrates their membership of a particular group, that is, the cultural territory to which they stake a claim. In the case of Example 1.3.1, the discourse is one of swearing – the mastery of a complex code which only insiders can fully understand, and which can be used to exclude outsiders. Thus, apparent insult is read as greeting or endearment between the initiated girls, but as real insult and exclusion when directed at the boy.

However, the two girls are not only members of the small culture of swearing girls on the bus. As with Parisa, Zhang and Ming in Units A1.1 and A1.2, they belong to a complex society which allows a multiplicity of choices. They could also define themselves as members of an age group, a nationality, an ethnic group, a social class, a religion, a scout group, an aerobics class, a hockey team, a school class group. We are all, as individuals, members of a vast number of different small cultural groups (Table A0.1.1, cell viii) and, hence, have a multiplicity of identities. An individual person can be at the same time a member of a family, part of which, through marriage, might be associated with a different country, the university where one did graduate studies, a professional group, part of which, through its activities, is international, a university department, a local community of artists, and so on; besides being a member of a particular nation, which in itself might be problematised by migration, heritage, displacement, war, and so on. With each identity a person has a certain communal bond with a group of other people: we are linked through a common experience, we have our icons, our ideologies and our communal history to draw on, and we encapsulate all of this in our discourses. Because all of us inhabit different cultural groups – we are in fact all unique in our cultural identities. This point is represented in the personal cultural trajectories domain in the grammar in Figure A1.2.1, where each of us form particular cultural identities as we encounter different small cultural groups and organisations as we travel through life.

Identity card

There is also a very strong sense of small cultural assertion in Example A1.3.1 – '*This* is how we *are*! We use bad language; we shock; we make boys feel uncomfortable; we don't care about annoying people around us'. And in the paragraph above we use the term 'define themselves' rather than simply 'are'. The two girls are not simply *being* members of a culture, they are *doing* the culture in order to *communicate* something to the people around them. In this sense, they are *playing* a particular identity card.

In a way they are playing with the cultural stereotypes expected by other members of their society. Swearing is 'often' considered a territory occupied only by males displaying their toughness. Indeed, it would seem that girls have invaded this traditional male territory and taken it over. They have also invaded the misogynistic male lexicon of derogatory terms for women – 'slag', 'bitch', 'tart', 'cow'. They thus subvert the potentially wounding power of these terms, neutralise them by their frequency of use, and convert them into the normal phatic functions of greeting and 'small talk'. And in so doing, they increase the shock effect by voicing yet twisting what the audience of bus passengers may consider taboo. On the other hand, these terms have become very much the domain of women generally in their in-talk. Whereas outsider men will use them at their risk.

The girls are very vocal and thus also occupy the acoustic space of the bus: the old notions of men not swearing in the presence of the 'weaker' and 'daintier' sex are completely challenged – indeed inverted here. This incident would seem to have a lot to do with the notion of 'girl power'. Further attack is made upon maleness by the bullying of the boy and the questioning of his sexuality. Again the weapons of reductionist and derogatory sexual labelling are used by the girls on the boy rather than vice versa.

Although we are not fully in control of the resources that make up our identity, and we cannot choose our ethnicity, our sex, etc., we can decide how to play the hand of cards that we have been dealt. We can work with the discourses available to us according to how we wish others to see us and how we wish to influence others' perceptions of the hand of cards we have been dealt. Indeed, through such discourse action over time these very cards can become viewed in different ways. This is true, for example, of how women have changed the way femininity is constructed and perceived over the last century, and how a range of marginalised groups work hard to establish themselves in mainstream acceptability. Identity is therefore not a stable concept, but one that is achieved through the skilled manipulation of discourses in society.

Territory

By being creative with the act of swearing, the girls are in effect marking a powerful new territory – an identity terrain which they occupy in their struggle for presentation of Self against the identities that are imposed upon them by others. This territory is fought over and at times conceded during interactions. In the case of Example A1.3.1, the act of swearing becomes a critical marker of this territory.

Figure A1.3.1 shows two sides to cultural identity. The left hand bubble represents a state of affairs, which, though imposed by the way in which society defines us – and indeed other societies define us, in the case of national cultural perceptions – can be seen as the resources of the material that we have to work with. In the case of the girls on the bus, these might comprise that 'traditional' notions that girls do not swear, but are sworn at. The right hand bubble signifies a dynamic movement away from this establishment, in which, through playing with the available resources, individuals or groups can create new identity and, indeed, create culture change. Although a similar process, this is subtly different to what can be seen in Unit A1.2, as represented in Table A1.2.1. There, cultural resources are used ephemerally to defend identity; here they are used to create the fabric of identity.

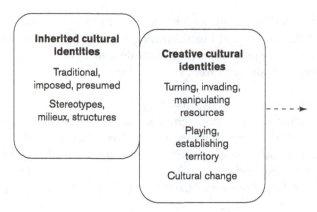

Figure A1.3.1 Two sides to identity

Communication

Being sensitive to and understanding others' cultural productions and the way in which they play with the various identities available to them (discourses on their identities currently available in the context of their interactions) is a crucial part of good intercultural communication. A good interpersonal communicator, therefore, needs to be aware of issues surrounding the concept of identity. Before we can communicate with people who are different to ourselves, we need to understand something about how they present themselves as being or belonging to certain groups. This goes deeper than the observations about Zhang in Unit A1.2, where we note that one should respect what people say about themselves and see this as an artefact of who they are without over-generalising. The creative element in Example A1.3.1 takes this further. Hence the first discipline for this unit must be that we should (numbering continues from previous unit):

10. Understand how people are creating and indeed negotiating their cultural identity in the very process of communicating with us.

We need, therefore, to see communication with anyone as a dynamically creative process. Also, this surely teaches us something about ourselves, which should be evident from all the examples in this theme – that the whole thing is of course a two-way process, as the next discipline suggests:

11. Appreciate that you are creating and negotiating your own cultural identity in the process of communicating with others.

Furthermore, as the process of communication is also personal – as all the examples in these units are to do with interaction between individuals, we should:

12. Appreciate that the creation and negotiation of cultural and personal identity are the same thing.

Task A1.3 Thinking about the girls on the bus

➤ Think of a situation you have been in which is like the girls on the bus example and describe it in similar detail.

➤ Explain how you can better understand one or more people in the situation with the help of Figure A1.3.1 and the disciplines listed above.

➤ What can you learn from this about intercultural communication?

➤ Connect the references to discourses in this example to *discourses of and about culture* in the grammar of culture in Figure A1.2.1, statements about culture in Unit A1.2, and the West as steward discourse regarding the story of Reza in Unit A3.1. Can you name any other discourses of culture?

Theme 2
Addressing the Other

This theme will explore a major inhibition to communication by looking at how so easily we can construct and reduce people to be less than what they are. Continuing from the first three units within the Identity theme, the angle on communication will be how we must discipline our own perceptions if we are to communicate successfully, but the three units in this theme will look more deeply at the forces which prevent us all from seeing people as they really are. The weight of responsibility is on 'us' to understand ourselves, rather than on essentialist categories of 'them'.

UNIT A2.1 COMMUNICATION IS ABOUT NOT PRESUMING

Falling into culturist traps

Experience

Continuing to follow the principle that we should try to understand people before we can communicate with them, in this unit we explore how easy it is to be misled by our own pre-conceptions, and to fall into the trap of Othering. As with Unit A1.3, we use an example in which the participants belong to the same society to demonstrate how the tendency to reduce the foreign Other is deep within the roots of society generally. We hope therefore to show how even easier it is to misconstruct people from other societies. Consider this experience:

Example A2.1.1 The Smith family?

A while ago John had neighbours, the Smiths, who, by their own declaration, belonged to a religious group that was not part of the mainstream. John took this as a matter of fact because Mr Smith told him so several weeks after moving in during a residents' meeting. However, from the very first impression he had of them he suspected something of the sort. There were six children. The girls and Mrs Smith were dressed in long dresses with aprons, which came down to their mid-calf, and wore headscarves over long hair. The boys had long shorts with braces [US suspenders] which also came down to mid-calf. Mr Smith was clean-shaven except for a beard around his chin.

As they were moving in John could see that their furniture was like old-fashioned wooden school furniture; and they didn't seem to have a television, stereo or video. There was, however, a piano and John could hear them making their own music for entertainment in the evenings. This reminded John of the image of the religious community in the Hollywood movie *Witness*.

Several events took place after the family moved in which began to reveal the way in which John was thinking about them. One afternoon John was in his garage pottering about when Mr Smith came out and got into his large people carrier. John guessed he was waiting for the rest of his family before going out with them. He really was amazed when Smith turned on the car's CD player and listened to music. John had thought that because they didn't have a television or stereo in the house, their religion forbade them to listen to such things.

It was the time when the whole country seemed involved in the events surrounding the wedding of a popular member of the royal family. Mr Smith's parents were staying with them; and Meltem, John's wife, had encountered Mr Smith's mother in the driveway. Mrs Smith senior told her that because there was no television or radio in her son's home, and no-one was allowed to read newspapers, it was difficult for her and her husband to find out what was going on, and felt they were missing out on seeing the wedding on television. Despite the incident with the car stereo, this confirmed to John that the Smith family were indeed religious fundamentalists who did not allow the watching of television, and that he had been right all along about how they abstained from modernity. John was therefore shocked and indeed concerned that it would be an inconsiderate invasion of their religious *culture* when Meltem suggested inviting Mr and Mrs Smith senior, and indeed the whole Smith family, in to watch the wedding on the television. He really felt that this invitation would put the whole Smith family in a very difficult position. It would be like inviting Muslims to eat pork. Meltem said that it would be impolite to invite Mr and Mrs Smith senior alone, and that anyway they all had the choice to refuse.

John was amazed again when the whole Smith family accepted the invitation and all ten of them came into his living room, the children sitting on the floor in a line in front of the adults, to watch the whole wedding. He was even more amazed when Mrs Smith junior later wrote Meltem a note to say that they had all really appreciated the opportunity.

Deconstruction

This example shows John reducing his neighbour according to a prescribed stereotype – very much as Parisa's colleagues reduced her to a stereotype in Unit A1.1. What makes this particularly significant is that it is so easy to fall into traps like this. It is therefore extremely important to deconstruct exactly how this can happen.

It seems clear from Example A2.1.1 that John had made a mistake, both about the nature of the Smith family and about how to communicate with them, whereas his wife, Meltem, had been successful at least to the extent of achieving significant interaction that seemed to be appreciated by both sides. In an attempt to explain why this happened we are going to explore the following interconnected concepts, some of which will be familiar, some less so, and link them with the concept of essentialism introduced in Table A0.1.1:

- Stereotype
- Prejudice
- Othering
- Culturism.

From stereotype to Othering

John had formed a *stereotype* based on his observation of wooden furniture, abstention from exposure to the media, what he considered to be austere clothing, a large family, Mr Smith's chin beard, and Mrs Smith's and the daughters' long hair, put together with the popular image of a religious group presented in a Hollywood movie. Many argue that it is natural to form stereotypes, and that they indeed help us to understand 'foreign cultures' – that they act as a template, or as an ideal type, against which we can measure the unknown. We disagree with this view. One reason is that we do not behave sufficiently rationally in intercultural dealings to be able to work with such templates objectively. A major reason for this is that stereotypes are often infected by *prejudice*, which in turn leads to *Othering*. This process is summarised in the top half of Figure A2.1.1. We have

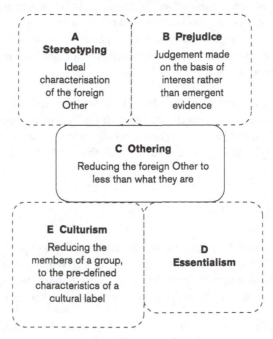

Figure A2.1.1 Constituents of Othering

chosen the words for the bubbles in the figure carefully because this is a complex, dangerous area.

The 'foreign Other' (bubbles A and C) refers not only to different nationalities, but to any group of people which is *perceived* as different – perhaps in terms of so-called ethnicity, religion, political alignment, class or caste, or gender. This is 'so called' ethnicity because this term is particularly relative and disputed (for example, Baumann, in Text B0.1.2). We also do not list culture because all the other things listed can be said to have cultures, or to be cultural. Interest (bubble B) could similarly be ethnic, religious, political, class or caste, or gender. This would colour, bias or infect the way in which the foreign Other is seen. Emergent evidence (bubble B) would be based on what can be learned on the basis of deeper understanding. This is clearly very difficult to achieve, as interest of one sort or another is always with us. Attempts are made in various types of social science. Reduction (bubble C) is where the different facets, the variety of possible characteristics and the full complexity of a group of people are ignored in favour of a preferred definition. In our view, as the figure implies, stereotyping, prejudice and Othering interact with each other; but it is the negative impact of the latter which makes the other two undesirable.

A feature of this process is the way in which information is brought from outside the situation, *a priori*. The reference to the Hollywood movie shows that it was images that John already had about particular religious groups that gave rise to his stereotype of his neighbours. If he had simply observed what he saw and heard of them *in situ*, without these prior images, he would have had a far more complex picture of them. To compound this, were perhaps his *a priori* negative feelings about particular types of religious behaviour – his prejudices – so that his final Othering of his neighbours reduced them to people who would *never* watch television, would *always* think it evil, and, by extension, would not *appreciate* the complexities of such popularised phenomena as a royal wedding on television. One may think, so what? – people from some religious sects *are* strange and odd, and restrict their behaviour and opt out of 'normal' life. The point is that he judged his neighbours, and categorised them, and decided what they would and would not be, *before* really investigating who they were as individuals.

Culturism

The bottom half of Figure A2.1.1 reveals another aspect of Othering, which addresses the issue of culture. Following our comment regarding the bubbles A and C above, the groups of people who we characterise as the 'foreign Other' can be said to share between them something cultural. The problem is that 'we' can very easily take this too far and allow the notion of 'culture' to become greater than the people themselves. Just as we too easily form stereotypes which can pre-define what people are like, we can *imagine* or *reify* 'cultures' as objects, places, physical entities within which and by which people live (Table A0.1.1, cell i). By reification we mean to imagine something to be real when it is not. Hence, essentialism is born (bubble D). Therefore, in Example A2.1.1:

■ John saw the Smith family as members of a religious culture, characterised by the stereotypical traits of austere appearance, disdain for modernity etc., which would govern all aspects of their behaviour. He thus saw them through the filter of 'in . . . culture' (Table A0.1.1, cell ix).

From essentialism there is just a small step to *culturism* (bubble E). This is similarly constructed to racism or sexism in that the imagined characteristics of the 'culture' (or 'women' or 'Asians') are used to define the person. Thus:

■ Whatever Mrs Smith did, John *explained* it as being her religious culture. And if she did something which did not fit the explanation, that she had somehow lost her culture, was no longer, or 'not really' a member of that culture, or had lost her culture.

Again, the reader might think this argument inconsequential, again, because 'everyone knows' that the people of 'that' culture 'are in fact like that'. Nevertheless, if one applied the same culturist rule to women, we would get:

■ Whatever Mrs Smith did, John e*xplained* it as being due to her being a women. And if she did something which did not fit the explanation, that she had lost her femininity.

Communication

The disciplines for intercultural communication arising from this unit carry the same basic message as those in the previous three units, except that here they can draw attention to the factors which help *prevent* us from misinterpreting other people's realities. In the light of the experience of this unit, we must therefore (numbered from previous unit):

13. Avoid falling into the culturist trap of reducing people to less than they are – in the same way as we must avoid racist and sexist traps.

Task A2.1.1 Thinking about the Smiths

➤ Think of a situation you have been in which is like the Smiths example and describe it in similar detail.

➤ Pinpoint where the elements of Othering depicted in Figure A2.1.1 show themselves in the situation, and who are the perpetrators and the victims.

➤ What can you learn from this about intercultural communication? How might you go about conforming to the discipline described above?

UNIT A2.2   CULTURAL DEALING

What we project onto each other

Experience

This unit looks at the problem of Othering on a macro scale when two communities of people come together and behave according to their images of each other. Consider this example:

Example A2.2.1 Tourists and business

Agnes has joined a tour group which is travelling through what she considers to be a very foreign part of the world visiting archaeological sites. The group is made up of tourists from a number of countries. They stay in a small hotel near one particular site for three days. It is 30 kilometres from the nearest town; but there is a village nearby. The villagers work in the hotel and have also set up a string of small shops in which they sell local handicrafts and souvenirs.

Agnes forms a brief relationship with François. She is really amazed at herself for succumbing to his charms. She thinks it is after all such a cliché. She has of course seen the film *Shirley Valentine*, in which a middle aged woman falls in love with a restaurant owner while on holiday. She has never ever had such a casual relationship before; but her marriage is struggling and she has come away to escape. She is also sure that François, who seems to her to be quite a 'womaniser', does this sort of thing with every woman tourist who comes along.

François is amazed at himself for getting involved like this. He is unmarried and has never had a relationship with a woman tourist before. He is engaged to be married, and has a high sense of personal morality. He has actually fallen in love with Agnes, but is at the same time smitten by remorse because he is being unfaithful to his fiancée, whom he also loves deeply. After a very short time he becomes horrified at Agnes' behaviour, in the way that she 'throws herself' at him. It must after all be true what everyone says about women from her culture – that they are loose, promiscuous, and have no morals.

They part in anger. She goes back to her fellow travellers and indulges more than ever in the stories of how men from his culture swindle tourists and mistreat their women. He goes back to his village and indulges more than ever in the stories of the corrupt foreigner.

Deconstruction

Here we can see François and Agnes getting into a very difficult relationship made more so by a complexity of personal and cultural complications. Basic concepts here are:

- When people from different backgrounds meet a middle culture of dealing is set up within which they interact, which is in turn influenced by respective complexes of cultural baggage.
- What people see of each other is influenced by the middle culture of dealing, which may be very different to what they think they see, which is a product of Othering.

Middle cultures of dealing

Example A2.2.1 can be interpreted not in the essentialist terms of this 'culture' and that 'culture' (Table A0.1.1, cell iii), but in terms of a far more complicated mélange of interacting and overlapping cultural entities (Table A0.1.1, cell vi). This is demonstrated in Figure A2.2.1.

Circles 2 and 4 represent the small cultures of the tourists and of the villagers *while* they are trading with the tourists. These are the cultures which initially come into contact with each other and which act as the primary source of information for

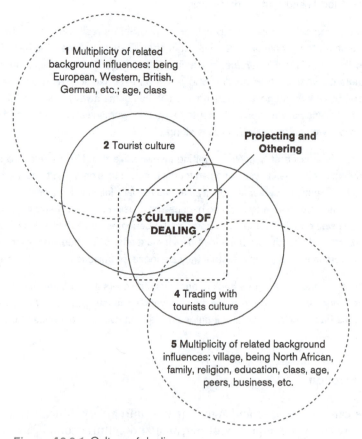

Figure A2.2.1 Culture of dealing

each group. The broader cultural influences of being tourists or villagers, from particular parts of the world, etc. are in the background in circles 1 and 5. What exactly these influences, as cultural resources, might be will also depend on the specific circumstances. In this case, village community and family might have a stronger impact on François because of their proximity, and being from a particular country on Agnes because of the group of people she is with as a tourist. The tourist small culture and the trading-with-tourists small culture (circles 2 and 4) are more temporary and yet specific to the activities in hand. Anyone who has seen a group of tourists, among whom are their own compatriots, will recognise that they are behaving very differently (in circle 2) to when they are at home (circle 1), forming a new type of cohesiveness among themselves with perhaps new artefacts such as cameras, water bottles, sun hats, back packs, and so on.

At the same time, the village trading culture (in circle 4) will have different characteristics to the culture of the village itself (circle 5), with perhaps use of languages, currencies, codes of politeness, and so on which are tuned to the foreign customer. This trading with tourist culture (in circle 4) may be seen as extensions or outcrop from the village culture (in circle 5); and it will not be the only one. Similar small cultures (circle 4) will grow when people go to school or university, travel to cities or deal with other people who come to the village – thus exemplifying that the village culture (circle 5) is always far from the confined exclusivity in the essentialist sense.

Bubble 3, in the centre of the figure represents a further extension of all the other cultures where the actual interaction between François and Agnes takes place. This is a culture of dealing because it is set up between the two interactants who enter into a relationship of culture making.

We do not wish to give the impression in this model of behaviour that the small cultures in circles 2–4 are 'sub-cultures' which are hierarchically subordinate, or deviant, to the respective 'parent' cultures (circles 1 and 5). A more open-ended picture seems more appropriate, in which the small cultures of the tourists, the village, the tourist–tourism business, and so on have a multiplicity of relationships both within and transcending larger entities (Table A0.1.1, cells iii–iv). Furthermore, Figure A2.2.1 presents only one way of seeing what happens between the villagers and the tourists. Another way of seeing this might be in terms of discourses, rather than small cultures, as discussed in Unit A2.2, and by Gee in Text B1.3.2. Whether these can be called discourses or cultures might depend on the degree in which they are represented by ways of talking or behaviour and artefacts.

This model of multiple cultures means that what François and Agnes actually *see* of each other is very much defined by the specific situation in which they meet. The cultural influences of the country from where Agnes comes, are only part of the picture. The culture of tourism is closer, and its influence is evidenced in Example A2.2.1 by Agnes' reference to the *Shirley Valentine* film, in which the behaviour of a middle-aged woman is changed by being away from home in an 'exotic' place. For François, it is the culture of trading with tourists which brings him into contact with Agnes, leaving the social influences of the village and his engagement relatively distant. When they actually meet, it is within the very new small culture of their dealing with each other that they see each other's behaviour directly. It could be argued that in this new small culture their behaviour becomes anomalous, sometimes mixed up, still approaching the competence people achieve in longer standing cultures, as they learn how to behave in this very new culture. Put more simply, they see each other very much out of character in this clumsy new culture.

Nevertheless, the basis upon which they *perceive*, or think they see each other is very different. Inaccurate Othering and culturism becomes rampant. Although Agnes, as a tourist, is behaving differently because she is on holiday, François explains her behaviour – as a 'loose' woman – according to the common stereotype of women from a certain part of the world that he brings from his village. Agnes similarly explains his behaviour – as a 'womaniser' – according to the common stereotype of men who live in a certain part of the world. They both thus totally miss that each of them are involved in intense moral struggle, precipitated by the strangeness of the situation in which they find themselves.

What needs to be realised here is that in a non-essentialist paradigm, we are not looking at the foreign Other as though it is locked in a separate foreign place. In all the examples used so far, there are people who are operating at cultural borders. Moreover, their struggle for identity is very much connected with this border activity – how they are being seen by people who do not know them. We showed in Units A1.3 and A2.1 that this is not just to do with people moving between different societies, but also between small cultures within a particular society. Figure A2.2.2 shows that what we actually see in a person's behaviour and what they say about themselves interacts *both* with the cultural resources they bring with them and the new cultural experience they encounter. Hence, Zhang's talk about The Code of Civility in Unit A1.2 is his projection onto the circumstances in which he finds himself in the foreign society of the masters programme.

What is particularly unfortunate here is that very often the resources we bring with us from our familiar cultural experience (right hand bubble of the figure), and which we then project onto the unfamiliar culture which we confront (left hand bubble) are very often stereotypes which arise from our own discourses about the

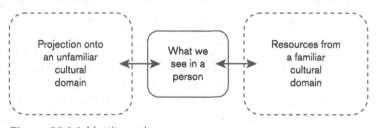

Figure A2.2.2 Identity on the cusp

Other. Then, after subsequently unsuccessful interaction with the Other, we return, like François and Agnes, to the same comfortable discourses – hence the two-way arrows in Figure A2.2.2.

Communication

As a result of this unit it is possible to build on the disciplines from Unit A1.3, which dealt with communication as cultural negotiation. From our understanding of the complex cultures surrounding communication, the following disciplines are helpful (numbering continued from previous unit):

14. Be aware that what happens between yourself and others is influenced very much by the environment within which you are communicating and your own pre-occupations.

15. Become aware of your own pre-occupations in order to understand what it is that people from other backgrounds are responding to.

This in effect means that we need to research ourselves just as much as we research those who are strange to us. This links with the disciplines in Unit A1.1 about building a thick description of the whole communication scenario.

Task A2.2.1 Thinking about cultural dealing

➤ Think of a situation you have been in where there is an element of cultural dealing and describe it, using Figure A2.2.1 to help you.

➤ Evaluate and try and improve on it so that it fits the situation you have described better.

➤ Explain how you can better understand one or more people in the situation with the help of Figure A2.2.2 and the disciplines listed above.

➤ What can you learn from this about intercultural communication?

UNIT A2.3 POWER AND DISCOURSE

We must be careful what we say

Experience

This unit considers how careful we must all be when talking about and to people who we consider to be Other, because we may be unaware of the power our words may carry. Indirectly, it will consider the issue of political correctness, a much contested concept. Consider this example:

Example A2.3.1 Understanding supervisor

Jeremy is a university lecturer. He was very pleased when he heard he was going to supervise Jabu, a student from a country that he had visited several years ago when he had been involved in a three-year science education project in secondary schools. He therefore felt he knew where she came from more than his colleagues. He felt he would clearly be the best person to help her to get through her research project. He had also read quite a few things on cultural differences, which interested him a great deal.

Jabu first met Jeremy during a class he was teaching on introducing science research. She was the only 'international' student there and felt quite angry when, during introductions, he announced to all the other students that he knew her 'context' very well. She was not sure whether it was something about his tone of voice – as though he was speaking about someone who had a handicap of some sort – or his speed of voice – as though she might not understand normal English – or that she was being separated out from of all the other students as needing some sort of special attention – which annoyed her. Or perhaps it was that he was making out that he understood her and was on her side. What could he possibly know about her and her background which would give him this right!? Even her closest friends at home did not presume that they knew her so well that they could speak for her like this – except perhaps her mother – and every daughter knows that story!

She could see at their first tutorial that he really was trying his best, but he still maintained his slow tone of voice. At least he wasn't shouting as some people did when they thought you might not understand. Then – he began to explain to her that he understood something about 'her culture', and that therefore he would be able to help her to meet deadlines and to 'understand concepts' that might be 'alien' to her. He even said that he knew what it was like, with her 'history', that she had to 'suddenly have to compete in every sphere'. It took her a moment to understand what he was getting at. Then she realised that he was having the ignorant audacity to be thinking that she might have difficulty keeping up with people from what she imagined he would call 'his culture'.

This sort of thing became the norm for their meetings. When she showed him work he always made a big thing about saying how well she had done – as though he was surprised that she could do it at all. Then there were lots of informal 'friendly' bits of conversation, in which he always put on a very 'kind' face, about 'food', 'rituals', 'marriage practices' and 'ceremonies' 'in her culture'; and once he even asked her if she 'was still in contact with her tribe'. He was also supervising a German student; and she was sure he never asked *him* about 'food', 'rituals', 'marriage practices', 'ceremonies' and 'tribes'.

One day Jabu really felt like giving up the whole thing and going home. She was walking down the corridor towards Jeremy's office. He was standing in the corridor talking to a colleague. He hadn't seen her; and he was saying, 'Well she does have some difficulty meeting deadlines; but of course that's something deep in her culture, isn't it'. She knew as a matter of fact that she was having no more difficulty than any of the other students; and anyway, even if she was, why should it have anything to do with her 'culture'? There was a Welsh student who always missed deadlines, and no-one would dare suggest this was anything to do with 'Welsh culture'.

Deconstruction

This is a case where there are clearly two very different perceptions of what is going on. Jeremy believes he is being supportive, inclusive and understanding, whereas Jabu feels she is being treated badly, and indeed the victim of racism. Jeremy is, we are sure, trying his best to do what he can for Jabu, but in our view he is making a basic mistake, which derives from his essentialist notion of her culture, that prevents him from dealing with her as she sees herself. Her predicament is similar to that of Parisa in Unit A1.1, though remains unresolved in this example. Jeremy falls into the same trap as John does in Unit A2.1, but in his naïvety he does not realise it, and this lack of realisation goes deep into his language. We shall discuss the details of this problem in terms of the following concepts:

- Thinking you are being understanding when in fact you are patronising
- False sharing
- Culturist language.

Being patronising

This is detailed in rows (a) to (c) in Table A2.3.1. Basically, in row (a), Jeremy does not base his understanding of Jabu on what he observes of her, but on pictures he, himself, has constructed from his own experience in South Africa. Here, he makes the usual essentialist mistake of imagining that everyone in South Africa is the same, and the basis of his construction in the first place is likely to have been stereotypical (Table A0.1.1, cells ix). His reading into 'cultural difference' also implies an essentialist fascination with comparable, collectible cultures as objects (Table A0.1.1, cell i). All of this drives his behaviour – talking not really to her, but to an image of who she is. Moreover, his treating her as a cultural category sets her apart from the other students (Table A2.3.1, row b). Making her 'special' inhibits her ability to integrate and makes her feel labelled as less capable than the other students (row c). This notion of 'special needs' is also strengthened by the essentialist idea that arriving in a 'new' culture, like learning a new language, puts Jabu in a deficit position. See for example Table A0.1.1, cells vii–viii, x. ('Special needs' is an issue which also affects the inclusion of children from diverse backgrounds and abilities within state education.)

Table A2.3.1   Difficult communication

Jeremy thinks he is being understanding and inclusive because:	Jabu feels patronised, Othered and the victim of racism because:
a He shows he understands her cultural circumstances and special needs.	She does not want to be made 'special' by someone who could not possibly understand. He has no right to presume she has special needs. He is treating her as inferior to others because of a limited understanding of who she is. She feels invaded.
b He rationalises her shortcomings in terms of 'her culture'.	He makes her a special cultural case. He implies the inferiority of what he has constructed as 'her culture'. He fails to imagine she could be like others.
c He speaks slowly and carefully.	Before he even meets her, he assumes she will have difficulty understanding. He treats her as though she is handicapped.
d He shows interest in 'her culture'.	He over-emphasises 'exotic' aspects which imply backwardness.
e He makes reference to cultural concepts she will understand.	He uses language which implies her inferiority.

The final straw for Jabu is when she overhears Jeremy in the corridor making what can be no less than a culturist comment – that her lateness in meeting deadlines is caused by her 'culture'. The blatant error in this judgement is revealed by Jabu's observation that she certainly is not being treated equally with other students. Indeed, it is Jeremy's over-generalisation that her lateness is a product of her 'culture' which prevents him from seeing a far more common explanation – that she is really more like other students than different to them.

False sharing

This category of Othering is complex. It corresponds with row (d) in Table A2.3.1. Again, Jeremy is probably right and sincere in wanting to share; but he is sharing with an image of Jabu which he has constructed, while the real Jabu exists in a very different world. What reveals Jeremy's mistake is Jabu's observation that if she were German, he would not be making references to 'marriage practices, ceremonies and tribes', and as German society must be complex, just like hers, he must have selected these topics when he talks to her because they have some sort of exotic value, which in turn implies, for her, some sort of backwardness. This type of Othering is often difficult to pin down. Jeremy could equally have cultural imaginations about German society, which would indeed be reflected in his choice of topics when talking to his German student – perhaps connected with being organised or militaristic. In Jabu's case, coming from a part of the world where there is a colonial history, there is indeed an expectation of another type of cultural imagination, akin to Orientalism in the Middle and Far East, where certain aspects of societies have been sensationalised by the West to feed a deep view that they are indeed 'backward' and 'lascivious'. (See the discussion of Orientalism in Unit B2.1.) The key word in Jeremy's choice of topics is 'tribe'. Although this term might be in common usage to refer to certain types of social grouping, perhaps even by Jabu herself, when used by Jeremy, it rings of 'primitive', lacking in state organisation and 'pre-literate', and colours his reference to the other things on his list. Therefore, 'wedding *practices*, ceremonies and rituals' become 'primitive'. Jabu is thus being 'tribalised' by Jeremy (see, for example, Nzimiro 1979; Wagner 1981: 29; Bauman, Text B0.1.2). This is therefore similar to the situation seen in Unit A1.3, where we see a group of schoolgirls using terms of abuse to create social cohesion which would be considered misogynistic if used by outsider men.

Culturist language

The significance of Jeremy's use of 'tribe' and 'practices' draws attention to the role of language in Othering (Table A2.3.1, row e). A major point here is that he does not seem to be aware of the effect of the language he is using; and investigating this hidden area takes us into critical discourse analysis and the uncovering of the way everyday talk hides our ideologies (Fairclough 1995; Wodak 2008). Although we do not have the full text of what Jeremy says to Jabu, from what we do have in Example A2.3.1, it is possible to see the traces of Jeremy's essentialist culturist ideology in some of his phraseology. Talking of helping Jabu to 'understand concepts' that might be 'alien' to her is not in itself particularly significant in a tutorial supervision context. However, when this is put alongside 'history' and that she would 'suddenly have to compete in every sphere', understanding concepts seems to become dependent on racial factors. This is certainly the connection which Jabu makes – 'keeping up' with his people.

This attention to language raises the issue of political correctness. What has become known as 'PC' in some circles has been attacked quite a lot for (a) preventing people from speaking their minds and stating the obvious, and (b) being over-sensitive to apparently innocent language which carries hidden racist or sexist references – for example, 'clearing the decks' being a non-PC gender-related phrase because it refers to the navy which is a male-dominated institution. (It refers to removing unnecessary objects from a warship's deck in preparation for battle – and it used to mean tidying up in preparation for a new activity.) While we would tend to agree with (b), where the sanitisation of language might indeed be being taken too far, we do not agree with (a). We really do feel that Jeremy needs to be extremely careful with his language. We certainly regard his statement that her inability to meet deadlines is connected with 'something deep in her culture' as something that needs to be 'politically corrected'. This not just Jeremy speaking casually in an unguarded moment when he thinks Jabu is not listening. The question tag, 'isn't it', is there to involve colleague in a discourse which is essentially racist and culturist. This type of unguarded language is thus in danger of normal-ising a potentially very destructive way of speaking and thinking about others. Responding again to objection (a) above, Jeremy may indeed be stating what seems to *him* to be obvious. The point is that, as Jabu rightly rationalises, what he says is *not* based on immediate empirical evidence, but on inaccurate stereotyping leading to prejudice (Figure A2.1.1, bubbles A–B).

We would therefore state that political correctness is very necessary in the sense that everyone needs to:

- ■ Take great care of connections they make between people, their behaviour and generalisations about the categories in which we place people – culture, gender and race being but examples
- ■ Be disciplined in considering evidence which is not connected to these categories.

The discipline in the second point is a form of *bracketing* – a device used in qualitative research for avoiding the easy answers which most readily spring to mind because of their presence in dominant discourse. Jeremy thus needs to be aware that he is already conditioned by an essentialist dominant discourse which will always tend to explain the behaviour of people from certain parts of the world in terms of their 'national' or 'ethnic culture'. If he really wants to help Jabu, he should attend to this rather than indulging unguardedly in his prior experience of her exoticness.

We think it is important to spend a moment to comment about the relationship between culturism and racism in this example. Basically, Jeremy is Othering and reducing Jabu to less than what she is by means of a prescribed image of what he thinks she is. Whether this is racist, culturist, or even sexist depends on which aspect of her persona, in his eyes, is the driving force behind his image of her. If it is her race, then this is racism. If it is her gender, then this is sexism. If it is her culture, then this is culturism. Although Jabu reads his attitude as racism, his primary interest is in her culture. Therefore, we see his reducing of her as culturism. At the same time, there is a body of literature that argues that in much of our everyday talk, reference to culture is a euphemism for race and in effect amounts to neo-racism (Delanty *et al.* 2008: 1; Spears 1999: 12–13).

Communication

This unit is very much about restraint. Learning from Jeremy's mistakes, we need to consider the following disciplines:

16. Avoid being seduced by previous experience of the exotic.
17. Monitor your own language and be aware of the destructive, culturist discourses you might be conforming to or perpetuating.

(Numbering is continued from the previous unit.)

Task A2.3.1 Thinking about Jabu

➤ Think of a situation you have been in which is like the Jabu example and describe it in similar detail.

➤ Explain how you can better understand one or more people in the situation with the help of Table A2.3.1 and the disciplines listed above.

➤ What can you learn from this about intercultural communication?

Theme 3
Representation

This theme will take a more macro look at how society constructs the foreign Other on our behalf.

UNIT A3.1   CULTURAL REFUGEE

We have been different to what we are now

Experience

This unit will look at the issue of migrants, not just because it is extremely important in today's world, but because the migrant predicament as cultural traveller with problematic status serves to teach us a lot about the nature of culture and cultural representation. Consider this example:

Example A3.1.1 Life before

When Martha first met Reza he seemed to her the typical newly arrived migrant, drably dressed and unsure of himself. She was new to teaching people like him but found a lot of support from conferences, colleagues and textbooks, and it made a lot of sense to her to follow the approach within which her job was not just to teach the English necessary for citizenship, but to empower her students by encouraging them to express their identity. Reza was a good example of this need. He was from a country that had been ravaged by civil war. She was lucky that there was so much information around in the media about the plight of people in his country. Martha felt that coming to the West would enable him to express himself and articulate his identity in ways he had never been able to before. She knew that even in the capital city of his country, people had absolutely nothing.

At first, as everybody said, Martha found Reza clearly unable to deal with the requirements of Western society. He was terribly prejudiced against basic freedoms. Even when she was sure he had the basic English he refused to talk about his culture, he seemed to resent having a female teacher, which one would expect from a culture where women were not even considered second-class citizens, and the only coherent statement she heard him make was that he would never let his daughter marry someone from her country. There was an odd incident she would always remember. He cut his finger rather badly. When he came back from the hospital he was extremely agitated and kept on talking about the nurse who had stitched it. Martha presumed that he just could not cope with being touched by a woman. Eventually she had to give up on him as a hopeless bigot.

Martha then met Reza a year later. He was sitting in the cafeteria while waiting for a friend who was signing up for her programme. Martha thought he looked somehow different – less angry and desolated. She accepted his invitation to sit down and have coffee. He told her he was working as a supervisor in a furniture factory. His English was better, and it seemed more appropriate now to ask him about his life before he was a migrant. She was astonished when he told her he was a judge, but that he hadn't been as successful as his sister, who was a university professor in the US, and his eldest daughter, who was specialising to be a gynaecologist in Moscow. He said he remembered her being annoyed with him in class, and that she needed to understand what a difficult predicament he was in at that time, entering a new country at the bottom of the system as a casual labourer, and feeling totally powerless and isolated – a member of the underclass of a Western country who found it hard to appreciate the 'freedoms' about which they had heard. He explained that although it might seem silly and unimportant now, the last straw had been the accident with his finger. All he had wanted to do at that point, despite everything that was happening there, was to return home to get it treated. She asked him why, when surely there was no decent medical care in his own country. Reza said that this is just one of the things that everyone misunderstood about where he came from. In fact, there were excellent hospitals there, where, despite the life-threatening political dangers, of course he would not be treated like a migrant who couldn't think. He finished by saying that he felt his greatest achievement in his new country was seeing his teen-age daughter doing well at school and taking part in the full range of activities that young people deserved. However, he also wanted to tell her that all those things did exist in his own country before the civil war.

Deconstruction

In this example we see Martha working with Reza, a migrant in her language class, according to representations of the foreign Other which are present in society. She then discovers that he is very different to these representations. Reza's plight is not dissimilar to that of several of the people who are culturally misunderstood in these units, and Martha is no more or less to blame for not seeing his reality than other people who misunderstand them. This unit does not tell a different story, but focuses on a different aspect of how cultural misunderstanding comes about – through the following sources of representation in influencing Martha in the way she sees Reza:

- Media images.
- Professional images.

To deal with this, we shall discuss the need to:

- Bracket popular representation.

Media images

A major source of Martha's prejudging of Reza, a migrant from a country torn apart by civil war, is the information she gets from her national media. In modern society we are constantly fed images of the foreign Other by the television, radio, internet and press, in the explicit form of news, documentaries and current affairs discussion, which report and describe people and events across the world, often with graphic visual material, and more subtly through the images of people and places that we see creatively manipulated in advertising and sensationalised journalism. Reza's country of origin would be an example of this. It is not, therefore, at all surprising that Martha should see Reza in these terms – derelict, war-ruined streets with little evidence of urban facilities, and a society in which women appear deprived of the most basic rights. These images, usually in the so-called developing world, are represented very selectively, and, despite the often well-wishing of journalists, what is chosen to be shown will be influenced by imaginations of the 'exotic', which are the basis of the reductive Orientalism discussed in Unit B2.1. Especially during the so-called 'Arab Spring' uprisings, the unprecedented numbers of refugees trying to enter Europe and coming out of the Syrian civil war, and the rise of the 'Islamic State of Iraq and Syria' (ISIS) in the 2010s, these images are more mixed, but will be selectively displayed. There are representations of middle-class and highly educated activists and migrants in street protests or walking destitute across Europe, and then European citizens joining ISIS and firing Islamophobia among Western populations as they are associated with hidden religious fundamentalism. Without knowledge of the complex histories of emerging extremism, it is hard for members of the public to make sense of this proliferation of images and to sort out the relationships between different types of people, religion and politics.

Among these images, it would still be easy for many people not to know, for example, that many Arabs are not Muslim, that many Muslim women do not wear the hejab and that many people in the so-called developing world do not live in traditional souqs, bazaars, shanty-towns or war-torn streets with livestock. It could be unknown that a large slice of the population all over the world own cars and computers, live in orderly suburbs, and dress and go about their daily business very much like 'we' do – and that, regardless of forms of dress, ordinary people everywhere struggle to a create civil society. Significant for Martha to know is that many migrants, though they have fallen on hard times because of war, political oppression or economic catastrophe, have, in the not too distant past, had sophisticatedly educated lives. Despite not owning cars and computers or not having the opportunity of formal extended education, they still have the intelligence and autonomy to make use of these resources when given the opportunity.

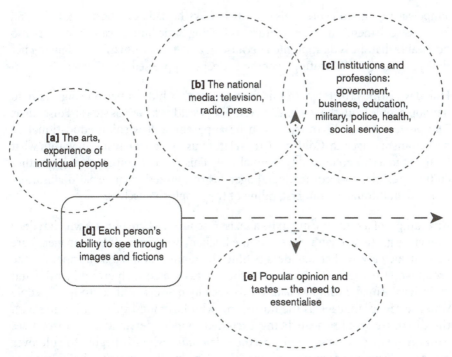

Figure A3.1.1 Forces of representation

What is perhaps strange is that while people may be naturally cynical about much of what the media shows us, they may well be often less critical of images of the 'exotic'. This is shown in Figure A3.1.1, which is our own interpretation of the relationships between the individual and forces of representation in society. The representations created by the media are in bubble (b). There is a subtle dialogue between this and the tastes and opinions of the public in bubble (e). The nature of this dialogue will vary from society to society, depending on the freedom of the media, but in the West, the representations in the media will very largely respond to public demand – and at the heart of this demand is the desire to essentialise.

Professional images

Apart from the possible Othering of the so-called developing world, the representations we see cannot be disconnected from a particular political point of view that depicts a derelict country in need of rescue by the West. During colonial times, images of the South and East as deficit cultures were often constructed, consciously or unconsciously, to justify 'civilising' conquest. This strategy for reproducing certain types of representation can, we think, be connected with the professional image which Martha gets from 'conferences, colleagues and textbooks'. In our view, the discourse of the professionalism which Martha employs also projects a 'civilising conquest' over refugee students. Instead of simply teaching Reza the language he needs to live and work in a new country, she is intent on 'empowering' him to 'express' his identity in ways 'he had never been able to before'. She thus sees 'them' and 'their culture' as lacking basic human capacities. It is also noticeable that she is disappointed because Reza is 'not a woman', thus denying her the opportunity of 'liberating' even more deeply 'oppressed' individuals.

Holliday (2013: 110) refers to this friendliness that hides a patronising desire to develop people from the so-called developing world as a West as steward discourse. The power of this discourse lies in its apparent well-wishing educational or developmental agenda. Collins (2016) relates this to higher education within what he refers to as 'interculturality from above'. This is an attempt to bring together cultural realities to feed neoliberal agendas of marketised internationalisation, rather than through an understanding of the people themselves.

An example of *a discourse* might be a sexist discourse, where phrases which reduce women (e.g. 'the woman's place is in the kitchen', 'women can't be managers') are used in such a way that the ideas behind them are promoted as normal for the group who use them. Discourses can thus be associated with group identity and exclusivity. Anyone who has had to mix socially or work with a group of people who use sexist language as the norm, and who has found that not joining with the discourse would mean being excluded, will understand how discourses work. A sexist discourse would become *dominant* when it begins to rule over other discourses in a larger group or society. The media can play a significant role in promoting discourses and making them dominant. There is a similar relationship here between popular tastes and opinions and professional representations (Figure A3.1.1, bubbles e and c) as there is with the media. In bubble (c) we have also listed other institutions and professions which produce representations of the foreign Other, all of which, in turn, to varying degrees, with their own strong discourse of reality, feed, influence and provide the content for the media in bubble (b).

Bracketing popular representations

The relationship between bubbles (b), (c) and (e) in Figure A3.1.1 therefore implies an almost hegemonic set of beliefs and images in which the mainstream opinion, tastes, media and institutions of a society collude to produce established representations of the foreign Other. By hegemonic we mean achieving a domination, which pervades all aspects of society to such a subtle degree that it may be invisible. There can, however, be breakthroughs, the source of which we have placed on the left of the diagram. This is, of course, an extremely simplistic representation in itself of very complex social forces, but we wish to make the simple point that the individual actor (bubble d) in whatever society is able to form her or his own images and break away from – see through – the established essentialism. Some of the resources, which can be used here (bubble a), have already been exemplified in these units. The conference colleagues in Unit A1.1 are introduced by Parisa to a film and see an alternative (to the established) picture, which reveals a more complex reality of who she is. Janet and John in Units A1.2

and B2.1 arrive at such pictures through encounters with individual people in Zhang and Ming and the Smith family, as do the observers of the schoolgirls in Unit A1.3. Something happens that makes us bracket the easy answer and look at things differently. We have listed the arts generally in the bubble because we think that it is in this domain – broadly from quality television drama through to music and painting, and indeed, more critical television documentary – more critical, creative images *can* come. We have not listed travel and international contact because, as we see with Jeremy in Unit A2.3, and Agnes and François in Unit A2.2, *contact* with 'other cultures' may confirm rather than question the essentialist point of view.

Returning to Martha's experience, there were several cultural presumptions she formed in her initial encounter with Reza that she will need to reassess in the light of her second encounter. She explained both his unease in class and his dissatisfaction with regard to his hospital visit as misogynous dislike of contact with female teachers and nurses. Apart from one statement about not wanting his daughter to marry someone from his new country, these presumptions stem directly from the overall cultural stereotype of his country of origin and all its male population being entirely in support of limiting women's rights.

It is entirely on the basis of this background that Martha judged Reza's behaviour. That he was uneasy in class and at the hospital, he confirms himself, but the explanations for this could be many, and in effect she had no direct evidence arising from the situation itself to support misogyny. In the second encounter with Reza, he explains his reason for discomfort in class and in the hospital as to do with being a newcomer in very difficult social circumstances. His statement about how he left his country to give his daughter better opportunities also goes against Martha's assumption about his attitude towards his daughter. Indeed, feeling isolated and a member of the underclass in his new country might well make him cautious about his daughter integrating into a society seen from that point of view. The hospital incident is significant because Martha had simply assumed that there was no infrastructure in his country of origin. She had also assumed that there was no-one there who had the social sophistication to deal with their own identity – that this was the exclusive domain of Western society.

All of these assumptions about Martha and Reza are, of course, grey areas and rough generalisations. However, it is not difficult to imagine that a major reason why Martha saw Reza as a bigoted misogynist was that he did not respond to her strategy to reconstruct him. In effect, he was neither a misogynist nor in need of reconstruction. In terms of a methodology for understanding, she did indeed observe him closely, but her observation may have been clouded by a certain prejudice.

Communication

The disciplines within this theme need to focus on our awareness of the images from our own society that influence the way we see other people. This takes us further into the need for us to research ourselves. Taking heed of the experience in this unit, when communicating with others, we therefore need to consider the following disciplines:

18. Be aware of the media, political and institutional influences in your own society which lead you to see people from other cultural backgrounds in a certain way.
19. See through these images and fictions when we encounter people from other cultural backgrounds, and always try to consider alternative representations.

(Numbering continues from the previous unit.)

 Task A3.1.1 Thinking about Reza

➤ Think of a situation you have been in which is like the Reza example and describe it in similar detail.

➤ Explain how what happens in the situation can be understood in terms of the types of images and representations described in the Deconstruction section and Figure A3.1.1.

➤ Explain what you therefore need to know in order better to understand people like Reza. Refer to disciplines listed above.

➤ What can you learn from this about intercultural communication?

➤ Where can you see examples of the West as steward discourse? Think also about the way in which Parisa's colleagues say 'well done' in Unit A1.1.

UNIT A3.2 COMPLEX IMAGES

We have no idea how deeply we get things wrong

Experience and deconstruction

In this unit we will look more deeply at some of the profound errors of representation of the foreign Other within our own society. The images we will show present a familiar picture, but what we need to do is to fathom the unfamiliar which they hide. In this unit we are not going to present a description of one event, but instead a series of descriptions of different media events. While fictionalised, they are based on events that really took place. These are, of course, our personal impressions of them, coloured by our desire to undo essentialism. We are also in this unit mixing the Experience and Deconstruction sections, which will allow us better to deal with each example in turn.

The first example speaks for itself:

Example A3.2.1 Whose art?

A discussion was taking place on television about a new exhibition of paintings. Some art critics were arguing that this was a major development within the cultural life of a minority group to which the artists belonged. Two of the artists, who were also present, kept on saying that they thought that this was not a minority thing, but that it contributed to the international scene because of how the paintings were influenced by and spoke back to a particular international art movement. No one seemed to pick this up. It was as though whatever they said was being ignored, and they fail to make any impact in the discussion.

This television discussion might not seem particularly problematic to the majority of viewers, who would most probably see things in the same way as the majority of the discussants; that this was all about a minority art scene. However, what we wish to point out is that the art critics fail to pick up on the point the painters were making because it does not conform to a dominant discourse – that art produced by a minority group belongs only to that minority group. The following definitions are our own:

- **Dominant discourses** are ways of talking and thinking about something which have become naturalised to the extent that people conform to them without thinking.
- **Naturalisation** occurs when a social phenomenon becomes sufficiently routine and natural to be internalised into everyday 'thinking-as-usual'.

Naturalisation is very similar to institutionalisation (where new behaviour becomes established practice in an institution), reification (where something that is only an idea is considered real), and routinisation (where new behaviour becomes a routine). All these processes can happen by themselves as part of the natural way in which society works, or be socially engineered by managers, spin doctors, governments, the media, political parties, or anyone who has influence over other people. There has already been references to discourses of culture in Unit A3.1. The people who speak against the dominant discourse, in this case the two artists, are promoting a *counter discourse* that is trying to prevent the dominant discourse from being naturalised. They might be compared to Parisa in Unit A1.1 and Reza in A3.1, who try hard to counter the dominant West as steward discourse, which fails to see them as autonomous in their own right.

Dominant discourses can be so *naturalised* that people become unaware of them (Fairclough 1995: 36). In Example A3.2.1, the dominant discourse is such that the argument of the two artists does not seem to be opposed as much as simply not heard. This may be because the ideas the artists express does not correspond with what the other discussants normally think about. In other words, their ideas do not conform to the thinking-as-usual of the other people. Thinking-as-usual is a term used in sociology to mean what people have got used to thinking of as being normal.

It can also be argued that the dominant discourse in this example is essentialist because it states that something that comes from a particular culture only belongs to that culture, whether a national culture or any other culture (ix in Table A0.1.1).

The next example shows how the media can feed dominant discourses about cultural stereotypes. It is in two parts, the first looking at a travelogue and the second seeing a probable effect of this:

Example A3.2.2 Country image

Part 1

A well-known television travel correspondent is doing a series of programmes on countries in a particular region. At the end of her programme on one of the countries she is filmed standing on the border. Pointing over the border, she announces that her next programme will take her to this very different, 'fundamentalist' neighbour. This is followed by footage of women wearing extreme religious clothing in a downtown market area.

Part 2

Matthew recently visited the same country, which he knew well, with a group of colleagues, all of whom were well travelled and sensitive to issues of Othering. Nevertheless, he found himself on the edge of a discussion of how the dress code for women visitors might be relaxed because there was 'now' a new President. The implication was that 'now' the country might be more modern ('= liberal' '= less fundamentalist' '= allowing women to cover less'). Matthew had been there fifteen years before when the then, previous government, had prohibited female university students from wearing the Islamic headscarf on the campus, but he did not feel it appropriate to bring this up on the edge of this casual conversation as they were getting on the conference bus. He thus allowed the dominant discourse to rule.

The views of Matthew's colleagues, who were not at all familiar with the country, were fed by news items and documentaries of the type described in part 1 of the example. It would not be surprising if the correspondent in part 1 did not herself purposely *choose* to *select* only the footage of religious-looking women. There might have been a range of possible footage to choose from, and it might have been the editors who chose what they thought was more sensational. On the other hand, the dominant discourse is so strong that she probably did not think about selecting other available footage from the country – of young men and women, intensely conscious of high European fashion, which they integrate into their own styles, walking by elegant boutiques and sitting in restaurants. And, of course, it might not occur to someone with these dominant views that people wearing the traditional dress of the region might not be 'fundamentalist' at all. The outcome with Matthew and his colleagues was that his colleagues had picked up a dominant discourse. Although he had something to say that would counter the discourse, he did not feel that he could do this without spoiling the relationship. The discourse therefore persisted.

A very similar dominant discourse is present in the next example:

Example A3.2.3 Traffic problems

The same country, as described in the previous example, was later featured in a popular tourist guide series, which has the reputation of being progressive and culturally sensitive. There is a reference to traffic problems in the capital city. It is commented that the inhabitants of this country are 'just beginning to learn to use traffic lights'.

The reference to traffic lights is motivated by, what appears to the guide's authors, to be a less improper use of traffic lights than might have been observed in the past. Matthew, from the previous example, might know that it is indeed true that the use of traffic lights in the capital is different to their use in, say, Britain. One can observe, for example, that motorcyclists will sometimes position themselves in front of motorists, in front of the line at which motorists have stopped, and, indeed, the line itself might be interpreted liberally by some motorists. It might also be true that in recent years the practice has become more like that of Britain. It is, however, factually inaccurate that the citizens of the capital city are just learning to use traffic lights. The culture of traffic lights use is as longstanding as it is in any Western country, but different. The rules for use are as sophisticated, but because they look different to the newcomer or tourist observer, they are depicted as being primitive. If there *is* a change in the behaviour at traffic lights, it might be more of a result of globalisation than anything else.

As tourism to more 'exotic' locations becomes more accessible, tourist guides become a more influential part of the media that influences the way in which we see each other. As with the case of Matthew's well-travelled colleagues in Example A3.2.2, a significant twist in the first part of Example A3.2.2 is the intended intellectual sensitivity of the text, which is thus all the more likely to draw the discerning reader into the discourse. The issue of tourism in a post-colonialist discourse is taken up in Unit A2.2, and is discussed in Urry (2002).

The next example moves into the more politically sensitive domain of conflict between different populations within a particular country that has a high profile on world media.

Example A3.2.4 School children

There is a short piece on a news programme about how school children are coping with the atmosphere of threat from a nearby community. The school and the children look affluent and middle class. Those who are interviewed speak calmly and articulately. This is followed by footage from the community from which the threat is thought to be coming: people throwing stones at soldiers in an urban setting with dust, rubble and unfinished building sites.

This is a very complex case. One of the author's major feelings at the time of seeing these news items was how easy these contrasting images made it for a middle-class viewer, like himself, to identify with the (to him) familiarly middle-class image of the school children, who seemed 'normal', 'calm' and (presumably) therefore more 'civilised' than that of the stone-throwing 'other' community. In fighting this seduction, he also wondered why we do not see comparable images of middle-class members of the 'other' community in the media, which might help to break the dominant discourse of 'them' as 'terrorists and fundamentalists' – very similar to that discussed above, in Example A3.2.2, generated by 'fundamentalist' street scenes. On the other hand, there are complex issues of identity here. Who are *we* to presume the images by which *we* would like other people to be represented – simply in order for me to undo *our* reductive preoccupations?

The final two examples are also sensitive, in that they are connected with the emotions surrounding personal abduction and abuse. Each of the cases deal with a serious issue that it is the responsibility of the media to reveal. In the next example the women and children in question are clearly suffering. The question is, how is the cause of their suffering represented, and is it a simple one-sided matter?

Example A3.2.5 Abducted children

A television documentary tells a story of a group of women travelling to the country where their ex-husbands come from to see their children who have been 'abducted' by the ex-husbands. The men are characterised as despotic; they do not respect prior agreements; they will imprison their children; women and children in their society have no rights.

The real anguish of the women in this example has to be respected. However, the documentary, which is carried out by a production company that has a particular reputation for being critical, is one-sided in that there is no discussion of the complex cross-cultural history of each relationship, which must have led up to this state of affairs. There is no discussion of the point of view of the husbands, who are rarely heard to speak. Some or all of the traits of the husbands might have been true in some or all of the cases in the documentary, but there is no exploration of the possibility that they might not. Exploration of any of these issues would have implied a diversity in 'their' foreign society – perhaps as diverse as 'our' own society – which the discourse of Othering does not allow (Table A0.1.1, ix). Thus, the essentialist packaging of the foreign Other is perpetuated. It seems strange that the level of sophisticated analysis one might expect of the documentary was suspended in this case.

There is also a degree of sensationalism present in Example A3.2.5. A media message is sensational when it exaggerates particular features in order to appeal to the emotions. There was perhaps no *intention* in this documentary to be sensational. Indeed, the emotions connected with the abduction of children are real and do not need to be exaggerated. However, the documentary could be criticised for exoticising and sensationalising the husbands as distant and alien imprisoners of women and their children, instead of as ordinary men with different principles and laws governing child custody.

Our final example demonstrates a similar case of people being exoticised sensationally as imprisoners of women:

Example A3.2.6 Abuse of women

On a radio discussion programme is an item about the abuse of women by their husbands. However, it quickly becomes apparent that the focus of the item is families from a particular minority group. Another radio discussion features an academic from the same minority background, who makes the point that outsiders to the 'mainstream culture' of the country might well think that it is characterised by paedophilia, given the quantity of discussion of this issue in the national media.

This was an important item in that such abuse should be revealed and its causes discussed. It may indeed be the case that such abuse is more common within families from this particular minority group than within other families. However, the phrase 'in their culture' was used in such a way as to imply that abuse of women was a default feature of this 'culture'. 'Arranged marriages' were also referred to, and one immediately sees how the packaging of this particular 'foreign' Other begins to be formed. Othering of the community might have been far from the agenda of the journalist involved, but it was deep in the discourse of the item. The Othering discourse around 'arranged marriages' rarely refers to the practice that might be considered to be common in élite Western communities where money, property and dynasty are at stake. Neither will it draw attention to the fact that 'arranged marriage' might not be a bad thing, or that not all marriages within the communities with which they are associated are 'arranged', because these facts are not part of the packaging. Adrian Holliday recalls his friend from a northern town in Britain commenting that the common concept of 'arranged marriages' does not sit easily with the image of 'liberated young Asian women who jump on the bus with me each morning'. Perhaps we feel that they are not 'real' (like Parisa in Unit A1.1). It is the second news item, in Example A3.2.6, which shows us the reality of this reductive distortion.

Communication

In this unit, it is important to build on the advice of Unit A2.1 and look deeper into some of the origins of essentialist prejudice in the media. From all the examples in this unit we can see that it is important to think about dominant discourses (numbering continued from last unit):

20. Be aware of dominant discourses which are easily perpetuated by the media, and which lead us to 'think-as-usual' that familiar images of the foreign Other are 'normal'.

From Example A3.2.5 and Example A3.2.6 especially, we can see how prejudice is sometimes hidden behind intellectual sensitivity:

21. Be aware that even images projected by sensitive, intellectual, 'critical' sources can seduce our own sensitivities and intellects into thinking that they are 'true'.

From Examples A3.2.5 and A3.2.6 especially, we can see that there is often a hidden sensationalism:

22. Although sensationalism in the media is something we know about and guard against, you need to appreciate how deeply it exists in our traditional views of the foreign Other.

 Task A3.2.1 Thinking about representation

➤ Think of a situation you have been in or observed which is like one of the ones presented in this unit and describe it in similar detail.

➤ Provide an examples of naturalisation in the description and try and link it with a dominant discourse.

➤ Thinking about the disciplines listed above, consider how far we really do need to search out hidden forces.

➤ What can you learn from this about intercultural communication?

UNIT A3.3   THE PARADOXES OF INSTITUTIONAL LIFE

Things may be more complex and quite different to first appearances

Experience

Much has been written about institutional cultures and about how people in different so-called national cultures conduct events, like business meetings, differently. The everyday reality of complex institutions seems, however, to be quite different, and different kinds of common representations seem to lack substance.

Example A3.3.1 Department or national culture?

Act 1 Betrayal

Wang had been working in the University Quality Office for three years and, while finding the institution strange, had made good friends and felt she was liked and appreciated. She had previously come to the country as a doctoral student in the Management Department and felt she had got to know the higher education system well.

Then, suddenly, everything began to fall apart. She had believed that she had funding to go to a staff development event in another city. She had already paid the conference and accommodation fee when she received an email from the department administrative assistant to say that a decision had been made that she was no longer able to go. She was horrified. She knew it must be the department head's decision, and yet she had had a meeting with him earlier in the day and he had said nothing about it.

She had coffee with her friend Pieter who was a lecturer in the Management Department. She told him that she was very confused here because people appeared friendly and then betrayed this friendship. Pieter felt it must be hard for her coming from a collectivist society where group loyalties were much stronger. (They had both studied the work of Hofstede and Triandis when they were students in the Management Department.)

Pieter also tried to explain that people often had to carry out actions that they did not feel comfortable with and that Wang's head of department may well have been in some committee where it had been decided that staff development budgets had to be cut, and then he had been too embarrassed to tell her face to face. He might even have forgotten due to the massive pressure of work that everyone had. Nevertheless, Wang left the conversation with a feeling of deep betrayal. She had imagined that people in this country had a high sense of honour and straightforwardness in personal and professional relationships. This had indeed been her experience when she was a Management student.

Act 2 Complexity

Several months later Wang changed her views about what had happened to her. Since the event with the conference fee she and two colleagues from her department had been doing some joint work with the Sociology Department – to help them develop their quality systems. This experience had been problematic in two respects. No matter how much she and her colleagues tried, with emails, documents and meetings, several key people in the Sociology Department totally failed to understand the systems they were trying to introduce. Moreover, they found attending Sociology meetings impossible because the Sociologists, who had a high reputation for research, spent all their time discussing who was going to be in which research group, without any discernable conclusion, and never got any further in the meeting agenda. Also, a lot of people were late or didn't turn up for the meetings – which blew the well-known theory about punctuality among people from this country.

Wang concluded that even after being in the University a number of years, she was just beginning to understand its complexity, that different departments had very different cultures, which her colleagues who were born and brought up here often found just as mystifying as she did. She had also learnt that several of her colleagues had been treated in exactly the same way as she had with the conference fee issue, and kept on telling her how 'incomprehensible' it all was. Regarding her own perception of being foreign, she was learning that she had drummed up ideas about being 'from a different culture' as a way of coping. In fact, what she had learnt most about the 'strange culture' of this country was that universities were just as complex and inefficient as universities at home. Actually, she felt more culturally competent than some of her colleagues who came from here because she had a broader, international experience of institutional life. Indeed, she found that personal management, negotiation and overall organisation skills she brought with her from working in organisations at home were particularly useful, and sometimes influenced her colleagues.

Deconstruction

In this example there are two competing narratives, which are represented in Table A3.3.1. In the first act the essentialist narrative, which has underpinned the chauvinistic theme of culturism in previous units, dominates, and Wang feels culturally strange and marginalised. This is a narrative of inability. It is based

Table A3.3.1 Two narratives

	Essentialist	Critical cosmopolitan
The institution	Institutions in different countries are essentially different because they reside in different national cultures. This factor is considered more significant than the cultural differences between departments within institutions in any society.	Universities in different national settings are equally complex, with internal cultural variety and the potential for internal miscommunication.
Wang	Lacks experience. Has difficulty understanding and coping with institutions in collectivist national cultures where there is less group loyalty.	Has a broader cultural experience with which to understand and cope with a strange institution. Has skills learnt in organisations in one society that are useful, can contribute, and, indeed, can influence cultural practices in an institution in another country.

on the common notion in intercultural studies that people who come from so-called *collectivist* national cultures are disadvantaged in institutional contexts in so-called *individualist* cultures because they have loyalties to the group, which make it hard to cope with creative, 'active' decision-making. See the full discussion of individualism and collectivism in Triandis (1995), Text B3.5.2.

Critical cosmopolitanism

The critical cosmopolitan narrative is very different to essentialism in that it:

■ acknowledges a fluid cultural complexity with blurred boundaries, with diversity as the norm
■ recognises a deep inequality between the Centre and the Periphery
■ considers that Periphery cultural realities need to struggle for recognition, but have the potential to claim the world.

(See for example Beck and Sznaider 2006; Delanty 2006; Delanty *et al.* 2008; Grande 2006, and Holliday 2011, 2013.)

> **Note:** *Critical* cosmopolitanism needs to be distinguished from what some writers call *global* cosmopolitanism, which supports a Western market-led picture of globalisation (for example, Bhabha 1994: xiv; Canagarajah 1999; Fairclough 2006: 40). The terms *Centre* and *Periphery* need to be used with caution, and for Adrian Holliday only make sense as psychological concepts. Hannerz (1991) defines the relationship between Centre and Periphery as one of giving and taking meaning within an unequal global order. This can be applied strategically or emotionally to different groups of people, events or attitudes at different times, and is particularly meaningful to the people who feel they have been placed in a Periphery position at a particular time.

From the critical cosmopolitan viewpoint, on the right of Table A3.3.1, the illusory aspects of the essentialist narrative become clear. Wang's abilities, which come to light in the second act of the example – the manner in which she copes, along with her colleagues who were born and brought up there, and actually begins to see that she brings cultural skills from her own country, and from a broader perspective of travel, which are both relevant and contribute – indicate that there is not the cultural 'problem' that she first imagined. Indeed, the way in which she reflects on mystifying cultural practices makes her seem no less or more individualist than her colleagues.

Whether or not Wang really comes from 'a collectivist culture', and whether or not this prevents her from coping, it is *assumed* that this is the case. There is thus a powerful, polarised, national cultural representation that influences not only the explanations that Pieter brings to what has happened to Wang, but also influences a large, dominant slice of intercultural communication management training. The assumption is strengthened by Wang's, like Zhang in Unit A1.2, collusion with the essentialist view of herself. She uses the notion of collectivism as a cultural resource to rationalise her own feeling of betrayal. A romanticised view of the 'culture' of her adopted country embodied in her previous academic department, expressed towards the end of the example, is another cultural resource that strengthens the essentialist view. Wang thus seems to indulge in self-marginalisation, as with Zhang's dependence on The Code of Civility.

The cosmopolitan narrative opens up the possibility that Wang's cultural abilities are not confined, but are able to transcend national boundaries, which are considered blurred and negotiable. Indeed, the illusion that she may not have this potential is due to its struggle for recognition against the dominance of the essentialist narrative. This struggle has already been evidenced in the example of Parisa in Unit A1.1.

The cosmopolitan narrative also opens up the possibility that the university in which Wang works is also more complex than a contained sub-set of an individualist national culture. Wang's experience indicates that there are also marked cultural differences between different departments in the university, which are sufficient to create serious miscommunication and mystification even for her colleagues who were born and brought up there. It becomes apparent that there is a complex of small cultures. As such, there emerges an equivalent complexity to the institutions she is familiar with in her country of origin. Indeed, it is at this closer level of detail that commonalities can be found. This author's own brief experience of hearing her colleagues speaking about familiar institutional inconsistencies, incompetent colleagues, mystification at the small cultures of other departments, unexpected events, and so on evidences this fact.

Underlying universal cultural processes

This picture of a cultural mélange, the complexity and detail of which can be familiar across national divides, raises the possibility of culture negotiation abilities, which everyone needs to get along in any society, as one moves from such different cultural realities as home to school to work, between jobs, communities and so on. These abilities relate to the discourse identities discussed in Unit B1.3 with reference to the work of Gee and colleagues. At the small culture level there are, therefore, underlying universal cultural processes that underpin all cultural realities. They are represented in the central domain of the grammar of culture in Figure A1.2.1, and will be argued to be the basis of intercultural travel and competence in Holliday (2016) in Text B3.6.2. It is these shared processes that Wang is able to tap into in the strange university of her adopted country, which she has brought with her, once she has seen through and put aside the individualism–collectivism façade. Furthermore, it can certainly be argued that the process of self-marginalisation is itself part of this set of underlying universal cultural strategies.

Cultural realism

This does not mean to say that there are no national social structures which influence people. The notion of cultural realism is important here (Holliday 2011: 192; Kumaravadivelu 2007: 143). This recognises that people everywhere are brought up with the facts of national structures, such as education, institutions and media, but that they also have the potential to see through and transcend them, as suggested in Figure A3.1.1. There will be cases where this ability is repressed by political and even educational and institutional systems, but the lack of opportunity to express does not mean that the potential is not there.

Communication

The disciplines which emerge as paramount for Wang, and indeed for her friend, Pieter, are therefore as follows – once again taking the numbering on from the last unit:

23. Believe that people from different cultural backgrounds can have the underlying cultural ability to understand, be competent in and contribute to your own cultural scene.
24. Understand that while people might be deeply influenced by the social structures of their nation, this does not mean that they are confined by them.

Task A3.3.1

➤ Consider small cultural differences within the organisation in which you work. From this, think about the intercultural skills you have acquired to deal with these, and how this can prepare you for working in other locations no matter how foreign.

➤ Think of cases where you or people you know have contributed to and perhaps even improved local cultural practices by importing practices from other places.

➤ Consider cases where these contributions have not been noticed or recognised because of cultural prejudice.

➤ Consider cases where people have travelled away from countries where they have been restricted because of oppressive political or other systems – and have then excelled in the very activities in which they had previously lacked the opportunity to participate.

➤ How might such an observation impact on the common prejudice that if someone does not openly express critical thought in, say, a classroom, it is thought that they don't know how to be critical?

➤ Under what circumstances might someone express their criticality through being silent? What underlying universal cultural processes may be in operation here, and what might drive you to similar behaviour elsewhere?

➤ Relate all of these tasks to the examples seen so far in Section A.

UNIT A3.4 DISCIPLINES FOR INTERCULTURAL COMMUNICATION

At the end of this last unit in Section A it is now possible to put together all the discipline from this whole section in Table A3.4.1. These disciplines have been derived from analysis of the situations discussed throughout the section. The right hand column provides a summary which clarifies their relationship with each of the three themes which run throughout the book. Along with further discussions connected with the readings presented in Section B, these disciplines will be taken forward to Section C where they will be realised in research projects.

Table A3.4.1 Disciplines

Discussion	Statement	Summary
	Identity	
Unit A1.1	1. Respond to people according to how you find them rather than according to what you have heard about them. 2. Avoid easy answers about how people are. Bracket – put aside simplistic notions about what is 'real' or 'unreal' in your perception of 'another culture'. 3. Appreciate that every society is as complex and culturally varied as your own. 4. Learn to build up thick descriptions of what happens between you and others – to work out how to communicate as you go along.	Seek a deeper understanding of individual people's identity by: a) avoiding preconceptions b) appreciating complexity c) not over-generalising from individual instances.
Unit A1.2	5. When people are in a difficult, strange environment, they can close ranks and exaggerate specific aspects of their cultural identity. 6. Different cultural resources can be drawn upon and invoked at different times depending on the circumstances. 7. What people say about their cultural identity should be read as the image they wish to project at a particular time rather than as evidence of an essentialist national culture.	Achieve this by employing *bracketing* to put aside your preconceptions, *thick description* to enable you to see complexity, and an appreciation of *emergent data* to signal the unexpected.

Table A3.4.1 continued

Discussion	Statement	Summary
	8. While respecting whatever people say about their own cultural background, take what they say as evidence of what they wish to project rather than as information about where they come from.	
	9. Take what people say about their own cultural background as a personal observation which should not be generalised to other people who come from the same background.	
Unit A1.3	10. Understand how people are creating and indeed negotiating their cultural identity in the very process of communicating with us.	
	11. Appreciate that you are creating and negotiating your own cultural identity in the process of communicating with others.	
	12. Appreciate that the creation and negotiation of cultural and personal identity are the same thing.	

Othering

Unit A2.1	13. Avoid falling into the culturist trap of reducing people to less than they are – in the same way as we must avoid racist and sexist traps.	Seek a deeper understanding of the prejudices, pre-occupations and discourses which lead you to Other.
Unit A2.2	14. Be aware that what happens between yourself and others is influenced very much by the environment within which you are communicating and your own pre-occupations.	Use this to enable bracketing and to manage your own role in communication.
	15. Become aware of your own pre-occupations in order to understand what it is that people from other backgrounds are responding to.	
Unit A2.3	16. Avoid being seduced by previous experience of the exotic.	
	17. Monitor your own language and be aware of the destructive, culturist discourses you might be conforming to or perpetuating.	

Table A3.4.1 continued

Discussion	Statement	Summary
	Representation	
Unit A3.1	18. Be aware of the media, political and institutional influences in your own society which lead you to see people from other cultural backgrounds in a certain way. 19. See through these images and fictions when we encounter people from other cultural backgrounds, and always try to consider alternative representations.	Seek a deeper understanding of the representations of the foreign Other which are perpetuated by society.
Unit A3.2	20. Be aware of dominant discourses which are easily perpetuated by the media, and which lead us to 'think-as-usual' that familiar images of the foreign Other are 'normal'. 21. Be aware that even images projected by sensitive, intellectual, 'critical' sources can seduce our own sensitivities and intellects into thinking that they are 'true'. 22. Although sensationalism in the media is something we know about and guard against, you need to appreciate how deeply it exists in our traditional views of the foreign Other.	
Unit A3.3	23. Believe that people from different cultural backgrounds can have the underlying cultural ability to understand, be competent in and contribute to your own cultural scene. 24. Understand that while people might be deeply influenced by the social structures of their nation, this does not mean that they are confined by them.	

Although for the most part the disciplines related directly to the substantive knowledge required for successful intercultural communication, there is also a research methodology, focused on bracketing, thick description and emergent data, which comes directly from mainstream qualitative research. This will be the main approach presented in Section B.

SECTION B
Extension

Units in Section B are centred on texts concerned with issues introduced in Section A, which will also be explored further in Section C of the book. Each unit comprises an introduction, one or more texts accompanied by tasks, and a commentary, in which we point to related issues and perspectives of other writers. For each unit there are suggestions for further reading. Units B0.1, B0.2 and B0.3 serve as an introduction to Section B. Units B0.1 and B0.2 are concerned with a number of issues which we will explore in more depth later in the section, and which were introduced in Section A – for example:

- How our understanding of ourselves and of different people, and of the relationships and communication between these individuals, is often framed by the language (or 'discourse') that we use when we speak or write.
- How we tend to group people together under simplistic labels, while not considering the implications of doing so.
- How the language we use all too often exaggerates the differences between people rather than the similarities.
- How the mass media often engages in simplifying issues and exaggerating differences.
- How the ways 'cultures' and 'communities' are referred to, and talked and written about, often serve particular vested interests.

Unit B0.3 aims to provide an overview of intercultural communication by highlighting older and more recent perspectives in the field. Units B1.1 to B1.5 explore different aspects of and approaches to identity and consider what identity might mean for the individual, as well as how the individual may construct identity, in the contemporary world. Units B2.1 to B2.5 are concerned with 'Othering', and with how images of the Other, in both the literal and metaphorical sense, continue both to dominate understandings of, and inter-action with, people of different cultural identities. Units B3.1 to B3.5 focus on representation of different individuals and groups in the media, online, in academic and business discourse, and in intercultural training. Unit B3.6 is concerned with considering how we can move beyond the narrow representation and Othering of individuals and cultures in intercultural training.

We have employed a number of criteria when selecting texts for inclusion, as follows:

- Accessibility – the capacity of texts to be accessible to the reader who may not have specialist knowledge of issues being discussed.
- Richness – the capacity of texts, on the other hand, to introduce key concepts and raise important issues in terms of the themes of the book: identity, Othering, and representation.
- Relevance – the capacity of texts to introduce concepts and raise issues which are of relevance to readers studying or working in a range of disciplines or fields.
- Variety – the capacity of texts to provide a variety of perspectives, and to be taken from a variety of genres.

As research in various sub-fields in the related disciplines of cultural studies, media studies, and applied linguistics has demonstrated, the selection of a text is in itself significant, and reflects a certain personal standpoint. The texts in Section B do indeed reflect our own interests, and, in some cases, our own experiences, and we have sometimes included personal reflections in introductory sections and commentaries. Taken together, the texts reflect our belief that it is engaging with the ideas of others that plays an important part in understanding ourselves and our own contextual realities. 'Engagement' does not necessarily involve 'agreement'; we do not expect you to agree with all the ideas in the texts, and we do not do so ourselves.

With regard to the tasks designed to accompany texts, these are designed as a way of helping you to consider the implications and applications of issues raised, and perspectives provided in the texts and to consider them particularly as they relate to yourself. We, like anyone else writing tasks to accompany texts, are open to accusations of leading you towards certain conclusions and positions. We have tried to avoid doing so, and have deliberately made tasks generally open-ended, but we are aware that the very questions we have asked you to consider will inevitably reflect our own preoccupations and concerns.

Introduction

UNIT B0.1   'CULTURE' AND 'COMMUNITY' IN EVERYDAY DISCOURSE

The first text in this unit was written by the social anthropologist Ulf Hannerz, who is particularly concerned with how the term 'culture' is used in everyday discourse, and emphasises the need to 'keep a critical eye on the varieties of culturespeak both among ourselves and in society at large' (1999: 396).

Ylanne-McEwen and Coupland (2000: 210) state that 'studies aiming to describe "intercultural" communication should ideally be linked to studies of how individuals and social or cultural groups define themselves and others'. The second text, by sociologist Gerd Baumann, is an extract from such a study, which was the result of extensive ethnographic research carried out in Southall in west London, England.

Task B0.1.1

➤ The word 'culture' is used in many different ways (often in combination with other words) and with a variety of different meanings.

➤ Note down a number of different uses of the word 'culture' (as well as 'cultural') which you have come across recently in the media and everyday use.

Hannerz, U. (1999) 'Reflections of varieties of culturespeak.' *European Journal of Cultural Studies* 2/3. pp. 393–407 (extracts)

Text B0.1.1
U. Hannerz

A sunny morning a few years ago, at my summer house in southern Sweden, with a national election season approaching, I found a leaflet in my mail box. In blue letters against a yellow background (the colours of the Swedish flag), an extremist group in a nearby town argued that the country had turned from a folkhem, a 'home of the people', into a 'multicultural inferno'.

One could reflect that this suggests two things about the place of the culture concept in contemporary discourse. One is that 'culture' is no longer a notion occurring mostly among the well-educated, within the confines of their scholarly, intellectual, and esthetic [sic] preoccupations. Increasingly it, and other concepts deriving from it, seem to be just about everywhere, from public commentary and political agitation through organisational consultancy to commerce and advertising. And there are no real barriers separating different uses and different users. Researchers and policy makers now share the term 'multiculturalism' with ethnic minority politicians, as well as with the xenophobia activists claiming to represent a silent majority. One has to be sensitive, consequently, to those refractions of meaning which may occur as a vocabulary of culture moves between contexts.

The other thing to note, with regard to that suggestion of a 'multicultural inferno', is that while 'culture' in the past was probably a term with mostly consensual and positive overtones, it now very often shows up in contexts of discord – 'culture clash', 'culture conflict', 'culture wars'; and perhaps also, at a different level, 'culture shock'. A major reason for this, no doubt, is that culturespeak now very often draws our attention to what are taken to be the interfaces between cultures; a tendency which in its turn has much to do with that polymorphous global interconnectedness through which such interfaces become increasingly prominent in human experience.

Scrutinising culturespeak

. . . Cultural study is not only a summarising label for all those inquiries we conduct into the wide range of things we consider cultural, but also (not least in the present period) a study of popular theories, prototheories and quasitheories of culture.

Cultural fundamentalism is only one of these. They may develop in different contexts, shaping themselves to meet different requirements, and they need not be all malignant. I mentioned above the concept of 'culture shock', diffusing widely in the late 20th century as a way of referring to the kind of emotional and intellectual unease that sometimes occurs in encounters with unfamiliar meanings and practices. Rather facetiously, I have also occasionally referred to the growth of a 'culture shock prevention industry'. The proper term for its practitioners, I should quickly note, is 'interculturalists' – a new profession of people working commercially as trainers and consultants, trying to teach sensitivity toward cultural diversity to various audiences through lectures, simulation games, videos, practical handbooks and some variety of other means. From an academic vantage point one may be critical of certain of the efforts – they may seem a bit trite, somewhat inclined toward stereotyping, occasionally given to exaggerating cultural differences perhaps as a way of positioning the interculturalists themselves as an indispensable profession . . .

It would seem helpful to make more continuously visible how both persistence and change in culture depend on human activity; and how in contemporary, complex social life, the combined cultural process, and the overall habitat of meanings and practices in which we dwell, is the outcome of the variously deliberate pursuit by a variety of actors of their own agendas, with different power and different social and spatial reach, and with foreseen or unanticipated consequences. Such an approach to cultural process would be a challenge to each of us, layperson or scholar, to try and work out what ingredients go into situations that may puzzle us or annoy us . . .

The attention to processes and people may also help unpack the assumption of the unitary, integrated culture which may not be unique to cultural fundamentalism but which goes well with it. We have an old habit of speaking about 'cultures', in the plural form, as if it were self-evident that such entities exist side by side as neat packages, each of us identified with only one of them – this is indeed a time-worn implication of at least one 'anthropological culture concept'. And the notion of 'cultural identity' often goes with it. It may well be that some considerable number

U. Hannerz

of people really live encapsulated among others who share most of the same experiences, ideas, beliefs, values, habits, and tastes. Nonetheless, it appears increasingly likely that many people have biographies entailing various cross-cutting allegiances – they share different parts of their personal cultural repertoires with different collections of people. And if there is an 'integrated whole', it may be a quite individual thing. Under such circumstances, people may well value some parts of these personal repertoires more highly than others, identify themselves particularly in terms of them, and identify in collective terms more strongly with those other people with whom they share them. It could also be, on the other hand, that they may resist attempts to categorise them unidimensionally in terms of any single cultural characteristic.

. . . and the point here must be that whatever is most enduring is not necessarily also at any one time most central to people's cultural preoccupations, and to their sense of who they are. There are now surely many different ways of being more or less Christian, more or less Muslim, more or less Confucian; and of being at the same time some number of other things. Most significantly, finally, an emphasis on process may entail a subversion of a kind of mystique of cultural difference which seems to be an important part of cultural fundamentalism.

Task B0.1.2

➤ In the text Hannerz writes that '. . . while "culture" in the past was probably a term with mostly consensual and positive overtones, it now very often shows up in contexts of discord'.

➤ In looking back at the notes you made in Task B0.1.1 on different uses of the words 'culture' and 'cultural', do the examples you listed reflect Hannerz's view that today the term 'culture' has negative overtones?

Task B0.1.3

➤ In the text Hannerz also writes that 'It would seem helpful to make more continuously visible . . . how in contemporary, complex social life, the combined cultural process, and the overall habitat of meanings and practices in which we dwell, is the outcome of the variously deliberate pursuit by a variety of actors of their own agendas . . .'

➤ What 'actors' and 'agendas' do you think Hannerz is thinking of?

Task B0.1.4

➤ Considering a society you have lived in or are familiar with, which different communities would you say there are, and what makes these communities distinct from other communities?

Baumann, G. (1996) *Contesting Culture*. Cambridge: Cambridge University Press. pp. 1–2, 4–6 (extracts)

Having myself migrated to Britain at the age of twenty-one, I had been puzzled for a long time by the way in which immigrants were portrayed in the British media, in political rhetoric, and, not least, in the academic literature . . . in Britain (this) ethnic reductionism seemed to reign supreme, and the greater number even of academic community studies I read seemed to echo it. Whatever any 'Asian' informant was reported to have said or done was interpreted with stunning regularity as a consequence of their 'Asianness', their 'ethnic identity', or the 'culture' of their 'community'. All agency seemed to be absent, and culture an imprisoning cocoon or a determining force. Even their children, born, raised, and educated in Britain, appeared in print as 'second-generation immigrants' or 'second-generation Asians', and, unlike the children of white migrants like me, were thought to be precariously suspended 'between two cultures'.

This latter commonplace in particular I failed to understand. I could not work out why they should be suspended between, rather than be seen to reach across, two cultures. More importantly, which two cultures were involved? Was there a homo-geneous British culture on the one hand, perhaps regardless of class or of region, and on the other hand some other culture, perhaps one which was shared with their parents? If so, how were these parental cultures defined: was it on the basis of regional origin or religion, caste or language, migratory path or nationality? Each of these could define a community, a culture, and an ethnic identity in the same breath, it seemed . . .

. . . The answers to my confusion could, I thought, be found only by field-work: I rented a house in the centre of Southall, where I lived for the next six years, and from there involved myself in the life of the suburb. My agenda, as in all fieldwork, was open: live locally, socialise locally, find local things to do, and let yourself in for whatever comes. At the same time, keep a daily research diary, write fieldwork notes, and, not least, keep a personal diary in order not to confuse private concerns with the documentation of other people's doings and sayings . . .

Adult Southallians were no less relativist than their children in discussing culture and community. Even assuming that community was a matter of birthplace, as the dominant discourse so often does, some Southallians could, among friends, squeeze a laugh out of the absurdities of ethnic classification. 'See me friend Jas here', said Phil, an Englishman, and pointed to his drinking-mate at the Railway Tavern bar, 'he's an Asian, but he's born in Africa, so I'd say he's an African. And me, I was born in Burma, so I'm the Asian here, aren't I. And Winston here, you think he's a West Indian: he's the only one of us born in this town, so he's the Englishman born and bred!' Attributions of culture and community can clearly not be reduced to one factor alone. Rather, all but the most single-minded of adult Southallians, it turned out, regarded themselves as members of several communities at once, each with its own culture. Making one's life meant ranging across them. I did find a few people who said: 'I am a Muslim and nothing else', 'I am a Christian and have no other community', or 'I am an African from the Caribbean, but as African as the people born in Africa' . . . Nevertheless, the vast majority of all adult Southallians saw themselves as members of several communities, each with its own culture. The same person could speak and act as a member of the Muslim community in one context, in another take sides against other Muslims as a member of the Pakistani community, and in a third count himself part of the Punjabi community that excluded other Muslims but included Hindus, Sikhs, and even Christians. In this way, they echoed the awareness of shifting identities that young Southallians had alerted me to. Matters got more confusing, however, as fieldwork progressed. Some Hindu parents would claim that 'all Sikhs are Hindus'; some Sikh parents would dissociate themselves from the Sikh community and describe their culture as 'British–Asian, basically, whatever the religion you're from'; and Muslim friends would argue with pride that the local mosque was in itself a multi-cultural community. Clearly, all these utterances could be discounted as if they were mere figures of speech. But when an ethnographer collects more of them by the week, should one not ask what makes these usages any less important, authentic, or truthful than the usages that equate culture with community; community with ethnic identity; and ethnic identity with the 'cause' of a person's doings or sayings?

. . .The dominant discourse relies on equating community, culture, and ethnic identity, and its protagonists can easily reduce anybody's behaviour to a symptom of this equation. So long as its human objects can be logged under some ethnic identity other than, say, British, German, or American, it can even claim to speak 'for' them, 'represent' them, explain them to others. The ways in which Southallians spoke about each other and about themselves added up to a very different message: culture and community could be equated in some context, but were not the same in others. What the word 'identity' might mean in any one context, was a question of context.

Task B0.1.5

➤ Baumann and Hannerz make similar points concerning how individuals do not see themselves in uni-dimensional terms; Baumann writes that people see themselves 'as members of several communities at once, each with its own culture', and that 'making one's life meant ranging across them', while Hannerz writes that 'many people have biographies entailing various cross-cutting allegiances' and 'share different parts of their personal cultural repertoires with different collections of people'.

➤ Do you agree with Baumann and Hannerz?

➤ If so, what 'communities' do you feel you are a member of, and how does your own life mean 'ranging across' these communities? Or, in the words of Hannerz, which 'cross-cutting allegiances' does your own biography involve? What are the significant different parts of your own 'personal cultural repertoire', and with which 'different collections of people' do you share these?

Task B0.1.6

➤ Baumann refers to 'ethnic reductionism' in the British media, political rhetoric, and academic literature, which consists of 'equating community, culture, and ethnic identity'.

➤ Can you think of examples in the media, political rhetoric, and academic literature where such 'ethnic reductionism' is apparent?

Commentary

A recent paper by van de Vijver *et al.* (2015), which investigated a multicultural community in Antwerp, Belgium, comes to similar conclusions to Baumann (1996). The paper concludes that: 'conventional studies of identities in the diaspora may need to be more adapted to the changing environment in which identities develop' and that there are 'a multitude of identity domains that are important' (p. 54).

The crucial point to come out of both of the texts in this unit is that 'culture' and 'community' (and, indeed, 'cultural identity') are *not* concepts that exist independently and somehow abstracted from how these terms are used by any individual in society and by the media, politicians and academics. Moreover, there are tangible consequences for any society of how such terms are used.

A number of writers have been interested in the notion of 'community'. One common reference is to the 'symbolic' community: 'the community as experienced by its members does not consist in social structure or in "the doing" of social behaviour. It inheres, rather, in "the thinking" about it. It is in this sense that we can speak of the community as a symbolic, rather than a structural construct' (Cohen 1985: 98). Central to the work of Benedict Anderson (1983) is that communities, and particularly national communities, are 'imagined', while for Barthes (1970) communities, and particularly national communities, are represented in terms of 'cultural myths'. The rise of information communication technology has of course seen increasing interest in the notion of the 'virtual' community.

UNIT B0.2 'CULTURE' – DEFINITIONS AND PERSPECTIVES

Much of the debate on 'culture' in the last fifty years or so has been concerned with challenging models of culture which have emanated from the field of anthropology. Such a model is that of Tylor (1871), for whom 'culture' is 'that complex whole which includes knowledge, belief, art, morals, law, customs, and any other capabilities and habits acquired by man as a member of society'. There has been unease with, and debate about, both what culture is seen to 'include' in such a model, and the notion that culture is 'acquired'. The first text in the unit, by Brian Fay, provides a summary of differences between 'standard' and 'complex' views of culture. In the second text Adrian Holliday offers an alternative to the 'standard' view of culture in his discussion of 'essentialism' and 'small cultures'.

 Task B0.2.1

➤ Read the following definitions of 'culture'.

➤ What do you think the writers mean by their descriptions?

> Which, if any, of the descriptions do you feel successfully captures the *complete* or a *partial* meaning of 'culture'?

- A culture is 'a text the vocabulary and grammar of which its members learn' (Fay 1996: 55).
- 'Culture is a verb' (Street 1991).
- Culture is 'an evolving connected activity, not a thing' (Fay 1996: 62–3).
- 'Believing . . . that man is an animal suspended in webs of significance he himself has spun, I take culture to be those webs' (Geertz 1973: 5).

Fay, B. (1996) *Contemporary Philosophy of Social Science: A Multicultural Approach*. Oxford: Blackwell. pp. 55–60 (extracts)

Text B0.2.1
B. Fay

According to a standard view, a culture is a complex set of shared beliefs, values, and concepts which enables a group to make sense of its life and which provides it with directions for how to live. This set might be called a basic belief system (note that such a belief system can include items which are fully explicit and others which are not, and can include matters of feeling and deportment as well as discursive claims about the world). In perhaps the most influential variant of this standard view, culture is pictured as a text the vocabulary and grammar of which its members learn. Indeed, in this view, becoming a member of a particular culture is a process of enculturation conceived as learning to read the culture's basic text and making it one's own.

This standard view asserts the further claim that in becoming the carriers of a specific cultural tradition individuals become the people they are. That is, by internalising a particular belief system and its attendant forms of feeling and interaction a person acquires the basics of his or her identity. A culture penetrates its individual members mentally (so that they possess a certain mind-set), physically (so that they possess certain basic bodily dispositions), and socially (so that they relate to one another in certain characteristic ways). This penetration produces in them their distinctive capacities and characteristics. In this holistic way identity is a function of enculturation . . .

So far I have been speaking as if culture consisted of a coherent set of beliefs (a 'text'). But this is a mistake. Any culture complex enough to warrant the name will consist of conflicting beliefs and rules which offer mixed, contested, and ambiguous messages to its followers. The reason for this derives in part from what I have already said about cultural rules and agency: rules require interpretation, and interpretation requires reflexive analysis and judgment on the part of agents. Besides, cultural beliefs and ideals apply to people in differential positions of power. The meaning of a rule for a powerful member of an elite often will not be the same for, nor will it have the same outcome on, a member of a group who is on the periphery. Moreover, cultural norms and ideals result from histories of struggle in which significant voices are silenced. As a result, various members in a cultural group will have heterogeneous histories, divergent interests, and antagonistic interpretations. Far from being coherent unities uniformly distributed throughout a society, cultures are rather tense loci of difference and opposition . . .

Another important fact about cultures is that they are essentially open. Cultures are ideational entities; as such they are permeable, susceptible to influence from other cultures. Wherever exchange among humans occurs, the possibility exists of the influence of one culture by another. (Even when such influence does not occur it is because those in one culture consciously reject the foreign or strange culture: but this rejection is itself another way the alien culture interjects itself into the home culture.) Human history is in part the story of the ways different cultural groups have rearranged cultural boundaries by expanding contacts, tolerating outsiders, and fashioning interactive arrangements. Even the creation of stricter boundaries involves mutual impact. The human world is not composed of a motley of independent, encapsulated, free-floating cultures; rather, it is one of constant interplay and exchange . . .

. . . consider the deeper cultural rhythms by which you live. Your conceptions of time, of space, of power, of beauty, of agency, of sociality, of knowledge have all been deeply affected by importing, responding to, transforming, and borrowing the cultural meanings and values of others different from you.

Task B0.2.2

➤ Fay writes that 'Any culture . . . will consist of conflicting beliefs and rules which offer mixed, contested, and ambiguous messages to its followers'. Within a small or large culture you know well, what conflicting beliefs and rules can you identify?

➤ How do you think 'the cultural meanings and values of others different from you' that Fay refers to have affected your own conceptions of:

- Time?
- Space?
- Beauty?
- Knowledge?

In Section A, the notion of 'essentialism' was introduced. The third text in this unit suggests that 'essentialism' is often the natural 'default position' of how people view cultures and illustrates how a 'non-essentialist' view involves a shift from a 'large' to a 'small' culture perspective.

Holliday, A. R. (2005) *The Struggle to Teach English as an International Language*. Oxford: Oxford University Press. pp. 17–24 (extracts)

Essentialism

Essentialism presumes 'that particular things have essences which serve to identify them as the particular things that they are' (Bullock and Trombley 1997: 283). The most common essentialist view of culture is that 'cultures' are coincidental with countries, regions, and continents, implying that one can 'visit' them while travelling and that they contain 'mutually exclusive types of behaviour' so that people 'from' or 'in' French culture are essentially different from those 'from' or 'in' Chinese culture. This psychogeographical picture also presents a hierarchical onion skin relationship between a national culture and elements within it, so that 'Egyptian school culture'

70

is a subset or subculture of 'Egyptian education culture', and so on. At the more macro level, 'Kenyan culture' becomes a subset of 'African culture'. Common variations on this geographical theme are the association of 'cultures' with religions, political philosophies, ethnicities and languages, where 'Islamic culture', 'black culture', and 'English language culture' take on the same essence of containment. (See Keesing 1981, 1994; Holliday 1999a; Holliday *et al.* 2004).

Much of this essentialism will seem natural and normal to many readers, because it is in many ways the default way of thinking about how we are different from each other. It is however problematic because if we think of people's behaviour as defined and constrained by the culture in which they live, agency is transferred away from the individual to the culture itself, so that we begin to think that 'German culture believes that . . .', and that 'she belongs to German culture, therefore she . . .'. There is only a short, easy distance from this essentialist way of thinking to the chauvinistic stereotyping inherent in culturism which allows us to arrive at statements like 'in Middle Eastern culture there is no concept of individualised critical thinking' [pp. 17–18].

I do not wish to give the impression that cultural essentialism is only practised by the dominant West. People from the East and the South also essentialise their own cultural identities for a number of reasons – to reaffirm that their 'culture' survives, despite Western domination, through the display of traditional dress, dances, rituals of state, arts festivals, tourist performances, and so on (Keesing 1994: 306–7), to play the 'culture card' to maintain and acquire power (Sarangi 1994: 416), to reinforce nationalist imagery (Sakamoto 1996: 113; Kubota 1999: 9) and to appeal to a Western market (Moeran 1996).

In my experience it is indeed often colleagues and students from outside the English-speaking West who talk most enthusiastically about their own circum-stances as 'the situation in country X culture'. A Chinese student once told me that some of her compatriots admitted feeding their British tutors with exoticised accounts of 'Chinese culture' because it seemed to be what was expected. On the one hand, I know from experience of being a foreigner in other people's countries, that this sort of exaggeration of Self to suit people's perception of Other can help one to gain acceptance (Holliday *et al.* 2004: 10–15). On the other hand, it seems unfortunate that this desire to assert identity presents an over-simplified reality which both feeds native-speakerism and contributes to its adoption outside the English-speaking West.

I see it as seriously problematic that English-speaking Western tutors collude with this over-generalised self-Othering by accepting such statements as 'true' because they come from people who must be authorities on every aspect of their 'culture' because 'they' are all the same and know everything about each other. It is part of a general tendency for middle-class people from comfortable societies to enjoy the opportunity of 'discovering another culture' and to think that by talking about 'cultures', and admiring their 'exotic' qualities, they are 'accepting' and 'being tolerant' and 'understanding' of them. Jordan and Weedon (1995: 149–50) assert that the 'commodification' of 'racial and cultural difference is a marked feature of the radical twentieth-century avant-garde'. 'Other cultures' similarly become objects to be 'nice' about instead of groups of real people with whom we can interact and be equally people. I was once horrified to hear, while working as a curriculum consultant in India, an Indian colleague say that 'we' considered 'them' as 'all Indians together'. This 'liberal multiculturalism', which 'celebrates cultural difference as an end in itself' in terms of superficial 'artefacts, festivals, and customs' results in a bland 'cultural tourism' which obscures 'issues of power and privilege' (Kubota 2004: 35, citing Derman-Sparks) [pp. 21–2].

In the non-essentialist view, culture is not a geographical place which can be visited and to which someone can belong, but a social force which is evident wherever it emerges as being significant. This concept of culture falls somewhere within the critical, constructivist, symbolic and 'verb' views of culture (Roberts *et al.* 2001: 54). It is something that flows and shifts between us. It both binds us and separates us, but in different ways at different times and in different circumstances. I am not suggesting that there is no such thing as cultural difference, but that this difference is not locked into essentialist cultural blocks. There are many aspects of our behaviour which are 'culturally different'. It is possible to say that 'there is something culturally different' about the way in which someone might behave, but this may be as much to do with the *small cultures* of family, age, occupation or other social background factors as with *large cultural* differences in nationality (Holliday 1999a: 240). Where cultural difference is connected with nationality, it does not necessarily follow that all people of that nationality will behave similarly. We must therefore be wary not to use these differences to feed chauvinistic imaginations of what certain national or ethnic groups can or cannot do – as exotic, 'simple', 'traditional' Others to our complex, 'modern' selves.

A non-essentialist, small culture approach considers any instance of socially cohesive behaviour as culture. Cultural significances can thus be found in particular football teams, types of restaurants, individual universities and departments, and, indeed, in professional cultures such as TESOL. This conceptualisation is not dissimilar to the expression of culture as related to the basic fabric of social activity in discourses, literacies, and institutions as expressed by a range of critical writers (Fairclough 1995; Clark and Ivanič 1997; Gee 1997; Lankshear *et al.* 1997). In this view, the world is made up of a vast complex of shifting, overlapping, swirling, combining and splitting cultures; and to imagine that they are organised into regional hierarchical blocks is an ideological, political, or chauvinistic act.

My approach to culture and to culturism is concerned with how people construct for themselves the realities of others, and how culture is itself socially constructed.

A world in which realities are socially constructed can however work in different ways: either we construct, or we are constructed by the discourses of culture [pp. 23–4].

 Task B0.2.3

➤ What do you think of the following statements in the Text B0.2.2?

- ■ 'Essentialism will seem natural and normal because it is in many ways the default way of thinking about how we are different from each other'.
- ■ 'I do not wish to give the impression that cultural essentialism is only practised by the dominant West. People from the East and the South also essentialise their own cultural identities for a number of reasons'.
- ■ 'The world is made up of a vast complex of shifting, overlapping, swirling, combining and splitting cultures'.

➤ In the extract it is written that 'A non-essentialist, small culture approach considers any instance of socially cohesive behaviour as culture' and that 'cultural significances can thus be found in particular football teams, types of restaurants, individual universities and departments, and, indeed, in professional cultures such as TESOL'.

➤ What factors may be 'culturally significant' in making one of the following a 'small culture':

- ■ A particular football team;
- ■ A particular type of restaurant;
- ■ A particular type individual university or department;
- ■ A particular type of professional culture such as TESOL?

➤ Think of other particular 'small cultures'. What factors may be 'culturally significant' in making these 'small cultures'?

Commentary

Any study of culture will inevitably be complex and there are no easy off-the-peg definitions. It is, indeed, off-the-peg definitions that prevent a consideration of the complexities of culture, and prevent us approaching culture as a dynamic and interactive process.

Taking a '*small culture*' approach makes the study of intercultural communication more complex since it means that it opens up the possibility of research into intercultural communication among and between individuals in small social groupings, characterised, for example, by social class, disability, gender, sexuality, profession, special interests, personal interests, beliefs and value systems, and specific communication norms.

A starting point for research into the complexities of culture is suggested by Alasuutari (1995: 135–6), who states that 'the researcher must be able to see beyond the horizon of the self-evident' and needs to 'generate why-questions': 'In an ethnographic study of a foreign culture the why-questions will often stem from the researcher's own failure to understand why the people concerned are living the way they do, or why they think the way they do'; however, 'when you are looking at something that is closely related to your own culture, most things will often appear more or less self-evident or trivial'. For Baumann (1990: 15–16), a necessary first step in attempting to research 'culture as a dynamic and interactive process' and 'how cultural identity is nowadays lived and experienced' is 'defamiliarisation', a process which 'takes us away from our comfortable, limited, commonly accepted and often unconsidered opinions about what everybody and everything is like and makes us more sensitive to the way that those opinions are formed and maintained. It alerts us to the ways that things which at first sight appear obvious and 'natural' are actually the result of social action, social power or social tradition'.

UNIT B0.3   CURRENT AND PREVIOUS APPROACHES TO THE STUDY OF INTERCULTURAL COMMUNICATION

The field of intercultural communication, like any academic discipline, is influenced by certain 'discourses', discourses that change and shift, are challenged and resisted. As Kumaravidivelu emphasises in the first text intercultural communication is 'a fairly new field of academic activity' with its origins in the middle of the last century. Today intercultural communication can be said to be an academic discipline and those involved in teaching, learning, researching and writing about intercultural communication are a 'community of practice'. For Hyland (2000), communities of practice are not 'monolithic and unitary' but 'comprise competing groups and discourses, marginalised ideas, contested theories, peripheral contributors and occasional members' (p. 9). In this unit we explore in particular the 'competing discourses' and 'contested theories' in the field of intercultural communication.

 Task B0.3.1

➤ Before you read Text B0.3.1, consider:

■ The first extract by Kumaravidivelu includes the quotation from Hall (1959) that 'culture is communication and communication is culture'. What do you think Hall means by this and do you agree with him?

■ From your previous reading in the field of intercultural communication, have you come across the 'big names' of Edward Hall and Geert Hofstede and their widely known theories?

■ How might these theories be open to criticism or 'contested'?

Text B0.3.1
B.
Kumaravadivelu

Kumaravadivelu, B. (2008) *Cultural Globalisation in Language Education*. Yale: Yale University Press. pp. 212–17 (extracts)

Intercultural communication is a fairly new field of academic activity. It was born from the rubble of World War II when, as the leader of the winning Allied forces, the United States found its international diplomacy, commerce, and trade expand to unprecedented heights. Government officials, diplomats, business leaders, and other Americans sent to work overseas realised that their lack of knowledge of foreigners' cultural practices and communication styles impeded their effective functioning. To address this problem, Congress passed the Foreign Service Act in 1946, which facilitated the establishment of the Foreign Service Institute. The Institute hired a team of anthropologists, psychologists, and linguists to develop methods and materials for training government officials in intercultural communication. It was this team that laid the foundation for the field of intercultural communication, thus making the field a truly American invention.

Among the scholars the Institute hired were anthropologist Edward Hall and linguist George Trager. Drawing freely from their respective fields, they jointly produced a Foreign Service Institute training manual titled *The Analysis of Culture* (Hall and Trager 1953). In it, they presented a matrix for mapping a foreign culture along certain dimensions the most important of which was communication, both verbal and nonverbal. A central anthropological linguistic concept that guided their work was the Sapir-Whorf hypothesis, which posited a close connection between language and reality and between language and cultural thought patterns . . . They also believed that since cultures are created and maintained mainly through language, language has an inherent capacity to provide a window into cultures, and therefore it should be possible to draw useful insights into intercultural communication by analysing and understanding language communication. To a large extent, the importance they gave to the role of language in general and to the Sapir-Whorf hypothesis in particular continues to characterise the field of intercultural communication even today.

Hall expanded the initial insights presented in the training manual and wrote a book called *The Silent Language* (1959). This seminal work became so influential that it is considered to be 'the founding document in the new field of inter-cultural communication' (Rogers, Hart and Miike 2002: 11). In it, he focused on interpersonal communication among people of different cultural backgrounds. Declaring unequivocally that 'culture is communication and communication is culture' (Hall 1959: 186), he highlighted the importance of factors such as personal space and the sense of time, and how they affect intercultural communication. He also emphasised nonverbal communication, such as gestures, and their role in intercultural understanding. In this and other works, he posited several dich-otomous cultural parameters and drew sharp distinctions between, for instance, low-context societies (e.g. the United States), where communication is premised upon explicit verbal statements, and *high-context* societies (e.g. Japan), where communication relies crucially on nonverbal, contextual cues or even on silence; and between *polychronic* cultures (e.g. west Asia), where time is conceptualised as flexible and circular, prompting individuals to attend to multiple events and tasks simultaneously, and *mono-chronic* cultures (e.g. the United States), where time is considered fixed and linear, encouraging individuals to handle events and tasks sequentially and on time.

Hall's emphasis on interpersonal communication, including nonverbal communication, was in part necessitated by his chief task of helping Foreign Service officers 'to go overseas and get results' (Hall 1959: 35). He realised that 'what was needed was something bold and new, and not more of the same old history, economics, and politics' (p. 36). Therefore, he departed from the mainstream anthropological approach, which focused primarily on a culture's broader social, political, and religious systems, and instead concentrated on the microlevel dynamics of face-to-face interaction between individuals, such as tone of voice, gestures, time and spatial relationships, etc. Intercultural training based on such inter-personal factors helped the members of the Diplomatic Corps prepare to face their communicational challenges in alien nations.

Apart from the Diplomatic Corps, yet another government agency that found the studies on intercultural communication useful was the Peace Corps. Founded in 1961 by the Kennedy administration, the Peace Corps aimed at sending American volunteers to work with local communities in several newly independent, developing countries [pp. 212–14].

. . . Insights derived from the studies on interpersonal communication across cultures conducted in the context of international diplomacy were also found to be immensely useful by the corporate sector. When trade and commerce with other countries expanded after the Second World War, the American business community found it necessary to train its overseas employees in several dimensions of intercultural communication, including negotiating, socialising, identifying communication breakdowns, avoiding cross-cultural misunderstanding, keeping proper eye contact and physical distance, minding body language and politeness formulas, and so on. Particular importance was given to American and Japanese intercultural communication because of extensive trade and personnel exchanges between the two largest economies of the world. As a result, 'today there are more studies of Japanese/American communication than of intercultural communication between any two other cultures' (Rogers, Hart and Miike 2002: 15). These studies, following the lead given by Hall, stressed the American/Japanese cultural differences such as individualism/collectivism, and low-context/high-context behaviours and their impact on intercultural communication. Also stressed were nonverbal communication patterns such as hierarchy-based bowing practices, facial expressions, and physical touching, which were considered to differentiate the two cultures in contact.

In emphasising the microlevel behaviours of face-to-face interactions between people of different cultures, Hall and other interculturalists departed significantly from traditional anthropological interests, and thus introduced a new and important component to the study of intercultural communication. But, in doing so, they generally adhered to the popular 'cultural difference' paradigm, which directed anthropologists' attention to variations in cultural beliefs and practices, instead of an earlier 'cultural deprivation' paradigm, which suggested that other cultures are somehow deficient and, therefore, disadvantaged and underdeveloped. Like other anthropologists, they too followed an ethnographic investigative technique that consisted mainly of participant observation, in which they systematically and directly observed cultural behaviours, and also of interviews with local cultural informants. Clearly, such a technique put a premium on the interculturalists' personal observation as well as on their critical interpretation of what they heard, observed, or experienced. The resulting accounts – mostly subjective and descriptive in nature – were then deemed to be the cultural construct of a particular cultural community.

During the 1980s, an empirical dimension was introduced to intercultural communication studies by Geert Hofstede, a social psychologist from the Netherlands. Using statistically oriented quantitative methods, he conducted a factor analysis of cultural values contained in survey responses from more than 116,000 IBM employees in forty countries and reported his findings in his influential book *Culture's Consequences* (Hofstede 1980). Based on this empirical study, he identified four dimensions of corporate culture: (a) inequality acceptance, that is, how people accept authority embedded in hierarchical relationships, (b) uncertainty avoidance, that is, how people feel threatened by, and therefore avoid, ambiguity, (c) social role, that is, how the gendered role relationship between men and women is prevalent in the corporate sector, and (d) individualism versus collectivism, that is, how individuals relate to the company they work for or the community they belong to. Hofstede unhesitatingly extended these corporate cultural behaviours to larger society as well.

The fact that the interculturalists profiled intercultural communication differences generated out of data collected from governmental and corporate players and overgeneralised them to the entire population has resulted in justifiable criticism (see Martin and Nakayama 2000, for a review). Even in cases where they approached cultural informants from nongovernment and non-corporate sources, the limited number of samples and the limited experience of informants responding to interview questions or to survey questionnaires easily rendered the findings unrepresentative of the cultures selected for study (Chuang 2003; Miyahara 2000). Moreover, the interculturalists also paid scant respect to the fact that human interaction, particularly intercultural interaction, embedded as it is in multiple layers across space and time, is a complex, ongoing process that cannot be reduced to expedient labels and convenient dichotomies. It cannot be captured in snapshots.

More than the methodological concerns, a crucial conceptual drawback of the intercultural communication studies popularised by Hall, Hofstede, and others is that it has been very much conditioned by Western perceptions of non-Western cultures. As George Renwick (2004: 450) has recently remarked: 'most of the theorists we have drawn on are Western. This can be illuminating, of course, but it is certainly limited and can be limiting.' It is limiting because most interculturalists treated European patterns of social and corporate communication styles as the norms against which those of other cultures were studied, analysed, described, and judged. In doing so, they were following a long-cherished sociological and anthropological tradition in which, as Oxford University cultural critic Robert Young (1995: 94) pointed out, 'civilisation and culture were the names for the standard of measurement in the hierarchy of values through which European culture defined itself by placing itself at the top of a scale against which all other societies or groups within a society, were judged.' Consequently, interculturalists seldom recognised that certain communication behavioural patterns of other, particularly Asian, cultures may not be satisfactorily explained by Western theories (Xiaoge 2000). But still they persisted with a solely Western interpretation of Eastern cultures. This has led to the charge that the field of intercultural communication is beset by Eurocentrism.

Several Asian scholars have asserted that, because of widespread Eurocentrism, the intercultural field remains anything but inter-cultural (e.g. Chuang 2003; Dissanayake (ed.) 1988; Kim 2002; Miike 2003; Starosta and Chen (eds) 2003). In a comprehensive review, Yoshitaka Miike (2003: 244) explains that Eurocentrism in the intercultural field 'refers to hegemonic Eurocentrism in which we structurally and systematically privilege certain theorising and researching methods of Western origin over others and disadvantage alternative possibilities of theorising and researching culture and communication phenomena. Eurocentrism in intercultural communication studies appears to manifest in our academic activities in at least three spheres: (1) theoretical concepts and constructs, (2) research material and methodology, and (3) otherisation in theory and research.' Since these three spheres cover major aspects of the field of intercultural communication, Asian scholars have stressed the need to radicalise the field's intellectual roots. They would, for instance, 'like to see the classical texts associated with Confucianism, Daoism, and Buddhism as well as the treaties associated with classical Asian aesthetics brought into discussion' (Dissanayake 1996: 10).

Western scholars too recognise the need to open up the field to non-Western thoughts. Toward that end, the prestigious *Journal of Cross-Cultural Psychology* dedicated an entire volume (#31, 2000) to discuss the problematic aspect of Western-oriented concepts and methods and to construct alternative paradigms of intercultural under-standing and training. Attempts such as this have resulted in growing optimism that 'as we continue our journey, we should be sure to explore carefully the perspectives of thinkers in other traditions and other regions of the world' (Renwick 2004: 450). One such perspective comes from scholars working in the field of post-structural/postcolonial studies [pp. 214–17].

Task B0.3.2

➤ Summarise the ways in which Kumaravidivelu believes widely recognised work in the field has helped broaden our understanding of intercultural communication.

➤ Summarise the criticisms Kumaravidivelu makes of widely recognised work in the field of intercultural communication.

➤ From your previous reading on intercultural communication, do you agree with the criticisms Kumaravidivelu makes?

Kumaravidivelu writes that the importance given 'to the role of language in general and to the Sapir-Whorf hypothesis in particular continues to characterise the field of intercultural communication even today'.

➤ Do you believe that a particular language *reflects* the world view of a particular 'culture' (for example, that the English language reflects a particular way of looking at the world and the people in it)? If so, in what ways?

➤ On the other hand, do you think that a particular language *determines* the world view of a particular 'culture' (for example, that the culture of the English-speaking world has an important influence on the form of the English language)? If so, in what ways?

In recent years the theories of Sapir and Whorf, and the work of those who have applied their theories, have come under increasing scrutiny and a number of reservations have been expressed. Gumperz (1996: 376–7), for example, writes that 'the assumption that our social world comes segmented into discrete internally homogenous language/culture areas has become increasingly problematic. Cultures are no longer homogenous and language divisions have become more and more permeable . . . speakers of the same languages may find themselves separated by deep cultural gaps, while others who speak distinct languages share the same culture. At the same time group boundaries are rapidly changing and less sharply marked. We can thus no longer assume that language and culture are co-extensive and shared understandings cannot be taken for granted. The one to one relationship between language and cultural variability must now be seen as an oversimplification.' Whilst few linguists would now accept the Sapir–Whorf hypothesis in its 'strong', extreme or deterministic form, many now accept a 'weak', more moderate, or limited Whorfianism, namely that the ways in which we see the world *may* be influenced by the kind of language we use. Chassy (2015: 50), for example, points to instances:

Wherein language actually affects the perceptions of others . . . By using one word instead of another . . . we can introduce a subtle nuance in the person's representation of the situation. We will not determine the thought, as the strong version of the Whorfian hypothesis would suggest, nor will we change the set of values that underpins the person's way of thinking, but we definitely can orient thinking. In this sense . . . we can say that language is a marker of identity and also contributes to shape our social perception of the self and of others.

The field of intercultural communication has in recent years embraced a greater range of perspectives from the social sciences and these have opened up to scrutiny how 'culture' has been defined by those coming from a linguistics or language teaching background. Risager (2015: 87), for instance, suggests that:

> People trained in language studies tend to see culture through the lens of language . . . you study language and 'its associated culture' . . . while [sic] among people trained in fields like anthropology or cultural studies this language-bound view of culture is not normally seen. The conceptualisation of culture in these fields may be very diverse, conflictual and contested, but the point of departure would seldom be that 'culture' is coterminous with 'language' – unless perhaps we are dealing with an interdisciplinary field like linguistic anthropology.

Despite a broadening of perspective in recent years, the ways in which 'culture' is defined in the field of intercultural communication continues to be problematic. De Fina (2015: 46), for example, writes that:

> Many studies of 'intercultural communication' have traditionally operated with a notion of culture that not only is not really problematised, but is also often equated with shared patterns of behaviour, beliefs and norms within groups defined mostly in terms of nationality or ethnicity. And a great deal of research on interculturality takes for granted, for example that 'cultural' differences run along national borders.

Collier (2015), who reflects on her thirty years as a researcher and writer on intercultural communication, and who has recently 'added a decidedly critical turn to my previous interpretive orientations' also continues to find many approaches to culture 'problematic' because 'cultural associations are presumed to predict social/psychological tendencies and binary patterns of conduct such as individualism or collectivism' and because 'culture is approached as if individuals 'carry' culture instead of enacting interculturality through dynamic representations, identifications, and relationships (p. 10).

Work by a number of researchers has focused critical attention on the work of a number of key figures in the field of intercultural communication. A study by Cardon (2008), for example, is critical of Hall's 'low-context and high-context' model that Kumaravadivelu mentions in Text B0.3.1 (which is referred to extensively in textbooks on intercultural communication), and points out that 'none of Hall's works about contexting have been published in refereed journals and they have escaped close scrutiny by other researchers' (p. 2). A number of other voices have also been raised in criticism of the work of Hofstede, and of the ways in which Hofstede's model has been used in business communication textbooks. Spencer-Oatey and Franklin point out that 'there is a fundamental concern in applying his findings to intercultural interaction: how can scores that are country-level averages be used to explain the influence of culture on individual behaviour?' (2009: 19).

Another model commonly cited in business communication textbooks is that of Trompenaars (1993), who sought to extend the work of Hofstede. In addition to the 'individualist/collectivist culture' dimension in Hofstede's model, Trompenaars believed the following dimensions to be important in intercultural communication in business environments:

- Universalist Cultures (people are logical and rational and there are universal rules which direct behaviour)/Particularist Cultures (people's behaviour is directed by interpersonal relationships and therefore rules tend to have less influence and are interpreted flexibly).
- Affective Cultures (emotions are displayed openly)/Neutral Cultures (emotions are not displayed openly).
- Specific relationships (work relationships are not carried over to relationships outside-work contexts)/Diffuse relationships (work relationships influence relationships in outside-work contexts).
- Achieving Status (status is on the basis of previous achievement)/Ascribing Status (status is ascribed to people based on such factors as gender, colour, age, etc.).
- Time as sequence (a linear approach to carrying out tasks so that tasks are handled in sequence)/Time as synchronisation (a non-linear approach to work with parallel tasks).
- Inner Directed (individuals seek to control their environments with the result that conflict is)/Outer Directed (individuals accept that their environments are directed by others for their greater good).

Trompenaars presented respondents from over fifty countries with a series of situations in which there were certain dilemmas and asked them to make choices regarding what they would do. The results were analysed according to the nationalities of the respondents. Sealey and Carter (2004) believe the conclusions Trompenaars drew to be 'conflationary, in that they attribute to 'countries' properties and powers which can only belong to human agents. They also elide beliefs . . . with behaviour. This kind of account is also potentially deterministic, suggesting that being born in a particular country will lead to an adherence to a particular set of values' (pp. 146–7).

Despite the previously mentioned criticisms of the work of Hall, Hofstede and Trompenaars, their work has introduced important factors which *may* be significant in any study of intercultural interaction. A problem has often been that other 'interculturalists' have simplistically adopted and applied the models of Hall, Hofstede and Trompenaars and have ignored many other aspects of definitions of 'culture' and the complexities of intercultural communication.

In recent years, the mass movement of people and increasing super-diversity in many parts of the world have played an important part in forcing a critical examination on the complexities of intercultural communication, and on questions of power, advantage/disadvantage and ideology. Sorrells (2011), for instance, calls for a greater attention to be paid to power, ideology and context in intercultural communication:

> We must reimagine the study of intercultural communication to account for the ways that historical and current conditions and relations of power are layered and stitched together in the context of globalisation.
>
> (p. 181)

A welcome advance in research in recent years has been towards a more in-depth micro-analysis of how power and ideology are realised through language and interaction in authentic examples of intercultural communication. The following extracts from Verschueren (2008) are one example.

Task B0.3.3

➤ Before reading the second text in this unit, consider two statements that Verschueren makes in the text:

- Intercultural communication is not something 'special' that is 'really different from other forms of communicative interaction'.
- 'an intercultural context is not to be equated with the sum of two different contexts, but essentially the creation of a new one'.

➤ What do you think he means by these two statements?

Verschueren, J. (2008) 'Intercultural communication and the challenges of migration'. *Language and Intercultural Communication 8/1:* 21–35. pp. 23–5 (extracts)

Text B0.3.2
J. Verschueren

It may seem trivial to posit that intercultural communication is first and foremost to be looked at *as* communication. Unfortunately, it is not. More often than not, the phenomenon is viewed as something 'special,' really different from other forms of communicative interaction, and not following the same general rules. Let me try to explain why such a view is misguided. I will do so with reference to three basic notions that we need for any linguistic-pragmatic description of communicative language use: *variability, negotiability* and *adaptability* (see Verschueren 1999).

First, *variability*. Speaking or using language consists in a concatenation of choices from a wide and variable range of options at various levels of structure, going from

J. Verschueren

the choice of a language (definitely relevant in many migration-related contexts, such as asylum procedures) to word choices, sound patterns and so on. What is always involved is *fundamental variability*, in the sense of different packages of options for the different people involved in an interaction, to the point where everyone basically speaks a different 'language.' This variability is not necessarily larger in intercultural contacts; it is the case that different types of variables come into play . . . [p. 23].

A second key notion is *negotiability*. There is no absolutely fixed relationship between linguistic forms and their functions. On the contrary, meaning is continuously negotiated interactively. The reason is that in communication more always remains implicit than can be said explicitly. Implicitness determines the points of departure in which what is said gets anchored. Hence speakers must continuously engage in the making of hypotheses about what it is that can be reasonably assumed to be 'given' or 'known'; and whoever interprets a message must in turn make assumptions about the nature of the utterer's presuppositions. The competence that enables people to do this is what psychologists call 'theory of mind', a typically human capacity that is developed by every child by a certain age and that functions as a *conditio sine qua non* for the use of human language. Also connected to this implicitness is the phenomenon of ambiguity. The result is that meaning in interaction is indeed always dynamically generated and negotiated. Just as with the property of fundamental variability, negotiability is also involved both in intra- as well as intercultural contacts.

Assume that the following question is asked: 'Where do you come from?' This seemingly simple question is multi-interpretable: it may refer to a country, a city, a university or a building. It is clear that this may lead to misunderstandings, but these are usually easy to remedy. Meaning negotiation is indeed a dynamic process that does not even stop when a conversation is over; consider, for instance, the description of a road, which is usually reinterpreted over and over in the course of following directions. Just as with variability, we are touching on a phenomenon that characterises all forms of verbal communication . . . [pp. 23–4].

. . . In order to explain the fact that language can still achieve its communicative purpose with a significant degree of success in spite of the use of variable means that cannot be interpreted mechanically, we rely on the concept of *adaptability*. Communicative means and their use can be continually retuned or adapted. That is why an intercultural context is not to be equated with the sum of two different contexts, but essentially the creation of a new one. A superficial example – chosen from a very practical domain for the sake of clarity – is that of the European businessman being prepared for a trip to China. During the training sessions he is told that the exchange of presents is important in China, but that the Chinese never open their presents out of fear of possibly being impolite when they might show, however slightly and however involuntarily, that they are not thrilled with what they receive. In the training process, one tends to forget that the Chinese are not 'cultural dopes' and they, just like Europeans, are not stuck in the habits that they grew up with. Consequently, they are also receiving preparatory training, in which they are told that Europeans do open their presents. The consequence is not hard to imagine: Qian opens his present, Peter does not, and neither of them realises what is happening – unless their reflexive capacities jump into action, the capacities which they both possess, and with which everyone should always be able to make a reassessment of every new situation. On this occasion these reflexive capacities will lead them to the conclusion that indeed a new context has emerged. Therefore, a static 'comparison' of 'cultures' . . . seems the worst possible basis on which to approach intercultural communication.

Briefly, the variability referred to with respect to the term 'intercultural' is not a distinctive feature that would produce a 'different' kind of communication, but only a specific and ever-changing configuration of points on diverse continua of variability that characterise every form of communication, thus leading to omnipresent negotiability and adaptability. The main objective of a pragmatic approach to intercultural communication is to investigate the way in which meaning gets generated in interaction. In order to do so, communicative events have to be approached from four angles. First, there is the angle of context, where any ingredient of a communicative event (whether at the level of physical social, or mental 'reality', or at the level of co-text and channel) is a potentially relevant aspect of context. Whether such an ingredient actually becomes relevant depends on the interactants' 'lines of vision' (that is, whether they 'orient' to them). Secondly, there is structure: contributions to the meaning-generating process can be made by choices at any level of linguistic structure. Context and structure together define the locus (extra- and intra-linguistic coordinates) of the phenomena to be described. Thirdly, the main task is to capture the dynamics of the processes involved in (interactive) meaning generation. These processes are 'dynamic' because, as explained above, they are not based on fixed form-function relationships, but on far-ranging negotiability. Fourthly, all those processes take place in a medium of adaptability, which is the human mind; we can use the term salience to refer to the status of the processes in relation to that medium. All of these angles have to be invoked when discussing verbal communication, whether or not it takes place in an intercultural setting [pp. 24–5].

Task B0.3.4

Verschueren gives the example of the European and the Chinese businessmen not relying on their previous understanding of how people in different cultural contexts behave, but instead using their 'reflexive capacities' and adapting to each other and creating a new context of communication.

➤ Can you think of other examples where you or other people you know have used their 'reflexive capacities' and have adapted to each other and created a new context of communication?

Verschueren also writes that 'contributions to the meaning-generating process can be made by choices at any level of linguistic structure' and refers to 'word choices, sound patterns and so on'.

➤ What other choices of linguistic patterns would you include in addition to 'word choices' and 'sound patterns'? What different 'choices' might be made in the scenarios outlined in Section A which contribute to the 'meaning-generating process'?

Verschueren writes that: 'any ingredient of a communicative event (whether at the level of physical social, or mental 'reality', or at the level of co-text and channel) is a potentially relevant aspect of context'.

➤ Think about what are the 'ingredients' of one or more of the intercultural communicative events in Section A of this book which may be 'relevant aspects of context'.

The work of Dell Hymes and others working in the field of 'ethnography of communication' has been instrumental in highlighting aspects of context at the level of the observable or easily identifiable 'physical' and 'social'. In recent years, those working within the field of discourse analysis have extended the discussion of 'context' beyond the observable or easily identifiable 'physical' and 'social' aspects of context to a deeper consideration of the nature and relative importance of all the different actions and activities that accompany language, and help express meaning, as well as what underlies language in terms of such factors as values, beliefs, attitudes, intentions, power, agency, political considerations and historical 'baggage'. One such discourse analyst is Van Dijk, who writes that 'it is not the context itself . . . that influences text and talk, but rather the *context models* of language users'. These context models,

> Represent how participants in a communicative event see, interpret and mentally represent the properties of the social situation that are now relevant for them. This is important, because it is precisely this subjective nature of context models that also allows for personal variation and contextual uniqueness – it is not the objective fact that speakers are women or men, white or black, young or old, or powerful or not, but how they see and construct themselves, in general or in the social situation.
>
> (Van Dijk 1998: 212)

Van Dijk (p. 214) proceeds to state that:

> In their ongoing construction, context models are constructed from information from the following sources:
>
> 1. a general schema, or goals or expectations about the current social situation;
> 2. activated previous models (being reminded of a previous conversation with X, reading the same newspaper in the same situation, etc.);
> 3. general personal beliefs about such a situation ('My neighbour always talks about his work and I don't like that');
> 4. socio-cultural knowledge and beliefs about communicative events;
> 5. previous parts of the ongoing discourse;
> 6. previous parts of the text.

In referring to 'a pragmatic approach to intercultural communication' Verschueren alludes to a rich field of work in cross-cultural pragmatics. Spencer-Oatey (2008), drawing on the work of Leech (1983), identifies a number of ways in which 'cultural differences in language use can have a major impact on people's assessments of appropriate language use', which include (in addition to 'fundamental cultural values'):

■ *Contextual assessment norms* – ('people from different cultural groups may assess contextual factors somewhat differently');

■ *Sociopragmatic principles* – ('people from different cultural groups may hold differing principles for managing rapport in given contexts – for example, some societies may value overt expressions of modesty in interactions with acquaintances and strangers, while others might prefer more "honest" evaluation. Similarly some societies may value explicit expressions of opinions and permit more open disagreement among new acquaintances than other societies do');

■ *Pragmalinguistic conventions* – ('people from different cultural groups may have differing conventions for selecting strategies and interpreting their use in given contexts – for example, two cultural groups may agree that an apology is necessary in a given context but may have different conventions for conveying it . . . people from one group may typically include an explanation, whereas people from another group may typically use acknowledgement of fault as a key component.');

■ *Inventory of rapport – management strategies* – ('every language has a very large inventory of rapport – management strategies').

(Spencer-Oatey 2008: 43–4)

In the final text in this unit, Martin and Nakayama present a model which attempts to account for the complexities of intercultural communication and to include those perspectives that Kumaravidivelu and Verschueren claim have often been ignored or downplayed in the field of intercultural communication.

Martin, J. N. and T. K. Nakayama (2008) 'Thinking dialectically about culture and communication.' In Asante, M. K., Miike, Y. and Yin, J. (eds) (2008) *The Global Intercultural Communication Reader.* **London: Routledge. pp. 81–5 (extracts)**

Text B0.3.3
J. N. Martin
and T. K.
Nakayama

Toward a dialectical perspective

The notion of dialect is hardly new. Used thousands of years ago by the ancient Greeks and others, its more recent emphases continue to stress the relational, processual, and contradictory nature of knowledge production (Bakhtin 1981; Baxter 1990; Cornforth 1968). Aristotle's famous dictum that 'rhetoric is the counterpart of dialectic' emphasises the significant relationship between modes of expression and modes of knowledge. Dialectic offers intercultural communication researchers a way to think about different ways of knowing in a more comprehensive manner, while retaining the significance of considering how we express this knowledge.

Thus, a dialectical approach to culture and communication offers us the possibility of engaging multiple, but distinct, research paradigms. It offers us the possibility to see the world in multiple ways and to become better prepared to engage in intercultural interaction. This means, of course, that we cannot become enmeshed into any paradigm, to do so flies in the face of dialectic thinking . . . [p. 81].

In intercultural communication research, the dialectical perspective emphasises the relationship between aspects of intercultural communication, and the importance of viewing these holistically and not in isolation. In intercultural communication

J. N. Martin
and T. K.
Nakayama

practice, the dialectical perspective stresses the importance of relationship. This means that one becomes fully human only in relation to another person and that there is something unique in a relationship that goes beyond the sum of two individuals. This notion is expressed by Yoshikawa (1987) as the 'dynamic in-betweenness' of a relationship – what exists beyond the two persons . . . [pp. 81–2].

A dialectical approach to studying intercultural interaction

. . . We have identified six similar dialectics that seem to operate interdependently in intercultural interactions: cultural–individual, personal/social–contextual, differences–similarities, static–dynamic, present–future/history–past, and privilege–disadvantage dialectics. These dialectics are neither exhaustive nor mutually exclusive but represent an ongoing exploration of new ways to think about face-to-face intercultural interaction and research.

Cultural–individual dialectic

Scholars and practitioners alike recognise that intercultural communication is both cultural and individual. In any interaction, there are some aspects of communication that are individual and idiosyncratic (for example, unique nonverbal expressions or language use) as well as aspects that are shared by others in the same cultural groups (for example, family, gender, ethnicity, etc.). Functionalist research has focused on communication patterns that are shared by particular groups (gender, ethnicity, etc.) and has identified differences between these group patterns. In contrast, critical communication scholars have resisted connecting group membership with any one individual's particular behaviour, which leads to essentialising.

A dialectical perspective reminds us that people are both group members and individuals and intercultural interaction is characterised by both. Research could investigate how these two contradictory characteristics work in intercultural interactions. For example, how do people experience the tension between wanting to be seen and treated as individuals, and at the same time have their group identities recognised and affirmed (Collier 1991)? . . . [p. 82].

Personal/social–contextual dialectic

A dialectical perspective emphasises the relationship between personal and contextual communication. There are some aspects of communication that remain relatively constant over many contexts. There are also aspects that are contextual. That is, people communicate in particular ways in particular contexts (for example, professors and students in classrooms), and messages are interpreted in particular ways. Outside the classroom (for example, at football games or at faculty meetings), professors and students may communicate differently, expressing different aspects of themselves. Intercultural encounters are characterised by both personal and contextual communication. Researchers could investigate how these contradictory characteristics operate in intercultural interactions.

Differences–similarities dialectic

A dialectic approach recognises the importance of similarities and differences in understanding intercultural communication. The field was founded on the assumption that there are real, important differences that exist between various cultural groups, and functionalist research has established a long tradition of identifying these

J. N. Martin
and T. K.
Nakayama

differences. However, in real life there are a great many similarities in human experience and ways of communicating. Cultural communication researchers in the interpretive tradition have emphasised these similar patterns in specific cultural communities. Critical researchers have emphasised that there may be differences, but these differences are often not benign, but are political and have implications for power relations (Houston 1992).

There has been a tendency to overemphasise group differences in traditional intercultural communication research – in a way that sets up false dichotomies and rigid expectations. However, a dialectical perspective reminds us that difference and similarity can coexist in intercultural communication interactions . . . [p. 83].

Research could examine how differences and similarities work in cooperation or in opposition in intercultural interaction.

For example, how do individuals experience the tension of multiple differences and similarities in their everyday intercultural interactions (class, race, gender, attitudes, beliefs)? Are these aspects or topics that tend to emphasise one or the other? How do individuals deal with this tension? What role does context play in managing this tension?

Static–dynamic dialectic

The static–dynamic dialectic highlights the ever-changing nature of culture and cultural practices, but also underscores our tendency to think about these things as constant. Traditional intercultural research in the functionalist tradition and some interpretive research have emphasised the stability of cultural patterns, for example, values, that remain relatively consistent over periods of time (Hofstede 1991). Some interpretive research examines varying practices that reflect this value over time (for example, Carbaugh's study of communication rules on Donahue discourse 1990a). In contrast, critical researchers have emphasised the instability and fleetingness of cultural meanings, for example, Cornyetz's (1994) study of the appropriation of hip-hop in Japan.

So thinking about culture and cultural practices as both static and dynamic helps us navigate through a diverse world and develop new ways of understanding intercultural encounters. Research could investigate how these contradictory forces work in intercultural interactions. How do individuals work with the static and dynamic aspects of intercultural interactions? How is the tension of this dynamic experienced and expressed in intercultural relationships?

Present–future/history–past dialectic

A dialectic in intercultural communication exists between the history–past and the present–future. Much of the functionalist and interpretive scholarship investigating culture and communication has ignored historical forces. Other scholars added history as a variable in understanding contemporary intercultural interaction, for example, Stephan and Stephan's (1996) prior intergroup interaction variable that influences degree of intergroup anxiety. In contrast, critical scholars stress the importance of including history in current analyses of cultural meanings.

A dialectical perspective suggests that we need to balance both an understanding of the past and the present. Also the past is always seen through the lens of the present . . . [pp. 83–4].

. . . How do individuals experience this tension? How do they balance the two in everyday interaction? Many influential factors precede and succeed any intercultural interaction that gives meaning to that interaction.

J. N. Martin
and T. K.
Nakayama

Privilege–disadvantage dialectic

As individuals, we carry and communicate various types of privilege and disadvantage, the final dialectic. The traditional intercultural communication research mostly ignores issues of privilege and disadvantage (exceptions include Pennington 1989; Gallois *et al.* 1995), although these issues are central in critical scholarship. Privilege and disadvantage may be in the form of political, social position, or status. For example, if members of wealthy nations travel to less wealthy countries, the intercultural interactions between these two groups will certainly be influenced by their differential in economic power (Katriel 1995). Hierarchies and power differentials are not always clear. Individuals may be simultaneous [sic] privileged and disadvantaged, or privileged in some contexts, and disadvantaged in others. Research could investigate how the intersections of privilege and disadvantage work in intercultural encounters. Women of colour may be simultaneously advantaged (education, economic class) and disadvantaged (gender, race), for example (Houston 1992). How are these various contradictory privileges and disadvantages felt, expressed, and managed in intercultural interactions? How do context and topic play into the dialectic? Many times, it may not be clear who or how one is privileged or disadvantaged. It may be unstable, fleeting, may depend on the topic, or the context.

Dialectical intersections

So how do these different dialectics work in everyday interaction? These dialectics are not discrete, but always operate in relation to each other (see Figure B0.3.1). We can illustrate these intersections with an example of a relationship between a foreign student from a wealthy family and a US-American professor. Using this example we can see how contradictories in several dialectics can occur in interpersonal intercultural interaction. In relation to the personal/social–contextual dialectic, both the student and professor are simultaneously privileged and disadvantaged depending on the context. In talking about class material, for example, the professor is more privileged than the student, but in talking about vacations and travel, the wealthy student may be more privileged.

To focus on another set of dialects, if the topic of international trade barriers comes up, the student may be seen as a cultural representative than an individual and, in this conversation, cultural differences or similarities may be emphasised. When the topic shifts, these relational dialectics also shift – within the same relationship.

. . . This approach makes explicit the dialectical tension between what previous research topics have been studied (cultural differences, assumed static nature of culture, etc.) and what should be studied (how cultures change, how they are similar, importance of history). The dialectical perspective, then, represents a major epistemological move in our understanding of culture and communication.

Martin and Nakayama give the example of a relationship between a foreign student from a wealthy family and a US-American professor and of how 'contradictories in several dialectics' can occur in interpersonal intercultural interaction between them.

➤ Return to the scenario in Section A, Unit A3.1 (Reza and Martha) and think about the 'contradictories in several dialectics' that might occur in this example of interpersonal intercultural interaction.

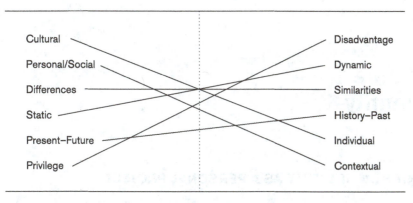

Figure B0.3.1 Intersections of six dialectics of intercultural interaction

➤ Think of other examples of relationships in which 'contradictories in several dialectics' can occur in interpersonal intercultural interaction.

Martin and Nakayama write that, 'a dialectical approach to culture and communication offers us the possibility ... to become better prepared to engage in intercultural interaction.'

➤ In what practical ways do you think a 'dialectical approach' helps individuals to become better prepared to engage in intercultural interaction?

Commentary

The dialectical perspective of Martin and Nakayama represents an attempt to account for the possibility that intercultural communication is 'a complex, ongoing process that cannot be reduced to expedient labels and convenient dichotomies' (Kumaravadivelu 2008). In doing so, it attempts to integrate what Humphrey (2007) has summarised as 'the three main conceptual perspectives to the study of intercultural and cross-cultural communication': the 'social psychological perspective' (related to the work of Hall and Hofstede, and others who have developed further their ideas); 'the critical perspective' which 'focuses more on macro-contexts, such as the political and social structures that influence communication' and within which 'scholars pay attention to the influence that context, including socio–historical context, and ideological aspects of power, oppression, and emancipation in society may have on our intercultural interaction'; the 'interpretive perspective' that 'challenges the definition of culture and the ideological nature of intercultural communication research' according to which scholars 'argue that there is a need to recognise the complexity of the subject matter being addressed', that 'culture is created and maintained through communication' and 'different layers of culture can intertwine in complex ways'.

Theme 1
Identity

UNIT B1.1   IDENTITY AS A PERSONAL PROJECT

In recent years in the broad field of cultural studies there has been a growing interest in questions of identity. Questions commonly discussed include:

- How is the identity of any one individual created?
- In the creation of individual identity what factors are salient and how do these factors interact?
- To what extent is any one individual's identity a matter of personality and to what extent do influences from the sociocultural context impact?
- How much commonality of identity is there, first, between two individuals who inhabit the same physical and sociocultural space and, second, between two individuals who inhabit very different physical and sociocultural spaces?
- How far is identity fixed and stable?
- If identities do change what factors are responsible for such change?
- How far is individual identity influenced by global forces?
- How far is individual identity influenced by information technologies?
- What is the relationship between language and identity?
- In what ways does identity impact on communication?

The term 'identity' defies precise definition and crosses traditional boundaries between disciplines in the social sciences. Increasingly in recent years there has been an emphasis on the interrelationship of culture and *identity*, as well as on the longer established emphasis on the interrelationship between culture and *behaviour*.

In this unit we consider a particular aspect of identity which has come to the forefront in recent years: that of identity being a personal project. The first text is by a Peruvian novelist, short story writer, playwright and essayist, Julio Ramón Ribeyro, while the second is by Anthony Giddens, a well-known social scientist.

 Task B1.1.1

➤ In what ways might identity be said to be 'a personal project'?

Text B1.1.1
J. R Ribeyro

Ribeyro, J. R (1972) 'Barbara' *from La Palabra del Mundo,* **collected short stories, translated by D. Douglas (1986) from** *On Being Foreign: Culture Shock in Short Fiction – An International Anthology,* **Lewis, T. J. and Jungman, R. E. (eds), Yarmouth, Maine: Intercultural Press (extracts)**

Despite the fact that he was a *mulatto*[1] named Lopez, he longed to resemble less and less a goalie on the Alianza Lima soccer team and increasingly to take on the appearance of a blond from Philadelphia. Life had taught him that if he wanted to triumph in a colonial city it was better to skip the intermediate stages and transform himself into a *gringo*[2] from the United States rather than into just a fair-skinned nobody from Lima. During the years that I knew him, he devoted all of his attention to eliminating every trace of the Lopez and zambo,[3] within him and Americanising himself before time could sentence him to an existence as a bank guard or a taxi driver. He had had to begin by killing the Peruvian in himself and extracting something from every gringo that he met. From all this plundering a new person would emerge, a fragmented being who was neither mulatto nor gringo, but rather the result of an unnatural commingling, something that the force of destiny would eventually change, unfortunately, for him, from a rosy dream into a hellish nightmare.

But let's not get ahead of ourselves. We should establish the fact that his name was Roberto, that years later he was known as Bobby, but that in the most recent official documents he is listed as Bob. At each stage in his frantic ascension toward nothingness his name lost one syllable.

First of all he had to eliminate every trace of the zambo in himself. His hair didn't cause any major problem; he dyed it with peroxide and had it straightened. As for his skin, he mixed starch, rice powder, and talcum from the drugstore until he found the ideal combination; but a dyed and powdered zambo is still a zambo. He needed to know how the North American gringos dressed, talked, moved, and thought: in short, precisely who they were.

In those days we saw him marauding about during his free hours in diverse locales which seemingly had nothing in common, except for one thing: they were usually frequented by gringos.

This phase of his plan was for him absolutely perfect. In the meantime, he was able to confirm that the gringos were distinguishable from others by the special way they dressed, which he described as sporty, comfortable, and unconventional. Because of his observations, Roberto was one of the first to discover the advantages of blue jeans, the virile cowboy look of the wide leather belt fastened by an enormous buckle, the soft comfort of white canvas shoes with rubber soles, the collegiate charm of a canvas cap with a visor, the coolness of a flowered or striped short-sleeved shirt, the variety of nylon jackets zipped up in front bearing an emblem of special significance, always influential and distinctive, and worn underneath, a white shirt also bearing an emblem of a North American university.

All of these articles of clothing were not sold in any department store but had to be brought from the United States, a place where he had no contacts. There were North American families who, prior to returning to the United States, announced in

---

1 *Mulatto* means someone who is a mixture of white and black.
2 *Gringo* is a term used to identify a (white) North American.
3 *Zambo* means someone who is a blend of native Indian and black.

the newspaper their intention to sell everything they had. Roberto showed up on their doorstep before anyone else, acquiring in this way a wardrobe in which he invested all of his savings.

With hair that was now straightened and bleached, a pair of blue jeans and a loud shirt, Roberto was on the brink of becoming Bobby.

★ **Task B1.1.2**

Ribeyro writes of Lopez 'killing the Peruvian in himself'. This assumes that his identity is in part defined by national culture (in his case, Peruvian culture).

➤ Do you think your own identity is in part defined by one or more national cultures? If so, in what ways and to what extent?

In the extract Lopez attempts to change his identity by changing his name, appearance and social contacts.

➤ Do you think it is possible to change your identity by changing these things? Have any changes you have made to your own name, appearance or social contacts affected your own sense of self-identity?

Text B1.1.2
A. Giddens

Giddens, A. (1991) *Modernity and Self-Identity: Self and Society in the Late Modern Age,* Cambridge: Polity. pp. 14, 81, 53–5 (extracts)

Today each of us lives a biography reflexively organised in terms of flows of social and psychological information about possible ways of life . . . 'How shall I live ?' has to be answered in day-to-day decisions about how to behave, what to wear and what to eat, and many other things [p. 14] . . . each of the decisions a person makes every day . . . are decisions not only about how to act but who to be [p. 81].

Self-identity is not a distinctive trait, or even a collection of traits, possessed by the individual. It is the self as reflexively understood by the person in terms of her or his biography. Identity here still presumes continuity across time and space: but self-identity is such continuity as interpreted reflexively by the agent. This includes the cognitive component of personhood. To be a 'person' is not just to be a reflexive actor, but to have a concept of a person (as applied both to the self and others). What a 'person' is understood to be certainly varies across cultures, although there are elements of such a notion that are common to all cultures . . .

The existential question of self-identity is bound up with the fragile nature of the biography which the individual 'supplies' about herself. A person's identity is not to be found in behaviour, nor – important though this is – in the reactions of others, but in the capacity to keep a particular narrative going. The individual's biography, if she is to maintain regular interaction with others in the day-to-day world, cannot be wholly fictive. It must continually integrate events which occur in the external world, and sort them into the ongoing 'story' about the self . . .

The 'content' of self-identity – the traits from which biographies are constructed – varies socially and culturally. In some respects this is obvious enough. A person's name, for example, is a primary element in his biography; practices of social naming, how far names express kin relations, whether or not names are changed at certain stages of life – all these things differ between cultures. But there are other more subtle, yet also more important, differences. Reflexive biographies vary in much the same ways as stories do.

Task B.1.1.3

➤ Do you see your own identity as a matter of keeping 'a particular narrative going' or would you use another metaphor?

➤ If you do believe identity is a matter of keeping 'a particular narrative going', then what does your own 'narrative' consist of?

➤ If you came up with another metaphor for describing your identity, explain this metaphor.

Task B.1.1.4

Giddens writes that although there are commonalities between cultures, 'what a "person" is understood to be' varies culturally. Wetherell and Maybin (1996: 221) point to some key assumptions 'which many people in countries such as the UK and USA would see as simply obvious and true, although they may want to add items to or qualify our list'. These are:

- A person is someone with a self-contained mind and consciousness: a unique individual who is separate and distinct from other people.
- Each individual has one personality or a consistent set of traits, characteristics, preferences or abilities which sum up that person's true nature.
- People own their thoughts and feelings. These are private, self-generated and organised within the inner self. Thoughts, feelings and internal states can, however, be expressed publicly through language, actions and through other symbolic means. Although people might struggle to find the right terms, their words reflect more or less accurately their internal states.
- People ... are the centre and source of their experience. Individuals initiate action and try to realise themselves (their plans, beliefs, desires) in the world.

➤ Do you think there is any truth in the assertion by Giddens that 'what a "person" is understood to be' varies culturally? Why/why not?

If so:

➤ If you live in a country 'such as the UK or USA', do you share and/or recognise the assumptions described by Wetherell and Maybin ?

Or:

➤ If you live in a country very different from the UK or USA, would you say there are different and contrasting assumptions about individual identity?

Commentary

Giddens believes that whereas the lives of individuals in previous generations were structured around 'life cycles' consisting of 'ritualised passages' (for example, particular birthdays of significance, festivals and marriage), in contemporary life individuals' lives are 'more and more freed from externalities associated with pre-established ties to other individuals and groups' (1991: 147) and are structured around 'open experience thresholds' (i.e. particular events and experiences in the individual's 'biography' which have particular significance). Giddens believes that in contemporary life 'life-planning' is of particular importance for the individual: 'Life plans are the substantial content of the reflexively organised trajectory of the self. Life-planning is a means of preparing a course of future actions mobilised in terms of the self's biography' (1991: 85).

The move away from 'traditional' means of defining identity has for some been a key feature of postmodernism. For Strinati (1997: 431), for example, postmodernism has seen 'the gradual disappearance of the traditional long-standing and once legitimate frames of reference in terms of which people could define themselves and their place in society, and so feel relatively secure in their own identities. These traditional sources of identity – social class, the extended and nuclear family, local communities, the "neighbourhood", religion, trade unions, the nation state – are said to be in decline as a result of tendencies in modern capitalism towards increasingly rapid rates of economic, geographical, political and cultural change.'

There remains an important question of how far an individual narrative of identity is influenced by, and intersects with, the socio–cultural milieux within which an individual is socialised and inhabits. Baynham (2015) writes of a tension in identity studies concerning the 'degree of agency attributed' to the individual (p. 70) and distinguishes between 'identity brought along' and 'identity brought about'. 'Identity brought along' refers to 'identity positions that are relatively stable and long-standing' (p. 69), which are 'often thought of as essentialised' and that are 'built up over time through many repeated encounters'. During these encounters identity is 'performed' or 'brought about', just as in a story, so that 'rather than seeing identity as somehow sitting behind the discourse and retrievable from it, we see identity both brought along and brought about as being performed in discourse' (p. 84).

UNIT B1.2 GLOBALISATION, COSMOPOLITANISM AND IDENTITY

In this unit, the first text by Mathews raises important questions as to whether the forces of globalisation have impacted on individuals' sense of identity. In the second text, Sobré-Denton and Bardhan (2013) review previous approaches to 'identity' in intercultural communication, and discuss the potential for individuals to develop 'cosmopolitan' identities that cross borders and have the potential to play a part in bringing about social and political change.

Before you read the text, do task B1.2.1.

Task B1.2.1

➤ How far, and in what ways, would you say your sense of your own identity has been affected by global trends and the flow of goods, people and images around the world?

Mathews, G. (2000) *Global Culture/Individual Identity: Searching for Home in the Cultural Supermarket.* **London: Routledge. pp. 19–23 (extracts)**

Text B1.2.1
G. Mathews

The cultural supermarket bears some resemblance to its metaphorical root, the material supermarket. Just as the material supermarket has been transformed as to the scope of its goods in recent years . . . so too has the cultural supermarket, thanks to television and computers. And just as in the material supermarket shelf space is unequally distributed – products like Coca-Cola being on the middle, easily seen shelves, other, less heavily advertised products being above the customer's head, and less noticeable – so too in the cultural supermarket. Those societies whose material goods are readily available in the world also have greater cultural influence in the world. 'The United States', writes Robert Bockock, '. . . has come to epitomise the modern [worldwide] consumer's dreamland', and certainly the world's cultural supermarket has more than its share of American 'goods,' in the influences of movies, music, and sports – America's celebrity culture, spread worldwide.

But the structure of the cultural supermarket is far more complex than this metaphor indicates; in its far-flung intangibility, it is more like a vast library than like a grocery store, more like the internet than like a map of nations of the world.

The information within the cultural supermarket may be categorised by its users in a number of different ways, but the two most readily available are (1) region of origin, and (2) realm of use. For most of the information in the cultural supermarket, we have some idea of where it comes from. This usually corresponds to culture as 'the way of life of a people,' as embodied in national culture: we refer to Indian music, Brazilian samba, French cuisine, and so on, in order to have a shorthand way with which to refer to these entities. These represent aisle signs, often of questionable validity but of considerable convenience, in labelling and dividing up the vast array of materials in the cultural supermarket for consumers' ease. As we will see, these claims may become particularly vital when applied to oneself; claims of 'Japanese' art or 'American' religion or 'Chinese' values may seek to make what may seem a choice from the cultural supermarket into one's underlying essence – they may seek to make a choice not a choice.

There is also the realm of use. We fashion ourselves from the cultural supermarket in a number of areas, among them our choices in home decor, in food and clothing,

G. Mathews

in what we read, watch, and listen to in music, art, and popular culture, in our religious belief, and in ethnic and national identity itself: whether, in the United States, to identify oneself as Hispanic–American or as American; whether, in Hong Kong, to be Chinese or Hongkongese. These different shapings bear differing degrees of personal significance: one's choice of home decor, for example ('That Buddhist mandala in the living room? No, of course I don't believe in that stuff. I just thought it looked neat'), may be of considerably less significance for one's sense of cultural identity than, for example, one's choice of religion, which may lie at the core of who one senses oneself to be. In this book, we will consistently see that the choices people make in the realms of artistic expression, religious belief, and cultural identity are of deep personal significance: we will find that choices from the cultural supermarket, unlike many choices from the material supermarket, are very often agonised over, for they may be of extraordinary importance to these people in defining what their lives are most essentially about.

The foregoing should not, however, be taken to mean that our choices from the cultural supermarket are free; rather, as earlier noted, our choices are restricted in a number of different senses. There is first of all the differential in receiving equipment for the cultural supermarket. One who is educated and affluent may possess optimal receiving equipment: access to and ability to make use of the repository of human thought contained in libraries, and access to the contemporary repositories of thought in the Internet and in mass media – the world assortment of newspapers, magazines, and compact disks available at key outlets throughout the world. A person with such advantages may make full use of the cultural supermarket, but many of the people in the world cannot – their access to the cultural supermarket is more limited, confined to whatever echoes of the cultural supermarket may reach their particular corner of the world. No doubt more people from rich societies than poor societies, and more people from the upper, affluent, educated classes in every society than the lower, poorer, less-educated classes have this optimal receiving equipment. It may be that the less sophisticated the receiving equipment you have, the more likely that you will be manipulated down the standard paths of Coca-Cola, Marlboro, Rambo, Doraemon, although there are certainly exceptions to this; and as anthropologists often note, how consumers in different societies actually interpret these various products may differ substantially from the plans of marketers.

Beyond this, there is the fact that the choices each of us makes as to cultural identity are made not for ourselves but for performance for and in negotiation with others: we choose ourselves within the cultural supermarket with an eye to our social world. One's cultural identity is performed in that one must convince others as to its validity: one must have the knowledge and social grace to convince others that one is not an impostor. Efforts to this effect may be seen in many different social milieux . . . from the Japanese salaryman/rock musician who wears a short-hair wig to his office rather than get his hair cut, so that he can convince his fellow rock musicians that he is 'for real,' to the American spiritual seeker who pursues various religions despite the scorn of her husband, snickering that she 'goes through religions like she goes through clothes,' to the mainland Chinese woman in Hong Kong who wears expensive fashions but not with quite enough of a sense of style to disguise her mainland background from the disdainful eyes of Hong Kong people.

A wide range of cultural identities in this world is available for appropriation; but although culturally the world may be wide open, socially it is not. One's cultural choices must fit within one's social world, which is more limited. In a typical middle-class American neighbourhood, I could probably become a Buddhist without alarming

G. Mathews

my neighbours, but I could not become an Islamic fundamentalist; I may study the Mbuti pygmies in an anthropology text, but were I to express beliefs such as theirs to my co-workers, I would at best be seen as eccentric, at worst as a lunatic. One's social world – outside one's mind, and more, as resident within one's mind – acts as a censor and gatekeeper, selecting from the range of possible cultural ideas one might appropriate only those that seem plausible and acceptable within it. One's social world particularly constrains one's choices in terms of such factors as class, gender, and age. The elderly woman who wears a miniskirt and the working-class kid who uses fancy foreign words are likely to learn quite rapidly, if they have any sensitivity at all to the cues of their social world, about the inappropriateness of their cultural choices.

Despite these strictures, there is often the effort to bring into one's social world what Pierre Bourdieu terms 'cultural capital': knowledge from the cultural supermarket that one can display to one's social credit, justifying and bolstering one's social position. One's interest, at least within some segments of American society, in Indian ragas as opposed to top 40 hits, or in Tibetan Buddhist writings as opposed to evangelical Christian tracts, is a way of advertising cosmopolitan discernment: my far-flung tastes may well be the servant of my local strategy of impressing the people around me. The matter of what from the cultural supermarket can provide status in a given social milieu is highly complex. Each social milieu has its rating system for information and identities from the cultural supermarket; individuals seek to attain maximum credit and credibility, not only through consumption within the existing cultural rating system, but also through bringing in new information and identities, whose high status they seek to establish. The criteria for the establishment of such status are thus highly specific and flexible; individuals play the game with an extraordinarily acute sense of its implicit rules and strategies.

But all this is not to claim that there is absolutely no room for individual choice from the cultural supermarket. Why does one person thrill to Bach, another to juju? Why does one person become a Christian, another a Buddhist? Why does one person revel in her ethnicity, while another spurns that ethnicity? Why does one person travel the world while another stays home? Much can be predicted about our choices by considering such factors as social class, educational level, income, gender, and age, as well as our personal histories, but not everything can be predicted. We are not slaves to the world around us, but have (in a social if not a philosophical sense) a certain degree of freedom in choosing who we are. This freedom may be highly limited, but it cannot be altogether denied.

Task B1.2.2

Mathews suggests that 'our choices in home decor, in food and clothing, in what we read, watch, and listen to in music, art, and popular culture' all help to fashion our identities.

➤ Do you think that your own identity has been partly fashioned by such things, and if so, how important are they to your own sense of identity?

➤ In your own 'social world' what from the 'cultural supermarket' can 'provide status'?

➤ What 'cultural ideas' are *not* 'plausible or acceptable' in your own 'social world'?

There is no doubt that for many of us our world is very different, in many respects, from that of previous generations. Yet, despite the myriad changes, questions at the core of debate in the social sciences remain unanswered: those of how much freedom individuals have to fashion their own identities (in other words, the degree of agency individuals have), and, on the other hand, of how far individuals' thoughts, values and identities are determined and constrained by the values of the social structures, economic realities and mass media of their cultural milieux. These questions Mathews touches on in the last two sentences of the extract.

A number of writers have made similar links between consumption and identity. In linking consumption with identity, it is not simply a question of identity being formed through the acquisition of consumer goods. As Mathews suggests, it is what objects *mean* to individuals rather than the objects themselves which are significant. Gabriel and Lang (1995: 89) write of the 'stories' which the individual 'reads into' consumer objects; for them this is the particular nature of 'Western' consumption so that 'identity becomes vitally and self-consciously enmeshed in stories which are read by consumers themselves into innumerable, relatively mundane, mass produced objects which they buy, use or own'. Bourdieu's ideas on consumption and identity have been especially influential, and his theory of 'cultural capital' has been widely discussed in relation to discourse and to issues of advantage and disadvantage.

A key question is how in different contexts individuals' identities are influenced by the forces of globalisation and the relations of power in the multiple processes of globalisation. Sorrells (2013, cited in Sobré-Denton and Bardhan 2013: 3) writes that 'Through advances in technology – and open markets, people from around the globe with different cultural, racial, national, economic, and linguistics backgrounds are coming into contact with each other; consuming each others' cultural foods, products and identities' (pp. 26–7).

 Task B1.2.3

➤ Do you believe that identities can be 'consumed' through the multiple processes of globalisation? If so, in what ways?

Text B1.2.2
M. Sobré-
Denton and
N. Bardhan

Sobré-Denton, M. and Bardhan, N. (2013) *Cultivating Cosmopolitanism for Intercultural Communication*. London: Routledge. pp. 1–2, 52–3, 55–6, 59, 62 (extracts)

Despite much technological progress and the effusive promotion of market ideology as the solution for a better planet, our world remains a vastly uneven place. It is a place where some cultures and countries continue to benefit at the expense of others. Within countries the disparities between the privileged and the marginalised continue to widen. But what if another world were possible, one where we value difference, shun oppression of the cultural Other, strive for peace, work collectively to protect the

M. Sobré-
Denton and
N. Bardhan

earth as a single entity, build intercultural alliances for social and global justice, engage more in difficult intercultural dialogues and believe in the importance of communicating ethically and critically as global citizens? . . .

As intercultural communication scholars, we can look for some ways to accomplish this within our own field. Communication is action and it can transform perceptions and bring about change for the sake of local and global justice. But first we need to ask what it means to communicate ethically and critically across cultural difference and global citizens [p. 1].

We have wondered why the communication discipline, specifically intercultural communication, has paid scant attention to the promise of cosmopolitanism and its ethical vision . . . Cosmopolitanism helps us to get to the heart of some of the central concerns within the field of intercultural communication – culture, differences, power, identity and the need for alliance-building across differences – and it does so by questioning divisive cultural boundaries and nation-state-centric thinking. We live and communicate within nation-states, across nation-states, and within the flows and disjunctures of a larger interconnected world (Appadurai 1996). The time is ripe for exploring the potential of the cosmopolitan moral vision in intercultural communication within the context of globalisation [pp. 1–2].

The topic of identity has increasingly become a focus in the field of intercultural communication since how we perform and communicatively co-construct identities lies at the heart of intercultural communication . . . In today's conditions of postmodern and postcolonial globality, heightened movement (actual or virtual) across cultural borders is increasingly interrupting the power of national culture to remain a hegemonic identity category (Appadurai 1996; Rosenau 2004). People can and are simultaneously identifying with sub and supranational culture entities (including virtual communities), and this is leading us away from a stable place-based view of 'identity' to one of 'identities' that extend and shift across place and space (Hall 1997; Shome 2003, 2010). One major form of culture and identity movement occurs through travel and migration . . . In addition to actual travel, exposure to images, ideologies and information about other cultures through those who travel, the media and online sources is also a form of cultural movement that is widening our imagination about the world as a whole and the cultural beings who inhabit it . . . Our multiple senses of Self and Others are turning cultures into identities into multidimensional ongoing projects that are caught up in the play of various dialectics and registers of power, vacillating in particular directions depending on context [pp. 52–3].

What we can take away from (earlier) theories of identity in intercultural communication is that identities are multidimensional, relational, open to change and negotiable through communication . . . What we don't get so much from these theories, some of which are work in progress, is sufficient focus on issues of power hegemony, privilege, spatial context, cultural deterritorialisation/reterritorialisation and the notion of difference. While context is acknowledged, it is generally studied as stable and unchanging . . . and larger historical structural and political forces that impact identity-related communication are not investigated in depth [pp. 55–6].

The critical postmodern and postcolonial approaches to cultural identity highlight the roles of power and difference in intercultural communication, two issues that are central to the more recent postcolonial turn in cosmopolitan thought . . . They suggest that identities are not set in stone, and that they can be performatively and communicatively reconfigured to bring about changes in perceptions about difference in ways that could open up possibilities for forming alliance across cultural divides.

M. Sobré-
Denton and
N. Bardhan

In other words, how we perform identities can interrupt and gradually change oppressive power hierarchies and structures – from the ground up. This move from identity as something people passively 'possess' to something they 'do' that can always be changed is a hopeful note for conceiving cultural identity and communication in cosmopolitan terms [p. 59].

Simply put, cosmopolitanism, when conceived of as intercultural communication, can introduce another layer of identity, that of critical global citizenship, to all our other cultural identities and affiliations' [p. 62].

★ Task B1.2.4

➤ Sobré-Denton and Bardhan write about the 'move from identity as something people passively "possess" to something they "do"' (p. 62). What do you think they mean by this? Can you think of ways in which you might 'do' identity?

➤ Sobré-Denton and Bardhan refer to the process by which 'we perform identities can interrupt and gradually change oppressive power hierarchies and structures – from the ground up' (p. 59). Thinking about your own local context, do you think how individuals 'perform identities' can interrupt and gradually change oppressive power hierarchies and structures – from the ground up? What about in the global context?

➤ If so, can you think of examples in recent societies and/or communities of how oppressive power hierarchies and structures have been interrupted or gradually changed from the ground up by how people 'perform' identities?

➤ The term 'critical global citizenship' is used in the text (p. 62). What do you think 'critical global citizenship' might involve?

Commentary

The notion of 'cosmopolitanism' has in recent years become a key issue in the field of intercultural communication and sociology. In a study of the discourse of parents of children attending an international school in Holland, Weenink (2008) distinguishes between 'dedicated' and 'pragmatic cosmopolitans'. For the dedicated cosmopolitan the following attributes were seen as important: 'the ability to look beyond borders'; to be flexible and 'prepared to adapt to the situation'; 'being open to foreign cultures'. Parents who were 'pragmatic' cosmopolitans, however, had a more restricted and instrumental perspective; they:

> Often had international work experiences and therefore saw the advantages of appropriating an international orientation . . . But they did not relate this to a vision of the world without borders that is open . . . or a dedication to cultural openness.

> (2008: 1096)

The instrumental nature of pragmatic cosmopolitanism can arguably lead to what Featherstone terms 'shallow cosmopolitanism' which involves 'dabbling rootlessly in a variety of cultures' and an 'incapacity to form lasting attachments and commitments to places and others' with a 'restless pursuit of experiences, aesthetic sensations and novelty over duties, obligations and social bonds' (2002: 1). This is in contrast to a 'dedicated' cosmopolitanism which for Kurasawa (2011: 279) is 'a capacity of multiperspectivism' which involves the ability to 'move between and be able to decode a wide array of divergent socio-cultural practices and belief systems, as well as to be familiar with the self-understandings of various groups across the world' (quoted in Sobré-Denton and Bardhan 2013: 6).

UNIT B1.3   DISCOURSE AND IDENTITY

In the first text De Fina emphasises the importance of the 'stories' that people tell about themselves and their lives, and reflects a growing importance given to the role of narrative in defining identity. An important point made by De Fina is that 'what defines people as members of a group is not only the content of their stories, but the way in which they use socially established resources to tell them'.

What defines people as members of groups, and how people draw on 'socially established resources' is also the concern of James Gee, the writer of the second and third extracts from his book *An Introduction to Discourse Analysis: Theory and Method* (1999). Gee writes that 'when we speak or write we always take a particular *perspective* on what the "world" is like. This involves us in taking perspectives on what is "normal" and not; what is "acceptable" and not what is "right" and not, what is "real" and not; what is the "way things are" and not; what is the "way things ought to be" and not; what is "possible" and not; what "people like us" or "people like them" do and don't; and so on and so forth, again through a nearly endless list' (1999: 2).

De Fina, A. (2006) 'Group identity, narrative and self-representations.' In De Fina, A., Schriffin, D. and Bamberg, M. (eds) *Discourse and Identity.* Cambridge: Cambridge University Press. pp. 351–5 (extracts)

Text B1.3.1
A. De Fina

The last decade has seen a growing interdisciplinary interest in the formation, negotiation, and development of identities. This new focus on identity is, at least partially, the product of the intensified contact between different communities brought about in post-modern societies by such social processes as globalisation and massive migrations. The multiplication of the occasions for contact with *the other* has brought with it a problematisation of the concept of identity itself and an effort to understand the relationship between people's sense of membership in a community, the beliefs and social practices that define that sense of membership, and its expression and manifestation in social behaviour.

For discourse analysts and sociolinguists the challenge has been to show not only the centrality of the role of language in the construction and transmission of identities, but also the concrete forms in which and through which language practices index such identities [p. 351].

A. De Fina

Identities in narrative

The stress on narrative as the locus for the study of identities is not new in discourse analysis. Researchers in the field have shown that by telling stories, narrators are able not only to represent social worlds and to evaluate them, but also to establish themselves as members of particular groups through interactional, linguistic, rhetorical and stylistic choices. Thus, for example, researchers in narrative have related identities to cultural ways of telling (Blum-Kulka 1993; Ochs and Taylor 1995) or culturally determined schemata (Wood 1999; Kiesling, this volume), to the choice of particular strategies such as reported speech (Hill 1989) or detail (Johnstone 1990), to the use of performance devices in general (Bauman 1986), to the degree of discourse integration of stories (Sawin 1999), to the choice of language or language variety in the telling (Bucholtz 1999b; Holmes 1997). These studies of narrative have shown that what defines people as members of a group is not only the content of their stories, but the way in which they use socially established resources to tell them . . .

Another way of analysing the relationship between identities and narrative has been to examine how linguistic resources are used by narrators to index their positioning with respect to social categories such as gender, ethnicity, or race (Bucholtz 1999b; De Fina 2000, 2003; Kiesling, this volume; Moita-Lopes, this volume). Analyses of the use of these kinds of social constructs in stories have shown that narrators give situated meanings to categories describing race, ethnicity and gender, that these categories are often inter-connected in intricate ways in the discourse of narrators, and that the latter negotiate through stories their sense of belonging or opposition to groups represented by those categories. The studies just discussed support a widely accepted social constructionist conception of identity in which identity is seen as situationally motivated and achieved (Bauman 2000: 1). Within this vision . . . people do not possess one identity related to the social categories to which they belong, but rather they present and re-present themselves, choosing within an inventory of more or less compatible identities that intersect and/or contrast with each other in different ways and in accordance with changing social circumstances and interlocutors. Social constructionist perspectives have also influenced our view of identity construction and attribution as a process grounded in different kinds of social practices and activities. In that sense, it has become generally accepted that different types of narratives emerging in different types of interactional contexts provide specific loci for the construction of particular inventories of identities. The recognition of the 'polyphonous' (Barrett 1999) nature of identity should not, however, lead to a vision of the construction of identity as an entirely creative and locally managed process, since . . . the identities that people display, perform, contest, or discuss in interaction are based on ideologies and beliefs about the characteristics of social groups and categories and about the implications of belonging to them. These ideologies and beliefs underlie in complex ways the discourse produced in interaction by social actors. Thus, situated displays of identity relate in many ways to the more general identities that are built by social groups.

Identity and categorisation

Among recent developments in identity studies, one of the most influential is an approach that focuses on categorisation as a central discourse process for the construction and negotiation of identities. As categorisation reflects ways in which members of a culture organise experience into categories with associated features, the analysis of how these processes are managed in discourse, that is, of how categories for identification are produced and made relevant by participants in interaction, has become one of the main areas of interest within this kind of analysis of identity [pp. 352–4].

Among the most important principles proposed within this approach are the centrality of the local occasioning of identity categories, the stress on the activities that make relevant certain identity categories, and the idea that the use of categories in discourse is consequential for the interaction at hand (see Antaki and Widdicombe 1998a: 3) [p. 354].

Many discourse analysts look at identities as built and negotiated in discourse, agree on the situated nature of the processes of attribution and negotiation over identities, and consequently reject a conception of identity as a stable feature characterising individuals or groups independently of social activities and interaction. However, recognising the centrality of interaction and of member's orientation to the study of identity, does not, in my view, automatically entail the rejection of the existence of cognitive aspects in the management of identity categories and concepts, nor does it resolve the analytic problem of how categories are interpreted by interactants, given that much of what is being conveyed about category membership is a matter of shared understanding and implicit meanings. Thus, the study of categorisation and identity should avoid two equally misleading assumptions: one is that the meaning of categories is exclusively managed at a local level and is in some sense 'manifest' only within the interaction at hand; the other is that speakers hold in their minds a certain number of well-defined categories with associated meanings and that all they do in specific interactions is apply them. Analysts need instead to be able to link local identities to shared ideologies and beliefs, but they also need to account for the fact that the construction and presentation of identity is a process in constant development and that one of its crucial sites of negotiation is interaction. It is indeed in concrete social activities and within specific instances of discourse that shared categories and beliefs about identity become the object of resistance, alternative formulations and renegotiation [pp. 354–5].

Task B1.3.1

In addition to the 'formation' and 'development' of identities, De Fina refers to the 'negotiation' of identities.

➤ In what ways are identities 'negotiated' in De Fina's view?

De Fina writes that: 'what defines people as members of a group is not only the content of their stories, but the way in which they use socially established resources to tell them.'

➤ What do you think she means by 'socially established resources'?

De Fina also writes that: 'people do not possess one identity related to the social categories to which they belong, but rather they present and re-present themselves, choosing within an inventory of more or less compatible identities that intersect and/or contrast with each other in different ways and in accordance with changing social circumstances and interlocutors'.

➤ Think about your own 'identities'. What does your own 'inventory of identities' consist of, and how do the different 'identities' 'intersect and/or contrast with each other in different ways and in accordance with changing social circumstances and interlocutors'?

➤ The process that De Fina refers to as 'choosing within an inventory of identities' is a common theme among those who advocate a discourse approach to intercultural communication.

De Fina refers to researchers who have related identities to 'culturally determined schemata'. Hargie *et al.* (1994) define schemata as ways in which 'information is gleaned, stored, organised into a framework representing the world as experienced by the individual and used to interpret current events' (p. 21) and identify five broad types of schemata (p. 22):

1. 'self-schemata (= knowledge of ourselves)';
2. 'event schemata' which 'represent the sequence of events that characterise particular, frequently encountered, social occasions such as ordering a meal or buying a newspaper';
3. 'role schemata' which 'involve concepts according to which we expect people, based on occupation, gender, race and so forth, to abide by certain norms and behave within set parameters of appropriate conduct';
4. 'causal schemata' which 'enable us to form judgements about cause-effect relationships in our physical and social environment, and to adopt courses of action which such schemata make possible';
5. 'people schemata' which are 'organised sets of knowledge about the features and characteristics of others and they therefore facilitate social categorisation'.

The term 'scripts' is sometimes used synonymously with 'schemata' but is often used to signify how 'schemata' are activated in communication. Thus Wierzbicka (1998) writes that scripts 'have to do with culture-specific norms for saying what one thinks, saying what one wants, and saying what one feels, norms for telling people what one wants them to do and what they have to do; for saying that one doesn't want to do something; for saying bad things about people and for saying good things about people; for telling people that one thinks the same as they do, or that one doesn't think the same, and so on.' Wierzbicka proceeds to state that: 'Cultural scripts . . . are not meant to describe how all people behave in a given society, but rather to articulate certain norms that people in a given society are familiar with (on a conscious, semi-conscious or unconscious level), and that serve as a shared frame of reference for a given speech community (whether one chooses to go along with them or to reject them)' (1998: 245).

In more recent work, De Fina (2015) focuses on the importance of power in the ways identities are 'expressed and negotiated'. Drawing on Agha (2009), she distinguishes between 'enregistered' and 'emergent' identities. The former are identities that are allocated to an individual and related to the cultural group(s) that an individual belongs to and to the socio–cultural milieu(x) that an individual inhabits, and tend to be stereotypical. These identities are drawn on by both those in more powerful and those in lower-status positions. Emergent identities are 'new ways of presenting yourself' and represent breaks from one's own past experiences and dominant stereotypes (p. 59).

The ways in which individuals construct identities and how identities are constructed is the key theme of much of the work of James Gee. In one interview, Gee stated that 'I am not a big fan of the word "culture" – too many meanings and gets us sometimes to think at too large a scale and miss important intergroup differences. I am more a fan of Discourses in the sense of socially recognisable identities and activities' (2008: 97). In Text B1.3.2 he explains what he means by 'Discourses' as 'socially recognisable identities and activities'.

Gee, J. P. (1999) *An Introduction to Discourse Analysis: Theory and Method.* London: Routledge. pp. 12–13, 17–18, 37 (extracts)

Text B1.3.2
J. P. Gee

I want to develop several 'tools of inquiry' (ways of looking at the world of talk and interaction) ... The tools of inquiry I will introduce in this chapter are primarily relevant to how we (together with others) build identities and activities and recognise the identities and activities that are being built around us . . . The tools to be discussed are:

(a) '*Situated identities,*' that is, different identities or social positions we enact and recognise in different settings.
(b) '*Social languages,*' that is, different styles of language that we use to enact and recognise different identities in different settings; different social languages also allow us to engage in all the other building tasks above (in different ways, building different sorts of things).
(c) '*Discourses*' with a capital 'D,' that is, different ways in which we humans integrate language with non-language 'stuff,' such as different ways of thinking, acting, interacting, valuing, feeling, believing, and using symbols, tools, and objects in the right places and at the right times so as to enact and recognise different identities and activities, give the material world certain meanings, distribute social goods in a certain way, make certain sorts of meaningful connections in our experience, and privilege certain symbol systems and ways of knowing over others . . .
(d) '*Conversations*' with a capital 'C,' that is, long-running and important themes or motifs that have been the focus of a variety of different texts and interactions (in different social languages and Discourses) through a significant stretch of time and across an array of institutions.

[Gee states later in the book that he uses 'Conversation' to mean 'the range of things that count as 'appropriately' 'sayable' and 'meaning-able', in terms of (oral or written) words, symbols, images, and things, at a given time and place, or within a given institution, set of institutions, or society, in regard to a given topic or theme (e.g. schools, women's health, smoking, children, prisons, etc.)' and refers to the work of Foucault (1985) (p. 37).]

J. P. Gee

When you speak or write anything, you use the resources of English to project yourself as a certain kind of person, a different kind in different circumstances. You also project yourself as engaged in a certain kind of activity, a different kind in different circumstances. If I have no idea who you are and what you are doing, then I cannot make sense of what you have said, written, or done.

You project a different identity at a formal dinner party than you do at the family dinner table. And, though these are both dinner, they are none the less different activities [pp. 12–13].

Making visible and recognisable who we are and what we are doing always involves a great deal more than 'just language.' It involves acting-interacting-thinking-valuing-talking- (sometimes writing-reading) in the 'appropriate way' with the 'appropriate' props at the 'appropriate' times in the 'appropriate' places.

Such socially accepted associations among ways of using language, of thinking, valuing, acting, and interacting, in the 'right' places and at the 'right' times with the 'right' objects (associations that can be used to identify oneself as a member of a socially meaningful group or 'social network'), I will refer to as 'Discourses,' with a capital 'D' . . . 'Big D' Discourses are always language plus 'other stuff.' There are innumerable Discourses in any modern, technological, urban-based society: for example, (enacting) being something as general as a type of African-American or Anglo-Australian or something as specific as being a type of modern British young second-generation affluent Sikh woman. Being a type of middle-class American, factory worker, or executive, doctor or hospital patient, teacher, administrator, or student, student of physics or of literature, member of a club or street gang, regular at the local bar . . . are all Discourses.

The key to Discourses is 'recognition.' If you put language, action, interaction, values, beliefs, symbols, objects, tools, and places together in such a way that others recognise you as a particular type of who (identity) engaged in a particular type of what (activity) here and now, then you have pulled off a Discourse (and thereby continued it through history, if only for a while longer). Whatever you have done must be similar enough to other performances to be recognisable. However, if it is different enough from what has gone before, but still recognisable, it can simultaneously change and transform Discourses. If it is not recognisable, then you're not 'in' the Discourse.

Discourses are always embedded in a medley of social institutions, and often involve various 'props' like books and magazines of various sorts, laboratories, classrooms, buildings of various sorts, various technologies, and a myriad of other objects from sewing needles (for sewing circles) through birds (for bird watchers) to basketball courts and basketballs (for basketball players). Think of all the words, symbols, deeds, objects, clothes, and tools you need to coordinate in the right way at the right time and place to 'pull off' (or recognise someone as) being a cutting-edge particle physicist or a Los Angeles Latino street gang member or a sensitive high-culture humanist (of old).

It is sometimes helpful to think about social and political issues as if it is not just us humans who are talking and interacting with each other, but rather, the Discourses we represent and enact, and for which we are 'carriers.' The Discourses we enact existed before each of us came on the scene and most of them will exist long after we have left the scene. Discourses, through our words and deeds, carry on conversations with each other through history, and, in doing so, form human history.

Think, for instance, of the long-running and ever-changing 'conversation' in the U.S. and Canada between the Discourses of 'being an Indian' and 'being an Anglo' or of the different, but equally long-running 'conversation' in New Zealand between 'being a Maori' and 'being an Anglo' (or, for that matter, think of the long-running conversation between 'being a British Anglo' and 'being an American Anglo'). Think of the long-running and ever-changing 'conversation' between creationists and biologists. Think of the long-running and ever-changing 'conversation' in Los Angeles between African-American teenage gang members and the L.A. police . . . Intriguingly, we humans are very often unaware of the history of these conversations, and thus, in a deep sense, not fully aware of what we mean when we act and talk . . . [pp. 17–18].

Task B1.3.3

At the beginning of Text B1.3.2, Gee refers to 'Situated Identities', in other words 'different identities or social positions we enact and recognise in different settings.'

➤ Think of different identities you have enacted and/or might enact in the following settings:

■ As a member of the family at a family gathering (e.g. a wedding, funeral, or formal birthday celebration).
■ As a witness in a criminal trial in a court of law.
■ As a job applicant at a job interview.
■ As a sports supporter at a sporting event at which an individual or team shares the same nationality as you and is representing that nation.

➤ What different styles of language did you employ/might you employ in such settings?

➤ What thoughts, actions, patterns of interaction, values, feelings, beliefs were/ would be integrated or underlie the language used in these settings?

➤ What symbols, tools and objects accompanied/might accompany the language in such settings?

Task B1.3.4

➤ Consider how one of more of the following individuals mentioned by Gee might 'pull off' a Discourse and describe what this Discourse comprises: a politician; a movie star; a pop star; an artist; a doctor; a hospital patient; a teacher; a member of a club or street gang; a sports fan.

Task B1.3.5

➤ What do you think Gee means when he writes that: 'It is sometimes helpful to think about social and political issues as if it is not just us humans who are talking and interacting with each other, but rather, the Discourses we represent and enact, and for which we are "carriers." The Discourses we enact existed before each of us came on the scene and most of them will exist long after we have left the scene'?

➤ What social and political issues can you think of both in your own context and globally that are Discourses which you are a 'carrier' of?

Text B1.3.3
J. P. Gee

Gee, J. P. (1999) *An Introduction To Discourse Analysis: Theory and Method*. London: Routledge. pp. 49–50, 68–9, 78 (extracts)

Thinking and using language is an *active* matter of *assembling* the situated meanings that you need for action in the world. This assembly is always relative to your socio-culturally-defined experiences in the world and, *more or less*, routinised ('normed') through cultural models and various social practices of the sociocultural groups to which you belong [p. 49]

Cultural models

We can distinguish (at least) the following sorts of cultural models:

■ Espoused models, that is models which we consciously espouse;
■ Evaluative models, that is models which we use, consciously or unconsciously, to judge ourselves or others;
■ Models-in-(inter)action, that is models that consciously or unconsciously guide our actions and interactions in the world.

Furthermore, cultural models can be about 'appropriate' attitudes, viewpoints, beliefs and values; 'appropriate' social, cultural and institutional organisational structures; 'appropriate' ways of talking, writing, reading, and communicating; 'appropriate' ways to feel or display emotion; 'appropriate' ways in which real and fictional events, stories, and histories are organised and end, and so on and so forth. Cultural models are complexly, though flexibly organised. There are smaller models inside bigger ones. Each model triggers or is associated with others, in different ways in different settings and differently for different socio-culturally defined groups of people. And we can talk about 'master models', that is sets of associated cultural models, or single models, that help shape and organise large and important aspects of experience for particular groups of people, as well as the sorts of Conversations we discussed' [p. 68–9].

Cultural models as tools of inquiry

Cultural models . . . lead us to ask, when confronted with a piece of talk, writing, action, or interaction, questions like these:

■ What cultural models are relevant here? What must I, as an analyst, assume people feel, value, and believe, consciously or not, in order to talk (write), act, and/or interact this way?

- Are there differences here between the cultural models that are affecting espoused beliefs and those that are affecting actions and practices? What sorts of cultural models, if any, are being used here to make value judgments about oneself and others?
- How consistent are the relevant cultural models here? Are there competing or conflicting cultural models at play? Whose interests are the cultural models representing?
- What other cultural models are related to the ones most active here? Are there 'master models' at work?
- What sorts of texts, media, experiences, interactions, and/or institutions could have given rise to these cultural models?
- How are the relevant cultural models here helping to reproduce, transform, or create social, cultural, institutional, and/or political relationships? What Discourses and Conversations are these cultural models helping to reproduce, transform or create? [p. 78].

Task B1.3.6

➤ Go back to Section A of the book and re-read one or more of the following examples in the 'Experience' sections: A1.1.1, A1.2.1, A1.3.1, A2.1.1, A2.2.1. Use the 'Cultural Models as Tools of Inquiry' described above in the second extract from Gee's book to analyse what is described in these examples.

Commentary

Other writers have defined 'Discourse' (and 'discourse') differently to Gee. Jaworski and Coupland (1999: 1–3) review the changing definitions of 'discourse' and means of discourse analysis and highlight the increasing importance given to discourse as a means of constructing reality. The writer whose ideas underlie much of the work carried out on Discourse Analysis is Foucault, to whom Gee makes reference in Text B1.3.2. Foucault is interested in the interrelationship of Discourse and Power, and, in particular, the way in which individuals are unaware of how they are 'constituted' by Discourses. He writes that:

> Each society has its regime of truth, its 'general politics' of truth: that is, the types of discourse which it accepts and makes function as true; the mechanisms and instances which enable one to distinguish true and false statements, the means by which each is sanctified; the techniques and procedures accorded value in the acquisition of truth; the status of those charged with saying what counts as truth.
>
> (1980: 131)

UNIT B1.4   DISCOURSE, IDENTITY AND INTERCULTURAL COMMUNICATION

In this unit we consider the implications of and applications to the field of intercultural communication of the ideas of De Fina, Gee and others who have written on discourse and identity. The first text is by Scollon and Wong Scollon (2002) who 'take the position that in any instance of actual communication we are multiply positioned within an indefinite number of Discourses (in the Gee sense) or within what we have called discourse systems.' In taking this position Scollon and Wong Scollon, like Gee, are wary of terms such as 'culture': 'The subject of "intercultural communication" is beset by a major problem, since there is really very little agreement on what people mean by the idea of culture in the first place . . . Cultures do not talk to each other; individuals do. In that sense all communication is interpersonal communication and can never be intercultural communication' (2001: 138) (a similar point to that made by Verschueren, whose ideas we explored in Unit B0.3.

In the second text, Celia Roberts and Srikant Sarangi analyse a sample of interpersonal communication between a doctor and patient through an approach they call 'theme-oriented discourse analysis' which 'looks at how language constructs professional practice' and in which 'analytic themes drawn primarily from sociology and linguistics shed light on how meaning is negotiated in interaction' (2005: 632).

Text B1.4.1
R. Scollon
and S. Wong
Scollon

Scollon, R. and Wong Scollon, S. (2003) 'Discourse and intercultural communication'. In Schriffin, D., Tannen, D. and Hamilton, H. E. (eds) *The Handbook of Discourse Analysis*. Oxford: Blackwell. pp. 543–5 (extracts)

While researchers have arrived at the position from rather different directions, perhaps we can say that a strongly unifying theme of discourse analysis and intercultural communication in the present decade is that all communication is constitutive of cultural categories. From this point of view the focus has shifted away from comparison between cultures or between individuals to a focus on the co-constructive aspects of communication.

With this change of focus has come a change in assumptions about the purposes of research and of the entities upon which analysis should be focused. Rather than seeking an explanation of how given identities and meanings are communicated or fail to be communicated, what is sought is an understanding of how identities and meanings are constituted in and through the interaction itself. The role of culture and other a priori categories in this model is as historical and cultural archives of tools through which social actions are taken by participants.

We have called our own approach to intercultural communication a 'discourse approach' (Scollon and Scollon 1995) and we have preferred to call what we do 'interdiscourse communication'. We take the position that in any instance of actual communication we are multiply positioned within an indefinite number of Discourses (in the Gee sense) or within what we have called discourse systems. These discourse systems would include those of gender, generation, profession, corporate or institutional placement, regional, ethnic, and other possible identities. As each of these discourse systems is manifested in a complex network of forms of discourse, face relationships, socialisation patterns and ideologies, this multiple membership and identity produces simultaneous internal (to the person) and external contradictions. Thus, we argue, it is as important a research problem to come to understand how a

R. Scollon
and S. Wong
Scollon

particular person in a particular action comes to claim, say, a generational identity over against the other multiple identities also contradictorily present in his or her own habitus (Bourdieu 1977, 1990) as it is to try to come to understand any two individuals as positioned as culturally or ethnically different from each other. An interdiscursive approach to intercultural communication has led us to prefer to set aside any a priori notions of group membership and identity and to ask instead how and under what circumstances concepts such as culture are produced by participants as relevant categories for interpersonal ideological negotiation.

For us, this approach to intercultural communication as discourse analysis has led to what we would now call mediated discourse (R. Scollon 1995, 1997, 1999; Scollon and Scollon 1997, 1998; S. Scollon 1998). A mediated discourse perspective shifts from a focus on the individuals involved in communication, and from their interpersonal or intercultural or even interdiscursive relationship, to a focus on mediated action as a kind of social action. The central concern is now not persons but social change.

In conclusion, we might sketch out quite roughly how these different approaches would handle a characteristic research problem. The approach implied by the title of this chapter would assume first that individuals are members of different cultural groups and that their communication can be studied as a problem in communication through a discursive analysis of the characteristic communication of members of those groups. Thus a cross-cultural approach would begin with the problem that a German was to communicate with a Chinese. This might be derived from business or diplomatic concerns on the practical side or from an anthropological or social psychological perspective on the theoretical side. In either case, one might expect that experimentally designed studies or quantitative survey studies would be set up to test differences in values, perceptions, the typical structure of genres, rates of speaking and of turning over turns, gestural and other nonverbal communication systems, or of world view and ideology.

An intercultural or interactional sociolinguistic approach would identify people from these different groups who are in social interaction with each other. Through a close analysis of the discourse actually produced, the analyst would first identify breakdowns in communication, then try to find the sources of the breakdowns in the language used as well as in the misinterpretation of contextualisation cues. Differences between the participants would most likely be understood as arising from a history of socialisation to different groups and therefore a misunderstanding of contextualisation cues in the actual situation of communicating with each other.

A mediated discourse approach would begin by asking why the problem was posed in the first place as a problem in communication between members of different cultural or other discourse-based groups. The primary question would be: what is the social action in which you are interested and how does this analysis promise to focus on some aspect of social life that is worth understanding? This concern with social action would treat the group identities of the participants as problematical only to the extent that such membership can be shown to be productive of ideological contradiction, on the one hand, or that the participants themselves call upon social group membership in making strategic claims within the actions under study, on the other. Thus the analysis would not presuppose cultural membership but rather ask how does the concept of culture arise in these social actions. Who has introduced culture as a relevant category, for what purposes, and with what consequences?

In this sense a mediated discourse analysis is a way of erasing the field of inter-cultural communication by dissolving the foundational questions and reconstituting the research agenda around social action, not categorical memberships or cultural genres. Conversation or narrative or talk itself is not given pride of place. Discourse is just one of the ways in which social action may be mediated, albeit commonly a very significant one. Thus culture is possibly relevant when it is empirically an outcome (or means) of actions taken by social actors, but to start from culture or intercultural (or interdiscourse) memberships is to start with a theoretical commitment in groups which is not a primary conceptual entity in mediated discourse theory; groups such as cultures are taken to be the outcomes of social actions and of histories but to have no direct causal status in themselves.

 Task B1.4.1

➤ What do understand by the following statements in the text by Scollon and Wong Scollon:

■ 'All communication is constitutive of cultural categories'.
■ 'What is sought is an understanding of how identities and meanings are constituted in and through the interaction itself'.
■ 'Groups such as cultures are taken to be the outcomes of social actions and of histories but to have no direct causal status in themselves'.
■ 'The role of culture and other a priori categories in this model is as historical and cultural archives of tools through which social actions are taken by participants'.

Another example of a 'discourse approach to intercultural communication', which takes a predominantly 'intercultural or interactional sociolinguistic approach' and which also considers how 'actions' are 'productive of "culture" or of membership in particular discourses or communities of practice' is the analysis of a 'medical encounter' in the United Kingdom by Celia Roberts and Srikant Sarangi in Text B1.4.2.

In this paper Roberts and Sarangi provide a number of data examples of doctor–patient interaction, including 'Data example 3'.

 Task B1.4.2

➤ Before reading the example of doctor–patient interaction, read the first extract below which consists of 'a number of analytic concepts, drawn primarily from linguistics and sociology' and which 'provide the theoretical back-drop' and 'relate to the overarching preoccupation with how meaning is negotiated and how the outcomes from these negotiations feed into assumptions and knowledge' (p. 634).

Roberts, C. and S. Sarangi (2005) 'Theme-oriented discourse analysis of medical encounters'. *Medical Education* **39: 632–40. pp. 634–8 (extracts)**

Text B1.4.2
C. Roberts and
S. Sarangi

Interactive frames and footing

Framing works as a filtering process or membrane through which general values and principles of conduct are reworked to apply to the particular encounter in hand. These frames trigger inferences by constructing possible scenarios. For example, doctors may have different frames from patients as to what counts as healthy or not. Related to this is the idea of 'footing'. Goffman reworked the general idea of 'putting something on a proper footing' to describe the way in which during an interaction the roles and relationships of participants can change. He also talks about 'participant frameworks' in which people align themselves to others by the way they manage their talk in the context of a given activity.

Contextualisation cues and inferences

Talk only has meaning in context and this has to be actively constructed as the interaction proceeds. Contextualisation cues are the hidden underbelly of this meaning making. They are the signs that invoke the context that gives each utterance a specific meaning. They channel the inferencing processes in a particular direction by calling up the frames and affecting the footing of each moment of an interaction. These linguistic and prosodic signs include words such as 'so' and 'well', intonation, stress, pausing and rhythm. They tend to be used unconsciously and their function in establishing or reinforcing social relations and negotiating shared meaning goes largely unnoticed.

Face and facework

There is a ritual element to interaction that is concerned with the fragility of social relations. We spend a lot of time in talk 'saving face' – both our own and that of others. This is largely done through politeness strategies which determine how direct or indirect to be and how far to claim relative closeness and informality or relative distance and formality. Disagreeing with more powerful people or managing uncertainty, for example, involve politeness strategies. So, a stark request or attempting to challenge or disagree are softened, or mitigated, by phrases such as 'I think' or the use of auxiliary verbs such as 'could' or 'would'.

Social identity

Our social identity includes our gender, our social standing, regional and ethnic backgrounds and so on. These identities are brought into the encounter but are also brought about in it. For example, we can make our powerful status or our ethnicity more or less relevant in the interaction. This 'performed social identity' affects how we get along together in an encounter and how we judge each other. Shared ways of speaking or finding something in common can oil the wheels of the interaction and create a positive assessment of the other.

C. Roberts and
S. Sarangi

Rhetorical devices

Rhetoric is the use of language to influence or persuade. Although associated with political speeches (Martin Luther King's 'I have a dream' is perhaps the most famous modern example), these patterns of argumentation are used routinely as part of institutional encounters. Rhetorical devices include the organisation of talk around contrasts, repetition of words and grammatical structures, metaphor, analogy, reported speech and lists (often of 3 items). Rhetorical devices and styles are often crucial in the assessment of speakers and, in medical settings, of patients and their conditions . . . [pp. 634–5].

Different ethnic groups, whether they use English as their heritage language or not, may use culturally specific styles of communicating which are different from local or standard English (which are themselves culturally specific). These different ways of speaking combine both linguistic and rhetorical styles and affect both how speakers talk and how they interpret others' talk. Differences include: how personal or impersonal to be, what to stress and what to play down, how direct to be in self-presentation, how to sequence responses, choice of words and idioms, and a range of prosodic features, including intonation and rhythm. The content and style of talk is also determined by assumptions and values based on shared experience, such as how to relate to the doctor's perceived authority . . . So both background knowledge and ways of speaking may be different. These differences can not only lead to overt misunderstandings, but also to difficult or uncomfortable moments and to some of the small tragedies of everyday life: for example, when patients do not get access to scarce resources. The key question is: how does diversity affect interpretation of meaning in interactions and how do differing interpretations lead to misunderstandings and potentially less favourable outcomes for less powerful groups? [p. 637].

 ## Task B1.4.3

➤ While reading Data Example 3, consider what factors that Roberts and Sarangi highlighted in Text B1.4.2 may be significant in trying to understand the interaction. In particular consider:

■ Do the doctor and patient have different 'frames' (for example, principles concerning how a doctor and patient should conduct themselves in a consultation or other 'assumptions or values' which influence the interaction)?

■ How do the doctor and patient 'manage the interaction' and attempt to 'align themselves to each other'?

■ In more detail, what specific 'contextualisation cues' (that is, linguistic and prosodic signs including words such as 'so' and 'well', intonation, stress, pausing and rhythm) are used to attempt to establish or reinforce social relations and to negotiate shared meaning in the doctor-patient interaction?

■ How personal or impersonal, direct or indirect are the doctor and patient in the interaction?

■ What issues or factors do the doctor and patient stress and what do they play down?

■ Do the doctor and patient succeed in 'sharing ways of speaking' and 'finding something in common'?

■ Do the roles and relationships between the participants change during the interaction? If so, in what way(s)?

DATA EXAMPLE 3

In the following example, a young mother (M) from Somalia has brought her baby daughter to see the family doctor (D) because she has been suffering from diarrhoea. At this stage in the consultation, the doctor has already taken a brief history from the patient's mother and, before examining the baby, has asked her some initial questions about breast-feeding.

1	D	little bit (.) right so you're virtually stopped (.)
2		so what sort of questions have you got in your mind for me today (.)
3		what do you want me to do
4		(..)
5	M	mm no: [she say]
6	D	[today]
7	M	eh: the lady she say if you want to contacting doctor eh: you want eh: talk him
8	D	yeah =
9	M	= I say yes I am happy with e- with [you]
10	D	[right] right ok =
11	M	= because (.) definitely when I am coming with you
12		when I go back I will go back happy
13	D	((laughs)) I hope so
14	M	because I will look to see you and your doctor K (.)
15		I like it
16	D	good =
17	M	= (cos) when when I come in will come in the you know ((tut))
18		when I go back my home I'm happy
19	D	right
20	M	((laughs))
21	D	so you want me to- (.) check her over

[pp. 637–8]

➤ Now read how Roberts and Sarangi analyse Data Example 3:

At line 1, the doctor uses a number of contextualisation cues to show that she is about to shift topic from discussing breast-feeding. She pauses, uses the discourse marker 'right' and sums up the patient's contribution. She then moves, at line 2, to eliciting the patient's concerns in classic patient-centred mode. However, patient-centred models have not been designed for intercultural communication. Shared decision making assumes that, through talk, the patient and doctor will tune into each other's way of thinking. But what happens when talk itself is the problem, as is the case here?

The mother may well have missed the contextualisation cues that mark the shift in topic and this exacerbates the difficulty in processing the questions in lines 2–3. But the main difficulty seems to be that she cannot interpret the shift in frame marked by these open questions. She responds with a negative and then refers to the 'lady' (probably the receptionist) and how she is happy to see this particular doctor. This is the beginning of a narrative account about coming in to see the doctor rather than an analytical account of her concerns. Unlike the mother in Data Example 1, here M offers a life–world account that can contribute to a potential frame mismatch. M then reformulates her perception of the doctor twice more (lines 12 and 18). This repetition of how she likes this doctor and her colleague seems to shift the topic from the question she asked the receptionist (about seeing the doctor) to some general display of satisfaction. This may be because she is uncertain of how to take the doctor's elicitation and/or because she sees it as culturally appropriate to praise her. This is not the footing that the doctor had anticipated. When there is only a minimal response from the GP at line 19 ('right'), the mother laughs. The doctor then speaks *for* the patient in line 21, thus undermining her original attempt to be patient-centred and shifting back to a more orthodox frame in which she pushes on with the next phase of the consultation.

This short extract shows us several things. Firstly, we cannot take interpretive processes for granted in intercultural communication. When there is no obvious coherent link between a question and answer, we have to look outside, to ethnographic data to answer the question 'What is going on here?' In this instance, it is important to know that the baby's mother comes from a rural area of Somalia, where strictly hierarchical relationships exist between medical professionals and other healers and their patients. Empowerment, participatory encounters and shared decision making are not in the frame. Secondly, we can see how talk itself can be a problem and so widely held models of good practice, which assume that more talk means better communication, may not hold in intercultural encounters. Finally, related to this, is the fact that in order to increase shared decision making, doctors resort to metacommunication – more talk about talk – as in lines 2–3. As the notion implies, this is a more abstract and more general level of talking which seems to cause particular problems for patients with limited linguistic competence in English.

In the video feedback session, the doctor commented on how she had used patient-centred questions in a mechanical way and that it was 'worrying' that she had not been aware at the time that these questions had, paradoxically, created more misunderstandings. She had also identified the mother who, along with her baby, was also registered with this doctor, as an anxious patient. The misunderstandings that arose in this consultation might well feed into this social evaluation. The mother's failure to produce an analytical response to the doctor's elicitations was part of her 'performed social identity' as someone perceived as responding (over) emotionally to her situation. An alternative interpretation might be that she was concerned that the doctor might see her as over-anxious (not aware perhaps that in Somalia her baby daughter's condition might be life-threatening) and wanted to mitigate this by declaring how happy she was with this doctor [p. 637–8].

Task B1.4.4

Roberts and Sarangi state that: 'widely held models of good practice, which assume that more talk means better communication, may not hold in intercultural encounters'.

➤ Can you think of other 'intercultural encounters' in institutional contexts, in which there is the assumption that 'more talk means better communication', can lead to 'overt misunderstandings', and less favourable outcomes for particular individuals?

Commentary

The study by Roberts and Sarangi is a valuable addition to work in health communication. Research by Suurmond and Seeleman in Holland (2006) has highlighted a similar 'shared decision-making' model of doctor-patient consultation which can disadvantage immigrants, while research by Rosenberg *et al.* involving doctors in Canada (2006), concluded that there was a basic lack of awareness of cultural factors that can impact on healthcare:

> Many physicians did not provide any evidence of knowing that culture can have effects in all of the following domains: communication behaviours, relationship to time and space, social and family organisation, the meaning of work, health beliefs and practices, the meaning of food, sexuality and reproduction, religion and spirituality and death and dying.
>
> (p. 242)

The increasing recognition in recent years of the importance of considering questions of power and advantage in intercultural communication has important implications for healthcare in multicultural societies. Chiarenza (2012: 78), for example, writes that:

> We need to modify the way the concept of culture is used in health care, going beyond mere ethnicity and race to include intersections of ethnicity, race, gender, age, class, education, religion, sexual orientation and physical ability. We should move the focus of our analysis from minority cultures to the dominant cultures in society, in order to understand how the unequal distribution of power allows certain groups and not others to acquire and maintain the majority of resources.
>
> (p. 78)

Canada is one country in which issues of advantage and disadvantage are being seriously addressed. In 2012, the Health Council of Canada carried out research into cultural issues relating to the healthcare of Aboriginal people and produced a report (2012) that calls for and outlines strategies to address the inequalities experienced by minorities in the Canadian system.

UNIT B1.5   IDENTITY AND LANGUAGE LEARNING

The learning of a second or additional language, especially when it is 'forced' upon an individual by a (permanent) move to a new language-speaking community is a process that is inextricably linked to issues of culture and identity. In the first text in this unit, Pellegrino Aveni considers the 'deprivation and/or alteration of the self' experienced by 'students who travel abroad to learn a new language and new culture', while in the second text, Aneta Pavlenko and James Lantolf provide an interpretation of parts of the autobiographical study *Lost in Translation: A Life in a New Language* written in 1989 by Eva Hoffman (along with interpretations of other autobiographical studies by writers originally from Central or Eastern Europe). Pavlenko and Lantolf (2000) describe Eva Hoffman's book, in which she details the processes involved in adapting to life in North America and in learning English following her emigration with her family from Poland to North America in 1959, as 'the most detailed and insightful description of second language socialisation and acculturation to date' (pp. 163–4). In their interpretation Pavlenko and Lantolf are particularly interested in how in Hoffman's account (and in those of the other autobiographical studies they analyse) 'identities are reconstructed and life stories retold' in the process of learning an additional language in a new cultural context. They point to how there are two phases in the reconstruction of identity: 'the initial phase of loss' and 'the phase of recovery and reconstruction'. It is with a more detailed description of these two phases that the text begins.

Task B1.5.1

➤ Before reading the two texts, consider the following questions:

- How important would you say it is to learn the language, language variety, or dialect of any cultural context if you are to fully understand its culture?
- How far has your own learning of a new language involved taking on a 'new identity'?
- What factors relating to 'culture' and 'identity' do you think can facilitate or inhibit the learning of a new language?

Text B1.5.1
V. Pellegrino
Aveni

Pellegrino Aveni, V. (2005) *Study Abroad and Second Language Use.* Cambridge: Cambridge University Press. pp. 9–16 (extracts)

Second language learners, whose knowledge of cultural conventions and communication skills in the new language may be particularly novice, might find conversation partners responding to them in unexpected ways, such as simplifying and slowing their speech excessively or speaking more loudly, as if to compensate for a loss of hearing. Madeline Ehrman and Zóltan Dörnyei (1998) appreciate this point, writing, 'language learning frequently entails new thought processes, identity, and values that can present a threat to learners' (p. 184). For example, Mamie, one of the many students we will encounter here, relates the following experience:

V. Pellegrino
Aveni

The second day we did a whirlwind tour of the city but I soon got tired of her pointing things out to me and repeating everything 3 or 4 times like I was blind, deaf and stupid. I couldn't enjoy anything because she just kept rattling on and treating me like I was five years old. Why do people always assume that if you are speaking with an accent that means you don't understand and are slow and stupid too?

Stripped of the comfortable mastery of their first language and of cultural and societal adroitness, learners in immersion environments, such as study abroad, often report feeling as if those around them may perceive them to be unintelligent, lacking personality or humour, or as having the intellectual development of a small child [p. 9].

The intimate relationship between self and language is most acutely felt by those in the position of language surplus or deficit, that is, by those with skills in more than one language and by those who possess no language at all. François Grosjean (1982) writes of the change in personality bilinguals often experience when using different languages in different environments, writing, 'some bilinguals report that when they change language they feel they are changing their attitudes and behaviours' (p. 279). He also notes that identity can be bound to language on the part of the observer as well, explaining that bilingual children closely identify those around them with the languages they speak and tend to become frustrated and even angry when the 'wrong' language is used (198). Charlotte Burck (1997) also recognises the distinct 'individual identity' given the speaker by each language he or she speaks, noting, 'languages have embedded cultures with very different constructions of self ... bilinguals may hold considerable contradictions in their experiences' (p. 74) [pp. 12–13].

For students who travel abroad to learn a new language and new culture, this deprivation and/or alteration of the self comes as with the shock of using the second language. The learner's self becomes trapped behind the communication barrier that results, and only an altered picture of the self, one filtered through this new, incomplete language, is projected by the learner. Moreover, the cultural frame of the new environment causes the presented self to be reinterpreted through yet another filter of meaning. Learners become disadvantaged in their ability to assimilate new information, develop their social networks, and present their self, when their own frame of reference becomes marginalised by the prominent frame of the new culture [p. 14].

The behaviours and perceived opinions of others become the individual's mirror, and the individual attempts to view the self through what he or she believes to be the eyes of interlocutors.

Thus, the self is defined not only by the individual from within, but also by the society within which the individual resides. The self is formed through the perceptions of individuals, perceptions shaped by personal experience and interaction with others, society, and culture and is stored within the memory. The self takes on multiple forms within a single individual; it is dynamic and formative, changing with the needs of the moment. Language plays a fundamental role in the development, manipulation, and expression of the self. Yet what happens to individuals who choose to study abroad in order to develop their skills in a foreign language and their knowledge of a foreign culture? How does the sudden deficit in linguistic skills and cultural knowledge affect the individual's ability to establish and maintain a 'real' self in any approximation of the 'ideal'? How does the nature of this changeable and complex self affect one's ability to use the new language and, thus, acquire the new language?

How does the new language affect the presentation of self, and what changes within the self are necessary for the learner to grow in the foreign language? [pp. 15–16].

 Task B1.5.2

➤ Do you agree with Ehrman and Dörnyei (1998) that 'language learning frequently entails new thought processes, identity, and values that can present a threat to learners'?

➤ How far do you agree that when people 'change language they feel they are changing their attitudes and behaviours'?

➤ Consider the questions posed by Pellegrino at the end of the extract (when she is writing about an individual who chooses to study abroad in order to develop their skills in another language and their knowledge of another culture):

■ 'How does the sudden deficit in linguistic skills and cultural knowledge affect the individual's ability to establish and maintain a "real" self?'
■ 'How does the nature of this changeable and complex self affect one's ability to use the new language and, thus, acquire the new language?'
■ 'How does the new language affect the presentation of self, and what changes within the self are necessary for the learner to grow in the foreign language?'

Pavlenko, A. and J. P. Lantolf (2000) 'Second language learning as participation and the (re) construction of selves'. In Lantolf, J. P. (ed.) *Sociocultural Theory and Second Language Learning.* Oxford: Oxford University Press. pp. 162–73 (extracts)

The initial phase of loss can be segmented into five stages:

■ loss of one's linguistic identity ('careless baptism', according to Hoffman 1989)
■ loss of all subjectivities
■ loss of the frame of reference and the link between the signifier and the signified
■ loss of the inner voice
■ first language attrition.

The phase of recovery and (re)construction encompasses four critical stages:

■ appropriation of others' voices
■ emergence of one's own new voice, often in writing first
■ translation therapy: reconstruction of one's past
■ continuous growth 'into' new positions and subjectivities.

Second language learning: phase of loss

The first step on the route to self-translation, identified by Hoffman (1989), is a name change, often imposed. Due to this 'careless baptism' from Ewa and Alina, the author

A. Pavlenko and
J. P. Lantolf

and her sister become 'Eva' and 'Elaine'. What follows is a shattering loss of their linguistic identity:

> Nothing much has happened, except a small, seismic mental shift. The twist in our names takes them a tiny distance from us – but it's a gap into which the infinite hobgoblin of abstraction enters. Our Polish names didn't refer to us; they were as surely us as our eyes or hands. These new appellations, which we ourselves can't yet pronounce, are not us. They are identification tags, disembodied signs pointing to objects that happen to be my sister and myself . . . [They] make us strangers to ourselves.
>
> (Hoffman 1989: 105)

At stake in the renaming process is, as Hoffman's commentary especially makes transparent, not merely a phonological problem to be overcome with some practice. It is about the conversion of subjects, actively embedded in their world, into objects no longer able to fully animate that world. In other words, it is about loss of agency in the world – an agency, in large part, constructed through linguistic means . . .

Loss of agency is not only about severing one's union with the world inhabited by others, it is, and perhaps more profoundly so, about losing the connection to one's own inner world – the world of the mind. This is attested in several of the writers we examined, but it is most explicitly, and painfully, evidenced in the words of Hoffman:

> I wait for that spontaneous flow of inner language which used to be my nighttime talk with myself . . . Nothing comes. Polish, in a short time, has atrophied, shrivelled from sheer uselessness. Its words don't apply to my new experiences, they're not coeval with any of the objects, or faces, or the very air I breathe in the daytime. In English, the words have not penetrated to those layers of my psyche from which a private connection could proceed.
>
> (Hoffman 1989: 107)

In the Text B1.5.2 passage Hoffman seems to be in a semantic twilight zone in which her inner speech in Polish has ceased to function, while the inner speech sparked by English, her new language, has yet to emerge. From a sociohistorical perspective, then, she has no way of organising and making sense of her experiences . . .

For a time, Hoffman's heroine is forced to live in a split universe, where the signifier has become severed from the signified. Ewa deeply mourns her inability to describe the world around her; her new words are simple referents without any conceptual systems or experiences to back them up:

> The words I learn now don't stand for things in the same unquestioned way they did in my native tongue. 'River' in Polish was a vital sound, energised with the essence of riverhood, of my rivers, of my being immersed in rivers. 'River' in English is cold – a word without an aura. It has no accumulated associations for me, and it does not give off the radiating haze of connotation. It does not evoke.
>
> (Hoffman 1989: 106)

Often, the inability of the 'new' language to intimately name the world (both inner and outer) is *accompanied by a deterioration* of that same ability in the native language . . .

A. Pavlenko and
J. P. Lantolf

The impact of the unravelling of a self is forcefully captured in Hoffman's words:

> Linguistic dispossession is a sufficient motive for violence, for it is close to the dispossession of one's self. Blind rage, helpless rage is rage that has no words – rage that overwhelms one with darkness. And if one is perpetually without words, if one exists in the entropy of inarticulateness, that condition itself is bound to be an enraging frustration.
>
> (Hoffman 1989: 124)

Recovery and (re)construction: second language becoming

The initial step toward recovery and reconstruction of a self . . . is the appropriation of others' voices . . . We observe the beginnings of the recreation process in the following excerpt from Hoffman:

> All around me, the Babel of American voices, hardy mid-western voices, sassy New York voices, quick youthful voices, voices arching under the pressure of various crosscurrents . . . Since I lack a voice of my own, the voices of others invade me as if I were a silent ventriloquist. They ricochet within me, carrying on conversations, lending me their modulations, intonations, rhythms. I do not yet possess them; they possess me. But some of them satisfy a need; some of them stick to my ribs . . . Eventually, the voices enter me; by assuming them, I gradually make them mine.
>
> (Hoffman 1989: 219–20)

. . . Eventually, a new voice and with it a self gradually emerges. At first the voice is often captured in writing, in many cases in a diary, a private activity conducted in a public language, which grants 'the double distance of English and writing' (Hoffman 1989: 121). For Hoffman her diary is a crucial stepping stone toward recovery of agency. It bestows upon her a new, English, 'written self' (*ibid.*). Because this self exists primarily in writing, it is experienced not as a fully agentive self, but as an 'impersonal' and 'objective' self, and even though Hoffman remarks that 'this language is beginning to invent another me' (*ibid.*), she is at first unable to deploy the quintessential indexical pronoun of agency, 'I'. Instead she is 'driven, as by a compulsion, to the double, the Siamese-twin 'you' (*ibid.*).' Although at this point in her story, she acknowledges Eva as her public persona, she has not yet identified Eva with 'I' in her private mental domain . . .

Step by step, Hoffman's Ewa/Eva discovers and inhabits the new cultural space, learning to preserve appropriate distances, read subtle nuances, and act according to new cultural scripts. Slowly Ewa's second voice acquires increasing strength; Eva becomes a person in her own right, arriving at the realisation that:

> This goddamn place is my home now . . . I know all the issues and all the codes here. I'm as alert as a bat to all subliminal signals sent by word, look, gesture. I know who is likely to think what about feminism and Nicaragua and psychoanalysis and Woody Allen . . . When I think of myself in cultural categories – which I do perhaps too often – I know that I'm a recognisable example of a species: a professional New York woman . . . I fit, and my surroundings fit me.
>
> (Hoffman 1989: 169–70)

A. Pavlenko and
J. P. Lantolf

. . . With regard to the bilinguals' narratives considered here, we believe that the problem confronting these individuals is the conflict that arises when they attempt to bring their past into the present. Their personal narratives and, consequently, their 'self' were constructed in a time and place constrained by conventions that differ from conventions of their present time and place. Thus, they have no way of making sense of the present and this, in turn, gives rise to the cognitive and affective dissonances reported in the narratives.

To overcome this difficulty, they are forced to reorganise, and, in some cases, organise anew, the plots of their life stories in line with the new set of conventions and social relationships sanctioned by the new community in which they find themselves. The result is the formation of new ways to mean (that is, make sense of their experiences and of who they are). Without this restructuring, these individuals would remain on the margins of the new community in which they reside (but not live) . . .

At one point in her story Hoffman writes that her parents, in their new Anglo cultural setting express their frustration at no longer knowing how to rear their own children:

> They don't try to exercise much influence over me anymore. 'In Poland, I would have known how to bring you up, I would have known what to do,' my mother says wistfully, but here, she has lost her sureness, her authority. She doesn't know how hard to scold Alinka [Eva's sister] when she comes home at late hours; she can only worry over her daughter's vague evening activities.
>
> (Hoffman 1989: 145)

At another point, Hoffman talks specifically about her loss of past and being trapped in the present and thus being unable to make full sense of her world and her place in it:

> I can't afford to look back, and I can't figure out how to look forward. In both directions, I may see a Medusa, and I already feel the danger of being turned into stone. Betwixt and between, I am stuck and time is stuck within me. Time used to open out, serene, shimmering with promise. If I wanted to hold a moment still, it was because I wanted to expand it, to get its fill. Now, time has no dimension, no extension backward or forward. I arrest the past, and I hold myself stiffly against the future; I want to stop the flow. As a punishment, I exist in the stasis of a perpetual present, that other side of 'living in the present', which is not eternity but a prison. I can't throw a bridge between the present and the past, and therefore I can't make time move.
>
> (Hoffman 1989: 116–17)

Task B1.5.3

> ➤ Have you had any experience of being in an unfamiliar cultural context in which a language, language variety, or dialect unknown or unfamiliar to you was the normal language of communication, and which you needed to learn?

➤ If so, did you:

- Experience the same feelings Eva Hoffman describes?
- Experience the need to 'reconstruct' an identity, and, if so, did this involve the two phases described in the text by Pavlenko and Lantolf?

 Task B1.5.4

➤ Pavlenko and Lantolf state the following in the text: 'her inner speech in Polish has ceased to function, while the inner speech sparked by English, her new language, has yet to emerge'.

➤ Do you believe that language consists of 'inner speech', as well as what might be called 'outer speech'?

➤ If so, what are the implications for the learning and teaching of an additional language?

 Task B1.5.5

Eva Hoffman writes that 'I know . . . all the codes here. I'm as alert as a bat to all subliminal signals sent by word, look, gesture'. Another account by a writer, Shirley Geok-lin Lim, who made her life in the United States, provides a graphic example of how words, looks, and gestures mark one as an outsider, even when you can communicate in the normal language of communication in that context (1996: 300–1):

> There are many ways in which America tells you you don't belong. The eyes that slide around to find another face behind you. The smiles that only appear after you have almost passed them, intended for someone else. The stiffness in the body as you stand beside them watching your child and theirs slide down the pole, and the relaxed smile when another white mother comes up to talk. The polite distance as you say something about the children at the swings and the chattiness when a white parent makes a comment. A polite people, it is the facial muscles, the shoulder tension, and the silence that give away white Americans' uneasiness with people not like them.

➤ Think of a particular speech community or ('small') culture that you are a member of or are familiar with. What looks and gestures are specific to this ('small') culture or speech community, what do they mean, and how do they mark one as an 'insider' or 'outsider'?

➤ Have you had similar experiences to those described by Shirley Geok-lin Lim?

➤ What are the implications for those who work with people who need to adapt to life in a new cultural context and, at the same time need to learn an additional language to function in this cultural context? Consider the following: teachers (in general); language teachers; people working for government and non-governmental agencies (e.g. the police, social services support personnel, health professionals).

Commentary

The discussion by Pavlenko and Lantolf of 'inner speech' draws on the work of a number of theorists, including Vygotsky and Bakhtin. A prime interest of Vygotsky is the relationship between thought, meaning and words. In his seminal work, *Thought and Language* (1986: 218), Vygotsky writes that: 'Thought is not merely expressed through words; it comes into existence through them. Every thought tends to connect with something else, to establish a relation between things. Every thought moves, grows and develops, fulfils a function, solves a problem'. Hoffman writes that 'this language (i.e. English) is beginning to invent another me'. The notion that language *invents* rather than *defines* a person links with the ideas of Bakhtin (1984: 201), who writes that 'when a member of a speaking collective comes upon a word, it is not as a neutral word of language, not as a word free from the aspirations and evaluations of others, uninhabited by others' voices. No, he receives the word from another's voice and filled with that other voice. The word enters his context from another context, permeated with the interpretations of others. His own thought finds the word already inhabited.'

Another interesting interpretation of Eva Hoffman's autobiographical study is by Wierzbicka (1994), who focuses on how 'different cultures have different attitudes towards emotions' (p. 156) and highlights in detail such differences in Polish and 'Anglo' cultures, with examples from Hoffman's book to exemplify these differences. We have reservations, however, about the views expressed by Wierzbicka: is it useful and appropriate to talk of large 'Polish' and 'Anglo' cultures (or even of 'Anglo-American' and 'Anglo-Australian' cultures which Wierzbicka mentions); can language itself be responsible for differences in attitudes, and orientations towards emotions and feelings? In connection with the first reservation, it is perhaps significant that near the end of the book Eva Hoffman describes herself not in terms of 'Anglo' or 'Anglo-American' culture, but in terms of a much smaller culture: 'When I think of myself in cultural categories – which I do perhaps too often – I know that I'm a recognisable example of a species: a professional New York woman' (pp. 169–70).

Norton and Toohey (2011) write that:

> more recent work on language learner identities adopts poststructural understandings of identities as fluid, context-dependent, and context-producing, in particular historical and cultural circumstances.

(pp. 419–20)

An investigation by Benson *et al.* (2013) of Hong Kong students' English language learning in Anglophone study abroad contexts explored in depth the role of identity from a poststructuralist perspective. Two facets of identity are seen as especially significant: 'reflexive' and 'imagined' identity. The former 'includes both the learners' conceptions of their second language ability and their actual capacity to use the language in various contexts of interaction' (p. 20), while the latter 'are linked to goals and expectations, and can be understood as representations of who the students expect or would like to become in the study abroad setting' (p. 22). The conclusion of the study was that the development of the students' second language development during the period of study abroad 'depended largely on whether or not they succeeded in bridging this gap between reflexive and imagined identity by projecting identities as competent English users of English that would be recognised as such by local English speakers' (p. 166).

Theme 2
Othering

UNIT B2.1   OTHERING – FOCUS ON JAPAN

Possibly more popular manuals have been written about visiting, living in and working in Japan, than any other country. Text B2.1.2 in this unit is an extract from such a manual, written specifically for members of the US business community who are doing business in Japan. Text B2.1.3, written by Japanese social scientist Yoshio Sugimoto, raises interesting issues that relate to the views expressed by the writer of Text B2.1.2, Boyé Lafayette De Mente.

Unit B2.1 is the first unit relating to Theme B, 'Othering'. In Text B2.1.1 reference is made to the work of Said, whose work (1978, 1993) has been largely respons-ible in both academic and in more public circles for focussing attention on the processes in which those nations and their people on the 'peripheries' of the world, and particularly those who have been colonised and dominated by one or more of the European powers, have been framed by the Discourses of the colonisers. In *Orientalism* (1978: 4) Said states his belief that 'the Orient' is a social construct, 'an idea that has a history and a tradition of thought, imagery and vocabulary that have given it reality and presence in and for the West'. In addition, 'Orientalism depends for its strategy on . . . flexible positional superiority, which puts the Westerner in a whole series of possible relationships with the Orient without him ever losing the relative upper hand'. It is the nature of this 'flexible positional superiority' that is the basis of 'Otherisation', as Edgar and Sedgwick (1999) suggest in the following text.

Edgar, A. and Sedgwick, P. (1999) *Key Concepts in Cultural Theory*. London: Routledge. p. 266

Text B2.1.1
A. Edgar and
P. Sedgwick

The Other

. . . In the context of theories of culture, perhaps the most prominent contemporary use of this notion has been made by Said. In these terms, the Other may be designated as a form of cultural projection of concepts. This projection constructs the identities of cultural subjects through a relationship of power in which the Other is the subjugated element. In claiming knowledge about 'orientals' what Orientalism did was construct them as its own (European) Other. Though describing purportedly 'oriental' characteristics (irrational, uncivilised, etc.) Orientalism provided a definition

A. Edgar and
P. Sedgwick

not of the real 'oriental' identity, but of European identity in terms of the oppositions which structured its account. Hence, 'irrational' Other presupposes (and is also presupposed by) 'rational' self. The construction of the Other in Orientalist discourse, then, is a matter of asserting self-identity: and the issue of the European account of the Oriental Other is thereby rendered a question of power.

Text B2.1.2
Boye Lafayette
De Mente

Boyé Lafayette De Mente 'Beware of using logic in Japan!' (2005) from *Japan Unmasked*. Clarendon: Tuttle Publishing (extracts)

TOKYO – The cultural canyons between Japan and many Western countries – the United States in particular – remain broad and deep, despite more than half a century of massive interaction on every social, economic and political level.

From an American viewpoint, one of the most irrational and frustrating of these cultural chasms is the difference between the Japanese and American view and use of logic – ronri (roan-ree) in Japanese – a difference that has an especially profound effect on political as well as economic relations between the two countries.

As is well known, Americans and other Westerners pride themselves on thinking and behaving in a logical manner . . .

Still today, few things turn older Japanese off more rapidly and more completely than for someone to take a purely logical approach to personal, business and political relations. They regard positions and presentations that are based on logic as being cold and calculating, as failing to take into consideration the human and spiritual element.

On innumerable occasions, I have sat in on presentations by visiting American business [sic] that were perfect examples of logical reasoning only to see the Japanese side become increasingly uncomfortable and withdrawn, unable to reconcile their own values with the rationale of the Americans.

Japanese logic is based on cultural imperatives that have to do with creating and sustaining the kind of cooperative, harmonious relationships on which their society was based for many centuries . . .

The main point of difference in Western logic and Japanese ronri is that in its Japanese context logic does not necessarily equate with rationalism. It can, in fact, fly in the face of reason so long as it satisfies a human or spiritual element that the Japanese hold dear.

In Japanese dialogue it is perfectly logical to conceal one's real thoughts and intentions (honne/hoan-nay) behind a public facade (tatemae/tah-tay-my) by using words and phrases that are so abstract they are meaningless, or that give a false impression.

In such cases, which are the rule rather than the exception in most formal situations, it is left up to the listener to divine the true meaning or intentions of the speaker – a process that requires comprehensive knowledge of the Japanese language and culture; a skill that the Japanese refer to as haragei (hah-rah-gay-ee) or 'the art of the stomach,' which could be translated into English as reading the other person's mind.

It is also logical in the Japanese concept of things for responsibility to be diffused among a group rather than placed on an individual . . .

When serious mistakes or criminal activity do occur in a Japanese company or government organisation, it is Japanese logic for the head of the group to take

Boyé Lafayette
De Mente

responsibility and resign in a symbolic gesture that makes it possible to maintain the facade of harmony in the organisation.

Misrepresenting things, telling lies and engaging in other cover-up activities are logical in the traditional Japanese environment – logical when their purpose is to protect the group and the system . . .

The two main sanctions used by the Japanese system to enforce conformity to Japanese logic are bullying and ostracising. The bullying by co-workers and superiors can be sadistic and continuous. The ultimate tactic is to completely ostracise the guilty party.

Of course, most Japanese are perfectly capable of logical thinking in the Western mould, but their attitudes and behaviour are controlled by the groups they belong to, and with rare exceptions they are not brave enough, strong enough or foolhardy enough to break the codes that bind them.

Task B2.1.1

> Do you believe that Text B2.1.2 is an example of Othering as described by Edgar and Sedgwick in Text B2.1.1?

> More specifically:

- To what extent are the Japanese 'designated as a form of cultural projection of concepts'?
- Is there in Text B2.1.2 'a relationship of power in which the Other is the subjugated element'?
- Is there any suggestion in Text B2.1.2 that 'irrational' Other presupposes (and is also presupposed by) 'rational' self'?

Sugimoto, Y. (1997) *An Introduction to Japanese Society.* Cambridge: Cambridge University Press. pp. 1–4, 11–13 (extracts)

Text B2.1.3
Y. Sugimoto

Multicultural Japan

Suppose that a being from a different planet arrived in Japan and wanted to meet a typical Japanese, one who best typified the Japanese adult population. Whom should the social scientists choose? To answer this question, several factors would have to be considered: gender, occupation, educational background, and so on.

To begin, the person chosen should be a female, because women outnumber men in Japan: the 1990 census shows that sixty-three million women and sixty million men live in the Japanese archipelago. With regard to occupation, she would definitely not be employed in a large corporation but would work in a small enterprise, since fewer than one in eight workers is employed in a company with three hundred or more employees. Nor would she be guaranteed life-time employment, since those who work under this arrangement amount at most to only a quarter of Japan's workforce. She would not belong to a labour union, because less than a quarter of Japanese workers are unionised. She would not be university-educated . . .

Y. Sugimoto

The identification of the average Japanese would certainly involve much more complicated quantitative analysis. But the alien would come closer to the 'centre' of the Japanese population by choosing a female, non-unionised and non-permanent employee in a small business without university education than a male, unionised, permanent employee with a university degree working for a large company.

When outsiders visualise the Japanese, however, they tend to think of men rather than women, career employees in large companies rather than non-permanent workers in small firms, and university graduates rather than high-school leavers, for these are the images presented on television and in newspaper and magazine articles . . .

While every society is unique in some way, Japan is particularly unusual in having so many people who believe that their country is unique. Regardless of whether Japan is 'uniquely unique' in sociological and psychological reality, it is certainly unique for the number of Japanese publications which propagate the unique Japan argument. The so-called group model of Japanese society represents the most explicit and coherent formulation of this line of argument and remains the most influential framework for interpreting the Japanese and Japanese social structure. Put most succinctly, the model is based upon three lines of argument.

First, at the individual, psychological level, the Japanese are portrayed as having a personality which lacks a fully developed ego or independent self. The best-known example of this claim is Doi's notion of *amae* which refers to the allegedly unique psychological inclination among the Japanese to seek emotional satisfaction by prevailing upon and depending on their superiors. They feel no need for any explicit demonstration of individuality. Loyalty to the group is a primary value. Giving oneself to the promotion and realisation of the group's goals gives the Japanese a special psychological satisfaction.

Second, at the interpersonal, intragroup level, human interaction is depicted in terms of Japanese group orientation. According to Nakane, for example, the Japanese attach great importance to the maintenance of harmony within the group. To that end, relationships between superiors and inferiors are carefully cultivated and maintained. One's status within the group depends on the length of one's membership in the group. Furthermore, the Japanese maintain particularly strong interpersonal ties with those in the same hierarchical chain of command within their own organisation. In other words, vertical loyalties are dominant. The vertically organised Japanese contrast sharply with westerners, who tend to form horizontal groups which define their membership in terms of such criteria as class and stratification which cut across hierarchical organisation lines.

Finally, at the intergroup level, the literature has emphasised that integration and harmony are achieved effectively between Japanese groups, making Japan a 'consensus society' . . .

At least four underlying assumptions remain constant in these studies. First, it is presumed that all Japanese share the attribute in question – be it amae or miniature orientation – regardless of their class, gender, occupation, and other stratification variables. Second, it is also assumed that there is virtually no variation among the Japanese in the degree to which they possess the characteristic in question. Little attention is given to the possibility that some Japanese may have it in greater degree while others have very little of it. Third, the trait in question, be it group-orientation or kanjin, is supposed to exist only marginally in other societies, particularly in Western societies. That is, the feature is thought to be uniquely Japanese. Finally, the fourth presupposition is an ahistorical assumption that the trait has prevailed in Japan for an unspecified period of time, independently of historical circumstances . . .

Japanese culture like the cultures of other complex societies, comprises a multitude of subcultures. Some are dominant, powerful, and controlling, and form core subcultures in given dimensions. Examples are the management subculture in the occupational dimension, the large corporation subculture in the firm-size dimension, the male subculture in the gender dimension, and the Tokyo subculture in the regional dimension. Other subcultures are more subordinate, subservient, or marginal, and may be called the peripheral subcultures. Some examples are the part-time worker subculture, the small business subculture, the female subculture, and the rural subcultures.

Core subcultures have ideological capital to define the normative framework of society. Even though the life-time employment and the company-first dogma associated with the large corporation subculture apply to less than a quarter of the workforce, that part of the population has provided a role-model which all workers are expected to follow, putting their companies ahead of their individual interests . . .

The slanted views of Japan's totality tend to reproduce because writers, readers, and editors of publications on the general characteristics of Japanese society belong to the core subcultural sphere. Sharing their subcultural base, they conceptualise and hypothesise in a similar way, confirm their portrayal of Japan between themselves, and rarely seek outside confirmation. In many N*ihonjinron* writings, most examples and illustrations are drawn from the elite sector, including male employees in managerial tracks of large corporations and high-ranking officials of the national bureaucracy.

Core subcultural groups overshadow those on the periphery in inter-cultural transactions too. Foreign visitors to Japan who shape the images of Japan in their own countries interact more intensely with core sub-cultural groups than with peripheral ones. In cultural exchange programs, Japanese who have houses, good salaries, and university education predominate among the host families, language trainers, and introducers of Japanese culture. Numerically small but ideologically dominant, core subcultural groups are the most noticeable to foreigners and are capable of presenting themselves to the outside world as representative of Japanese culture.

Task B2.1.2

➤ What different perspectives on Japanese identity does Sugimoto provide that differ from those provided by Boyé Lafayette De Mente?

Task B2.1.3

Interestingly, Sugimoto writes that it is not just popular guides published *outside* Japan for those visiting, living in and working in Japan, that 'propagate the unique Japan argument', but numerous Japanese publications as well.

➤ Try to find examples of descriptions of the 'culture' of the country you live in published both in your country *and* in another country (you will find extracts from such guides on the internet, as I did in the case of Text B2.1.2).

➤ Do either or both of these guides propagate the argument that your country is 'unique'?

➤ If so, what is the nature of this uniqueness?

 Task B2.1.4

➤ What are the implications of what Sugimoto writes for how we understand and describe other cultures?

➤ What are the implications for those involved in 'intercultural' training programmes?

Commentary

Billig *et al.* (1988: 16) write that 'Many words are not mere labels which neutrally package up the world. They also express moral evaluations, and such terms frequently come in antithetical opposites which enable opposing moral judgements to be made.' The lexical choices made in Text B2.1.2 to describe the Japanese are good examples of how 'moral evaluations' and 'moral judgements' are expressed.

Recent research has challenged how Japanese people have been constructed and Othered. Brown *et al.* (2014) review research that challenges many of the ways that Japanese people have been represented and raise important questions as to the relevance of templates of individualism/collectivism, directness/indirectness hierarchy/egalitarianism for explaining differences between Japanese and American businesspeople. Clausen (2010) investigates intercultural communication involving Japanese and Danish workers in Danish-owned companies and their subsidiaries or partners in Japan. She found that while stereotypical national characteristics commonly found in intercultural communication literature and textbooks 'may be useful as background information for researchers and practitioners, they are insufficient to fully describe cultural encounters as they dynamically unfold over time' and 'while sophisticated stereotypes can serve to initially highlight differences in Danish and Japanese national characteristics, generalisation studies provide a static approach that fails to account for how perceptions and work identities are formed and how they may change over time' (p. 64).

UNIT B2.2 IMAGES OF THE OTHER

We live in a time when we are surrounded by visual images, both static and moving, in different forms of the media. In this unit we focus on 'image', both in its literal sense of visual representation, and in its broader sense of what Miriam Cooke terms 'preconception built on the weak and resilient foundations of myth and (visual) image'. In Text B2.2.1 Cooke explores how our preconceptions intervene in how we perceive of and communicate with each other, and writes specifically about the images held in 'the West' of Muslim women. Text B2.2.2 by Lei Guo and Summer Harlow reports on research into how African Americans, Latinos and Asians (who are inhabitants of the USA) are represented in YouTube videos.

Cooke, M. (1997) 'Listen to the image speak.' *Cultural Values.* Vol. 1/1. pp. 101–2, 104, 105, 106 (extracts)

Text B2.2.1
M. Cooke

I argue that the major block to respect of and communication with the unknown is preconception built on the weak and resilient foundations of myth and image.

Images are flat impressions that provide pieces of information. They are like photographs that frame and freeze a fragment of the real and then project it as the whole. What was dynamic and changing becomes static. Just as a snapshot provides a true, if partial, picture, so these cultural images contain some truth. That is why they are so hard to change. Just as the image of the amoral, free-living American woman epitomises for many pious Muslims all that is wrong with Western culture, so the image of the veiled woman encapsulates for the Western observer all the coercion imagined to mark Islamic culture. Women are easily turned by outsiders into emblems of their culture, for within the culture itself women are often made into custodians of their culture's values. No matter how many non-promiscuous, modest Western women the Muslim may meet, no matter how many assertive, independent, unveiled Muslim women the Westerner may meet, there is a possibility that the basic image will not change as these individuals come to be seen as exceptions to a rule that they thereby serve to reinforce. These images are the context of a first encounter between two people who know little if anything about each other.

Images we have of each other are always part of the baggage that we bring to dialogue. Sometimes we are at the mercy of the image our addressee has of us or chooses to invoke. Sometimes we hide behind the image. Sometimes we act as though neither of us had an image of the other. Sometimes, those ideal times, the image disappears and the contact is unmediated by the myth. Then we can act as individuals between whom messages pass easily regardless of the contact, code or context.

In September 1996, the Aspen Institute Berlin invited me to participate in a conference entitled 'The Images of Muslim Women in the West' . . . Throughout the summer I wondered why the image of Muslim women as passive and oppressed has so much power. I have come to believe that this is probably the case because 'Muslim Women' refers not only to a specific group but also to a general category. They are only sometimes both Muslim and women; they are often fused into a single category – Muslims in general and even so nebulous a concept as 'Islam', a term covering both the religion and the culture. However, regardless of whether the reference to 'Muslim Women' is specific women who happen to be Muslims, or slips seamlessly into the general (women who represent a faith and a culture), their look is the same: they are more or less exotic, more or less veiled, more or less armed. The meanings attached to their uniform appearance will differ depending on whether it is the Muslim or the woman who is being considered – a victim of patriarchy or a symbol of a fanatic faith. Since the general association with Islam is the most common, and Islam has long been negatively portrayed in the West, it is not surprising that its key emblem, women, should also be subject to sensationalist misrepresentation.

Most Muslim women and men live in Asia and Africa, hence they are not only Muslim but also Asians and Africans. When we think about them, try to represent them, and teach about them, we run the risk of confounding geographic, linguistic, racial, ethnic, religious and cultural categories. Thus, the fact that they are Syrian, Indonesian, Nigerian, Pakistani and American women, who speak dozens of languages and derive from a great many ethnic roots, becomes less significant than that they happen to practice a particular faith. After all, we can more easily identify as Muslim, rather than Egyptian or Pakistani, a woman we see in some form of purdah. The faith position overrides all other particularities to become the primary identity.

Journalists and scholars in the USA are fascinated by this assumed homogeneity of the Muslim world. Far from wanting to complicate this image, many seem intent on reinforcing it. The image is an object of desire. As Bhabha writes (1994), the stereotype 'gives access to an 'identity' which is predicated as much on mastery and pleasure as it is on anxiety and defense, for it is a form of multiple and contradictory belief in its recognition of difference and disavowal of it' [p. 75].

 Task B2.2.1

➤ Do you agree with Cooke that, when we meet a person for the first time, the images (that is, preconceptions) we have of people of a similar background will partly determine how we react to, and interact with, that person?

➤ How important a part do you think visual images we have come across of people of a similar background play in these preconceptions?

➤ Can you think of an occasion in your own experience when an individual from a different background has been seen by you or by someone else as an 'exception to a rule'?

 Task B2.2.2

Cooke writes that in the case of Muslim women, 'The faith position overrides all other particularities to become the primary identity.'

➤ Can you think of other groupings of people whose 'faith position' is seen as their 'primary identity'?

➤ Can you think of other examples of how in our perception of others the following 'positions' might be the 'primary identity'?

■ geographic; linguistic; racial; ethnic; gender; class.

 Task B2.2.3

➤ Before reading the extracts from the paper by Lei Guo and Summer Harlow on research into how African Americans, Latinos and Asians (who are inhabitants of the USA) are represented in YouTube videos, consider the following question:

■   Guo and Harlow write of a body of research which has shown 'that mainstream news media have helped perpetuate racial stereotypes by superficially covering minority groups, or ignoring them altogether' (p. 286). As YouTube allows ordinary users to upload videos, do you think that you will find that there is less racial stereotyping in YouTube videos of African Americans, Latinos and Asians living in the USA?

Guo, L. and Harlow, S. (2014) 'User-generated racism: an analysis of stereotypes of African Americans, Latinos, and Asians in YouTube videos'. *Howard Journal of Communications*, 25. pp. 281–302

Text B2.2.2
L. Guo and
S. Harlow

While studies on YouTube have burgeoned in recent years, very few of them empirically examined YouTube videos from the perspective of its potential as a new type of alternative media. This study seeks to fill this gap, investigating to what extent YouTube serves as an alternative medium by examining issues of race/ethnicity. Specifically, through a content analysis of YouTube's top 150 most-viewed videos about each of the three racial/ethnic groups—Blacks, Latinos, and Asians—this study explores whether the most popular videos on the site were citizen-generated or professionally generated, to what degree the videos challenged racist stereotypes, and how audiences responded [p. 282].

   Specifically, the following research questions are examined:

RQ1a: How do YouTube videos treat racial stereotypes in general?
RQ1b: What are the differences in how racial stereotypes are treated in videos of Blacks, Latinos, and Asians?
RQ2:   Which stereotypes are most frequent in YouTube videos' representations of Blacks, Latinos, and Asians, respectively?
RQ3a: Did ordinary citizens or professional organisations upload the YouTube videos?
RQ3b: Did ordinary citizens or professional organisations produce the content of the YouTube videos?
RQ3c: How does the fact of who uploaded/produced the YouTube videos affect how the videos treat racial stereotypes?

Given that audience interaction (e.g., 'likes' vs. 'dislikes,' comments) is also an integral part of YouTube, this study further examines:

RQ4:   How do audiences react to racial stereotypes in YouTube videos?

Method

This study used a content analysis to examine popular English-language YouTube videos that are concerned with three racial/ethnic groups: Blacks, Latinos, and Asians . . . The top 150 most-viewed videos (excluding cartoons or videos without people) from each racial category then were selected, resulting in a sample of 450 videos.

L. Guo and
S. Harlow

Because of broken links and removed or repeated videos, in the end 445 videos in total were analyzed. Also, because the view counts on videos change on a daily basis, our sample reflected the most-viewed videos by December 2011 when the searches were conducted . . .

To answer RQ1A and RQ1B . . . researchers coded whether the video contained any racial stereotypes, which of the three groups' stereotypes were present, whether the video reinforced/perpetuated those stereotypes, and whether it challenged them. Videos were coded as reinforcing/perpetuating stereotypes if they portrayed these stereotypes as truthful, accepted, or taken for granted. Videos were coded as challenging stereotypes if they portrayed non stereotypical images or overtly questioned stereotypes. Videos were also coded for the race of the main actors/characters portrayed in the video . . . The researchers coded for whether the main actors/characters were Blacks, Latinos, Asians, or Whites, or whether the video contained a mix of races [p. 289].

To answer RQ2 . . . coders looked for specific stereotypes, based on the literature, about Blacks, Latinos, and Asians. Coders were trained to identify Black stereotypes including 'law breaker' (i.e., criminals, gangsters, drug dealers, violent, dangerous); 'uneducated/unintelligent;' 'poor' (i.e., welfare, jobless, lazy); 'rapper/entertainer' (i.e., hip hop dancer); 'athlete/athletic;' and 'appearance/language and pronunciation' (i.e., pants falling down). Latino stereotypes coded included 'law breaker;' 'uneducated/unintelligent;' 'poor;' 'illegal immigrants' (i.e., 'aliens/wetbacks' and 'anchor babies'); 'sexualised women' (i.e., exotic Latina women, sexually seductive, teen mothers); and 'appearance/language and pronunciation' (i.e., sombreros). Asian stereotypes included 'yellow peril' (i.e., economic competitors); 'model minority' (i.e., academic and economic high achievers, hard-working, business-oriented, law-abiding, successful, etc.); 'nerdy' (i.e., workaholic, techy, lack creativity and feeling, quiet, fans of comic books/animations); 'perpetual foreigner' (i.e., more 'Asian' than 'American,' inassimilable, 'fresh off the boat,' eat rice all the time, use chopsticks); 'sexualised' (i.e., exotic, sexually seductive, passive femininity, manipulative 'dragon ladies,' asexual); 'Kung Fu warriors' (i.e., everybody in Asia is a martial artist); and 'physical appearance/language and pronunciation.'

For RQ3A–3C . . . coders determined whether the video had been uploaded to YouTube by a professional company or organisation, an ordinary individual user/a group of individual users, or 'other.' If the video was uploaded by ordinary user(s), coders then considered whether the video was originally made by ordinary citizens (e.g., citizen journalism, personal video diaries and commentaries, amateur-directed videos or presentations, remixed video) or originally produced by professionals (e.g., news clips, music videos, taped performance), or 'other.'

For RQ4 . . . coders counted the number of view counts, the number of comments, and the number of 'likes' and 'dislikes' for each video [pp. 289–90].

Results

In general, analysis showed that Blacks were the main characters in about 17% of the videos, Latinos in about 24%, Asians in 25%, and Whites in roughly 12%. The main characters in the remaining videos were a mix of races, at about 22%. Males were the main actors/subjects of about half (46%) of videos, and females 25%. The rest were a mix of genders. Most videos (31%) fell into YouTube's category of 'comedy,' 28% were 'entertainment,' 12% were 'people and blogs,' 9% were 'news and politics,' and the

L. Guo and
S. Harlow

rest were a mix of YouTube's other categories, such as 'film,' 'education,' 'how to,' 'sports,' 'travel and events,' 'science and technologies,' and 'nonprofits.'

Answering RQ1A–1B . . . results showed that more than three-fifths of videos (64%) included racial stereotypes. Further, of those, 85% reinforced or perpetuated racial stereotypes, and just 15% challenged racial stereotypes. In videos with stereotypes about Blacks, 70% reinforced the stereotypes, whereas 30% challenged them. Among videos containing Latino stereotypes, 99% reinforced those stereotypes and almost none—just 1%, or one video—challenged them. The videos coded as having stereotypes about Asians reinforced those stereotypes 91% of the time, and just 9% challenged stereotypes (p. 290).

In answer to RQ2 . . . the analysis showed that among videos with stereotypes about Blacks, the most frequent stereotype seen was that of 'lawbreaker,' appearing in about 57% of videos . . . As the second most salient stereotype, the stereotypical portrayals of Blacks' physical appearance and languages appeared in more than 40% of the videos that included African American stereotypes. For videos containing Latino stereotypes, the stereotype of sexualised/exotic women was most common, in 69% of these videos. 'Lawbreaker' was the next most frequent stereotype, appearing in 20% of videos with Latino stereotypes. In videos with stereotypes of Asians, the most frequent stereotype, found in 69% of such videos, referred to their physical appearance and language pronunciation. The second-most common stereotype, 'sexualised Asians,' was present in 28% of the videos [pp. 291–2].

Answering RQ3 . . . analysis demonstrated that 86% of the analyzed videos were uploaded by ordinary individuals or groups, and the remaining 14% were uploaded by professional organisations. Results showed that whether a video was uploaded by professional organisations or by ordinary users was not significantly related to whether the video included racial stereotypes, or whether the videos reinforced or challenged racial stereotypes [p. 292].

In general, per RQ4 . . . results showed videos with stereotypes generated significantly more view counts than videos without stereotypes (p. 293).

This study found that it is ordinary citizens—rather than professional organisations and companies—who uploaded and made the majority of the most popular videos on YouTube, at least for those about race/ethnicity included in the study. However, this study also found that citizen-generated videos are not necessarily critical in content. Despite—or perhaps because of—the fact that YouTube is mostly open to any type of content from anyone, the majority (64%) of the most popular videos about Blacks, Latinos, and Asians included some kind of a racial stereotype, and the overwhelming majority (85%) of those reinforced or perpetuated racial stereotypes. Only 15% were coded as challenging stereotypes, indicating that YouTube cannot be considered mainly as an alternative medium where racism is challenged. Rather, analysis suggests that the video sharing site to a large extent reproduces the racial hierarchy and maintains the status quo. Based on the analysis of the most popular race/ethnicity related videos, the study shows that YouTube caters to representations of race and stereotypes as fodder more for entertainment than for any actual contestation of power [p. 296].

. . . In general this study found that the same racial stereotypes emphasised in mainstream media were also popular in YouTube. In fact, because these videos often portray racial stereotypes, it is as though YouTube provides a space for ordinary users to amplify their prejudices—especially considering the incentive that such videos can usually attract a great number of views.

L. Guo and
S. Harlow

With respect to the audiences' reactions to the analyzed YouTube videos, it is somewhat disheartening that videos with racial stereotypes generated more view counts and more comments, suggesting that the public is interested in consuming an online spectacle of race (Nakamura 2008). It should also be noted that, while videos with racial stereotypes attracted significantly more views and comments, these videos were also found to generate significantly more 'dislikes.' In addition, when Black stereotypes were present, videos that reinforced Black stereotypes generated significantly more 'dislikes' than videos that challenged the stereotypes. These findings suggest that YouTube might serve as a potential alternative space for individuals, at least for viewers, to openly voice their opinions against racist ideologies [p. 298].

To conclude . . . this study suggests that YouTube instead to a large extent strengthens the racial hierarchy as emphasised in the mainstream media.

Task B2.2.4

➤ Analyse how minority groups in your own context are represented on YouTube.

➤ Does YouTube serve as a 'new type of alternative media to challenge the stereotypical representations of racial minority groups' in your own context?

Commentary

Kellner and Kim (2010) believe YouTube can 'provide the potential that individuals can empower themselves in relation to dominant media and culture and can provide the oppressed with ever more liberating forum for the counter-hegemonic politics of culture'. However, they balance their argument in emphasising 'the ways that media and technology generate social reproduction and can be part of an apparatus of social domination' (p. 6). Bouvier (2015) asks the question of whether the use of YouTube, Twitter, Facebook and other social media has encouraged 'a retreat into the comfort of being with those who share our existing opinions' (p. 154) and argues that:

Multicultural discourse studies needs to study social media to look at . . . the way that ideas and values are shared or not shared, and consider the linguistic tools and modes deployed to do so. And importantly, it needs to engage with the wider issue of power.

(p. 150)

UNIT B2.3 POWER AND THE OTHER IN INTERCULTURAL COMMUNICATION

In this unit we focus on how individuals categorise others and how this has important implications for intercultural communication and for social justice.

Text B2.3.1 features an analysis of the discourse of 'otherisation' in interviews of fifteen waiters ('servers') in a particular restaurant in a southern city in the USA. Text B2.3.2 is by Richard Dyer, who argued in an important work in 1997, that 'we have not yet reached a situation in which white people and white cultural agendas are no longer in the ascendant'.

There are a number of terms in the text that require explanation before you read Text B2.3.1:

- 'Red flags' – easily recognisable characteristics.
- 'Rednecks' and 'bubbas' – Mallinson and Brewster provide the following definition: 'The *Dictionary of American Regional English (DARE)* defines "redneck" as a "poor, White, rural Southerner – used with a very wide range of connotations, but now [especially] applied as a [derogatory] term for a White person perceived as ignorant, narrow-minded, boorish, or racist"'. *DARE* does not include an entry for 'bubba'. However, the *American Heritage Dictionary* (4th ed.) lists it as a regionalism and a slang term and defines it as 'a white working-class man of the southern United States, stereotypically regarded as uneducated and gregarious with his peers'.
- 'John Deere hats' – hats like a baseball caps with large peaks on which the name and logo of the company 'John Deere' appears. The John Deere Company is famous for manufacturing farm tractors and other agricultural machinery.
- 'Dale Earnhardt shirts' – The Dale Earnhardt Company produces a range of t-shirts and other apparel some of which have images related to activities such as motor racing and American football emblazoned on them.

Task B2.3.1

➤ While reading the interview in the first extract from Text B2.3.1 analyse what 'strategies of negative other-presentation' Nate uses when he talks about blacks, Latinos and rednecks.

Mallinson, C. and Z. W. Brewster (2005) '"Blacks and bubbas": stereotypes, ideology, and categorisation: processes in restaurant servers' discourse'. *Discourse and Society* 16/6: 787–807. pp. 792–802 (extracts)

Text B2.3.1
C. Mallinson
and Z. W.
Brewster

Interviewer: What sort of red flags *per se* do you look for when reading the patrons regarding tipping?

1 *Nate:* I hate to say it because it sounds like I'm really judging people, I guess
2 it really is judging people, I don't want to sound racist or anything, but you
3 know, it's, you see people that are quote rednecks or something like that or ah
4 other races.

Interviewer: What races?

5 *Nate:* Um, black, um Latinos are traditionally bad tippers. Saturday night I
6 had a table with like six Latinos. One was kind of translating for everybody
7 else and just ordered the biggest meals on the menu [and was like] do this, do
8 this. Desserts for everybody at the table, drinks you know, you want you want
9 okay I want a margarita, go ahead and make it, just like that. And then 140
10 dollar check and they leave like three dollars. And every time they're just
11 asking for something. Every time you come back to the table they feel, it's
12 almost like they feel obligated that if you're there they need to ask for
13 something and it seems like black people are the same way. But I mean there
14 are some really nice people so you can't judge it every single time. It's just
15 you'll get a feel for it after. I guess after you start taking tables for a little
16 while, the more they request, it's almost a good rule, the more they ask for the
17 less they are going to leave you. It really seems that way a lot of times.

Interviewer: Are there any other red flags that you have experienced?

18 *Nate:* Oh, overalls (laugh). John Deere hats, you know, Dale Earnhardt
19 shirts, things like that . . .
20 Rednecks, they actually shock me sometimes, but for the most part 75 to 80
21 per cent of the time rednecks are just terrible as far as, I don't like to listen to
22 them talk as far as, I mean, I have a bit of a country accent. I talk country
23 sometimes but I mean these guys are horrible and they seem so ignorant when
24 I'm talking to them. And on top of that of course you're going to get a rotten
25 tip and it just, you know.

Task B2.3.2

➤ Now read the analysis by Mallinson and Brewster. Do you agree with their analysis?

➤ Did you identify any strategies that Mallinson and Brewster do not identify?

Lines 1–4

. . . Nate answers the interviewer's question by presenting his standpoint about two social groups. The scope of his statement begins broadly; however, as Nate prepares himself to specify the patron type he is referring to, he issues four consecutive disclaimers (including apparent apology and apparent agreement; ll. 1, 2) and employs the tactics of hesitation and euphemism to mitigate these statements about rednecks and racially unspecified patrons (ll. 3, 4). Note the literal use of otherising talk (l. 4) as Nate linguistically marks social distance and establishes 'white' as the unmarked race.

When probed by the interviewer to specify what 'other races' of patron he is referring to, Nate constructs an argument to support his opinions.

Lines 5–17

In this segment, Nate zeros in on black and Latino patrons as the focus of his discussion about poorly tipping minority ('other race') patrons. He uses a common tactic that is part of the strategy of negative other-presentation to present evidence for his claims: he tells a story that implicates cultural difference in his perceived exploitative relationships with Latinos – and, by extension, blacks. Using words like 'traditionally' (1.5), he implies that his experiences are not unusual or biased; rather, they have happened to 'most' servers and so his assertions should not be interpreted as being personally contrived, unreasonable, or unfounded. He also provides specific numbers about the money involved in the transaction (II. 8–10). This particularisation has the semantic-rhetorical effect of casting Nate as an objective and credible reporter with quantitative 'evidence' to support his claims. Throughout this second part of Nate's excerpt, we again see otherising talk that constructs both minority groups as homogeneous, needy and perhaps even greedy (II. 11–13). Accordingly, Nate implies . . . a disclaimer of reversal. Without having to offer any evidence regarding the tipping practices of black patrons, Nate leads the listener to infer that black patrons, like Latinos, are likely to tip poorly, and that he is the victim of the exploitative transactions.

Lines 18–25

At the same time, however, Nate uses disclaimers as part of his complementary strategy of positive self-presentation to disavow, deny, and mitigate the racist tones of his statements. Anti-generalisations (II. 18–19) mitigate his claims and disavow the possibility that any of his assertions are founded on shaky ground or possible exceptions to the rule. Indeed, Nate frames his argument using the language of 'rules'. He first admits the possibility of exceptions (l. 14), then constructs a general rule (II. 16, 17), and finally acknowledges some uncertainty about the evidence he has presented (l. 17), again perhaps as a move to garner credibility.

After a follow-up question by the interviewer, Nate moves beyond overt discussions of race and tipping practices to elaborate on his previous assertions about the undesirability of 'redneck' patrons (l. 3).

In contrast to his discourse about black and Latino patrons, Nate begins his talk about rednecks by delineating a list of cultural stereotypes about rednecks (II. 18 19) rather than immediately renaming his reference group. Like Taylor, we see that Nate assumes shared cultural knowledge among himself, the interviewer, and larger society that these symbols index redneck culture and marks these characterisations with laughter.

Nate's discourse about rednecks is overtly derogative. He takes few pains to appear objective or unbiased and only rarely mitigates his statements (II. 20–21); instead, he is direct and even takes a moralistic stance toward them (l. 23). He uses otherising talk (II. 20, 21, 23) along with rhetorical tactics such as hyperbole and dramatisation to exaggerate his characterisations of redneck patrons and emphasise differences between himself and them. Nate also de-emphasises similarities between himself and rednecks, even though, as he grudgingly acknowledges, they are of the same race, live in the same region, and speak a similar dialect (II. 22–23). (The fact that Nate dislikes Southern speech even though he admits his own speech is sometimes similar is not unlike the attitudes of Preston's (1993) southern Indiana respondents toward the Kentucky dialect.) Only at the end of the excerpt does Nate mention poor tipping, which, for him, is simply another redneck behaviour – 'on top of' their speech – that he cannot tolerate.

Nate's discourse indicates that servers may not feel the need to engage in the complementary strategy of positive self-presentation to mitigate their negative other-presentations about rednecks to the same degree that they do with regard to minority patrons [pp. 792–4].

Mallinson and Brewster draw the following conclusions from their analysis of the fifteen interviews:

The servers draw on stereotypes made available by the dominant discourses of racism and capitalism. They articulate them, following the logic of negative other-presentation as well as positive self-presentation (to a greater or lesser extent, depending on patron type). By engaging in strategies to separate themselves sociopsychologically from stigmatised social groups, mark social distance from them, and emphasise positive characteristics about themselves, the servers create what Wodak (1997b) calls a 'discourse of difference'. They also use these stereotypes to form cognitive expectations about future interactions with these social groups, and, in so doing, they maintain, support, and reproduce larger ideologies of white supremacy [p. 801].

 Task B2.3.2

Mallinson and Brewster write that: 'cognitive expectations . . . may cause servers to provide inferior service to these patrons'.

➤ In what other ways may 'cognitive expectations of stigmatised social groups' lead to 'inferior service' or disadvantage?

Mallinson and Brewster refer to Wodak's notion of 'discourse of difference'. Related terms are 'order of discourse' and 'disorder in discourse'. The notion of 'order of discourse' in the work of Foucault has been adopted by some applied linguists, and chiefly Wodak (1996) and Fairclough, who defines the term (2001) as:

a social structuring of semiotic difference – a particular social ordering of relationships amongst different ways of making meaning . . . One aspect of this ordering is dominance: some ways of making meaning are dominant or mainstream in a particular order of discourse, others are marginal, oppositional or 'alternative'.

(p. 235)

Wodak (1996) is interested in 'disorders of discourse' and in how:

disorders in discourse result from gaps between distinct and insufficiently coincident cognitive worlds: the gulfs that separate insiders from outsiders, members of institutions from clients of those institutions, and elites from the normal citizen.

(p. 2)

It is the 'particular social ordering of relationships' and the gulfs between 'whites' and 'non-whites' that Dyer highlights in Text B2.3.2.

Dyer, R. (1997) *White*. London: Routledge. pp. 1–4 (extracts)

Text B2.3.2
R. Dyer

Racial imagery is central to the organisation of the modern world. At what cost regions and countries export their goods, whose voices are listened to at international gatherings, who bombs and who is bombed, who gets what jobs, housing, access to health care and education, what cultural activities are subsidised and sold, in what terms they are validated – these are all inextricable from racial imagery . . . Race is not the only factor governing these things . . . but it is never not a factor, never not in play . . .

There has been an enormous amount of analysis of racial imagery in the past decades, ranging from studies of images of, say, blacks or American Indians in the media to the deconstruction of the fetish of the racial Other in the text of colonialism and post-colonialism. Yet until recently a notable absence from such work has been the study of images of white people. Indeed, to say that one is interested in race has come to mean that one is interested in any racial imagery other than that of white people. Yet race is not only attributable to people who are not white, nor is imagery of non-white people the only racial imagery . . .

As long as race is something only applied to non-white peoples, as long as white people are not racially seen and named, they/we function as a human norm. Other people are raced, we are just people. There is no more powerful position than that of being 'just' human. The claim to power is the claim to speak for the commonality of humanity. Raced people can't do that – they can only speak for their race. But non raced people can, for they do not represent the interests of a race. The point of seeing the racing of whites is to dislodge them/us from the position of power, with all the inequities, oppression, privileges and sufferings in its train, dislodging them/us by undercutting the authority with which they/we speak and act in and on the world.

The sense of whites as non-raced is most evident in the absence of reference to whiteness in the habitual speech and writing of white people in the West. We (whites) will speak of, say, the blackness or Chineseness of friends, neighbours, colleagues, customers or clients, and it may be in the most genuinely friendly and accepting manner, but we don't mention the whiteness of the white people we know . . .

For most of the time white people speak about nothing but white people, it's just that we couch it in terms of 'people' in general. Research – into books, museums, the press, advertising, films, television, software – repeatedly shows that in Western representation whites are overwhelmingly and disproportionally predominant, have the central and elaborated roles, and above all are placed as the norm, the ordinary, the standard. Whites are everywhere in representation. Yet precisely because of this and their placing as norm they seem not to be represented to themselves as whites but as people who are variously gendered, classed, sexualised and abled. At the level of racial representation, in other words, whites are not of a certain race, they're just the human race.

We are often told that we are living now in a world of multiple identities, of hybridity, of decentredness and fragmentation. The old illusory unified identities of class, gender, race, sexuality are breaking up; someone may be black *and gay* and middle class *and* female; we may be bi-, poly- or non-sexual, of mixed race, indeterminate gender and heaven knows what class. Yet we have not yet reached a

R. Dyer

situation in which white people and white cultural agendas are no longer in the ascendant. The media, politics, education are still in the hands of white people, still speak for whites while claiming – and sometimes sincerely aiming – to speak for humanity . . .

We may be on our way to genuine hybridity, multiplicity without (white) hegemony, and it may be where we want to get to – but we aren't there yet, and we won't get there until we see whiteness, see its power, its particularity and limitedness, put it in its place and end its rule. This is why studying whiteness matters.

⭐ **Task B2.3.3**

➤ Does Dyer's description of how 'We (whites) will speak of . . .' reflect your experience of how white people speak?

> We (whites) will speak of, say, the blackness or Chineseness of friends, neighbours, colleagues, customers or clients, and it may be in the most genuinely friendly and accepting manner, but we don't mention the whiteness of the white people we know.

➤ Do you think the same point applies to how other groups in power speak of others less powerful?

⭐ **Task B2.3.4**

➤ Dyer's book was written in 1997. Do you think the views he expresses are still valid? If so, can you think of concrete examples that support his views?

⭐ **Task B2.3.5**

➤ Think of a cultural context familiar to you.

➤ Do one or more groups in positions of power seek to erase their own cultural identity while emphasising the 'culture' of one or more subordinate groups?

➤ If so, how is the 'culture' of the subordinated group(s) emphasised?

⭐ **Task B2.3.6**

➤ What are the implications of what Dyer writes for:

- how we research our own and other cultures?
- how we write about our own and other cultures?

Commentary

Notions of 'difference', 'presence', and 'absence' are key concepts in the work of Jacques Derrida, whose ideas have had widespread influence on the work of others, in a number of related fields, interested in questions of signification, representation, and Othering.

Derrida emphasises (1982: 213) how 'Western culture' has tended to promote the dominant poles of a system of binary distinctions to the exclusion of the other, terming this 'metaphysics':

> Metaphysics – the white mythology which reassembles and reflects the culture of the West: the white man takes his own mythology, Indo-European mythology, his own *logos*, that is, the *mythos* of his reason, for the universal form of that he must still wish to call Reason.

A key notion of Derrida's is that of '*difference*', which Gergen (1999: 27) summarises thus:

> Language is not like a flowing stream, but is divided into discrete units (or words). Each word is distinct from all others. Another way of talking about these differences is in terms of binaries (the division into two). That is, the distinctiveness of words depends on a simple split between 'the word' and 'not the word.' The meaning of 'white,' then, depends on differentiating it from what is 'non-white' (or 'black' for instance). Word meaning depends, then, on differentiating between a *presence* and an *absence*, that which is designated by the word against what is not designated. To make sense in language is to speak in terms of presences, what is designated, against a backdrop of absences . . . the presences are privileged; they are brought into focus by the words themselves; the absences may only be there by implication; or we may simply forget them altogether. But take careful note: these presences would not make sense without the absences. Without the binary distinction there is no meaning.

What is more, as Hall (1997: 235) writes:

> For Derrida there are very few neutral binary oppositions. One pole of the binary, he claims, is usually the dominant one, the one which includes the other within its field of operations. There is always a relation of power between the poles of a binary opposition.

'Deconstruction' is a complex term used by Derrida which has been employed in different ways in linguistic, literary and cultural studies. For Denzin (1994: 196) 'deconstruction is an effort to penetrate the world of lived experience where cultural texts circulate and give meaning to everyday life. It is necessary to show the gap that separates the world of everyday meaning from the worlds that are inscribed about that world by various cultural authorities, including newsmakers, social scientists, novelists, and filmmakers.'

UNIT B2.4   POWER AND THE OTHER IN EDUCATIONAL CONTEXTS

In the first part of this unit the focus is on how the English language itself is a key factor in debates on 'otherisation' and, in particular, on how certain varieties of English are dominant and unmarked forms. In the first text, Shuck (2006) reports on a study she carried out involving interview research with fifty-two first-year undergraduate students at a university in the southwest of the USA. The purpose of Shuck's study was to ascertain to what extent the casual conversation of 'White, middle-class, native-English-speaking, US-born college students' reflects public discourse about the use of 'non-English' or 'nonstandard English'. In the second text Lee Su Kim, a Malaysian applied linguist, describes her own experience as a graduate student in a university in the USA. In the second part of the unit the focus is on 'otherisation' in a university TESOL department in the United Kingdom.

Text B2.4.1
G. Shuck

Shuck, G. (2006) 'Racialising the non-native English speaker'. *Journal of Language Identity and Education*, 5/4: 259–76. pp. 262–73 (extracts)

Many native English speakers draw on colonialist discourses, particularly spatial metaphors of place and images of exotic, primitive natives, as they imagine the least likely speaker of English. The ideology of nativeness relies on the notion of place as a dimension along which native and non-native English speakers may be discursively imagined: Native English speakers are from 'here,' whereas non-native speakers must be from far away. Example 4 arose during a discussion of foreign instructors who might be acceptable as university instructors in the United States:

Example 4

Joe: . . I'm I'm not saying he [an instructor] has to be a native English spea/ker./
G: /Ah./. . OK.=
Joe: =uh, . . he can be . . . from— . . or she—
G?:   /mhm$^\lor$/
Joe: . . . /can be/from . . . I don't know, <u>some little island somewhere</u>.?:|softly] /@/
Joe: . . . /they/just have to have a certain level of . . . uh proficiency.

Joe constructs an image of someone who might not ordinarily be considered a proficient English speaker: someone 'from some little island somewhere.' Remoteness not only from English-dominant communities but also from civilisation forms an integral part of his argument. The reference to an island in a discussion of language proficiency, for those who hold an ideology of language that associates English with civilisation, subtly evokes an image of a primitive, brown-skinned island-dweller who speaks an exotic language. This association is easy for Joe to make because colonialist discourse already has within it the discursive means for imagining the superiority of one social group over another. As Said (1978) and Pennycook (1998) point out, dominant models of race always underlie the perpetuation of colonialist discourse.

. . . The language of 'special treatment' arose in more than one interview during discussions of the integrated, multilingual English composition class and of the English-Only movement. Such racialised discourse is further projected onto a model of education as competition, which tends to construct the majority—the invisibly privileged—as an oppressed group. Non-native English speakers are frequently represented as 'holding [native speakers] back' in settings in which educational resources (teacher help, time to cover material, etc.) are thought to be finite and therefore the object of competition between groups (Shuck 2001). When educational resources are seen as limited, only the unmarked group's educational possibilities are seen as threatened. If students marked by language background are in a class with 'regular' students, the former are described as having special interests that will impinge on the rights of the otherwise invisible majority. English-Only proponents similarly see the use of languages other than English as an affront to the ideal 'color-blind' society, and thus imagine any attempt to nurture the use of those languages as catering to the needs of special interests. The following excerpts (Examples 5 and 6) highlight this discourse as it is used in discussions of multilingual classes:

Example 5

Mary: . . . that if . . you go into a class like that, . . . you know, <u>they're gonna cater to the needs of the people that . . . DON'T know exactly what's going on.</u>

Example 6

Amy: maybe [‘I'm an international student’] shouldn't . . be written . . right at the top, because <u>I don't think . . special: . . . help should be given to them.</u>

In Example 5, the people who 'don't know what's going on' are non-native English speakers. In Example 6, Amy is referring to the composition placement exam, which she suggests would be most equitable if it did not identify international students as potentially needing any kind of extra help. Here, the ideology of education as competition, the discourse of reverse discrimination, and the ideology of nativeness converge. Because the United States is imagined to be monolingual, those who are not in that monolingual majority are imagined as outsiders or a minority group who might claim discrimination and demand special treatment.

The discourse of discrimination is also linked to colonialist discourses that rely on adult-child images to describe the relations between the unmarked group (native English speakers) and the marked group (non-native English speakers). Amy, the same student who argued against offering special help for non-native English speakers, also came up with a string of paternalistic analogies concerning the relations between native and non-native speakers, on one hand, and relations between parents and children, as well as between 'normal humans' (her phrase) and people with developmental disabilities, on the other (Shuck 2001). Drawing again on Gal and Irvine's (1995) notion of recursiveness, we see that the hierarchies between White and Black, parent and child, and native and non-native speakers are naturalised as though they all followed naturally and logically from each other. This is clear in Example 7. Amy agrees with her partner (Joe) that a combined class would benefit non-native English speakers more than native speakers:

Example 7

Joe: .. I I think it would be fun, .. for me, but I think it would be a lot .. more beneficial for them.=

Amy: =right.=

Cindy: —me too.

Amy: . . . you know, we were studying <u>this</u> in . . . um .. psychology last semester, on how . . . typically, . . . the oldest child in the family, .. is .. the smartest. [. . .] a- w- .. we talked about it, it makes a lot of sense, when . . . um the oldest child is born, .. he's around parents, . . . only . . . typically . . . when the second child is born, .. he's around parents, . . . AND the other child. . . which is typically . . . close in age. . . . um, . . . having that .. lower mental ability^v .. of . . . the second child, arou:nd the baby^v

G: /mhm^v/

Amy: /while he's/learning^v [. . .] . . . he tends to learn a lot of what he knows, . . . from the other child. . . . which is a lower . . . capacity, . . . than what the parents have.

G: .. mhm.=

Amy: =and—so I <u>understand that theory</u>, and in a way, . . . it would be I think more beneficial to the international student, than .. the native speaker.

Amy's use of 'this' and 'that theory' (both underlined) at the beginning and end of her turn naturalises the connection between babies' cognitive development and the experience of non-native English speakers in an integrated English class, making it seem as though the theory she learned in psychology (and surely has simplified or even misinterpreted) was in fact a theory of second language acquisition. She simply and uncritically erases the complexity of multilingual students' linguistic knowledge and renders them comparable to children with 'lower mental ability.'

This hierarchising of native and non-native English speakers has a far more extreme form: the xenophobic discourse represented by one interviewee's (Cindy's) use of the reactionary imperative, 'Go back to Mexico.' This only appeared once in this form in my data (Example 8), but the 'love it or leave it' discourse provides linguistic structures that other interviewees drew on to make similar comments in other contexts. Here is the canonical form, underlined:

Example 8

Cindy: they need to be able to function in society. . . . you know <u>if they . . . if they want to speak Spanish</u>, .. and .. function in their society, well, you know, th- . . . (you can? then?) <u>go back to Mexico</u>, you know?

Here, the imperative is encased in an *if/(then)*-clause structure. In Example 9, another student similarly relied on the imperative and added a rhetorical question (underlined).

The primary speaker (Kelli), like Cindy in the previous example, is also talking about immigrants who apparently refuse to learn English.

Example 9

Kelli: I can't imagine anyone . . living here, who would be intentionally trying NOT to learn . . the language, 'cause <u>then</u>,
Sara: /that's true./
Kelli: . . <u>why /are you here</u>./
Sue: //yeah,//
Kelli: //<u>like</u>,// . . . <u>leave</u>.

Kelli's shifting from 'anyone' to 'you' allows her, syntactically, to use the imperative, 'Leave,' which draws directly on xenophobic discourse.

Example 10 is remarkably similar to Examples 8 and 9, with a variation of the question 'Why are you here,' a conditional clause, and a hint of the injunction to 'go back to [where you came from].' The students in Example 10, however, were not talking about immigrants refusing to learn English. The first speaker, Tim, has just blamed the English composition program for its 'backwards' decision to separate US and international students. By the last two lines in this short excerpt, however, the blame seems to shift to the international students, who are seen as potentially isolating themselves:

Example 10

Tim: =I . . well I think . . . whoever . . you know, separated the classrooms, is—
Ann: . . . doesn't exactly understand <u>why they're here</u>. They're here to . . get the American—=
Tim: =yeah.
Laura: . . . <u>Why didn't they stay where they were from</u>, if they wanted to be . . . isolated still.

The similarities between the structure of Laura's comment and that of the canonical xenophobic argument are too striking to ignore. Ann initially embeds in her turn a variation of 'Why are you here' although without the accusatory tone. Laura, however, borrows the question form and approximates nationalistic discourses more closely in a particularly accusatory way: 'Why didn't they stay where they were from . . . ?' No longer is the apparent segregation of international students the fault of unaware administrators, as it was only moments earlier in the clause, 'whoever [. . .] separated the classrooms.' Now the international students are agents rather than objects, who are imagined as hypothetically wanting to be isolated. The form of Laura's question derives from the same kind of 'Love it or leave it' argument made by Cindy in Example 8: 'If they want to speak Spanish and function in their society [i.e., be isolated] . . . go back to Mexico.' Laura is able to draw on xenophobic discourse, whether or not she intends to argue that international students should go back to where they came from, for two primary reasons. First, the forms are easily accessible because they are well established in dominant ideologies of nationalism and assimilation. Second, those ideologies are directly interconnected with the construction of group boundaries, especially along ethnic or linguistic lines. As long as international students are seen as outsiders and linguistic minorities in the United States, they are subject to the same kind of exclusionary discourse [pp. 269–73].

Shuck provides a summary of binary features expressed by students she interviewed in Table B.2.4.1:

In commenting on the research findings summarised in Table B2.4.1, Shuck states that 'By investigating how everyday speakers discursively accomplish the process of marking and unmarking individuals and groups, we can better understand how racialisation is often a subtle practice deeply embedded in the way we speak.' She proceeds to ask the question: 'How does it happen that language background, race, and nationality become conflated in this way?' and argues that speakers 'rationalise social and linguistic differentiation as natural or explainable in terms of biology or some universal truth' (pp. 261–2).

Task B2.4.1

➤ In your own experience has there been a similar dichotomy in the discourse of 'native' speakers of English when talking about 'non-native' speakers of English, whether this has been in an educational, work-based or social setting?

Table B2.4.1 Some components of the native/non-native dichotomy (p. 262)

Native speakers	Non-native speakers
Are American	Are international
Are experts in English	Are novices in English
Are White or Anglo	Are non-White or non-Anglo
Are ahead/faster	Are behind/slower
Are up to speed	Hold everyone else (native speakers) back
Are compared to parents and 'normal humans'	Are compared to young children, the mentally disabled or 'emotionally disturbed,' and those who don't care
Take normal classes	Take easy classes that cater to them
Have no accent or have regional ones	Have accents
Are perfectly comprehensible	Are incomprehensible
Have little or no responsibility for communicating effectively with non-native speakers	Have full responsibility for communicating effectively with native speakers
Have no culture	Have culture

➤ Shuck refers to how the majority and 'invisibly privileged' group of 'native speakers' of English construct themselves as an oppressed group. Can you think of other examples of how the majority 'construct themselves as the oppressed group' in everyday or media discourse?

➤ Shuck refers to a '"love it or leave it" discourse' in Examples 8, 9 and 10. What other examples of a '"love it or leave it" discourse' have you come across in everyday or media discourse?

➤ Shuck's research focused on 'the normalisation of Whiteness, American-ness, and nativeness in certain prestige varieties of English'. When considering 'prestige varieties' of languages other than English consider how this 'normalisation' process operates.

In Text B2.4.2, a graphic example of the 'native/non-native dichotomy' is provided by Lee Su Kim when studying as a postgraduate student at a university in Texas.

Lee Su Kim (2007) *A Nyonya in Texas: Insights of a Straits Chinese Woman in the Lone Star State*. Singapore: Marshall Cavendish. pp. 77–9 (extracts)

Text B2.4.2
Lee Su Kim

The other day in a discussion group at a Graduate class at the University, I was annoyed at how 'insular' a bunch of Americans were. They were mainly Anglo-American school teachers. They lamented how these Asian learners of English 'just can't get their sounds right.' I was particularly incensed at the American professor teaching the particular class who should have known better. Instead, she reinforced their views and commented, 'Yeah, they just don't get it. I tell my ESL students to say "Fried Rice" and they say, "Yeah, that's what I said, Flied Lice"!' Some members of the group sniggered.

I was bothered by that comment, particularly at the sniggering. I couldn't let it go just like that. I had to point out that it wasn't because of the stupidity of the Asians, but that their tongues were unfamiliar with the sound 'r' as it does not exist in their language.

I piped up, 'You know, one can put the shoe on the other foot too. You guys can't pronounce a lot of sounds that exist in other languages as well. For example, many of you can't pronounce a common Chinese surname 'Ng'. It's all to do with the tongue and its familiarity with certain sounds.'

I had a number of Malaysian friends there with the surname 'Ng' who ended up being called Angie because the Americans can't enunciate the sound 'Ng' (pp. 77–8).

If only the Americans knew how many of us have had to change our Chinese names and take on American ones, not because we are smitten with these 'Christian' names but simply because we can't bear the daily mutilation of our Chinese names, I thought.

What I was trying to convey to the group really was that it wasn't so pat and simple—not being able to pronounce certain words in English for certain cultural groups could be because of the influence of their native languages. Different peoples have different phonological systems in their language and if one group has problems pronouncing the words of another language, it was merely because of our diversity and differences, not stupidity!

The American woman professor glared at me. I could sense her wrath for trying to show her up. I must have been an annoyance because I did not conform to the stereotype of the quiet, reticent Asian student. I participated actively in class (speaking out frequently), and asked questions which many Asian students seldom did. I made friends with people as people, and refused to cling to just the 'safety' of Asian friends. I could speak and write in perfect English and here I was challenging them and even telling them about how our tongues and brains were wired! [pp. 78–9].

To my surprise (not really anymore, actually), instead of an ensuing discussion in class, they just listened stumped, as if it couldn't even sink in, and then changed the subject altogether. It would have been interesting to pursue the discussion further. But that was it—end of discussion. No one wanted to go to down that unknown road any farther. Perhaps for fear that one's ethnocentricity would show up . . .

I wanted to say, 'Hey c'mon, ask me questions . . . open your minds . . . don't you want to know more about what I'm trying to share with you? The rest of the world knows so much about America . . . at least be a little interested in the rest of the world.'

The class continued in its little safe ethnocentric journey [p. 79].

 Task B2.4.2

➤ In what ways does the experience described by Lee Su Kim reflect the 'Native/ Non-native Dichotomy' in Table B2.4.1 in Shuck's paper B2.4.1?

In Text B2.4.3 the focus is on the experience of postgraduate students studying for a postgraduate qualification in TESOL in a British university. The authors, Sarah Rich and Salah Troudi, explain that:

> The term *racialisation* . . . draws a distinction between a static conception of race as the drawing of boundaries between people purely on the basis of physiological differences and an understanding of race as a 'floating signifier' (Rattansi 2005: 272) that can be applied differently at different times. That is to say, racialisation highlights a need to understand race (and thereby racism) as a situated, socially constructed response to sociocultural, political, and historical conditions at a given point in time.

Rich, S. and S. Troudi (2006) 'Hard Times: Arab TESOL students' experiences of racialisation and Othering in the United Kingdom'. *TESOL Quarterly* 40/3: 615–27. pp. 618–24 (extracts)

The study sought to address the following research question: How far and in what ways do Arab Muslim students perceive racialisation to be significant to their experiences of Othering in a TESOL community in the United Kingdom? . . . The research tools we . . . selected for this explorative study—an open-ended questionnaire and interviews—were designed to help us collect informative qualitative data.

Participants

The five Saudi students who took part in this study . . . were participating in a masters in TESOL education programme . . . and were seen to represent all the Saudi students

S. Rich and
S. Troudi

in the faculty because they were all male, Muslim, Arab, and in their late twenties, came from different regions of Saudi Arabia, and had all completed their education to the undergraduate level there . . . [p. 618].

Forms of Othering and racism perceived by the participants

Accounts of Othering based on non-racial categories

All participants invoked the identity of international student or foreigner to account for the difficulties they initially experienced in negotiating the community's cultural practices. This identity position was brought up in the context of the difficulty they felt in negotiating the requirement for independent study, a more interpretive style of teaching, and the assessment processes. Thus, for example, Mohammed said, 'The problems I face here are because I'm an international student. All international students feel the same,' and Karim stated, 'People here look at you first as a foreigner.'

Although Mohammed consistently saw international student as the primary identity category affecting his experiences throughout the programme, the other four participants also saw gender, culture, ethnicity, nationality, and religion as influencing their experiences to different extents and at times as intersecting in complex ways. For example, Saif and Karim both felt that gender was important to the ways other students interacted with them, and they linked gender to nationality, ethnicity, and religion. As Karim stated:

> You know we are all male Saudis here. They [the other students] I think maybe they have a bad impression of men, they don't say it but I feel it. They ask me why in Islam they marry four wives, I try to answer but I feel uncomfortable.

Saif too mentioned how other students quizzed him on the treatment of women in Saudi Arabia and wondered how they found marriage partners in such a 'closed society'. In describing his experiences, Ali invoked ethnicity, culture, and religion. Thus he claimed:

> Sometimes, not sometimes, many times, I would be questioning attitudes you know a lot, whether this person did that to me because I'm from the Middle East. A smaller or no beard with more smiles eases the misconception of many towards me. Many feel that due to what they hear about strict Islamic practices.

Ahmed's account offers a clear example of how an event within the community was instrumental in shifting his initial investment in a position of *international student* to a stronger alignment with national, ethnic, racial, cultural, and religious identity positions. This he described in the following way:

> I remember once during the first semester I came late to one of the classes and one of my teachers came to me and whispered, 'In our culture we respect time but I don't know about your culture.' That means an insult to my culture so I wished that X punished me or kicked me out but don't say something about my culture. After I heard what X said to me I hated that module really.

153

S. Rich and
S. Troudi

This led Ahmed to become aware of his racialised identity. According to him:

> Before [this event] I didn't see myself as a Muslim Arab Saudi. I saw myself as an international MEd student. But after my experience, after four or five months I found it mixing as TESOL student and as a Muslim, but mostly Muslim.

Accounts of Othering based on racism

In contrast to the accounts just presented, one participant, Saif, a Saudi of African origin, explicitly invoked the category of race in describing his experiences as he progressed through the programme. Although like the others, he claimed to have initially foreground [sic] the identity of *international student* and foreigner in making sense of his experiences, he pinpointed interactions with two different tutors as leading him to conclude that he was being subjected to racial discrimination.

In the first critical incident, Saif described how a tutor had suggested that he had copied part of his assignment from a book. He remarked on how he felt upset, because he hadn't understood what *paraphrasing* meant and the tutor had assumed that 'Arabs have limited knowledge, are lazy, and do cheating a lot.' In the second incident, which occurred shortly after the first, Saif described a conversation he had had with a different tutor who suggested that he might be overusing tutorial support at the expense of other students in the group. He saw this incident as reinforcing his view that he was being subjected to what he called 'special discrimination,' that is, Otherised in particular ways on account of his colour. As he remarked, 'I was really shocked you know when X [the tutor] said I signed up too much. I asked myself why X said this to me. I felt sure X wouldn't say this to other students.' Saif went on to claim that both of these instances were examples of racism done in what he called 'a professional way.' To him, the tutors achieved this professional racism by cleverly using institutional practices to disguise it.

The impact of political events and Islamophobia on Othering

Although explicit associations between the discourse of Islamophobia and recent political events involving Muslims and Arabs did not feature in participants accounts of their experiences within this particular community, all the participants except Mohammed alluded to the impact of events in a general sense on their experiences of living and studying in the United Kingdom. Saif, for example, felt these things meant that Saudi students in general were likely to have an especially hard time in the United Kingdom. Thus, he remarked that he felt sure there was a direct link between the fact that so many of the perpetrators of the 9/11 attacks were Saudi citizens and the way Saudi students were treated in higher educational institutions in the United Kingdom. As he said, 'Saudi students get especially bad treatment because everyone thinks we might all be terrorists.' He went on to describe a number of meetings he had attended with Saudi students studying at different universities in the United Kingdom who, he claimed, shared his views.

Ali and Karim talked of the emotional impact of Islamophobic discourses on the ways they interpreted their experiences and a tendency toward a kind of paranoia (*waswasa* in Arabic) in their dealings with others. Thus Ali remarked:

> What is going on around the world politically and what is going on in the Middle East is always looming in the back of my mind. When they ask me where I am from I say, 'I'm from Saudi Arabia.' Some of them smile, they say, 'Oh, Saudi Arabia.'

S. Rich and
S. Troudi

They are joking, but I know that joke it has something inside it . . . looking down at you as a terrorist.

Ahmed's accounts also provided some insights into how the effects of these Islamophobic discourses led him to develop a kind of counter-discourse that entailed prioritising national, ethnic, cultural, and religious aspects of his identity as a way of resisting negative representations of Muslims and Arabs in the press. As he said, 'I'm proud of my identity myself. I mean my religion, my people, my nation. If they don't think we are good people, that wouldn't affect me inside. That would maybe increase my love to my top, my identity.'

Implications for inquiry into racialisation

Undertaking this small-scale study has led us to a deeper understanding of the complexity inherent in undertaking research into racialisation and Othering in TESOL communities.

First, it has led us to question how explicitly participants need to invoke racialisation in order for us to claim that they experience their identities as racialised. That is to say, although we are mindful of a need to acknowledge Berard's (2005) point that the relevance of race should not be overplayed when interpreting data such as ours, we suggest that despite the fact that only one participant referred to race in his accounts of Othering, the foregrounding of religion, culture, and ethnicity in these accounts is evidence of racialised Othering taking place. In making this claim, we adopt the position taken by a number of writers, such as Blackledge (2003) and van Dijk (1993), namely, that these participants' accounts of Othering need to be understood as constructed against the backdrop of their lived experiences of marginalisation and inferiorisation as Arab Muslims in the wider community in which a racialised Islamophobia is increasingly evident.

Second, the findings have led us to consider the ways in which TESOL community practices may contribute to an experience of racialised Othering. Two participants, Ahmed and Saif, perceived specific incidents as having led them to reconstruct their initial understandings of their positioning in racialised terms. These incidents led them to a shift from perceiving of themselves as international students to a marginalised and inferiorised position on account of their culture, colour, ethnicity, and nationality. Though it may be open to debate as to whether community practices were necessarily racist, a key point of learning for us is the recognition that these practices may be construed as such by learners already sensitised to societal and global discourses of racism. Thus, undertaking this study has highlighted the need to be aware of subtle linguistic nuances when interacting with learners from different ethnic and cultural backgrounds. Moreover, we should be mindful of the need to exercise self-reflexivity with regard to our academic practices and the Western normative approaches to which we adhere, such as the way we approach the issue of plagiarism (Pennycook 1996). That is, we must remain alert to the ways in which our discourse may hide 'the old hierarchy of racial superiority that determines which form of cultural product or practice is the norm or deviant' (Kubota 2001: 28).

Third, undertaking this study has deepened our understanding of the challenges in investigating racialised Othering and posed a number of questions. For example, how does the position of a researcher affect the nature of the data generated? If researchers are insiders in the communities they are researching, how might this position affect the extent to which learners feel able to explicitly invoke racialisation in their accounts? In addition, how far does a shared sense of linguistic, ethnic, and cultural identity between an interviewer and participant influence the ways and extent to which learners articulate their understanding of Othering as racialised? Does a shared sense of identity enable learners to foreground racialisation in their accounts? Might it also lead them to overplay the significance of racialisation? Finally, how does asking learners to articulate a sense of racialised Othering in a foreign or second language affect the nature and quality of data generated? [pp. 620–64]

 Task B2.4.3

➤ Shuck in Text B2.4.1 reported on how the term 'international student' was a marked form which was aligned against 'American student', the dominant pole of the binary. Rich and Troudi provide further evidence of how being viewed as an 'international student' immediately places students in a deficit position ('Mohammed said, "The problems I face here are because I'm an international student. All international students feel the same," and Karim stated, "People here look at you first as a foreigner."'). In recent years there has been an increasing internationalisation of higher education in different parts of the word. What implications are there for how higher education students who have come to another country to study are referred to and what are the broader implications for how universities ensure that students are not 'racialised'?

Task B2.4.4

➤ Rich and Troudi refer to 'academic practices and the Western normative approaches to which we adhere, such as the way we approach the issue of plagiarism'. Different interpretations of what plagiarism consists of have been a key issue in debates on academic writing. Sunderland-Smith (2005), for example, in reviewing studies in different parts of the world, found that 'there were widely differing conceptions of plagiarism by students, staff and Institutions' (p. 85). In what ways do you think 'conceptions of plagiarism might differ' in different contexts?

Task B2.4.5

➤ Rich and Troudi ask a number of important questions in the final paragraph which relate to all those researching aspects of culture and communication including:

- Does the position of a researcher affect the nature of the data generated?
- How far does a shared sense of linguistic, ethnic, and cultural identity between an interviewer and participant influence what research participants disclose and how they do so?

➤ The information that the reader is provided with is that: 'Sarah Rich is a lecturer in applied linguistics and directs a masters in TESOL programme at the University of Exeter, England. Her research interests and publications focus on issues of identity and learning and teaching in multicultural classrooms. Salah Troudi teaches applied linguistics and language education at the School of Education and Lifelong Learning at the University of Exeter, England. His research interests include teacher education, critical applied linguistics, and language policies. He coordinates the doctor of education in TESOL program in Dubai, United Arab Emirates.'

    ■ How might the positions of Sarah Rich and Salah Troudi, and their linguistic, ethnic and cultural identities (as far as you can tell from the information provided), have affected the nature of the data generated in the study reported in Text B2.4.3?

Task B2.4.6

➤ Think about other research on intercultural communication (including that reported on in this book). How might the positions of the researchers, and their linguistic, ethnic and cultural identities, have affected the nature of the data generated?

Commentary

A number of calls have been made for a 'critical pedagogy' that helps students understand how education systems promote powerful discourses and exclude minority voices. For Apple (1996), critical pedagogy is about 'generating agency' and its purpose is to 'provide tools to students, teachers, and others that enable them to see 'texts' as embodying both particular 'representations' of the social and natural world and particular interests', as well as enabling them to 'understand how such "texts" position them and at the same time produce unequal relations of institutional power that structure classrooms, staffrooms and educational policies' (p. 131). A critical pedagogy will, it is hoped, lead to 'critical literacy' among students (Muspratt *et al.* 1997).

UNIT B2.5   THE OTHER AND THE TOURIST GAZE

In Unit B2.5 we focus on travel literature. The writer of Text B2.5.1, Alastair Pennycook (1998), sees a 'remarkable continuity with colonial discourse' in travel literature on China (p. 180) and suggests that 'rather than disappearing, these discourses have remained fairly constant and indeed are enjoying a period of rejuvenation in conjunction with the continued global expansion of English' (p. 130).

In Text B2.5.2, Tita Beaven focuses on 'settler writing', in other words accounts written by those who have chosen to settle in places away from their places of birth and upbringing. Beaven specifically analyses the accounts of those settling in Spain, among which is the account of Chris Stewart, *Driving Among Lemons: An Optimist in Andalucia* (1999).

Text B2.5.1
A. Pennycook

Pennycook, A. (1998) *English and the Discourse of Colonialism.* London: Routledge. pp. 171–2, 174–5, 180 (extracts)

Just as Said (1978) identified a range of stereotypes dealing with the Arab world – the eternal and unchanging East, the sexually insatiable Arab, the Feminine exotic, the teeming marketplace, mystical religiosity, corrupt despotism, and so forth – it is possible to outline a similar series of stereotypes in writing on China: the exotic and eternal, the underdeveloped and backward, the paradoxically juxtaposed old and new, the crowded, dirty and poverty-stricken life, the smiling or inscrutable exterior hiding either bad intentions or misery, the passive Oriental and the despotic leader, the dullness of life under socialism, the uncaring nature of the Communist government, and so on. Such constructions occur across a broad range of writing, from textbooks to encyclopaedias. One domain in which they have a particular salience, and in which they have shown a remarkable resilience over time, is in travel writing . . .

I would like to look at Paul Theroux's (1988) *Riding the Iron rooster: By train through China*. Theroux is, of course, an old and respected hand at travel-writing: 'The world's pre-eminent travel-writer' (*Time*, 16 May 1988); one of 'the best of today's travel writers' (*The Economist* 1988). And yet, as Salzman discusses in his review of the book, there are many problematic passages:

> [At the railway station at Baoji] everyone hawked, everyone spat, sometimes dribbling, sometimes in a trajectory that ran like candle-wax down the side of a spittoon . . . They walked scuffingly, sort of skating, with their arms flapping, with narrow jogging shoulders, or else hustling petlike, with their limbs jerking. They minced, they plodded, they pushed, keeping their hands out – straight – arming their way – and their heads down. They could look entirely graceless – unexpected in Chinese.
>
> Mr Tian [his guide and translator for most of the trip] shrugged, shook my hand, and without another word walked off. It was the Chinese farewell: there was no lingering, no swapping of addresses, no reminiscence, nothing sentimental. At the moment of parting they turned their backs, because you ceased to matter and because they had so much else to worry about.
>
> It seemed to me that the Chinese . . . had no choice but to live the dullest lives and perform the most boring jobs imaginable – doing the same monotonous Chinese two-step from the cradle to the grave.

Such descriptions can be commonly found in writing on China. it is interesting to observe here how Theroux on the one hand dwells on practices such as spitting, and on the other, manages to make vast generalisations about Chinese life: 'the Chinese farewell', the 'monotonous Chinese two-step' and so on . . .

Chinua Achebe has remarked that travellers with closed minds can tell us little except about themselves (1975: 40). I would suggest that he is right up to a point here. Travellers and travel writers may indeed tell us more about themselves than the place they are travelling in, but that telling about the Self is a telling that is discursively constructed. We do not, therefore, learn much about the lived realities of other contexts, but we do learn a great deal about how the Other is constructed in Western discourses. What I think by now must be manifestly clear – a point that I have perhaps belaboured somewhat – is that there are a series of dominant discourses on China which, with a remarkable continuity with colonial discourses, constantly construct China in a very particular way, dichotomising and essentialising to create a stereotyped vision denying any lived experience of Chinese people.

Task B2.5.1

➤ Do you believe the very nature of travel writing makes it possible for a travel writer to give an account of what Pennycook calls the 'lived experience' of people and the 'lived realities of other contexts'?

➤ If so, what will this account consist of?

In recent years how readers respond to texts is, for some, as important as the actual content of the texts themselves. Thompson (1995: 213–14), for example, writes that '. . . whether mediated messages are ideological will depend on the ways in which they are taken up by the individuals who receive them and incorporated reflexively into their lives. Texts and media programmes which are replete with stereotypical images, reassuring messages, etc., may in fact be taken up by recipients and used in quite unexpected ways . . . one must consider the ways in which these messages are incorporated into the lives of recipients.'

Watson (1997: 90), on the other hand, believes that 'Readers . . . actively interpret texts but cannot interpret them in just any way they wish. The texts themselves contain "instructions" which yield strongly preferred readings.'

Task B2.5.2

➤ What is your point of view?

➤ Do you believe, for example, that descriptions in travel, and other, literature, such as those written by Theroux and highlighted by Pennycook, 'yield strongly preferred readings' or could they be 'taken up by recipients and used in quite unexpected ways'?

➤ If they 'yield strongly preferred readings' what might be the implications for how the Other is perceived?

➤ If they could be 'taken up by recipients and used in quite unexpected ways', what might be these 'unexpected ways' and what might be the implications?

Text B2.5.2
T. Beaven

Beaven, T. (2007) 'A life in the sun: accounts of new lives abroad as intercultural narratives'. *Language and Intercultural Communication* **7/3: 188–202. pp. 191–201 (extracts)**

Among all kinds of travel writing, for evident reasons, settler writing in particular tends to elaborate more in depth on the concepts related to crosscultural adaptation . . . Whether settlers end up staying permanently or not, they subscribe to what migration experts have termed the myth of no-return (O'Reilly 2002), and hence moves towards adapting to their new surroundings are seen as paramount. Therefore, their narratives typically expose, in the first instance, issues of culture shock such as conflict and stress in the process of intercultural adjustments (see Matsumoto *et al.* 2003) as well as other more positive instances of the experience. In reading settler writings the reader witnesses how the act of settling down in a new surrounding enables the fashioning of hybrid identities, which encompass the old and the new, the self and the other; that is, the reader is introduced to the fluidity of cultural identities and to how a new, third culture can be built [p. 191].

One of the discourses produced by settlers is the one articulated around the notions of 'Bad Britain' and 'Good Spain', where Britain often signifies,

> routine; dullness; monotony; greyness; cold; no hope for the future; a miserable old age; misery; modern life; rushing around; no time for pleasure; crime; selfishness; lack of caring; loss of community; lack of trust; poor health; poor education; and a poor welfare state.
>
> (O'Reilly 2002: 99)

and Spain is constructed as a site to be valued for its:

> natural resources, including climate and landscape, things offered by the settled British community (clubs, leisure, a welcoming community) and things offered by the Spanish community (respect for children and the elderly, friendliness, warmth, security and a slow pace of life).
>
> (O'Reilly 2002: 26)

Each of these idealised elements can be found in the settler narratives . . . however, although these constructions can be read as an indication of acceptance and valuing of the foreign environment (which, in turn, it is a positive sign of adaptability), they need to be looked at more critically as imbalanced perceptions of the two worlds [p. 192].

A second element of the positive construction of Spain in this kind of narrative suggested by O'Reilly is what the settled British community has to offer. There is evidence in the settlers' accounts that the authors and their families rely on and find help and support from some of their compatriots. For instance, Chris Stewart writes about the help they received from Georgina, 'a confident young Englishwoman with a peculiar Mediterranean way of seeming at ease with her surroundings [. . . who] had carved out a niche for herself acting as an intermediary between the farmers who wanted to sell their cortijos . . . and the foreigners who wanted to buy them' (Stewart 1999: 1); he also, for instance, mentions a British couple who acted 'as guides through the arcane web of Spanish administration for other foreigners buying property in the area' (Stewart 1999: 140). It is a recognition that they are not alone in dealing with the Other. However, it is also clear that the relationship with their compatriots is a complex one, as the authors explicitly want to distance themselves from other British settlers as well as from the visitors in the tourist areas and from the ghettoised expat communities . . . this rejection of their own cultural group seems necessary for their narratives, as it contributes to their idealised construction of the foreign cultural group to which they aspire to belong [p. 194].

Another valued aspect of living in rural Spain that is mentioned in the settler narratives is its simplicity, one which harks back to a straightforward, timeless way of conducting one's life, a trope of the discourse common to much travel writing (Galasinski and Jaworski 2003: 135). It is a simple existence, as opposed to the unduly complicated life in Britain; it is wholesome and natural, where Britain is fussy and superfluous. When they start unloading the things they have brought from England for their new life in the Alpujarran mountains, Stewart grows self-conscious in front of one of the local 'peasants':

> 'It's a thing for slicing eggs . . . an asparagus kettle. That? Oh that's a teacosy . . . for keeping tea-pots warm . . . a device for applying rubber rings to the balls of lambs, a pepper-mill, a food-processor . . . a wordprocessor . . .' I felt more and more abashed as, with my explanations, I laid bare the fripperies of our existence. It seemed somehow wanting when compared with the elemental earthiness of his (Stewart 1999: 58) [p. 195].

However, if Spain represents an unchanged, unmodernised society, this can some-times have slightly menacing connotations. Spain's own past is also a recurring theme, and there are numerous references to various 'sinister' aspects. For instance, the writers reveal the grotesque, the macabre, the barbaric, 'dark side' of Spain: the ubiquitous bull fighting, poor treatment of animals, gruesome tales of the *matanza* (the slaughter of the pigs), and even the foreignness of the food: for instance, Pedro, who owns the farm Chris Stewart is buying, likes to eat 'strong food': Strong food in these parts is chickens' heads, ham fat, pig's blood pudding, raw peppers and garlic, chumbos (prickly pear), stale bread and wine . . . This was Pedro's preferred diet. He offered me a chicken's head one morning, a ghastly-looking burnt thing with charred feathers on it that he had taken from the fire, waving it under my nose with a grin. 'Strong food for the guest of honour!' (Stewart 1999: 35). These are the elements that perhaps best signal the separation between 'us' and 'them'. And, as previously stated, these unexpected revelations in the construction of the two realities are critical for preparing the readers with their mediated encounter with the Other [p. 196].

Common reflections and actions in settler narratives explicitly refer to desires of integrating and adjusting. For instance, they narrate episodes that relate the awareness of differences in physical appearance, knowledge of other cultures and language proficiency . . . In spite of this strong desire for adaptation, there is also a growing awareness of cultural difference, and an understanding that some deeply held beliefs or tastes are culturally specific and hard to change [pp. 196–7].

One of the results of the intergroup contact that the authors and their families undertake is that the relationship with the culture of origin is constantly re-evaluated. The individual reactions to cultural contact that emerge in the narratives echo some of the four main responses that have been identified in the literature: 'passing', chauvinistic, marginal and mediating (Ward *et al.* 2001: 31) (Table B2.5.1).

Settlers seem to aspire to align themselves with some of the values and cultural practices of their hosts, whilst at the same time defining themselves as other, and

Table B2.5.1 Individual reactions to cultural contact

Response	Type	Multiple-group membership affiliation	Effect on individual	Effect on society
Reject culture of origin, embrace second culture	'Passing'	Culture 1 norms lose salience, culture 2 norms become salient	Loss of ethnic identity self-denigration	Assimilation, cultural erosion
Reject second culture, exaggerate first culture	Chauvinistic	Culture 1 norms increase in salience, culture 2 norms decrease in salience	Nationalism, racism	Integration friction
Vacillate between the two cultures	Marginal	Norms of both cultures salient but perceived as mutually incompatible	Conflict, identity confusion, overcompensation	Reform, social change
Synthesise both cultures	Mediating	Norms of both cultures salient and perceived as capable of being integrated	Personal growth	Intergroup harmony, pluralistic societies, cultural preservation

highlighting the aspects that make them different from the host society. For instance, against the traditional and perhaps somewhat backward qualities that the Spaniards are seen to represent, the British settlers embody the spirit of adventure, albeit a little self-consciously, as the following remark by one of Stewart's acquaintances suggests:

> 'I mean who the hell was going to buy a place that has no access, no running water, no electricity – and that huge patch of land to work? I must say I think it very bold of you to have bought it. Or maybe you are a complete lunatic?' 'I'm at least a half-lunatic', I volunteered. But we'll manage somehow. It's an exciting challenge, and anyway, it beats being an insurance clerk working in an office.
>
> (Stewart 1999: 31) [p. 199]

One of the central elements around which the British character is constructed is the British attitude to animals, and it is consistently used to define them in opposition to the Spanish other. Another, obvious, element is related to the ubiquitous cup of tea, which is contrasted with the Spanish wine. On arriving in their new Spanish home after an endless, tedious drive from England, Stewart and his wife exclaim:

What we needed was a cup of tea. If you're English, or for that matter Chinese, you always need a cup of tea at such moments, even if you're just moving into your new home on the continent.

(Stewart 1999: 56)

At the same time, these symbolic actions are presented, in some instances, in combination with learnt actions from the other, perhaps symbolic of the settlers' wish to synthesise both cultures in a new way of being, in a redefined self. Stewart, for example, relates a situation where, during a country walk, he and his wife bump into a British couple who live nearby and, after the initial resentment of finding that the remote area they had chosen to settle in was not as 'undiscovered' as they had thought, they 'forgave each other's origin' and shared 'tea followed by wine' [p. 200].

Towards the end of Stewart's account . . . we read how Stewart finally reconciles himself to accept, and celebrate, his own Britishness:

However much you may fight against it, if you live abroad where there are other expatriates, you become part of what is known as the Foreign Community. Initially, I struggled hard against this notion but as the years passed I grew more relaxed about my status as a foreigner and more willing to appreciate the ties that, by language, humour and shared experience, bound me to my compatriots.

(Stewart 1999: 182) [p. 200–1]

Task B2.5.3

➤ Beaven writes that: 'In reading settler writings the reader witnesses how the act of settling down in a new surrounding enables the fashioning of hybrid identities, which encompass the old and the new, the self and the other; that is, the reader is introduced to the fluidity of cultural identities and to how a new, third culture can be built'. Do you think that the extracts from Stewart's book provide evidence that there is a 'fashioning of hybrid identities' and that a 'new, third culture' is built?

Task B2.5.4

➤ In Table B2.5.1 Beaven presented a model of 'outcomes of intercultural contact' (from Bochner 1982). Do you think this is a valid representation of the different responses that people experience when they settle in a different cultural context? Why/why not?

Commentary

A number of studies have been carried out which investigate other ways in which tourist destinations have been represented and the 'hosts' in these destinations 'Othered'. Jaworski *et al.* (2003), for example, carried out research on holiday programmes on British television, and concluded that, with a few exceptions, 'Overall, the programmes seem to imply that tourists need have very little or no contact with their hosts, who can thus be eliminated from the tourist experience, or objectified under the scrutiny of the tourist gaze' (Urry 2002). If contact does occur, according to the holiday programmes, local people are there to help, serve and inform. This can be achieved through a series of brief, formulaic encounters, and even if they may require the use of a language other than English, a few textbook phrases will be sufficient to get by and satisfy the tourist's basic needs . . . In some cases, local people are portrayed as compliant and submissive. They accept the need to see things 'our' way and even if they don't, they are likely to be polite enough not to insist on our seeing *their* point of view' (p. 159).

Theme 3
Representation

UNIT B3.1 THE REPRESENTATION OF IDENTITY: PERSONALITY AND ITS SOCIAL CONSTRUCTION

In this unit we return to the question of individual identity, and particularly the question of personality and how personality is 'socially constructed'. Vivien Burr, the author of the first text, writes that 'The notion of personality is so firmly embedded in our thinking in contemporary western society that we hardly, if ever, question it' (1996: 17). Indeed, not only do we rarely question the 'western' model of personality, but we often assume that it can be universally applied to, and be a useful mechanism for understanding, individuals in all cultures.

The processes through which we perceive a person's personality are described by Sarah Hampson in Text B3.1.2, and we explore their implications for our perceptions of individuals and their behaviour across different cultural contexts.

Task B3.1.1

➤ Before you read Text B3.1.1, write down (in about 10 sentences) a description of the personality of a good friend.

Burr, V. (1996) *An Introduction to Social Constructionism*. London: Routledge. pp. 21–8 (extracts)

Text B3.1.1
V. Burr

Problems with the traditional view of personality

. . . The idea of 'personality' is one that we use in our everyday lives in order to try to make sense of the things that we and other people do. 'Personality' can then come to be seen as a theory (one held very widely in our society) for explaining human behaviour, and for trying to anticipate our part in social interactions with others. We could say that in our daily lives we act as if there were such a thing as personality, and most of the time we get by reasonably well by doing so. But it is a big leap from this to saying that personality really exists (in the sense of traits inhabiting our mental structures, or being written into our genetic material).

Another weak point in the 'personality really exists' argument is this. If personality does really exist in this way, then we are describing part of human nature. We should

V. Burr

expect to find 'personality' as we know it in all human beings, no matter what part of the world they inhabit or what period of history they may have occupied. But it is clear that all peoples do not subscribe to our western view. In some cultures, people account for their actions by reference to invisible spirits and demons and would find our idea that behaviour originates in personality a very strange one . . .

The uniqueness and private nature of much of what we mean by 'personality' is also not a feature of all cultures. For example, we tend to think of our emotions as private events that are bound up with the kind of people we are. A person with a 'depressive' personality might be expected to feel 'sadness' often. We imagine a 'caring' person to have 'loving' feelings. These feelings or emotions are thought of as the internal, private experience of individuals, and are intimately connected to the type of person they are. For example, anger is something we feel inside us, and which is manifested in the things we say and do. However, as Lutz (1982, 1990) has pointed out, this is not the case in all cultures. For the Ifaluk (Samoan and Pintupi Aborigine), emotion words are statements not about people's internal states but about their relationship to events and other people. The Ifaluk talk of song, which in translation comes out as something like 'justifiable anger'. This justifiable anger is not a privately owned feeling, but a moral and public account of some transgression of accepted social practices and values.

Of course we could claim that these cultural differences are due to differences in education and understanding. We could suggest that non-western cultures (and those of previous historical periods) do not have the benefit of our knowledge. What we would be doing then is making a claim about the truthfulness of our own view as opposed to the falsity of theirs. We would be saying 'We know that in fact people have personalities, and that the way people behave is heavily influenced by their personality. People in other cultures have not realised this yet, and they therefore hold a false view of reality.' This is to state the case rather strongly, but it makes the point that unless we have complete confidence in the 'personality really exists' view, we have to accept that personality may be a theory which is peculiar to certain societies at a certain point in time . . .

As I mentioned earlier, one of the fundamental assumptions of the common-sense view of personality is that personality is stable across situations and over time. However, this does not stand up to scrutiny when we examine our own day-to-day experience. Do you behave in the same way when you are in the pub with your mates and when you are taking tea with great-uncle Eric? (I'm sure you can find your own equivalents.) Do you talk to your closest friend in the same way as to your bank manager? Do you feel confident, outgoing and 'on the ball' when you are at a party with people you know? What about when you go for a job interview? These examples may look trivial and you will probably already be coming up with explanations for the differences. But the overall message is an important one. We think and feel differently depending on whom we are with, what we are doing and why . . .

The social construction of personality

What might it mean, then, to say that personality is socially constructed? One way of looking at this is to think of personality (the kind of person you are) as existing not within people but between them. This is hard to conceptualise at first, so I will give you some illustrative examples. Take some of the personality-type words we use to describe people: for example, friendly, caring, shy, self-conscious, charming,

V. Burr

bad-tempered, thoughtless. If you like, make your own list of words you could use to describe the people you know. I would predict that most of them will be words which would completely lose their meaning if the person described were living alone on a desert island. Without the presence of other people, that is, a social environment, can a person be said to be 'friendly', 'shy' or 'caring'? The point is that we use these words as if they referred to entities existing within the person they describe, but once the person is removed from their relations with others the words become meaningless. They refer to our behaviour towards other people. The friendliness, shyness or caring exists not inside people, but in the relation between them . . .

Next, think of a person you know, someone with whom you are more than just slightly acquainted. Think about how you are when you are with that person. Perhaps you feel that when you are with her or him you are level-headed and rational. She or he always seems to be leaping from one crisis to another and seems to be in awe of your apparent ability to take the world in your stride. The nature of the relationship between you is one of counsellor and client, or 'the strong one' and 'the weak one'. Now think of someone else with whom you are just the opposite. With this person you always seem to be pouring out your troubles, asking advice and taking the lead from him or her. Perhaps this particular example does not fit you, but you will be able to think of comparable ones. The point is that it makes no sense to ask which of these is the real you. They both are, but each version of 'you' is a product of your relationships with others. Each 'you' is constructed socially, out of the social encounters that make up your relationships.

Task B3.1.2

➤ Read the description you wrote down of your friend's personality in Task B3.1.1. Answer the following questions about this description:

➤ Does your description include in it any indication that your friend's personality might vary depending on: the situation your friend might be in; the different people your friend might be with; any reference to events, actions or behaviour that involve your friend?

➤ Consider the description of your friend's personality in light of what Burr writes in Text B3.1.1. How is your friend 'constructed socially'?

Hampson, S. E. (1997) 'The social psychology of personality'. In Cooper, C. and Varma, V., *Processes in Individual Differences*. London: Routledge. pp. 77–80 (extracts)

Text B3.1.2
S. E. Hampson

The following discussion of the observer in personality construction is organised according to a three-stage model of personality perception . . . In brief, the process of personality construction from the observer's perspective involves (1) the identification of behaviour, (2) the categorisation of behavioural acts, and (3) the attribution of personality. These three stages are usually, but not necessarily, sequential. Whether or not processing proceeds from stage 1 to stage 2, or from stage 2 to stage 3, depends upon the goals of the perceiver/observer. Many social interactions can take place

S. E. Hampson

without going beyond behaviour identification, and many more can be quite satisfactory without engaging in personality attribution . . .

Personality traits can be used by observers/perceivers to describe (categorise) behaviour, or to describe personality. Each use of traits involves different processes. However, psychologists are not always clear on this distinction, and there can be confusion if a study of act categorisation is interpreted as if it were looking at trait attribution, or vice versa. In act categorisation (stage 2), traits are used to describe behaviour. Instead of identifying behaviour (e.g., Jane is carrying John's shopping bag), we use a descriptive category (a trait adjective) to describe it (e.g., Jane is being helpful). The behaviour is categorised as an instance of a particular trait category. In person categorisation, the trait is applied to the person performing the behaviour, not just the behaviour itself (e.g., Jane is helpful). In everyday language, we may blur the distinction between the two uses of traits with no adverse consequences. Indeed, the tendency to use traits to describe persons when we really only mean to categorise behaviours may be another manifestation of the fundamental attribution error, which is the tendency to explain behaviour in dispositional terms and to ignore the part played by the situation . . .

Stage 1: Behaviour identification

The first step in person perception is to identify what it is that a person is doing. Behaviour identification precedes either use of the trait concept. For example, is the person running or walking? Is Jane carrying something? . . .

Stage 2: Act categorisation

Act categorisation can only occur after behaviour identification. It involves further identification of the behaviour as a member of a trait category . . .

Behaviours are composed of three kinds of features: behavioural (the actions that occur), situational (the context in which they occur) and motivational (the underlying motive they reflect), and these features vary in their prototypicality with regard to different trait categories. Motivational features are often key to categorising behaviour and, because motivations have to be inferred from the context and other information, they can be the cause of miscategorisations. A behaviour may appear to be a good member of one category (e.g., Jane carrying John's shopping is a good instance of the trait category helpful), however, if we knew more about the relationship between Jane and John, we might more correctly categorise Jane's behaviour as submissive.

Stage 3: Personality attribution

Personality attribution involves the application of the trait concept to the person performing the behaviour. For example, we describe people as helpful, submissive or altruistic . . . Unlike act categorisation, we do not usually make personality attributions based on just one piece of behaviour (although we may).

In addition, more specific theories can be developed for the conditions under which particular traits will be attributed to persons . . . For positive moral traits such as honesty, many behavioural instances are required to convince the observer that the person is truly honest, whereas for dishonesty, the observer may use just one behaviour to make a trait attribution. If you observe a pickpocket at work in a crowd, you are likely to make an immediate person categorisation (dishonest thief). This is an example of where a person categorisation is made simultaneously with the behaviour categorisation.

Task B3.1.3

➤ Can you think of occasions when you have made false trait attributions on the basis of misinterpreting single instances of behaviour?

Task B3.1.4

The processes involved in behaviour identification and act categorisation as described by Hampson are also salient when considering how we Other individuals who are different to us. This point is made by Gandy (1998) in the following passage:

> We categorise those we believe are different from us into category systems that have less variety than the systems we use for people we think are more like us. In addition, after we have categorised a person as a member of a particular group, that classification affects how we characterise their behaviour. The same behaviour performed by a member of another group will be characterised in different ways on the basis of the structure of beliefs we have already developed about these groups.
>
> (p. 53)

A similar point is made by Kimmel (2006) who sees misattribution as a key factor in negative stereotyping and intercultural conflict. He writes that it is difficult for most adults to:

> understand fully others whose mindsets are inconsistent with their own . . . When the communication and behaviours of 'foreigners' do not square with this mindset, they will usually attribute these communications and behaviours to undesirable character traits and motivations of the 'misbehaving' or 'unreasonable' foreigners, rather than attributing the 'inappropriate' acts and messages to cultural differences.
>
> (p. 629)

➤ Reread Examples A2.3.1 and A3.1.1 in Section A. How far are Gandy's and Kimmel's comments borne out in these examples?

Task B3.1.5

➤ What are the implications of what Burr and Hampson write in the two featured texts in this unit, and of the comments of Gandy and Kimmel, for how we perceive and interpret the behaviour and personalities, and how we ourselves behave, when we come into contact with individuals in or from cultures which are unfamiliar to us?

Commentary

Burr also refers in the text to how emotions are also socially constructed, a view shared by Strongman (1996: 220) who writes that 'Theory deriving from social constructionism . . . has it that emotions (or at least adult human emotions) come from the culture or social concepts . . . The strong form of the social constructionist view of emotion is that *all* human emotions are socially constructed – that is, they are based on beliefs and shaped by language, and ultimately stem from culture. The weaker view is preferred by most in this camp – that is, that some emotions are socially constructed and some are more socially constructed than others. Interest then centres on how any social construction occurs.' For Strongman it is also important to consider roles and situations and how in any one 'macro' culture there will be a complex interplay between different factors: '. . . cultural and institutional roles carry implicit and explicit prescriptions about what emotions should be *expressed* and *experienced* in particular situations, and to what degree these emotions should be *displayed*' (p. 223).

UNIT B3.2 SOCIAL CONSTRUCTIONISM AND SOCIAL REPRESENTATIONS

Unit B3.2 starts with another extract from Burr's introduction to social constructionism which considers how our perceptions of the world might be said to be 'socially constructed'. We also focus on a related notion, that of 'social representations'. Serge Moscovici, who is credited with introducing the concept of 'social representations', documented how terms used in the field of psychology, and specifically in psycho-analysis and psycho-therapy, had come to be used by French people in describing and explaining everyday behaviour and events (1976). Hewstone and Augoustinos (1998: 62) provide their own definition:

> Culturally agreed upon explanations eventually come to be regarded as common-sense explanations. Each society has its own culturally and socially sanctioned explanation or range of explanations for phenomena such as illness, poverty, failure, success, violence, crime, etc. People therefore do not always need to engage in an active cognitive search for explanations for all forms of behaviour and events. Instead, people evoke their socialised processing or social representations for expected and normative behaviour and events.

Crucially, social representations have an historical dimension; Moscovici (1998: 242) writes that they are 'the product of a whole sequence of elaborations and of changes which occur in the course of time and are the achievement of successive generations. All the systems of classification, all the images and all the descriptions which circulate within a society . . . imply a link with previous systems and images, a stratification in the collective memory and a reproduction in the language, which invariably reflects past knowledge, and which breaks the bounds of current information' (1998: 244). Sperber, who writes that 'To explain culture, then, is to explain why and how some ideas happen to be contagious' (1996: 1), attempts to construct his own model of social representations which we shall consider in Text B3.2.2.

Burr, V. (1995) *An Introduction to Social Constructionism*. London: Routledge. pp. 2–5 (extracts)

Text B3.2.1
V. Burr

You might think of these as something like 'things you would absolutely have to believe in order to be a social constructionist':

1. A critical stance towards taken-for-granted knowledge:

Social constructionism insists that we take a critical stance towards our taken-for-granted ways of understanding the world (including ourselves). It invites us to be critical of the idea that our observations of the world unproblematically yield its nature to us, to challenge the view that conventional knowledge is based upon objective, unbiased observation of the world. It is therefore in opposition to what are referred to as positivism and empiricism in traditional science – the assumptions that the nature of the world can be revealed by observation, and that what exists is what we perceive to exist. Social constructionism cautions us to be ever suspicious of our assumptions about how the world appears to be. This means that the categories with which we as human beings apprehend the world do not necessarily refer to real divisions . . .

2. Historical and cultural specificity:

The ways in which we commonly understand the world, the categories and concepts we use, are historically and **culturally** specific . . . this means that all ways of understanding are historically and culturally relative. Not only are they specific to particular cultures and periods of history, they are seen as products of that culture and history, and are dependent upon the particular social and economic arrangements prevailing in that culture at that time. The particular forms of knowledge that abound in any culture are therefore artefacts of it, and we should not assume that our ways of understanding are necessarily any better (in terms of being any nearer the truth) than other ways.

3. Knowledge is sustained by social processes:

If our knowledge of the world, our common ways of understanding it, is not derived from the nature of the world as it really is, where does it come from? The social constructionist answer is that people construct it between them. It is through the daily interactions between people in the course of social life that our versions of knowledge become fabricated. Therefore social interaction of all kinds, and particularly language, is of great interest to social constructionists. The goings-on between people in the course of their everyday lives are seen as the practices during which our shared versions of knowledge are constructed. Therefore what we regard as 'truth' (which of course varies historically and cross-culturally), that is, our current accepted ways of understanding the world, is a product not of objective observation of the world, but of the social processes and interactions in which people are constantly engaged with each other.

4. Knowledge and social action go together:

These 'negotiated' understandings could take a wide variety of different forms, and we can therefore talk of numerous possible 'social constructions' of the world. But each different construction also brings with it, or invites, a different kind of action from human beings. For example, before the Temperance movement, drunks were seen as entirely responsible for their behaviour, and therefore blameworthy. A typical response was therefore imprisonment. However, there has been a move away from seeing drunkenness as a crime and towards thinking of it as a sickness, a kind of addiction . . .

Task B3.2.1

➤ Think about the ways: (1) the different regions of the world are 'divided up', (2) people of the world are divided up into 'large cultures'.

➤ In what ways are these social constructs? What part do the news media and advertising play in promoting these social constructs?

Text B3.2.2
D. Sperber

Sperber, D. (1996) *Explaining Culture: A Naturalistic Approach.* Oxford: Blackwell. pp. 24, 32–3, 81–2 (extracts)

What are cultural things made of?

Let us start as simply as possible. Cultural things are, in part, made of bodily movements of individuals and of environmental changes resulting from these movements. For instance, people are beating drums, or erecting a building, or slaughtering an animal. The material character of these phenomena is, so far, unproblematic. But we must go further. Is it a musical exercise, a drummed message, or a ritual? Is it a house, a shop, or a temple? Is it butchery, or sacrifice? In order to answer, one must, one way or another, take into account the representations involved in these behaviours. Whatever one's theoretical or methodological framework, representations play an essential role in defining cultural phenomena. But what are representations made of?

Let us note, to begin with, that two types of representations are involved: mental representations and public representations. Beliefs, intentions and preferences are mental representations . . . Signals, utterances, texts and pictures are all public representations. Public representations have an obviously material aspect. However, describing this aspect – the sounds of speech, the shapes and colours of a picture – leaves out the most important fact, that these material traces can be interpreted: they represent something for someone.

Interpreting and explaining cultural representations

A representation sets up a relationship between at least three terms: that which represents, that which is represented, and the user of the representation. A fourth term may be added when there is a producer of the representation distinct from its user. A representation may exist inside its user: it is then a mental representation, such as a memory, a belief, or an intention. The producer and the user of a mental representation are one and the same person. A representation may also exist in the environment of its user, as is the case, for instance, of the text you are presently reading; it is then a public representations. Public representations are usually means of communication between a user and a producer distinct from one another. A mental representation has, of course, a single user. A public representation may have several . . .

Consider a social group: a tribe, the inhabitants of a town, or the members of an association. Such a group and its common environment are, so to speak, inhabited by a much larger population of representations, mental and public. Each member of the group has, in his or her head, millions of mental representations, some short-lived, others stored in long-term memory and constituting the individual's 'knowledge'. Of these mental representations, some – a very small proportion – get communicated repeatedly, and end up being distributed throughout the group, and thus have a mental version in most of its members. When we speak of cultural representations, we have in mind – or should have in mind – such widely distributed, lasting representations. Cultural representations so understood are a fuzzy subset of the set of mental and public representations inhabiting a given social group . . .

Public representations are generally attributed similar meanings by their producers and by their users, or else they could never serve the purpose of communication. This similarity of attributed meaning is itself made possible by the fact that people have similar enough linguistic and encyclopaedic knowledge. Similarity across people makes it possible to abstract from individual differences and to describe 'the language' or 'the culture' of a community, 'the meaning' of a public representation, or to talk of, say, 'the belief' that witches ride on broomsticks as a single representation, independently of its public expressions or mental instantiations. What is then described is an abstraction. Such an abstraction may be useful in many ways: it may bring out the common properties of a family of related mental and public representations; it may serve to identify a topic of research.

Task B3.2.3

Burr gives the example of how views of drunks and drunkenness are socially constructed, and how these social constructs have changed over time. She also talks of how 'typical responses' that have been made to drunks and drunkenness have also changed over time.

➤ In a 'social group' you see yourself as a member of, how have the social constructions of the following people and issues changed over time?

- Gays/Lesbianism and Homosexuality
- Divorcees/Divorce
- People who suffer from 'mental illness'/'Mental illness'
- Women who have abortions/Abortion
- Criminals/Crime

> What have been 'typical responses' to these people and issues in your social group at different times?

  ■ What particular 'cultural representations' (in Sperber's understanding of the term) of the people and issues are currently widely distributed in your social group, and what do 'typical responses' currently consist of?

Commentary

For Van Dijk there is a close relationship between social representations and ideologies. He defines (1998: 8) ideologies as 'the basis of the social representations shared by members of a group'. An important question concerning social representations is that of how far the individual is bound by networks of social representations. Oyserman and Markus (1998: 117–18) assert that 'individuals may resist or fail to incorporate . . . public and mutually constructed ideas . . . into their meaning-making systems', but state that more research is needed into 'how many individuals in a given socio-cultural niche must share' social representations and 'with what level of incorporation and understanding, and of how much resistance or outright negation can be tolerated within a given cultural system'. Augoustinos (1998: 165) claims, too, that 'people may not simply endorse or reject dominant views, but rather, develop complex configurations of thought in which some dominant ideological elements find expression in conjunction with individual and group-based understandings'.

UNIT B3.3   REPRESENTATION IN THE MEDIA – THE CASE OF 'ASYLUM SEEKERS'

In Unit B3.3 we focus first on the often narrow ways that those in the news media, sometimes unconsciously, represent others. In particular, we focus on the representation of those commonly described in the media as 'asylum seekers'. We start by considering two sentences in the novel *By the Sea* by the British-based writer Abdul Razak Gurnah (2001), two sentences which suggests that the language we use to describe those seeking refuge or asylum plays an important part in how we perceive them. In the first text in this unit, Teun van Dijk, who has written extensively about the ideological nature of discourse and about 'critical' approaches to discourse analysis, describes the role of discourse in a 'new' form of racism, and analyses specific techniques used in the media which help to promote it. In Text B3.3.3 Gail Moloney analyses the stereotypical representations of those seeking asylum in Australia in satirical press cartoons, and this is prefaced by a definition of stereotyping from O'Sullivan *et al.* (1994) *Key Concepts in Communication and Cultural Studies* (Text B3.3.2). With Text B3.3.4, a second extract from the paper by Verschueren that was featured in Unit B0.3, we move away from media representation of asylum seekers and immigrants and focus on the ways in which asylum seekers are subject to and expected to tell their 'stories' in particular ways, ways which have the result of immediately putting them at a disadvantage when in communication with individuals in positions of authority.

Task B3.3.1

In a passage near the beginning of Abdul Razak Gurnah's novel *By the Sea*, an individual who is fleeing his own country, has no visa or permission to enter the United Kingdom, and is hoping to be given permission to stay in the UK, arrives by air at Gatwick Airport, near London. The story is narrated by the new arrival:

> I am a refugee, an asylum-seeker. These are not simple words, even if the habit of hearing them makes them seem so.
>
> (p. 4)

Before you read B3.3.1:

➤ Consider in what ways 'refugee' and 'asylum seeker' are *not* 'simple words'

➤ What do you think the narrator means when he says that 'the habit of hearing' the words 'refugee' and 'asylum seeker' makes them seem simple?

Task B3.3.2

Before reading Text B3.3.1, consider the following question:

➤ If you were to carry out an analysis of how 'asylum seekers' are represented in written news reports media, the most obvious starting point is to analyse the words or phrases use to describe 'asylum seekers'. What other features of such reports would you analyse?

van Dijk, T. A. (2000) 'New(s) racism: a discourse analytical approach'. Second short draft (July 1998) accessed online at www.hum.ura. nl/2teun/racpress.htm of chapter published in Cottle, S. (ed.) *Ethnic Minorities and the Media.* Buckingham: Open University Press

Text B3.3.1
T. A. van Dijk

The New Racism

In many respects, contemporary forms of racism are different from the 'old' racism of slavery, segregation, apartheid, lynchings, and systematic discrimination, of white superiority feelings, and of explicit derogation in public discourse and everyday conversation. The New Racism (Barker 1981) wants to be democratic and respectable, and hence first denies that it is racism. Real Racism, in this framework of thought, only exists among the Extreme Right. In the New Racism, minorities are not biologically inferior, but different. They have a different culture, although in many respects there are 'deficiencies', such as single-parent families, drug abuse, lacking achievement values, and dependence on welfare and affirmative action – 'pathologies' that need to be corrected of course . . .

The role of discourse

Especially because of their often subtle and symbolic nature, many forms of the 'new' racism are *discursive*: they are expressed, enacted and confirmed by text and talk, such as everyday conversations, board meetings, job interviews, policies, laws, parliamentary debates, political propaganda, textbooks, scholarly articles, movies, TV programs and news reports in the press, among hundreds of other genres. They appear 'mere' talk, and far removed from the open violence and forceful segregation of the 'old' racism. Yet, they may be just as effective to marginalise and exclude minorities. They may hurt even more, especially when they seem to be so 'normal', so 'natural', and so 'commonsensical' to those who engage in such discourse and interaction . . .

Discourse analytical approaches

Discourse analytical approaches systematically describe the various structures and strategies of text or talk, and relate these to the social or political context. For instance, they may focus on overall topics, or more local meanings (such as coherence or implications) in a *semantic* analysis. But also the *syntactic* form of sentences, or the overall *organisation* of a news report may be examined in detail. The same is true for variations of style, *rhetorical* devices such as metaphors or euphemisms, *speech* acts such as promises and threats, and in spoken discourse also the many forms of *interaction* . . . These structures of text and talk are systematically related to elements of the social context, such as the spatio-temporal setting, participants and their various social and communicative roles, as well as their goals, knowledge and opinions.

The role of the media

There is no need to argue here the overall power of the media in modern 'information' societies . . . the power of the media is primarily discursive and symbolic. Media discourse is the main source of people's knowledge, attitudes and ideologies, both of other elites as well as of ordinary citizens. Of course, the media do this in joint production with the other elites, primarily politicians, professionals and academics. Yet, given the freedom of the press, the media elites are ultimately responsible for the prevailing discourses of the media they control.

This is specifically also true for the role of the media in ethnic affairs, for the following reasons:

(a) Most white readers have few daily experiences with minorities
(b) Most white readers have few alternative sources for information about minorities
(c) Negative attitudes about minorities are in the interest of most white readers
(d) More than most other topics, ethnic issues provide positive but polarised identification for most white readers, in terms of Us and Them
(e) The media emphasise such group polarisation by focusing on various Problems and Threats for Us, thus actively involving most white readers

(f)   Minority groups do not have enough power to publicly oppose biased reporting
(g)   The dominant (media) discourse on ethnic issues is virtually consensual
(h)   In particular there is little debate on the 'new' racism
(i)   'Anti-racist' dissidents have little access to the media.

In sum, when power over the most influential form of public discourse, that is, media discourse, is combined with a lack of alternative sources, when there is a near consensus, and opponents and dissident groups are weak, then the media are able to abuse of such power and establish the discursive and cognitive hegemony that is necessary for the reproduction of the 'new' racism. Let us now examine in some more detail how exactly such power is exercised in news and news-making.

News structures

. . . On ethnic issues, for which alternative sources of information are scarce, news on TV or in the press often provides the first 'facts', but at the same time the first 'definitions of the situation' and the first opinions – usually those of the authorities or other white elites.

Topics

Interestingly, whereas there are a large number of types of topic in the press, news about immigrants and ethnic minorities is often restricted to the following kind of events:

(1)   New (illegal) immigrants are arriving.
(2)   Political response to, policies about (new) immigration.
(3)   Reception problems (housing, etc.).
(4)   Social problems (employment, welfare, etc.).
(5)   Response of the population (resentment, etc.).
(6)   Cultural characterisation: How are they different?
(7)   Complications: Negative characterisation: How are they deviant?
(8)   Focus on Threats: Violence, crime, drugs, prostitution.
(9)   Political response: Policies to stop immigration, expulsion, etc.
(10) Integration conflicts.

In each of these cases, even potentially 'neutral' topics, such as immigration, housing, employment off cultural immigration, soon tend to have a negative dimension: Immigration may be topicalised as a threat, and most ethnic relations represented in terms of problems and deviance if not as a threat as well, most typically so in news about crime, drugs and violence minorities are associated with. On the other hand, many topics that are also part of ethnic affairs occur much less in the news, such as migrants leaving the country, the contributions of immigrant workers to the economy, everyday life of minority communities, and especially also discrimination and racism against minorities. Since topics express the most important information of a text, and in news are further signalled by prominent headlines and leads, they are also best understood and memorised by the readers. In other words, negative topics have negative consequences on the 'minds' of the recipients.

T. A. van Dijk

In general what we find is a preference for those topics that emphasise Their bad actions and Our good ones. On the other hand, Their good actions and Our bad ones are not normally emphasised by topicalisation (and will therefore also appear less in headlines or on the front page, if reported at all). This general strategy of positive self-presentation and negative other-presentation is prevalent in most dominant discourse about immigrants and minorities . . .

Local meanings

Derogatory words in racist discourse are well-known, and need not be spelled out here. The new racism, as described above, however, avoids explicitly racist labels, and uses negative words to describe the properties or actions of immigrants or minorities (for instance, 'illegal'). Special *code-words* (such as 'welfare mothers') may be used, and the readers are able to interpret these words in terms of minorities and the problems attributed to them. And it needs no further argument that attitudes about groups and opinions about specific events may influence the lexical choice of such words as 'riot' on the one hand, or 'urban unrest', 'disturbance' or 'uprising' on the other hand, as is also the case for the classical example of 'terrorist' vs. 'rebel' vs. 'freedom fighter'. Thus, most mentions of 'terrorists' (especially also in the U.S. press) will stereotypically refer to Arabs. Violent men who are our friends or allies will seldom get that label. For the same reason, 'drug barons' are always Latin men in South America, never the white men who are in the drugs business within the USA itself. In other words, when there are options of lexicalisation, choosing one word rather than another often has contextual reasons, such as the opinions of the speaker about a person, a group or their actions.

Modern linguistics and discourse analysis, however, goes beyond the study of isolated words, and also studies the *meaning of sentences* or sequences of sentences and their role in the text as a whole. Thus, sentence meanings also show what specific roles participants have, for instance as responsible agents, targets or victims of action. What we find in such an analysis is in line of the general strategy mentioned above: Minorities are often represented in a passive role (things are being decided, done, etc. for or against them), unless they are agents of negative actions, such as illegal entry, crime, violence, or drug abuse. In the latter case their responsible agency will be emphasised.

Much of the information in discourse, and hence also in news reports, is implicit, and supplied by the recipients on the basis of their knowledge of the context and of the world. Also in news and editorials about ethnic affairs, thus, many meanings are merely *implied or presupposed* and not explicitly stated. Because of social norms, and for reasons of impression management, for instance, many negative things about minorities may not be stated explicitly, and thus are conveyed 'between the lines'. For instance in a sentence like 'The rising crime in the inner city worried the politicians', it is presupposed, and not explicitly stated, that there is rising crime in the inner city, as if this were a known 'fact'.

★ Task B3.3.3

➤ Find at least one report from the media which focuses on those seeking to be given, or who have been given, permission to stay in a particular country after they have fled their own.

➤ How does this report provide the first 'definitions of the situation' and the 'first opinions' as well as the first 'facts'?

➤ What negative words and phrases are used in the report to 'describe the properties or actions of immigrants'?

➤ What specific roles does the report represent immigrants as playing?

➤ What part do the following play in negatively framing immigrants and asylum seekers: lexical choices; the overall organisation of the news report; the syntactic form of sentences; variations of style; metaphors and euphemisms; speech acts?

An interesting trend in the British media in recent years has been the tendency to distinguish between the 'genuine' and the 'bogus' asylum seeker (Lynn and Lea 2003). However, the 'genuine' asylum seeker is represented 'as being such a rarity as to be almost irrelevant' (Lynne and Lea 2003: 446). What is more, the 'genuine' asylum seeker is understood in terms of the negative otherisation of the 'bogus' asylum seeker. A good example of this appeared in an article by Penny Wark in the *Times Online* on 17th November 2004 which focused on Amin Buratee, an Afghan teenager threatened with deportation:

> Perhaps you think that his story is one of an asylum seeker who flees a blighted country, leeches off the British benefit system, engages in crime and deserves to be thrown out. Amin's story is much simpler than this. And what is remarkable is that over the past nine days almost everyone who has got to know him in Kent has rallied to campaign for him to be allowed to stay in Britain . . . No, Amin's story does not concern an abusive young man. Rather it is one that shows that if you are gentle and earnest, dignified and trusting—and you then come up against an inflexible system, in this case the immigration policy—you may be treated inhumanely. Amin, who is 18, has done nothing wrong, he has not broken any rules, he is not a criminal.

Stereotypes

Stuart Hall (1997: 268) writes that 'Stereotypes get hold of the few simple, vivid, memorable, easily grasped and widely recognised characteristics about a person, reduce everything about that person to those traits, exaggerate and simplify them, and fix them without change or development to eternity.' Moreover, stereotyping both reflects and promotes particular perspectives; O'Sullivan *et al.* in Text B3.3.2 refer to the historical dimension to stereotypes and to the 'power relations, tensions and conflicts' which underlie them.

Text B3.3.2
T. O'Sullivan,
J. Hartley,
D. Saunders,
M. Montgomery
and J. Fiske

O'Sullivan, T., Hartley, J., Saunders, D., Montgomery, M. and Fiske, J. (1994) *Key Concepts in Communication and Cultural Studies*. London: Routledge. pp. 299–300 (extracts)

Stereotyping is:

the social classification of particular groups and people as often highly simplified and generalised signs, which implicitly or explicitly represent a set of values, judgements and assumptions concerning their behaviour, characteristics or history.

In the field of social psychology stereotyping:

has been defined as a particular extension of the fundamental cognitive processes of categorisation, whereby we impose structure and make sense of events, objects and experience. The process in itself requires the simplification and organisation of diverse and complex ranges of phenomena into general, labelled categories. In so doing attention is focused on certain similar identifying characteristics or distinctive features, as opposed to many other differences. Stereotypes, however, not only identify general categories of people: national populations (e.g., the Irish), races (e.g., the Latin race), classes (e.g., the working class), genders (i.e. men or women), occupations (e.g., accountants) and deviant groups (e.g., drug takers), etc., they are distinct-ive in the way that they carry *undifferentiated judgements* about their referents. Whilst they may vary widely in terms of their emotional appeal and intensity, they generally represent underlying power relations, tensions or conflicts (i.e. the 'stupid' Irish, the 'excitable' Latins, the 'cloth cap' image, the 'dumb blond', the 'boring' accountant, the 'evil' junkie and so on). In short, they operate to define and identify groups of people as generally alike in certain ways – as committed to particular values, motivated by similar goals, having a common personality, make-up and so on. In this way stereotypes encourage an *intuitive belief* in their own underlying assumptions, and play a central role in organising common sense discourse . . .

A key stereotyping device of satirical press cartoons is caricature. Caricature, states Moloney, the author of Text B3.3.3, 'predominantly works at group level; the caricature of a person is representative of a group or institution' and 'it is this enigmatic leap from individual to group that affords the cartoon, and particularly the caricature, its power' [2007: 72].

In order to understand the cartoons (see Figures B3.3.1, B3.3.2 and B3.3.3) it is important to understand something of the context and of the 'power relations, tensions and conflicts' in that context. Moloney writes that; 'The imposed refugee and asylum-seeker identity is one informed by Australia's concern over border protection, nationalism and sovereignty'. More specifically, in August 2001, 433 Afghani people were rescued from their sinking boat close to Australia and the captain of the Tampa requested permission to land them in Australia, but the Australian government refused. Two months later another ship, the *SIEV-4* was found to be carrying asylum seekers and a political scandal ensued when the Australian minister of immigration produced what transpired to be false photographic 'evidence' that 'a number of the children had been thrown overboard in an attempt to get the Australian navy to rescue them and thus grant them asylum' [p. 65].

Figure B3.3.1
Editorial cartoon
in *The Australian*
referred to in
Text B3.3.3

Figure B3.3.2
Cartoon in
The Australian
referred to in
Text B3.3.3

Figure B3.3.3
Cartoon in
*Coffs Coast
Advocate*
referred to in
Text B3.3.3

Task B3.3.4

➤ Before reading the extract analyse the three cartoons on page 181 and think about:

■ The emotional appeal and intensity of the cartoons.
■ The ways in which 'attention is focused on certain similar identifying characteristics or distinctive features'.
■ What other 'highly simplified and generalised signs' there are in the cartoons and how these, 'implicitly or explicitly represent a set of values, judgements and assumptions' concerning the behaviour, characteristics and history of the people represented.

Text B3.3.3
G. Moloney

Moloney, G. (2007) 'Social representations and the politically satirical cartoon: the construction and reproduction of the refugee and asylum-seeker identity.' In Moloney, G. and Walker, I. (eds) *Social Representations and Identity: Content, Process and Power.* New York: Palgrave Macmillan. pp. 73–8 (extracts)

The construction of the editorial cartoon

This editorial cartoon [Figure B3.3.1] appeared in *The Australian* newspaper on Wednesday, September 5, 2001, when Prime Minister John Howard was 'relocating' the Afghani people rescued by the Tampa. A satirical commentary on the insensitivity of governments to the plight of asylum-seekers, the cartoon has, as Manning and Phiddian (2004) describe, indignation cartooning as its intent: the legitimacy and office are not the urgent issues; rather, the action and the manner in which the office is dealing with the issue are. This form of cartooning draws the reader 'emotionally and intelligently' into the issue (Manning and Phiddian 2004, 35). However, regardless of the cartoon's intent, it is the construction of the character that is the asylum-seeker that is important here.

The first point in such an analysis is social distance. Van Leeuwen (2000) argues that the distance in visual representation is symbolic of the relationship that 'society' has with the people in the image. Depicted as 'not one of us,' distance in the lens shot can convey notions of othering. For example, a long shot in which a person is positioned further back in the image connotes a social distance between the viewer and that person, particularly when that distance is differential to other distance shots in the image. In the cartoon reproduced above, the Afghani people are positioned farther back than both John Howard and New Zealand Prime Minister Helen Clark, indicative perhaps of the difference in our familiarity with these people (see van Leeuwen 2000). The synchronised pose of the asylum-seekers augments this social distance through typification, which itself is accentuated by the individuality conferred by the fine detail given in the portrayal of John Howard and Helen Clark. Helen Clark carries a handbag; John Howard wears a tie.

Physiognomic stereotypes—exaggerated noses and accentuated moustaches—are used to depict the asylum-seekers, denoting the ethnicity or country of origin of the group, despite the word 'Afghanis' being included in the cartoon text. With their uncanny resemblance to Saddam Hussein, these people may be from regimes associated with evil and terror, or they may quite simply be camel drivers from central Asia. Whoever these people are, the use of physiognomic stereotypes implies that they are not like us. The averted gaze of the asylum-seekers (from the viewer) signifies quite subtly that these people are not the viewer's problem (see van Leeuwen 2000, 2001). There is no need to engage with these people or, more importantly, to engage with their plight.

Similar constructions can be seen in the two cartoons . . . [Figures B3.3.2 and B3.3.3] which appeared respectively in the national *Australian* newspaper and the regional *Coffs Coast Advocate*. The cartoon . . . [in Figure B3.3.2] appeared on November 1, 2001, as comment on the Australian government's continued treatment of asylum-seekers. The one . . . [in Figure B3.3.3] appeared on August 13, 2004, as a comment on the treatment of refugees fleeing famine in Sudan. Both are examples of how caricature inadvertently begets a distant other, despite a cartooning style designed to engage the viewer with the issue (Manning and Phiddian 2004). The headscarf and physiognomic stereotype of an exaggerated nose in the cartoon . . . [in Figure B3.3.2] suggest that the asylum-seekers are central-Asian Muslims, while the infantile stereotype (large head and bulbous eyes) in . . . [Figure B3.3.3] intimates helplessness and naïvety. In both instances, the stereotyping and typification construct a social distance between the viewer and the people, augmented by a vertical distance that denotes asymmetrical power relations between asylum-seekers and the government in the cartoon in . . . [Figure B3.3.2], and between refugees and world institutions in the cartoon in . . . [Figure B3.3.3]. This symbolism conveys their dependency not only on these institutions but, of course, on the viewer, as well.

In all three of the cartoons reproduced in this chapter, the image is one of helplessness and dependency, but also, through typification, one that negates individuality, thus casting these groups as 'others' from the point of view of Australians . . . This cartooning style was a consistent feature of the 237 cartoons found across the three newspapers over the three-year period surveyed. Table B3.3.1 presents the frequency of the styles as found across the cartoons.

Commentary

Van Leeuwen's ideas on 'social distance' in visual representation, that are referred to by Moloney, are shared by van Ginneken (1998), who examined how news photographs 'frame' a subject, and how there are three physical dimensions to such framing: 'the direction in which the camera is pointed', the distance to the subject, and the vertical angle, in terms of whether a photograph 'looks up or down at a subject'. As regards the second of these, he writes that: 'the physical distance may or may not translate into psychological distance, and vice versa', and that:

> First World subjects are on average pictured from a shorter distance than Second or Third World subjects; the former tend to be more often identified as individuals, the latter remain largely anonymous. This adds to other mechanisms privileging our identification with the former rather than the latter.
>
> (p. 170)

Table B3.3.1 Frequency of cartooning characteristics in 237 cartoons

Cartooning characteristic	Frequency
Physiognomic Stereotype	
Large nose	63
Large mustache	46
Long beard	31
Bulbous eyes/infantile	30
Synchronised Pose	
Group with same feature	41
Group in same position or direction	57
Single individual	13
Presence of symbol or cultural artefact	
Boat	38
Detention center	42
Burqa (full)	6
Burqa (open face)	29
Headscarf	8
Turban	29
Robe	27
Symbolic distance and passivity	
Vertical distance from non-refugee	14
Horizontal distance from non-refugee	16
Bowed head or shoulders	19
Non-refugee is large	27

Halliday's influential social semiotic approach to the analysis of language has been increasingly applied to the analysis of visual images. Goodman (1996), for example, is especially interested in the notions of transitivity and modality and employs a Hallidayan approach in her analysis. As regards transitivity she writes that, in analysing a photograph, it is important to focus on: '*processes* (what is going on) and *participants* (the entities involved with what is going on) . . . *Participants* can be involved in material processes in one of two ways, as *actor*, that is as "the one who does the deed" or as *goal*, that is, as "the one to whom the deed identity done" or "to whom the event happens"' (p. 56). Kress and van Leeuwen (2001) have outlined a multi-modal approach to the analysis of discourse through which:

> the attempt is to understand all the representational modes which are in play in the text, in the same degree of detail and with the same methodological precision as discourse analysis is able to do with linguistic text.

(p. 258)

Moloney concludes that: 'The imposed refugee and asylum-seeker identity' in the three cartoons 'does not represent these people, their histories or their cultures. It is instead a vacuous, administrative identity that is a construction of how they are seen in relation to us. As an imposed social identity, the refugees and asylum-seekers represent a location in our social knowledge about these issues and an identity pre-determined before these people set foot on Australian soil' (p. 78). The talk of a 'predetermined' identity recalls Benedict Anderson's notion of the 'imagined community' (1983). An important factor in such 'imagining' is 'myth'. In much of his early work Roland Barthes was concerned with myths of nationality, particularly French nationality. For Barthes myth has a naturalising effect: 'myth is constituted by the historical loss of the quality of things; in it, things lose the memory that they were once made of . . . The function of myth is to empty reality . . . Myth does not deny things, on the contrary, its function is to talk about them; simply it purifies them, it makes them innocent, it gives them a natural and eternal justification . . .' (1973: 142–3). Such ideas have been influential to the work of those who have investigated how national and racial identity is constructed, such as Wodak *et al.* (1999) who analyse the discursive construction of Austrian national identity.

Task B3.3.5

➤ Find cartoons or newspaper/magazine photographs of asylum seekers and/or other minority groups in your own context and analyse them in detail.

➤ Does your analysis confirm the findings of Moloney?

➤ How far do these cartoons reflect 'power relations, tensions and conflicts' in your own context?

In Unit B1.3 we referred to De Fina's assertion that: 'what defines people as members of a group is not only the content of their stories, but the way in which they use socially established resources to tell them'. In the final text in this unit we return to the article by Verschueren, extracts of which were included in Unit B0.3. Verschueren considers how the 'stories' immigrants are asked to tell about themselves 'creates narrative inequalities in the asylum procedure'. Verschueren refers to events and procedures in Belgium, but the issues raised have relevance for all contexts in which people are seeking asylum.

Verschueren, J. (2008) 'Intercultural communication and the challenges of migration'. *Language and Intercultural Communication* 8/1: 21–35. pp. 31–4 (extracts)

Text B3.3.4
J. Verschueren

Consider the following:

> The story of the applicant is *not precise on many counts*. Thus, she could not specify *the family name* of a childhood friend with whom she stayed. She also failed to specify *the date* on which she was supposed to have escaped from Lagos.
>
> (De Morgen, 3.10.98 [translation and italics ours])

This fragment from a newspaper report on the death of a Nigerian asylum-seeker (Sémira Adamu, who was suffocated with a cushion used to keep her under control when put on an airplane to be deported to Africa) quotes the text of the official letter in which the rejection of her asylum application was announced. Interestingly, the central argument is textual: Sémira's story was *not precise on many counts*. What follows are two arguments, one referring to the absence of a precise recollection of a *family name*, the second of *a date*. Both elements are obviously 'details', not necessarily crucial to an understanding of the sequential ordering of events the story is supposed to contain. Also, they are both elements of an *encyclopaedic* and *documentary* nature, the sort of things people write down or keep in a diary or seek to document in other ways. They are the sort of things people can forget more easily than, for example, general experiential things such as a sense of danger, anxiety, stress or a general atmosphere in a place. When one has had a car accident, the accident itself is often remembered in fantastic detail – the sound of the crash, one's own position in the car, the sight of the other car coming closer – while other things such as the precise date, hour or clothes one was wearing may be a lot more difficult to remember.

Asylum-seekers are expected to remember everything, including details such as brand names and types of cars (not just 'Volkswagen', but 'a black Volkswagen Golf Turbo Diesel'), addresses, timetables, people's names, the precise moments of boats leaving the harbour, the shape of buildings and so forth. In the asylum procedure, the applicant's story is the centrepiece. Upon their arrival in Belgium, asylum seekers are interviewed about their motives for seeking asylum, about the trajectory they followed from their home country to Belgium, about the actual travelling process, the means of transport, the people who helped them, other people they met, about the actual situation back home. They can be – and mostly are – interviewed repeatedly, and a number of stylistic-generic expectations are imposed upon them:

(1) Perfect replicability of the story: it is expected of them that they are capable of reproducing *exactly the same story* again and again.
(2) *Linearity and logic* in the story: it needs to be told according to strict rules of chronology and coherence.
(3) The capacity to provide *details* for every part of the story: they need to be able to document every episode of the story by means of additional observations and facts.

The model for treating asylum seekers' stories is that of the forensic treatment of testimonies and affidavits. It presupposes preparation and planning on the part of the one who provides the statement: witnesses or the accused are supposed to 'get their story right' and fill it up from the start with all kinds of controllable elements such as time frames, reference points, people who can support their story.

The point is that this is a *literate* narrative tactic. The genre of 'testimony' requires a documentary record, textual or otherwise, and a capacity to tell stories in a particular way. It is a form of expert narrative, and experts such as lawyers often contribute significantly to shaping the story, placing the sequences in the correct order and documenting the episodes. It is a socio-culturally anchored way of speaking which can be imposed (and is imposed) as strictly normative in the procedure. Differing narrative norms and conventions, ranging from differing ways of telling stories to the

J. Verschueren

use of nonstandard accents or language varieties can all be picked up to sanction the story teller and create obstacles to justice (see for example, Jacquemet 1992; O'Barr and Conley 1996). It has been observed (by O'Barr and Conley as well as by Jacquemet; see also Briggs 1997) that court and legal proceedings involve complex ways of text ordering and text structuring, in which literate, matter-of-fact and detached text models are privileged over oral, anecdotal, emotional or experiential ones. Thus we meet narrative inequalities: only some stories, more precisely stories that bear particular kinds of textual characteristics, are accepted as 'good', truthful', 'reliable', while others are easily dismissed as 'not to the point', 'contradictory', outright 'unreliable' or even 'lies' (see Hymes and Cazden 1981); the person who tells them is in turn morally categorised as (un)reliable or (un)truthful.

Summarising so far, we see that legal qualifications of considerable weight and relevance, such as the truth-value of statements and stories and the moral qualities of the story teller, are embedded in particular, genre-specific ways of treating their texts and utterances, and that these ways of treating texts and utterances are strongly connected to society-specific customs and patterns of authority, as well as to forms of literacy and control over linguistic-communicative skills that belong to the realm of expert discourse. These are 'textualist' ways of treating stories and utterances, based on a language ideology of transparency and perfect replicability (Collins 1996). Consequently, asylum seekers experience considerable difficulties in handling these textual and narrative requirements.

Combined with a demand for high literacy skills – asylum seekers are confronted with a considerable amount of complex paperwork usually framed in a legalistic register – the requirement to tell their story in a particular genre-specific way creates narrative inequalities in the asylum procedure. The linguistic-communicative resources required to comply adequately with the procedure are exclusive resources, access to which is controlled by institutional channels (e.g. education) as well as by support from expert groups (lawyers, social welfare workers and so on). Non-members of Belgian society (in the sense of the 'typical society' sketched above) find it very hard to acquire these resources and often experience them as a priori obstacles to justice and participation in society. Knowing how to read and write (in a variety of genres) are mere preconditions for a complex of discursive practices that are highly sophisticated, extremely complex and yet crucial to obtaining rights and benefits. Their 'storytelling rights' (Hymes and Cazden 1981) are conditioned by access to storytelling resources which, in effect, require membership in the society they try to enter.

The field of tension that emerges, then, is one between a semi-legal frame of interpretation (with clear interpretation rules that lead to an evaluation of an asylum request and the ultimate decision) and the intrinsic properties of life stories (which do not match the almost inevitable rules handled in the procedure). The procedure can hardly avoid emphasising the collection of reliable facts, for which precision is important, and the soundness of the argumentation, for which coherence is crucial. Diametrically opposed to that is the context of the life stories that are told, a context that is usually confused and confusing and not fit for exact documentation. On top of that, there is the psychological pressure under which stories have to be told and answers have to be given, with stakes that are extremely high. Finally, there is the nature of life stories in general, which even under relaxed conditions often appear chaotic and always carry the potential of contradiction across a number of retellings [pp. 31–4]

Task B3.3.6

Verschueren writes that: 'the requirement to tell their story in a particular genre-specific way creates narrative inequalities in the asylum procedure'.

➤ In what other contexts in a new society do recently arrived immigrants need to develop 'storytelling resources' in order to attain 'membership in the society they try to enter'? What are the expected 'genre-specific ways of telling stories' in these contexts?

Commentary

The genre of 'testimony' that Verschueren refers to is the focus of a small but increasing amount of research into cultural factors in police interviews of suspects and witnesses and courtroom discourse which falls under the umbrella of 'forensic linguistics' or 'forensic investigation'. D'Hondt (2009), for example, examines such factors through an analysis of courtroom discourse in cases in Belgium in which defendants whose cultural identity is 'culturally other' and concludes that her research 'exposes a fundamental contradiction' in the way the Belgian legal system deals with crime and deviant behaviour: 'On the one hand, the law and the apparatus for implementing it pretend to be free of culture (and they have to feign such universality in order to function properly), but on the other hand the law and the legal system are inevitably also the product of a particular cultural tradition' (p. 826). Eades, who has undertaken a considerable amount of research into courtroom discourse (see for example, 2008a and 2008b), investigates a particular trial in Australia involving three Aboriginal boys and concludes that we not only need to understand 'cultural and linguistic features that are involved in conversational inferencing' but also 'the larger and political forces' at work, including questions of resistance (2005: 314).

UNIT B3.4 REPRESENTATION OF IDENTITY ONLINE

The internet has opened up previously unimagined possibilities for communication between individuals and 'communities' (in the broadest sense). Such communication has had an impact upon how we view ourselves and others, and how we represent ourselves to others online. Gergen (1996: 132) writes that 'With the proliferation of communication technologies, we are first exposed to an ever expanding vocabulary of being. No longer do we dwell within the boundaries of a single geographically contained community, a region, an ethnicity, or even a culture. We have not a single satisfying intelligibility within which to dwell, but through the process of social saturation, we are immersed in a plethora of understandings – the psychological ontologies of varying ethnicities, class strata, geographic sectors, racial and religious groupings, professional enclaves, and nationalities'.

In this unit two texts are featured; the first, by Burkhalter, is concerned with how racial identity is an important factor in usenet discussions, while in the second Fred

Dervin reports on his investigation of how university students in Finland and Latvia construct and represent identities in online chat.

Burkhalter, B. (1999) 'Reading race online: discovering racial identity in usenet discussions'. In Smith, M. A. and Kollock, P. (eds) *Communities in Cyberspace.* **London: Routledge. pp. 63–9, 72–3 (extracts)**

Text B3.4.1
B. Burkhalter

Racial identity

In face-to-face interaction an individual's physical characteristics, from skin colour to vocal patterns, help convey racial identity. Lacking such physical cues on computer networks, one might predict that discrimination on the basis of race, age, gender, sexuality, class, status, and group membership would disappear. Indeed, some participants use the lack of physical cues to claim any identity they want. An SCAA message suggests: 'You are welcome here! Come on in. Would you like a beer or something? The only true colour here is the monitor. Here I can be Black, White or Green.'

The sense of freedom when establishing an online racial identity derives from a persistent belief that racial categorisation is determined exclusively by corporeal traits. Although much sociologic and anecdotal evidence has challenged this belief, race is still popularly seen as a characteristic of bodies (Spickard 1992). The body does not reveal race irrefutably. Multiracial individuals chronicle incidents in which their physical attributes were variously interpreted. The question multiracial individuals are so often asked – 'what are you?' – displays the problematic relationship between physical characteristics and racial identity. The possibility of passing or being mistaken for a different race in face-to-face interaction is also evidence of the fallible relationship between observable traits and identity (Bradshaw 1992). Of course, answers to the question 'what are you?' must be appropriate to the individual's observable characteristics. Physical characteristics are a resource that permit and limit a range of interpretations, but they are only one medium among a variety of resources.

In online interactions, participants are reduced to textual resources, but these resources can be just as determinant as physical indicators are offline. The posts show that racial identity, although fixed differently than it is offline, is firmly established online [pp. 63–4].

Identity disputes

Over the course of a single message, authors may racially identify themselves in several ways. In the following message . . . which generated a small thread over a few days, the author employs a hodgepodge of identity cues:

Hi. I find that many African-Americans where I live (northern California) tend to act in a way they think they should act, rather than just be themselves. I'm acknowledging this because the reality is, the behaviour of the minority completely stands out, as opposed to the behaviour of the majority. I must say, that I am part African-American. i don't feel ashamed of this in any way, but I am ashamed of the African-American behaviour of many citizens in my area. I am proud of all the ethnicities my gene pool possesses, while at the same time, I am proud of the ethnicities I don't possess. I ACCEPT those who are different from me. Different is good: it is new. it is unique. it is you. it is me. Let me explain more of what hits home for me. I must say that I am extremely proud of my mom: She is African-American and she is an individual. She speaks proper English because she chose to get an education, no matter how difficult that path would be. She's had a tough life; she grew up poor in Michigan; her mother died when she was five; she lived in foster homes her whole life; she was looked down upon because of status and her pigmentation. She is a very beautiful person. There are many more hardships to tell about her, but my point is, she's African-American and she is an individual. I want to let African-Americans know that they don't have to act 'black'. It doesn't make you more of an 'African-American' to do things you think Black should do. I've had friends who felt that acting 'black' was cool, both black and white ones. Did you know much of what many people refer to as being black resulted from their overseers who were known as 'poor white trash'? It's true. They were the ones the slaves learned English from, yet many people don't realise this. Please let me know that the majority of African-American are not like the ones I see on Ricki Lake. They don't have attitudes, move their necks from side to side, wave their hands in people's faces, speak loud and improper English, don't listen to what people are saying, don't speak out vulgarly, don't resort to violence because they can articulate how they feel. I'm not trying to put down African-Americans, I want to recognise a problem in the United States. The more people group themselves in simplistic categories, based on skin colour, the harder it will be for ALL of us to get along, live as the HUMANS we are . . . Ask me what my culture is and I'll tell you 'I'm American' [pp. 67–8].

Racial identity and disagreement

. . . identity challenges do not occur often. However, when participants dispute an author's perspective they often challenge the author's identity. Though disagreements come in various forms, one recurrent practice for disputing an author's arguments involves challenges to an author's identity . . . respondents' challenges to an author's identity dispute the social position from which the author makes his/her claim. Instead of arguing with the author's view of the world by presenting a contrasting view, respondents attempt to invalidate the argument by invalidating the author's claimed social position. The first reply to the above post mentions little on the issue of Africans-Americans acting Black, instead focusing on the author's identity:

I'm acknowledging this because the reality is, the behaviour of the minority completely stands out, as opposed to the behaviour of the majority. I must say, that I am part African-American. I don't feel ashamed of this in anyway, but I am ashamed of the African-American behaviour of many citizens in my area.

emphasis on the 'part African-American'? why are you ashamed of people you don't personally know? (unless of course, you are referring to the [African-American] folks from your personal lineage?) do you bear the burden for speaking for the race you 'partially' belong to?

I am proud of all the ethnicities my gene pool possesses, while at the same time, I am proud of the ethnicities I don't possess. I ACCEPT those who are different from me. Different is good: it is new. it is unique. it is you. it is me.

ummm, excuse me but this little Pollyanna statement just negated the part where you wept tears over the behavior of total strangers. If different is good, you should absolutely love those [African-Americans] that are causing you such embarrassment, doncha think? me thinks you bear more pride for the paler side of your life. perhaps that is who is speaking in this message?

(pp. 68–9)

Consequences for race online

In online discussions, readers treat racial identities as entailing particular perspectives. Offline has a name for the imputation of a characteristic, attitude, belief, or practice based solely on someone's race – 'stereotyping'. An observer may use physical characteristics to impute a racial identity and from that impute a delimited set of beliefs and perspectives. For example, after I confirmed that I was Black in a recent conversation, the talk turned to professional basketball. My co-interactants assumed that a Black male would be interested in basketball. While this stereotyping is not surprising, imagine that, on hearing of their interest in basketball, I had assumed they were Black. This would also be stereotyping, but an unusual variety. Stereotyping in face-to-face interaction follows from an assumed racial identity. Online interaction differs in that the imputation tends to go in the other direction – from stereotype to racial identity.

A discrepancy arises when a person identified as a member of a particular racial group by his or her physical characteristics offers a perspective that is inconsistent with the stereotype of that group. In face-to-face interactions, such an inconsistency can be resolved by modifying the stereotype or seeing the person as an anomaly – rarely are the person's physical racial indicators disputed. In online interactions perspectives resist modification because participants confront an immutable text, whereas racial identifications can be challenged [pp. 72–3].

Task B3.4.1

Burkhalter states in the text that in face-to-face interaction 'an individual's physical characteristics, from skin colour to vocal patterns, help convey racial identity.'

➤ Consider what physical characteristics, as well as 'skin colour' and 'vocal patterns' can help to convey racial identity.

Task B3.4.2

Burkhalter writes in the text: 'the question multiracial individuals are so often asked – "what are you?" – displays the problematic relationship between physical characteristics and racial identity.' This problematic relationship is highlighted by Claudine Chiawei O'Hearn (1998: xiv), who writes that 'for those of us who fall between the cracks, being "black", being "white", being "Latino", is complicated . . .

Skin colour and place of birth aren't accurate signifiers of identity. One and one don't necessarily add up to two. Cultural and racial amalgams create a third, wholly indistinguishable category where origin and home are indeterminate ... What name do you give to someone who is a quarter, an eight, a half? What kind of measuring stick might give an accurate estimation?'

➤ Think of other individuals in the public eye and/or people you know personally who also 'fall between the cracks':

- ■ How do they define themselves?
- ■ How do others define them?

 Task B3.4.3

Burkhalter writes that 'authors may racially identify themselves in several ways. In the following message . . . the author employs a hodgepodge of identity cues'.

➤ Analyse the first usenet message in Text B3.4.1 (beginning 'Hi. I find that many African-Americans . . .'). How does the author of this message identify him/ herself? What 'identity cues' does the author employ?

In text B3.4.2, Dervin (2014) describes and analyses online synchronic chat tasks between students in a Finnish and a Latvian university, who were both studying aspects of intercultural communication. Dervin explains that in the Finnish university, 90 per cent of the students were international students, while in the Latvian university the students were all Latvian, 'though we need to bear in mind that Latvia has a Russian minority of 27%'. The online chat tasks were part of assessed coursework that focused on representations of Russia, 'as the country had played a major role in the area politically, economically, etc.'. The language of discussion was English as the courses were taught in English and before meeting online, 'the students sent to each other media articles on both Russia and their partner's country in English, accompanied by a short commentary on the representations they had found' (p. 197). In the extracts below Dervin first introduces what he calls 'Discourse Pragmatics' (DP) and then uses DP to analyse transcripts of the online interactions between a student from Latvia ('Paula') and a Hong Chinese student ('Rose').

 Task B3.4.4

Dervin writes that: 'An identity is constructed through negotiating representations with the "other"'.

➤ What do you think Dervin might mean by this in relation to online communication?

Dervin, F. (2014) 'Exploring "new" interculturality online'. *Language and Intercultural Communication* **14/2: 191–206 (extracts)**

Text B3.4.2
F. Dervin

What is DP?

. . . The name of the method is derived from a proposal by Zienkowski, Östman, and Verschueren (2011) to describe the many and varied pragmatic features of certain perspectives and approaches to discourse. Zienkowski (2011: 1) justifies the unification of discourse and pragmatics by explaining that there is not just one definition of these terms and that he wishes to 'lump them together' to promote more 'inter-disciplinarity and inter-theoretical cross-fertilisation' (Zienkowski 2011).

Two approaches that I have used in my research on the 'intercultural' are also included in Zienkowski *et al.*'s (2011) work: Énonciation (French pragmatics) and Polyphony (I use its dialogic 'parent').

French énonciation (often called French pragmatics) proposes different approaches to pragmatic issues in language use. Johansson and Suomela-Salmi (2011: 71) explain:

> enunciation deals with utterance-level meaning from the perspective of different linguistic elements. In other words, the activity of the speaker is the focus: on the one hand there are traces and indices left by the speaker in the utterance; on the other hand there is the relationship the speaker maintains with her/his interlocutor.

In short, énonciation approaches are interested in 1) How a person constructs her/ his discourse and 2) How s/he negotiates the discourse with others (intersubjectivity). One central aspect of énonciation is to consider a speaker as a heterogeneous subject, meaning an individual who positions herself/himself in interaction with others and who thus uses and manages various discursive and pragmatic strategies to construct the self, the other, surroundings, experiences, etc. (pp. 194–5).

Many and varied linguistic elements have been examined to analyse enunciation. Deictics (markers of person, time and space such as personal pronouns, adverbs, and verbs) are such elements, which allow speakers to 'stage themselves or make themselves manifest in utterances, or on the other hand may decide to distance themselves from it, leaving no explicit signs of their presence or manifesting their attitude in utterances' (Johansson and Suomela-Salmi 2011: 94). The same goes for utterance modalities, which can give us a clue about the attitude of the speaker toward what s/he is saying (adverbs, shifters, etc.). For example, deontic modalities mark an obligation and relate to moral and social norms (e.g.: You must do this) (Johansson and Suomela-Salmi 2011: 97). Nouns may also express the attitude of a speaker toward a person, a phenomenon, an object, etc. (Paul is a lazybones). It is easy to see how enunciative markers can help the researcher to analyze how people co-construct who they are when interacting but also reveal the sentiments they attach to these images. By working on pragmatic changes in discourse, Énonciation can also help us to identify instability: shifts, contradictions, corrections, potential manipulation, etc. [p. 195].

Dialogism

The writings of Bakhtin (1895–1975) and Vološinov have had a lot of influence on research in the humanities and the social sciences today. Having created the idea of

F. Dervin

Dialogism, Bakhtin's theory places the concept of voice at the center of discourse. Roulet (2011: 209) summarises the Russian philosopher's ideas as follows:

(1) there is constant interplay between multiple voices in discourse and society;
(2) any discourse is always associated with former discourses and voices;
(3) any discourse is always a reaction to previous discourses and thus enters into dialog with these discourses; and
(4) other persons are thus always present in what people say.

. . . Linguistically speaking, dialogism and thus the presence of other voices are marked by the apparition of certain linguistic markers: pronouns such as we; reported discourses (he said: '. . .'); passive voice (I was given a chance to do something); etc. Dialogists call reported discourse (direct or indirect), discourse representation (Roulet 2011: 210) as, being reported from another context, it represents and integrates discourses and actions in a different context. Certain phenomena such as irony, negation, or the use of certain discourse markers such as 'but' all signal dialogism, i.e. dialogs between voices [p. 196].

Presentation and discussion of results

Negotiating and 'defending' one's identity

What is noticeable from the beginning of the online encounters is that all the students come from a context which necessitates negotiating in order to convey identities that suit them – and avoid misidentification.

At the beginning of their discussion, Rose needs to explain to Paula that even though Hong Kong has been officially part of China since 1997, Hong Kong people do not always consider themselves to be Chinese – Paula labelled her as Chinese. In such situations, one should adopt a strategy that does not lead to face threat. In what follows, Rose wants Paula to note this identification.

Excerpt 1

Rose: you know, when people asked where i come from, i always say i come from Hong Kong, rather than saying i come from China and Hong Kong is totally different from China, although it's part of China and of course it's normal for you to have such perception

Paula: Well, I think, that not many people discriminate here in Latvia. I did not know anything about Hong Kong, later you looked up. I mean I looked for information.

Rose: what i mean is that the culture and lifestyles etc. are totally different, and beuase Hong Kong was the colony of British before 1997 and now back to China, that's why we Hong kOngers have such national identity

(The excerpts are reproduced as they appeared in the chats. No linguistic corrections from my side.)

A discursive pragmatic analysis shows that both students are 'walking on eggs' in what is negotiated here as the issues of identity and representation can be potentially face-threatening. Rose uses a dialogical strategy first to tell Paula the 'truth' about who she is: 'when people asked where I come from, I always say I come from

Hong Kong, rather than saying I come from China.' Dialogism appears in the reported representation 'ask me where', the modality 'always' and 'rather than.' The last two markers indicate voices that are contradicted by the Hong Kong student. Another example of her trying to protect Paula's face is the use of another modality, 'of course,' in 'of course it's normal for you to have such perception', signalling in a sense that she forgives her for placing her in the 'wrong box' and/or her being used to such misidentification. As an answer to Rose's corrections, Paula puts forward her 'Nation' ('not many people discriminate here in Latvia,' meaning people do not know about the status of Hong Kong). Here again, dialogism ('not many people') allows the speaker to protect her face and excuse her ignorance. Rose comes back to the scene to provide her interlocutor with more explanations, as if to convince her even more of the differences between Hong Kong and China. Linking back to what was said earlier about énonciation, it is clear here that both students leave 'traces and indices' that allow us to notice identification but also negotiate these elements to reflect 'the relationship the speaker maintains with her/his interlocutor' (Johansson and Suomela-Salmi 2011: 71).

A similar situation arises when the two students begin to talk about Russia, especially because of Latvia's special status in relation to its Russian minority. In what follows, Rose seems to be reflecting on her own use of certain words in a question she asks her partner:

Excerpt 2

Rose: so do you make any friends from Russia?
Paula: No, I do not have any friends in Russia, but I have Russian friends here, in Latvia.
Rose: haha . . . that's my meaning^^ i should have asked, 'do u hv any Russian friends?'

Having just talked about the fact that Latvia is quite close to Russia, Rose asks the question 'so do you make any friends from Russia?' Paula's response seems to be giving the impression to Rose that she has made a mistake. The use of a self-dialogical form, written with inverted commas ('I should have asked do u hv any Russian friends?'), marks this reflexivity. These are surely here acts of identity as the Latvian context is complex and necessitates discussing and negotiating to get the right picture.

Following this short excerpt, Paula gives more details about the situation in Latvia and the fact that 'Russians' and Latvians live together (NB: The word 'Russians' is between inverted commas here as, in the Latvian context, we talk about their ethnicity rather than nationality. Many 'Russians' in Latvia have a Latvian passport only):

Excerpt 3

Paula: Russians and Latvians live here side by side. I do not have anything against them until they have similar values and they love Latvia as I do. If they live here, they should be loyal to Latvia.
Rose: so why do they choose to live in Latvia? Any reasons behind?
Paula: When Russia occupied Latvia in 1940, Russia sent millions of Latvians to Sibiria to die, but then sent in Russians. Everyone who had some property or farm was sent to Siberia, because they were traitors, as Russia said. Actually our mutual history is very sad.
Rose: oh . . . i feel sorry to hear that . . .

In this excerpt, it is interesting to see how both students talk about a general entity, namely the Russians ('they'). Paula's claim 'I do not have anything against them' is modified by a restriction ('until they have similar values') and a comparison to herself ('and they love Latvia as I do'), showing clearly her own positioning in relation to assimilation and national identity – and Russians! Rose then asks her a question which also includes the Latvian Russians' voice ('so why do they choose to live in Latvia?'), which leads Paula to provide her with a bit of historical background. A represented discourse attributed to 'Russia,' which indicates dialogism ('because they were traitors, as Russia said'), allows her to give even more weight to the ghastly details she is giving – especially as the agent is a whole country, Russia (pp. 197–9).

When the pair (a) discusses the documents on Russia and the Russians that they had sent to each other, Rose asks Paula to tell her more about 'your feeling towards this material?' Paula's answer, which contains an evaluator at the end as if to excuse the content of her sentence ('Sad'), is twofold: 'Well, first – I was surprised. Secondly – that is how Russians present themselves. Sad.' In short, she explains the negative content of the documents by referring to the Russians' voices themselves. This is followed by Rose's surprise at Paula's attitudes toward these elements in the paper she has sent her:

Excerpt 8

Rose: i hv read your document, it seems that you don't like the Russian, is it true? may i know more about it? is there any historical reasons behind?

Paula: Not that I do not like them, but we have bad experience with them. Yes, it is also history.

Rose: and when i read that 'i have not plan to go there' i feel that you don't like this country or people so much

Paula: There are half of population Russians in Latvia. The older generation came here, but they do not want to learn our language, or integrate.

Rose takes many risks with her questions/comments in this excerpt: 'it seems that you don't like the Russian, is it true?'; 'I feel that you don't like this country or people so much.' These reveal that she has created an identity for Paula and Latvians: they have a problem with Russians. Her use of modalities 'it seems that,' 'I feel that,' and 'so much' allows her not to be too face-threatening and, in a sense, be sympathetic toward Paula. In her answers, the latter identifies with Latvians ('we have bad experience with them,' 'they do not want to learn our language') to support her opinions. Rose then continues to ask her questions about the Latvian-Russian relations, trying to obtain 'political' analyses from Paula – without success.

Interestingly, the whole discussion about Russia ends on a reflective section during which Rose and Paula realise why Russia was put at the centre of the task they had to perform:

Excerpt 9

Rose: after reading what you have written about the historical background about Latvia and Russia, i come to realise why Russia is chosen as the topic that we have to discuss!

Paula: Well, I was so suprised about the topic, that we need to discuss about Russia, but well, I can do that.

These conclusions could show that the students were able to 'enter into dialog' with themselves when they were doing the task and start to reflect on the goal of the activities ('I come to realise,' 'but well, I can do that,' but well marking a self-dialog here) [pp. 201–2].

Conclusions and future research directions

Many questions remain for exploring the use of DP in analyzing interculturality and implementing intercultural education online . . .

(1) What difference(s) would it make if the students had met face to face rather than online or both? . . .
(2) Could DP be used for intercultural training/education? . . .
(3) Could DP support lecturers in assessing their students in relation to the intercultural?

(p. 204)

Task B3.4.5

➤ Do you think the interaction between 'Paula' and 'Rose' would have been different if they had been chatting face to face? If so, in what ways?

➤ Do you think DP could be used in intercultural training? If so, in what ways?

A number of commentators have suggested that there is a danger that online communication, rather than develop intercultural competence, can have the opposite effect and reinforce subjective and stereotypical views. Marcoccia (2012) writes that 'for some the internet is a medium which facilitates intercultural communication, whereas others consider that online communication makes intercultural communication difficult or reinforces cultural standardisation at the expense of cultural diversity' (p. 353). In addition he writes that: 'many social researchers . . . have shown that internet-mediated communication, and particularly discussion forums, create a communication situation which is characterised by the reduction of participants' inhibitions and of collective social control. This characteristic is an obstacle to intercultural dialogue. In this sense, cyberspace is as much a space for spreading aggressiveness and hatred as for intercultural understanding' (p. 360).

Task B3.4.6

➤ How far do you think that online chat tasks, such as the one outlined above by Dervin, can help develop intercultural competence?

➤ How can those involved in intercultural education structure online chat tasks so as to promote 'intercultural dialogue' and the development of intercultural competence (and avoid 'sentimental stereotypes that can be manipulated to reinforce private interests')?

Commentary

Shuter wrote in 2012 that:

> New media (ICTs) are transforming communication across cultures. Despite
> this revolution in cross cultural contact, communication researchers have
> largely ignored the impact of new media on intercultural communication.
>
> (p. 219)

What's missing, according to Shuter, 'are lines of research on how ICTs
affect intercultural communication between individuals and groups. Research
on this topic challenges more than 50 years of intercultural communication
knowledge and theory rooted in twentieth-century paradigm of face-to-face
interaction'. This paradigm embraced a view of identity 'rooted in twentieth-
century assumptions about the origins of the self in relationship to others; that is,
social identity is based on group contact(s) that is fixed in space and time, producing
discernable social identity(ies) that varies in salience depending on the social
context(s)'. Shuter asks: 'in a new media era of perpetual contact . . . where
individuals live in virtual spaces with myriad others, is this perspective relevant and
sufficient for explaining the development and maintenance of cultural identity in
the twenty-first century?' and calls for 'a new field of studies called Intercultural
New Media Studies (INMS) which explores the intersections between ICTs and
Intercultural Communication' (p. 220).

UNIT B3.5 CULTURAL CONSTRUCTS IN BUSINESS AND
INTERCULTURAL TRAINING

Fleming (2009) writes that: 'traditional intercultural training guides or programmes
. . . are largely based on "what to do" and "what not to do abroad"' and are 'often
presented as one-way encounters' in which there is little consideration to 'the
possibility of a social encounter based on openness and healthy curiosity aimed at
mutual understanding'. In such guides and programmes 'snippets of information
acquired in formal training are sometimes viewed as a superficial passport to
success' (p. 7).

In this unit we start with a description by Phillip Riley of a workplace in which
simplistic models of cultural difference often promoted in intercultural training
guides or programmes have had a direct and negative impact on intercultural
understanding and subsequent working practices.

Text B3.5.1
P. Riley

Riley, P. (2007) *Language, Culture and Identity*. London: Continuum.
pp. 231–3 (extracts)

1)

In a factory in France owned and managed by foreigners, a poster was displayed and
used in training sessions in which the French were described as 'Cartesian', 'Abstract',

'Individualistic', 'Rethorical' [sic] and 'Preferring words to actions', whilst people of the employers' nationality were stated to be 'Practical', 'Pragmatic', 'Team players' who 'preferred actions to words'. When I was subsequently (and very belatedly) invited in to try to pour some oil on what had become very troubled waters, each side described the other as 'inefficient' and 'impolite'.

The closure of the factory the following year with the loss of over 600 jobs, after only eighteen months' full and highly profitable operation, was part of the world-wide slump in the telecommunications market and due to a take-over by a rival firm that simply wished to eliminate a competitor, but it is certainly not too far-fetched to see these ethos-related negative impressions and communicative misunderstandings as a contributory factor. They were largely due to the fact that the international company had decreed English as the sole working language for the enterprise. As far as any reflection had gone into this decision, it seemed to be based on the ideas that, first, English is the language of business and international communication so that there was no need for management and workforce to learn one another's languages and, second, that using a 'neutral' language like English would create a level playing-field for management–workforce relations. Nothing could have been further from the truth: the managers spoke fluent English, the workforce, almost without exception, very little. Some of them admitted that they had 'enhanced' their curriculum vitaes in this respect because they needed the work.

An additional problem was the fact that each side spoke an English which was rooted in their own cultural values and communicative practices. For example, French falling affirmative intonation patterns were perceived by the management as aggressive and impolite and the management's own intonation patterns were perceived by the workforce as 'surly', 'unfriendly' – and impolite.

Again, a system of management based on regular 'work-meetings' was implemented, but without any thought being given as to how this English expression might be interpreted by each side. In brief, the management saw work-meetings as an occasion for reporting on work that had been done, decisions and plans that had been made, and projects that had been carried out. Work-meetings, they believed, should last no longer than thirty to forty minutes and should consist of a series of reports from both sides, with little or no discussion. For the French, however, a work-meeting was seen as a meeting where the work would actually be done, the plans made, the decisions taken. It would, therefore, involve full discussion of policy and detail, and could be expected to last two to three hours. The management saw the French attitude as 'coming to the meeting with empty hands', 'laziness' and 'inefficiency', wasting in time lengthy and pointless discussions of 'things they should have thought about earlier'. The workforce saw the management as a group of authoritarian control-freaks who did not respect their expertise and whose old-fashioned methods were hasty and inefficient.

2)

Foreign consultants hired to train management-level staff in the Nordic travel industry attributed 'defects' in their communicative performance in meetings which are in fact related to turn-taking procedures, speed of delivery and argumentative strategies to 'poor presentation skills', rather than seeing them as different communicative norms aiming at the projection of an ethos in many ways distinct from their own. They also requested their trainees to simulate greeting and parting routines to show that they were 'warm' and 'friendly', which even those who accepted (some flatly refused) found unnecessary and excruciatingly embarrassing. ('Hugging!' said one in a tone of real disgust.)

One can only conclude that we need to take a hard look at the models underpinning so-called intercultural training (Scollon and Scollon (1992), is an especially powerful critique). Far from being culturally sensitive, they can be unconsciously naive attempts to transpose the trainer's communicative practices and values to the learner's behaviour, in which case they are ethnocentric, unethical and counter-productive. Any morally or pedagogically valid approach to inter-cultural training must be based on respect for and knowledge of the learner's culture and communicative economy and will take the form of observation, sensitisation and the negotiation of identities and 'mini-cultures', with the aim of participating in encounters where no participant is forced unwillingly to sacrifice their own ethos, culture or identity by being modelled in the image of another (Adami *et al.* 2003) [p. 231–3].

★ Task B3.5.1

Riley writes that foreign consultants hired to train management-level staff in the Nordic travel industry failed to take account of 'different communicative norms aiming at the projection of <u>an ethos</u> in many ways distinct from their own'.

➤ What do you think he means by 'ethos' and what variables might there be which influence the 'ethos' of a work organisation in a specific cultural context (in addition to those mentioned by Riley)?

Riley makes an important point about the dominance of English and the naïve belief held by the managers of the French telecommunications factory that the English language is a 'neutral' language.

➤ Do you believe that any language used in the 'global market place' can ever be 'neutral'? Why/why not?

A particularly common focus of intercultural trainers and consultants has been the distinction between 'collectivism' and 'individualism' and this distinction has trickled down into numerous popular guides for those visiting, living in and working in 'foreign' cultural contexts, or working in the 'global marketplace'. Text B3.5.2 includes introductory sections from a book by a social scientist, who has written widely on 'collectivism' and 'individualism', Harry Triandis. We will consider, in light of some of the perspectives in previous units in Section B, how valid such a distinction is and whether it is a valuable distinction in helping us to understand, work with and communicate with people from and in a variety of cultural contexts.

➤ Before we go on to consider how the terms 'collectivism' and 'individualism' have been defined, read the description of ten incidents that Triandis provides in Text B3.5.2 Extract 1.

Triandis, H. C. (1995) *Individualism and Collectivism.* **Boulder: Westview Press. pp. 1–2 (extracts)**

Text B3.5.2
H. C. Triandis
Extract 1

1. In Brazil, a waiter brings one menu for four people and gives it to the 'senior' member of the group, who orders the same food for all.
2. In France, each member of the group orders a different entree at a restaurant.
3. In India, a senior engineer is asked to move to New York, at a salary that is twenty-five times his salary in New Delhi, but be declines the opportunity.
4. In California, a senior engineer is asked to move to New York, at a salary that is 50 percent higher than his salary in Los Angeles, and he accepts.
5. On a street in Moscow, an older woman scolds a mother she does not know because she thinks the mother has not wrapped her child warmly enough.
6. In New York, a woman asks for help from passers-by to escape from the beatings that her boyfriend is giving her; but no one helps.
7. In Japan, a supervisor knows a great deal about the personal life of each subordinate and arranges for one of his subordinates to meet a nice girl he can marry.
8. In England, a subordinate does not mention to his supervisor that his father has just died.
9. In Germany, a man walks on the grass in a public park and is reprimanded by several passers-by.
10. In Illinois, a man marries a woman his parents disapprove of.

Task B3.5.2

Triandis asks the question: 'What do the . . . incidents have in common?'.

➤ Can you see anything that any of the ten incidents have in common with another/other of the ten incidents?

➤ Can you provide explanations for what is said/done and what is not said/done by individuals in the ten incidents described?

➤ What do you think the writer's purpose is in asking what the incidents have in common?

Now read extract 2 of Text B3.5.2.

Triandis, H. C. (1995) *Individualism and Collectivism.* **Boulder: Westview Press. pp. 2–3, 4–5 (extracts)**

Text B3.5.2
H. C. Triandis
Extract 2

As we analyse episodes of this kind, we find that they can be explained by two constructs: collectivism and individualism. The odd-numbered episodes reflect an aspect of collectivism; the even-numbered ones an aspect of individualism. The fact that ten so diverse social behaviours can be explained by just two constructs indicates that the constructs are useful and powerful . . .

Collectivism may be initially defined as a social pattern consisting of closely linked individuals who see themselves as parts of one or more collectives (family, co-workers,

H. C. Triandis

tribe, nation); are primarily motivated by the norms of, and duties imposed by, those collectives; are willing to give priority to the goals of these collectives over their own personal goals; and emphasise their connectedness to members of these collectives. A preliminary definition of individualism is a social pattern that consists of loosely linked individuals who view themselves as independent of collectives; are primarily motivated by their own preferences, needs, rights, and the contracts they have established with others; give priority to their personal goals over the goals of others; and emphasise rational analyses of the advantages and disadvantages to associating with others.

The reader will want some explanation of why the ten behaviours mentioned above reflect these constructs. Brazil, India, Russia, and Japan are collectivist countries, though in different degrees. France, the United States, England, and Germany are individualistic countries, also in different degrees. Nevertheless, one can find both collectivist and individualistic elements in all these countries, in different combinations.

In Brazil, the waiter assumes that the senior member of the group will decide what to eat and that ultimately consuming the same food will intensify bonds among the members of the group, whereas in France, the waiter infers that each person has personal preferences that must be respected.

In India, the engineer feels he must stay close to his parents and that New York is simply too far. If his father were dying, it would be the engineer's duty to be at his bedside and facilitate his passage to the other state. Under similar conditions in the United States, it is more likely that the parent would be placed in a nursing home. The parent and his son have their own lives and are independent entities.

In Russia it is assumed that the whole community is responsible for child rearing. If the parent is not doing an adequate job, an older person is responsible for upholding community standards. 'Putting one's nose in another person's business' is perfectly natural and expected.

One's supervisor in Japan is often like a father, one who is obliged to attend to the needs of his subordinates. Locating a suitable mate for a subordinate may be one of his duties. In England, where individualism is quite intense, the death of a parent may be private information not to be shared with a supervisor . . . Germany, though overall individualistic, is also collectivist in certain respects. The German episode is illustrative of collectivist behaviour. Walking on hard-to-grow grassy areas is a community concern, and witnesses to such 'deviant' behaviour may take action. In most cultures, people try to marry a spouse that their parents find acceptable. However, in very individualistic entities like the United States, it is assumed that people are independent entities and can marry someone regardless of parental disapproval. In individualist cultures marriage is an institution that only links two people and not their respective families. In collectivist cultures it links two families, in which case it is mandatory that the families find the mate acceptable . . .

One of culture's most important aspects is 'unstated assumptions'. The assumption that we are bound together into tight groups of interdependent individuals is fundamental to collectivism. The assumption that we are independent entities, different and distant from our groups, is fundamental to individualism. If we look at the ten examples, we see that such assumptions hold. The Brazilian waiter saw a group of interconnected individuals, with a 'senior' member who would order the food. The French waiter saw individual preferences as unrelated to group influences. The Indian engineer saw himself linked to his parents; the American engineer saw his parents as having a life of their own. The elderly Russian woman saw herself linked to the mother passing by; the new Yorkers saw no ties to the woman asking for help. The Japanese supervisor saw himself linked to his subordinates and thus felt that it was his duty to take care of their personal problems. The English subordinate saw himself not linked at all to his supervisor, so the supervisor had no inherent right to obtain private information. The German citizens saw themselves linked to the community and felt a need to defend it from a person who broke the rules. The Illinois man saw himself as a discrete entity, only weakly linked to his parents.

Task B3.5.3

➤ Look again at the descriptions of incidents 1, 2, 3 and 4 in Text B3.5.2.

➤ Change 'Brazil' to 'France' in description 1, and 'France' to 'Brazil' in description 2. Also change 'India' and 'New Delhi' to 'California' and 'Los Angeles' in description 3, and 'California' and 'Los Angeles' to 'India' and 'New Delhi' in description 4.

➤ Now that you have changed the descriptions, do you think that these incidents could occur in the other places?

➤ If you think they could occur in the other places, what implications does this have in light of the points made in extract 2 of Text B3.5.2?

Task B3.5.4

➤ Evaluate what Triandis writes above in relation to other ideas we have previously considered in texts in other units in Section B. Below are quotations from some of these previous units:

We have an old habit of speaking about 'cultures', in the plural form, as if it were self-evident that such entities exist side by side as neat packages, each of us identified with only one of them.

(Hannerz (1999) – Unit B0.1)

The dominant discourse relies on equating community, culture, and ethnic identity, and its protagonists can easily reduce anybody's behaviour to a symptom of this equation. So long as its human objects can be logged under some ethnic identity other than, say, British, German, or American, it can even claim to speak 'for' them, 'represent' them, explain them to others.

(Baumann (1996) – Unit B0.1)

Another important fact about cultures is that they are essentially open. Cultures are ideational entities; as such they are permeable, susceptible to influence from other cultures.

(Fay (1996) – Unit B0.2)

Cultural models as tools of inquiry

Cultural models . . . lead us to ask, when confronted with a piece of talk, writing, action, or interaction, questions like these:

- What cultural models are relevant here? What must I, as an analyst, assume people feel, value, and believe, consciously or not, in order to talk (write), act, and/or interact this way? . . .
- How consistent are the relevant cultural models here? Are there competing or conflicting cultural models at play? Whose interests are the cultural models representing? . . .
- How are the relevant cultural models here helping to reproduce, transform, or create social, cultural, institutional, and/or political relationships? What Discourses and Conversations are these cultural models helping to reproduce, transform or create?

(Gee (1999) – Unit B1.3)

When I think of myself in cultural categories – which I do perhaps too often – I know that I'm a recognisable example of a species: a professional New York woman.

(Hoffman (1989) – Unit B1.5)

Stereotyping . . . has been defined as a particular extension of the fundamental cognitive processes of categorisation, whereby we impose structure and make sense of events, objects and experience. The process in itself requires the simplification and organisation of diverse and complex ranges of phenomena into general, labelled categories. In so doing attention is focused on certain similar identifying characteristics or distinctive features, as opposed to many other differences.

(O'Sullivan *et al.* (1994) – Unit B3.3)

After we have categorised a person as a member of a particular group, that classification affects how we characterise their behaviour. The same behaviour performed by a member of another group will be characterised in different ways on the basis of the structure of beliefs we have already developed about these groups.

(Gandy (1998) – Unit B3.1)

Social constructionism . . . invites us to be critical of the idea that our observations of the world . . . unproblematically yield its nature to us, to challenge the view that conventional knowledge is based upon objective, unbiased observation of the world.

(Burr (1995) – Unit B3.2)

Commentary

It should be noted that the model developed by Triandis is more complex than is suggested in the short extract from his book included in this unit, and, indeed, he mentions the following: that the 'terms' 'individualism' and 'collectivism' are 'fuzzy and difficult to measure' (p. 2); that 'our assumptions are not universal' (p. 3), that 'there are people in each of the countries that were mentioned in the examples who would have acted very differently' (p. 3), and that 'what may be called "the situation" is very important' (p. 3).

Important questions arise, however, when such models are considered in light of what others have recently written about culture, cultural identity, and its represent-ation. An important problem when social scientists, such as Triandis, employ models along the individualism–collectivism dimension, often adding other dimensions, to explain how cultures and communities are constructed, is that, first, these 'constructs' are interpreted as 'facts', and second, that they are seen as the primary, and sometimes sole factors in cultural identity, by intercultural trainers, writers of textbooks on intercultural communication and writers of the numerous popular guides for those visiting, living in and working in 'foreign' cultural contexts.

UNIT B3.6   CHALLENGING CULTURAL CONSTRUCTS IN INTERCULTURAL TRAINING AND EDUCATION

In the last unit was Riley's assertion that: 'Any morally or pedagogically valid approach to inter-cultural training must be based on respect for and knowledge of the learner's culture and communicative economy and will take the form of observation, sensitisation and the negotiation of identities and "mini-cultures".' Such an approach is taken in intercultural training reported on in the first text by Prue Holmes (2015), who focuses on the experiences of a group of sixteen immigrants in New Zealand who are on a volunteer work-placement scheme which also involved a serious of workshops. There were two key research questions in her study: 1) What intercultural communication challenges do immigrants face during work-placement with co-workers and employers?; 2) How is intercultural communication facilitated/constrained in intercultural encounters in the workplace? In the second text Adrian Holliday (2016) introduces the notions of 'cultural blocks' and 'cultural threads' that can be found in narratives of university students studying abroad, and argues that 'if there is to be such a thing as intercultural training, it should be in how to focus on cultural threads and put aside cultural blocks'.

Task B3.6.1

Before reading the text, consider this question:

➤ What intercultural communication challenges do you think the immigrants to New Zealand might face when interacting with co-workers and employers in the workplace?

Text B3.6.1
P. Holmes

Holmes, P. (2015) '"The cultural stuff around how to talk to people": immigrants' intercultural communication during a pre-employment work-placement'. *Language and Intercultural Communication* **15/1: 109–24. pp. 112–20 (extracts)**

Of the 16 participants in the study, only one had previous work experience as a volunteer for 3 months. Twelve were females and four males; they were aged between 26 and 55 years. They came from Chile, China, Columbia, Fiji, India, the Philippines, the Republic of Congo, Sri Lanka and the United Kingdom (UK). The programme coordinator, from the UK, had lived in New Zealand for 9 years. Five employers were also interviewed to establish their perceptions of how immigrants experienced their work placements. Three employers had experienced employing immigrants, and two had previously hired immigrants from this programme [pp. 112–13].

An analysis of the interview data revealed the following two key themes: negotiating informal and non-hierarchical intercultural relationships, and constructing collegial relationships through intercultural communication.

Negotiating informal and non-hierarchical relationships

Hierarchies are present in the organisational structure of most workplaces, including the small businesses where these immigrants were placed. While employees respect and manage hierarchical relationships, the communication among and across individuals and groups tends towards informality and equality, for example, through the use of first names, ignoring titles and reciprocal communication (Holmes and Stubbe 2003). In the following example, the degree of informality, signalled by the 'yelling' at the employee, with the expectation that the yelling would be reciprocated, created complications regarding the employer–employee hierarchy and the expected response:

> If you have such a respect or hierarchy in an organisation then they treat you in some different way as well. They will never scream at you because they know you cannot do it back. But here, your boss could yell at you, so you have to yell back. Sometimes you have to adapt.

And the consequences:

> If you cannot get rid of this hierarchy in your mind, then your New Zealand supervisor would treat you as less significant because that is the way you present yourself.

One participant expressed feelings of discomfort when her boss praised her work:

> I don't feel comfortable when [my supervisor] says . . . I'm not used to praises because in [my country] we don't really do that. If you get something done you give it to your boss and he will say 'alright'. But [my supervisor] would say really nice things like 'perfect, very good' [also in front of others]. I don't feel comfortable because in our culture we don't do that and I just don't know how to respond.

The employer was also aware of her discomfort as he had created an open exchange with her in weekly meetings, where she was able to explain her attitudes and feelings around being praised. The employer explained:

> In some of those weekly meetings she said that she felt uncomfortable because I kept on saying 'good job, well done, I like this'. She was not used to that. Her boss would never ever say, 'good'. There was always something wrong. It took her maybe two or three weeks to get used to that.

The employer's attempt to make her feel valued and develop her confidence by praising her work was misunderstood by this participant, instead, resulting in feelings of awkwardness. In their home countries, immigrants can gauge the social position of others through language, background and the unspoken. But in New Zealand, they are likely to be unaware of these sociocultural-linguistic cues, or if they are aware, how to use them to their advantage [p. 114].

. . . Working autonomously, without the need for constant checking, also had to be negotiated. One participant commented on how she thought it important to check her work with her boss to avoid making a mistake:

> I do it correctly because I don't want to get a bad image. I always double-check everything. It is very stressful to do that, but I do that because I don't want to make a mistake because I want to be permanent.

By contrast, her employer found this need for constant feedback unusual and slightly irritating:

> She had been used to negative feedback and being told to check everything with her boss. I wonder if she slowly understands now that we prefer that she wouldn't check everything, but rather that she did it. She is extremely intelligent so she is not going to make big mistakes. From my perspective, it is slightly irritating to have someone check.

This participant's personal anxiety about her performance was linked to her desire to secure future employment, yet her need to have her work checked contradicted her employer's expectations that employees show independence, initiative and autonomy [p. 115].

Constructing collegial relationships through intercultural communication

A second major theme centred on the ways in which participants sought to build relationships with colleagues during and after work: through communication in tea breaks, engaging in small talk and a preference for face-to-face communication over email.

Tea breaks. These offer an opportunity for developing relationships, but joining the conversation required an ability to use the informal language register and familiarity with colleagues' topics of interest. Participants discussed the awkwardness and unfamiliarity of communicating in the New Zealand social idiom, and feelings of being excluded because they could not follow:

There are words they are using, bad words, swearing, but then it looks like they are happy using it. They are smiling while they are talking. So I feel that they are not talking against me. But sometimes if they are serious talking, you have this kind of feeling that they are talking about me.

And another participant:

With the group, outside the office, in the fresh air, they have this kind of group segregation, informal conversation. You find sometimes that not to listen to their swearing kind of things. I don't want to join their conversation anymore. So I better segregate, just commune with the nature. Because if you are going to join them, then you should use the words they are using, but I am not used to that.

These examples illustrate that conversational English outside of desk work proved challenging. Some participants had used English in the workplace in their own country, which they described as 'formal' English. For some participants who had been used to socialising with compatriots in their immigrant communities, the workplace highlighted the differences in communication styles. However, the coordinator explained the importance of sharing organisational rituals such as tea breaks as a way of socialising and promoting acceptance among local staff:

It is actually counterproductive for you settling in the workplace if everybody else is having morning tea and you stay at the desk working. People won't think here 'Oh, they are a really hard worker' . . . they might start to think 'Oh, why have they not wanted to mix with me and have morning tea?' In New Zealand . . . the social side of work and having morning teas is actually an important part of life. But migrants think 'If I stay and work, work, work, it's going to make me look good', and I say, 'Well, actually, it might not give the best impression. It might give the impression that you don't want to mix!' . . .

Engaging in small talk

Tea breaks necessitated the ability to engage in small talk. Some participants noted unfamiliarity with the practice of tea breaks and the self-disclosure it sometimes involves:

[In my home country] everything is quite straight-forward. People don't do a lot of small talk. They don't do tea break, and most time we keep our life professional.

Another participant described the sense of time wasting it implies, preferring direct communication:

It is taking forever to find out what people are actually trying to talk about. Here it is small talk first, and then they are coming to the point later on, and when they do it is 5 minutes talk. I guess sometimes my co-workers feel that I am quite straight-forward because I just I don't want to do the small talk first. I always say, 'Have you done that? Do you have that? Do you have this?'

[pp. 115–16]

The cultural stuff around how to talk to people

A participant used this phrase to describe the cultural complexities associated with email as opposed to face-to-face communication. While small talk and tea break communication required certain informality, participants felt that, in contrast, emails were 'cold' and 'serious':

> When managers write emails here it seems like it is very, very cold. But when you talk they seem very nice. They will say, 'How are you?' And all that.

The lack of non-verbal, contextual, affective cues available in emails created challenges in gauging their tone; consequently, face-to-face conversations seemed more manageable:

> I am still trying to understand when people are really serious, when they really mean it. When they are trying to be rude and I should respond on email and be colloquial or should I just talk to them. So that is something I still can't make out. On emails you don't know the person, don't know his background, his culture, or what day he is having.

An employer also commented on some immigrants' uncertainty around tone in emails:

> In an email she said to somebody, cold, somebody we never had any communication with in the past. It was a bit, it was really abrupt and kind of 'Please make an appointment!' and I was like, 'Oh my God, you don't do that, you have to try and build a relationship . . . not slam the door, so of course, that person never replied. [Employer]

The coordinator described situations where immigrants failed to realise that their formal email came across as 'quite demanding, just because that is the background they come from' (Co-ordinator). She also described situations where interns had sent her emails asking her the meaning of the email. These examples illustrate the complex sociocultural cues embodied in emails which, like other forms of workplace communication, need to be understood and learned.

Intercultural communication as disempowerment

The final theme concerns how participants found communication could sometimes leave them feeling disadvantaged, resulting in feelings of detachment and of being an outsider . . .:

> In my home country I am a different person. I am just talking, talking, but here I do my thing. I am a silent person. But it is a little bit hard. I was always accustomed to talking English very fluently and pronouncing properly. I used to talk like locals and in [my country] I was the native speaker who could speak very fluently English, so when I got here and people couldn't understand. It was very frustrating.

The linguistic competence participants experienced in their own country and workplace became 'incompetence' in the New Zealand workplace. They felt a lack of linguistic resources to express their thoughts and ideas in real-time communication, and an inability to grasp the illocutionary force of the message:

> I really like to talk, but if they ask some questions or talk about something, I can only give some simple word and they might think, 'ah, you don't like to talk with me', but that is not true.

> You feel a little bit stupid. You are used to understand everything in your first language. And then sometimes they treat you like, they look at you like 'aw, must be stupid'.

> Here [in New Zealand] 'thank you' and 'how can I help you', to express yourself, what you want to say. You want to help, you have to express it. In [country] it is not like that. In [country] everyone will know from my accent. Everybody will know from what words I have chosen. But here, English is not so much rich with the words.

Another participant, affirming the above experience, noted that 'English is not emotional'. Even understanding the appropriate non-verbal communication required, for example, in greetings – whether to shake hands, hug, kiss, shake hands or none of these – could create feelings of awkwardness, as one participant who had been living in New Zealand for 3 years commented:

> Every time I have to say hello you have that minute where you don't know how to say hello. I think it is still every time.

 Task B3.6.2

> ➤ To what extent did you predict the intercultural communication challenges immigrants might face when interacting with co-workers and employers in the workplace?

> ➤ How might the intercultural communication challenges vary depending on the context?

> ➤ What implications are there for intercultural training of employers, co-workers and immigrant workers in the New Zealand context Prue Holmes focuses on, and in other contexts?

Holliday A. R. (2016) 'Difference and awareness in cultural travel: negotiating blocks and threads' in *Language and Intercultural Communication* 16/3: 318–31 (extracts)

Cultural blocks

There has been a significant paradigm shift in the last decade regarding the nature of culture within the field of intercultural communication. This has resulted in an overthrowing of a more established view of the nation state, or national culture as the 'default signifier' of who we are (MacDonald and O'Regan 2011: 553) and 'from overarching templates to engagements with local knowledge and practice' (p. 563).

There do, however, seem to be softer and more radical versions of this movement, which, I will argue, emerge as two very different types of thinking that are characterised by the concepts of cultural blocks and threads respectively [p. 319].

Talking explicitly about cultural blocks allows researchers and cultural travellers to ask questions and get answers in a literal, factual manner, collecting information about different cultures. This could be something like this:

- 'How do people in your culture behave at mealtimes?'
- 'The whole family arrives on time and eats together; and show their appreciation of the person who has prepared the meal, who is normally the mother.'
- 'Oh, interesting. That's a bit different to my culture and others I have been to, where the whole thing is less formal and organised. But we can certainly learn from each other in this respect.'

I am not suggesting that the answers received in this type of exchange would necessarily just be taken at face value. We are all, I think, aware of the personal politics behind the way in which we and others talk about personal identities. It is instead the sorts of questions that are asked that indicate some sort of expectation that a certain type of information about culture is both available and likely to be forthcoming – as though this is somehow set aside from the complexity that we see elsewhere in social life . . . [pp. 319–20]

Cultural threads

Talking instead about threads of cultural experience focuses our attention on diverse aspects of our past that mingle with the experiences that we find and the threads of the people that we meet.

Cultural threads can be associated with the connections between the different parts of Holliday's grammar of culture represented in Figure A1.2.1 (adapted from Holliday 2013: 2 – see Unit A1.2). They are carried by the personal cultural trajectories (centre left), where we develop different senses of culture as we encounter different small culture environments through changing life events and pull threads of experience out from the cultural resources provided by the particular structures, that form our upbringing (on the left), and are coloured by the global position and politics that these also provide. The underlying universal processes (centre right) process these threads; and it is because these processes are common to all of us that we are able to make sense of each other's threads, which in turn help us make sense of our own, thus creating a common ground for sharing and enabling interculturality. It is this commonality that provides us with the basis to engage creatively with culture wherever we find it, and with each other, wherever we find ourselves.

The concept of cultural threads also represents the critical cosmopolitan discourse of culture that perceives the boundaries between national cultures to be political and ideological constructions (Delanty 2012; Delanty *et al.* 2008) and where cultural travellers can be resilient and activist global adventurers (Caruana 2014). This constructivism recognises that the researcher and participants in interviews co-construct what is being said and that the researcher is therefore implicated in the subjective power relations of the event (Block 2000; Miller 2011) . . . [pp. 320–1]

It would however be a mistake to suggest that cultural blocks and threads are focused on by different types of people depending on whether they are positivist or constructivist in orientation. In reality individuals can switch from one mode to the other within the same short statement . . . However, I will argue that cultural threads are actively employed to cross boundaries, while cultural blocks build boundaries and restrict cultural travel. For people who have been used to the cultural block mode as the most conscious, dominant mode of exchanging facts about different 'cultures', shifting to a cultural thread mode might require considerable discipline to think about people as potentially like oneself, with threads to share, rather than as mysterious members of another culture. (pp. 321–2)

Instead of looking for blocks, we follow the threads from who we are as people who have something to share to the implications of our circumstances, how we are brought up, where we live, and then perhaps to comparisons of politics, economy, city life, and so on. And we may in this way begin to see that we can have something to offer, to contribute in the foreign place where we find ourselves, and perhaps find understandings there that we can apply back to where we come from.

. . . The outcome is a conversation made up of a rich intertwining tapestry, with different threads that run between the interactants, some shared, some specific to a particular cultural domain, coming together or pulling apart at different stages of the conversation, with both parties, and perhaps those listening, noticing new threads and pulling in their own to help make sense. (p. 322)

Creative non-fiction

The second part of this paper will exemplify the discussion so far by means of a creative nonfictional narrative about three university students who come from a different country to the place where they are at university. I follow Agar (1990) in using creative nonfiction to mean a dramatisation of observed behaviour . . . The reason for employing creative nonfiction is to overcome the difficulty researchers have in capturing what they perceive might be going on in any one selection of data, which can lead to forcing evidence from a small number of verbatim extracts, especially in a short research paper (p. 79). Creative nonfiction may therefore have as much chance as any other form of text creation, where the aim of 'good ethnography' is to demonstrate 'how pattern is grown to enable comprehension of member-produced social action in the context of one world from the perspective of another' [p. 86].

In this sense, the narrative is not data in itself, but the result of analysis of data. Within a constructivist qualitative approach, the data is built from instances rather than samples and therefore cannot claim to be representative of any particular population of students. Its purpose is to illuminate the possibility of what might be going on rather than to establish the fact of what is going on, and in this sense to suggest areas for further investigation (Stenhouse 1985: 31). The narrative is therefore both a thick description in its own right and contributes to a thick description when put together with other studies [p. 324].

Gita, Hande and Francisca

The narrative is taken verbatim from Holliday (2013: 132–4) . . . Here I look at what the conversation between the characters tells us about cultural difference with references to conflicting thread and block modes of thinking . . .

The narrative is based on interviews and conversations with students away from home, with long-standing migrant residents, listening to their conversations, and my own experience of different cultural references when residing in different parts of the world. It is written in the cultural thread mode, and yet the friends are seen to be struggling with the cultural block mode of expression. The narrative opens with a conversation between two of the students about home:

> Gita and Hande talked about how they missed home. They both agreed that it was hard to find the ingredients they needed to cook the dishes they missed, and that there was just the temptation to rely on fast food and pizzas. They missed their families and the ambiance and the sounds of the streets in the medium-sized towns that they each came from.
>
> The conversation between Gita and Hande begins with very physical aspects of the environments that they come from . . . They have something in common regarding families they miss, the desire to cook and memories of small towns. We don't need to know which countries or national cultures to understand this. They thus draw threads from their past – personal cultural trajectories that they both recognise and bring them together. [p. 325]

How we wish to be seen

As their conversation continues, and Francisca joins in, there is the beginning of a conflict between cultural blocks, as the students consider events where they can show and exchange the content of their national cultures, and threads of experience where they play with forms that other people might consider not part of their 'cultures':

> Francisca asked Gita what she thought of these events which they both knew about where someone would cook their national food and invite friends round to taste it. Gita said it was great in many ways because other people would get some sort of idea where she came from. The problem was that people very quickly jumped to conclusion that this was all that she was. She described an occasion when friends had arrived and shown real surprise that she was playing what one of them referred to as 'Western' music. They very clearly thought that she had somehow learnt to like it since she had been here, good heavens: it was Bob Dylan, someone that her parents had played when she was a young child . . .

The event referred to here is what many students away from their home country might recognise as 'international events' where there is an invitation to share cultural arte-facts – perhaps not only food but also costumes, musical performance and so on. Despite the ostensible inclusivity of such events, they might be considered the epit-ome of the cultural block mode of thinking. Gita and Hande's anxiety that these events can result in Othering, or reducing individuals to simplified exotic references, is now well-catalogued in critical sociology, where a number of writers use various phrases to indicate their discomfort – 'the exotica of difference', 'to dress up in some native Jamaican costume and appear the spectacle of multiculturalism' (Hall 1991: 56), '"bou-tique multiculturalism"' (Kumaravadivelu 2007: 109, citing Stanley Fish), 'ethnic rites rather than ethnic rights' (p. 111). The terms they use imply a ritual of highly imaged intercultural show that is seductive and perhaps appealing as an initial response for people searching for opportunities to satisfy a feeling of unrecognised identities . . . The outcome can therefore be a 'liberal' multiculturalism that lacks criticality about the potentially very simplistic images of difference that it can generate. This lack of criticality can also easily fall into the neoliberal trap of an apparent discourse of action that serves only the Western power-base that creates it . . . [pp. 325–6]

This is not however a matter of a clear choice between block and thread thinking. Both may serve us at different times depending on our needs. Even though the threads running through our trajectories may or may not, in varying degrees, associate with the ritualised block artefacts of culture that we find ourselves sharing at 'International' events, we all have our own takes on these cultural artefacts that others hold up to define us with. At different times and for different reasons we may therefore wish to associate with their block connotations or not. Sometimes we ourselves may hold up the cultural artefacts of food, dress or festivals to say that this is what we are. For this reason, the particular cultural products domain of the grammar (right of Figure A1.2.1) also includes statements about culture. 'In my culture this is what we eat and this is how we eat it' therefore becomes a strategic cultural block statement used for particular effect at a particular time depending on the strategy we feel we need to use to project how we want to be seen at a particular time. In this sense, choosing to associate ourselves with cultural blocks is itself one of the threads we pull through our experience. The major point here is that it is not for others to impose these block definitions upon us. We can block define ourselves; but others must not [p. 327].

Knowing what it's like

In this longer section Hande and Gita continue to share what they miss about home, and move from what are arguably very real aspects of light, sounds, smells, cultural practices that collect around particular locations – their personal threads of cultural experience – to what they are being told about who they are with reference to the cultural block of collectivism:

> They went back to things that they missed and talked about how it was very hard for other people who had not been away from home like they were to understand what it was like to wake up imagining for a moment being in one's own country, with familiar smells of breakfast and the smells and sounds, and the colour of the light that one had grown up with. It was so hard not to find the food one was used to. They agreed that they could eventually work out how they were supposed to behave, and that they could even get used to having to try so much harder to make friends.
>
> Back to family life again, they began to talk about issues that they found in common – concerning boyfriends, family pressures for them to get married and so on; and there was a huge amount they had in common. They talked about this and decided that it was because these were fairly universal things – except perhaps for Western people. So what was the issue there? Was it in fact the case that the West was completely different to everywhere else? Was it after all the case that the world really was divided into individualist and collectivist cultures?
>
> Hande said that she had heard on several occasions people from the East and the South, when they met each other, even for a short period of time, say that 'you are like us'; and it had something to do with shared understandings about the nature of life, or something like that. Gita asked Hande if she thought it was to do with things like family loyalties and the issues that arose from that. Hande said she wasn't sure. Gita said she thought it might have something to do with a warmth that arose from all sorts of things that people had to deal with which meant they had to depend on each other more. Then she thought again and said that it might not be that at all, because she had heard Westerners talking about dealing with all

those things. The problem was that Westerners didn't think that foreigners could be like them, perhaps because of all this stuff about food and festivals, and being traditional and religious; and so they just kept their distance.

Hande and Gita weigh the evidence carefully regarding whether or not they belong to a cultural block that is different to that of the West. The outcome of their analysis is that, even though there are common experiences, a separate, collectivist, family-oriented East and South could be more a Western imagination than an actuality . . . [p. 328]

Conclusion: intercultural learning

. . . while cultural difference is a crucial phenomenon that derives from the social structures within which we are brought up, we have the potential through cultural travel to cross boundaries and find ourselves in new domains and at the same time engage positively, creatively and critically with the realities and the people that we find. These principles of interculturality are enhanced by a cultural thread mode of thinking and talking about cultural difference. However, it also emerges that special strategies are required to ensure that the thread mode takes place. This is especially the case because the competing block mode seems to come to us more naturally.

Therefore, if there is to be such a thing as intercultural training it should be in how to focus on cultural threads and put aside cultural blocks – how to ask the questions, to talk to people, to recognise the threads in one's personal cultural trajectory, to connect this to the threads of others, to find threads that one can relate to. A mirror of this is the training of intercultural researchers – in the basic ethnographic disciplines of qualitative enquiry. Researchers too need to learn how to contribute their own cultural threads in conversational interventions within interviews to bring out the threads of their participants. Such training could include a close analysis of conversations – an ethnomethodology of how thread conversations come about. [pp.329–30]

Task B3.6.3

➤ Can you think of times you have referred to the cultural artefacts of national 'food, dress or festivals' to say that 'this is what I am'?

➤ Do you think it is true that 'the block mode' comes to people more naturally than 'the thread mode'?

➤ How can intercultural training help a shift from a 'cultural block mode' to a 'cultural thread mode'?

Commentary

The two texts in this unit suggest ways of moving beyond a model-based approach in intercultural training whereby participants are encouraged to view behaviour and communication in terms of pre-taught cultural models or cultural templates. A key element in recent approaches to intercultural education is that individuals should focus on authentic instances of interaction, and consider in depth contextual factors, including how identities are played out and how power is a *sine qua non* of any intercultural encounter.

Halualani (2011) provides an example of such a course she taught at two universities in the USA. The first part of the course 'focuses on understanding and applying the building blocks of culture (world views, cultural patterns, beliefs, values, and attitudes)' and on the work of Hofstede and E. T. Hall 'and other scholars' frameworks of cultural patterns and communication styles'. She writes that:

> These theories reinforce and reify 'truths' they have already heard and known about regarding different cultures. The familiarity of it all is comforting, reassuring, and stabilising. Right after their midterm, however, I take my students on a much different road, a rocky road. Together we experience the limits of everything they had just learned about culture. Meaning, we take the information we learned about cultural patterns to its most logical conclusion and interrogate such knowledge further.
>
> (p. 49)

On this 'rocky road' the aim is for students to explore and develop a critical appreciation of power in intercultural communication. Specifically students are encouraged to consider a number of questions including: 'What dimensions, structures, and forces of power are embedded in my own intercultural encounters and relationships?'; 'What kind of power dynamic deeply exists in these encounters and relationships?'; 'How am I positioned in the intercultural relationships and encounters in my life?'; 'To what extent do I gain a power advantage and gain over others in some contexts than in others?' 'To what degree am I marginalised and put at a disadvantage in certain contexts over others?'; 'What can I do to change and mediate the power differences between individuals and cultural groups?' (p. 51).

SECTION C
Exploration

In Section C of the book, the focus is upon relating what you have read and learned in Sections A and B to your own personal circumstances and experiences. The aim is to develop reflection and strategies for action which will increase your awareness about how you may approach intercultural communication. This is achieved through research tasks. These can be carried out either in groups or individually, but the value of researching in small groups, perhaps with others from different cultural backgrounds, is that you can compare notes and at the same time learn from each other's cultural perspectives.

As with the rest of the book, this section follows the broad themes of Identity, Othering and Representation. Explicit links will be made to Sections A and B, but there will also be links you will need to make by yourselves as an index of your own theory development. Ideas and themes raised in the units in the previous sections are therefore further developed in the units in this section.

The intention is to offer you research tasks that will develop both your 'noticing' skills and your strategies in undoing and dealing with essentialist cultural prejudices. They are designed to help you observe, gather data and reflect upon the deeper nature of cultural difference and hence to enhance your communication skills. There will thus be specific reference to the disciplines for interpersonal under-standing which grow out of and are listed in Section A. This section of the book is based upon the premise that communication skills can be improved through analysis and reflection. Both to help you undertake the tasks, and also to underpin your communication skills, another aim of this section will be to develop a research methodology, which is in effect a methodology for raising awareness.

Another important premise is that you do not need to travel to 'other cultures' to collect data on intercultural communication and develop intercultural commun-ication skills. Cultural difference is everywhere and we all actually engage with it in our everyday lives. This can be seen in the texts in Section B, and is illustrated in several of the examples in Section A. We will consider instances of cultural difference that occur within and between societies, communities and institutions; and especially within the process of globalisation, *all* of these can be encountered within our own personal social settings. Section C therefore invites you to explore and develop your understanding of intercultural communication as an everyday activity.

Task C0.1.1 Establishing an approach

➤ Re-read the discussion of 'the tourist gaze' in Unit B2.5. Consider these points:

- Why may the notion of travelling *to* a culture be an essentialist one? Does it comes from the thinking that reduces and others the individual in the same way as sexism and racism? You may like to revisit Table A0.1.1 in Section A and recall what we say there.
- Think of your own experiences as a tourist visiting another culture. Note down the way in which you considered that there was something culturally different about the people in the destination you were in.

Throughout Section C we suggest you keep a research diary and note down the various results of the tasks you are asked to complete and your thoughts about your findings. You can then revisit your thoughts after completing the exercises to see if afterwards you have any different thoughts about your initial reactions.

An ethnographic approach

Task C0.1.1 is broadly ethnographic in approach. It is within an interpretive qualitative approach to research. This means that you begin researching everyday life by looking around you to see 'what is going on'. Your very basic research tools are observation and writing descriptions of what you see and hear in a research diary. These activities need, however, to be disciplined. Some of these disciplines are represented in the ones listed in Table A3.4.1 (Section A). They are also implied in the non-essentialist thinking outlined in Table A0.1.1. Here the researcher is asked to try very hard to put aside preconceptions and attempt to gain an understanding of things in their own terms. If you wish to read more about ethnography and the attendant disciplines of qualitative research and participant observation, there are many books available; accessible ones are Spradley (1980), Hammersley and Atkinson (1995) and Holliday (2016).

An important aspect of progressive forms of ethnography and qualitative research is the understanding that you as a researcher are, or become, part of the setting you are researching. You do not simply observe 'them' and 'their' behaviour, but, instead, how the participants in the setting interact with you. Understanding how you interact with other participants will also help you to understand what sort of people they are. An interesting book to read here is Coffey (1999). Adopting this approach is important if you are going to escape from an essentialist 'us'–'them' view of culture.

The disciplines listed in Section A therefore look in two directions. They consider both how we may look *outwards* at people who we perceive as culturally different to ourselves to gain an understanding of the complexities of their identities, and how we should look *inwards* at ourselves to understand how we may be imposing a view of what other people are on them. The outward and inward gazes are of the same order in that we are fundamentally the same as the *people* with which we wish to interact. We all have complex cultural formations which derive from complex societies. Thus, the inward and outward gazes will deeply interact and the distinctions between them will be over-simplistic. Tasks in this section are designed to develop an understanding of yourself which has a bearing on the development of the understanding of others.

Intercultural communication research task

At the end of most units there will be a research task specifically designed to investigate instances of intercultural communication within the framework of the disciplines outlined in Section A. This will connect the other issues and investigations within each unit to an intercultural communication event within your own milieu. The intercultural communication research task in each case will have the form expressed in Figure C0.1.1, though this form is of course designed to be adapted to individual needs.

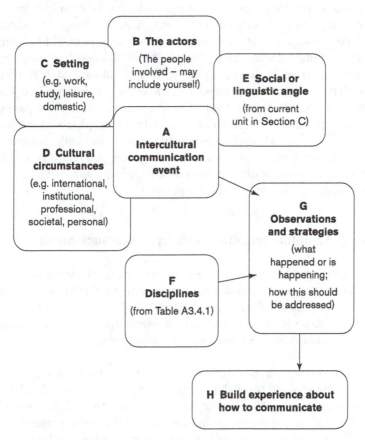

Figure C0.1.1 Format for intercultural research

The task will be focused upon an intercultural communication event of your choosing (as in Figure C0.1.1). You will begin the task by describing the overall scenario of the event in terms of **B** to **D** in the figure. You will be asked to address a particular angle **E**, which will arise from the discussion in the current unit, which may refer back to discussions in Section B of the book. You will be guided to apply particular disciplines and their attendant discussions from Section A. The overall approach to the task will be ethnographic in that, aided by the disciplines in **F**, the strategies in **G** will emerge by means of open-ended interpretation from observation.

The range of types of event covered by these tasks will depend on you, and will allow you to explore the intercultural domains in which you are interested. The examples in **C** and **D** show the possible width of choice, and are not exclusive. They are *working* categories, which only stand until better ones are found. They are *heuristic* in that they are there to help understanding, but do not represent real distinctions. It is as difficult and unsatisfactory to categorise settings and circumstances in this way as it is to categorise cultures. However, the following attempt to gloss them may be helpful. Work and study places could be companies, offices, building sites, schools or universities. Leisure settings could be football matches, clubs or cinemas. Domestic settings could be at home or in daily life which is not easily categorised. The event described in Unit A1.3, with girls on a bus, could be called domestic. International cultural circumstances would be where the 'difference' is connected with nationality; institutional, where it is connected with hierarchies, departments, territories, traditions or role and status differences, within work or study settings; professional, where difference is between groups of practitioners, such as doctors and nurses, geographers and historians, painters and ceramicists, engineers and academics, all clearly overlapping with institutional circumstances. Societal circumstances, which clearly overlap with the others, are to do with the structure of society, perhaps with gender, age, class, race, ethnicity, family, education, social condition, power, wealth, participation, and so on. Personal could be connected with interpersonal difference.

 Task C0.1.2 Exploring breadth of setting and circumstances

➤ Look at a selection of examples in Section A or in the texts in Section B. Explore how far you can categorise them in terms of setting and cultural circumstances. Look particularly for overlaps in the categories offered in Figure C0.1.1. Where there are categories in Figure C0.1.1 for which you cannot find examples in Sections A and B, find examples from your own experience.

➤ See if you can replace the categories in Figure C0.1.1 with better ones of your own. As you progress through the units in Section C, an overall task might be to redesign Figure C0.1.1. The important outcome of the intercultural communication research model in Figure C0.1.1 is H, the experience you build about how *to communicate*. As has been stated elsewhere in this book, we are more interested in mastering the *process* of intercultural communication than with the content of how to do it with individual 'cultures'.

Ethical considerations

Because you will be invited to research real events with real people, it is important to consider the ethics of this practice. It is best if you are able to confide in the people who take part in your investigation and to ask their permission. You may need to be prepared to share with them what you are finding out. In all cases, when sharing your findings with colleagues, it is essential to have anonymised as much as you possibly can; and you must tell the people in your research that you are doing this. There will, however, be occasions where your research is very casual and impromptu, with a minimum of invasion of people's privacy, and too unplanned for you to ask permission. For advice on these issues, consult Punch (1994).

Theme 1
Identity

UNIT C1.1   THE STORY OF THE SELF

Since childhood we have all been offered ways of understanding ourselves – from our family, education, friends and the society that surrounds us. In a sense we have been told who we are since our birth from a variety of sources. These messages may be contradictory, and so we may try to integrate these stories about what we are into a unified narrative of our own identity. This narrative is a key aspect of our sense of who we are – of our personal identity. As can be deduced from this perspective, the identity we assume is, at least in part, derived from the social context in which we live, the type of family we are born into, the education we receive and the friends that we are able to make as well as the society that surrounds us. This means that our identity is temporally and spatially framed or influenced. Who we feel ourselves to be is thus influenced by where and when we live our lives. To the extent that certain periods of history and certain geographical locations offer people living in them common features, our personal identity is, at least in part, shared with others from the same time period and location. Although the non-essentialist view promoted strongly in Section A encourages us to look at individuals, it cannot be denied that culture is nevertheless basically a phenomenon which involves individuals sourcing their identities from commonly held 'group' resources. The exercises in Section C are designed to make you critically aware of this process as it applies to you and to the development of your skill as an intercultural communicator.

The following research task involves age groups. This will serve to demonstrate both that cultural difference can operate within as well as between societies and the way in which you, as a member of an age group, may be culturally constructed.

Task C1.1.1 Exploring age

➤ Interview people from different age groups. Select three adults of different ages: one in the 20–30-year-old age bracket, one in the 40–50-year-old bracket and one in the 60+ age bracket. Think of general topics to broach with these participants concerning the belief systems they feel they either subscribe to or feel people of their generation subscribe to.

Research questions and informants

Before beginning your investigation it is important to decide several things. You need to have an overall research question to which you are looking for an answer. This provides a sense of direction and purposefulness to your research. At the same time, the questions must be sufficiently open-ended to allow you to respond to people according to how you find them rather than according to what you have heard about them (Discipline 1, Table A3.4.1). This relates to an important principle in qualitative research – allowing the unexpected to emerge. In this task, two possible questions are:

1. Are age groups 'culturally' different?
2. In what ways are age groups culturally different?

Consider which of these two questions best fulfils Discipline 1. Create more suitable questions if you need to.

Next you need to decide who exactly you are going to interview. This choice will depend on who you have access to and who would be good informants from each age group. These decisions will also depend on convenience and how much time you have. It is also important to realise the limits of your investigation. What you investigate will hopefully offer you insights and develop your understanding of the question you are researching, but you cannot say that what you interpret from the limited data you obtain is in any sense definitive and necessarily generalisable to other researchers and samples of populations. On the other hand, if others undertaking similar small-scale investigations derive insights similar to yours, then this acts to strengthen your findings. This is why researchers need to read one another's work.

Within an interpretive qualitative approach to research, we can learn from small instances of social life. The aim is not to prove how things are, but to make us think again and question our preconceptions.

Asking questions

Here are some interview questions that may be helpful.

1. When you were young, was it expected that young people should show respect to their elders?
2. Did you show this respect? How? Why? Why not?
3. What about now? Do you think there has been a change?
4. What do you think about this?

If you ask questions that distance the participant from their purely personal circumstances, that is, by asking them questions about what others believed or did rather than questions such as 'Did *you* show respect to your father?', you are more likely to obtain a more general picture of the views held by certain generations.

You may like to choose other topics to ask questions on, for example, sexual mores and behaviour, and attitudes to foreigners. The questions you choose are tools you use to try to 'unlock' underlying beliefs – which becomes your data. As they are tools (or instruments) you need to experiment until you find ones that work for you. You may elect to try to uncover such data using another strategy: you may ask the interviewee to tell you three things that were better in the past for young people than today and three things that are better now. You will then need to follow up the responses with probing questions to uncover why the interviewees hold the particular views they espouse. This allows you to attempt to try to uncover the values and beliefs each interviewee claims to hold. The methodology you choose is up to you, and is based upon your relationship with the interviewees and what you feel most comfortable with. The important thing is that you have thought through your approach before you undertake the interviews so that you know what you are aiming to achieve.

Organising the research task

It is a good idea when undertaking a research project to draw up a timetable for the research. There are different ways to organise Task C1.1.1 depending on the number of people involved. Table C1.1.1 is an example timetable where the research task is done as a group project. Note the columns which refer to discussions. Looking for emerging patterns between each stage of interviews, which guide further interviews,

Table C1.1.1 Research timetable

	First week	Beginning of second week	Second half of second week	Beginning of third week
Interviewer 1	Interviews with: Participant 1 Participant 2 Participant 3	Discussion between interviewers and analysis of data looking for patterns in the data that can be further investigated (probed).	Interviews with: Participant 1 Participant 2 Participant 3	Discussion between interviewers and analysis of data and gathering together of findings from interviews.
Interviewer 2	Interviews with: Participant 4 Participant 5 Participant 6		Interviews with: Participant 4 Participant 5 Participant 6	
Interviewer 3	Interviews with: Participant 7 Participant 8 Participant 9		Interviews with: Participant 7 Participant 8 Participant 9	

assures that Discipline 1 is applied. If you are going to do follow-up interviews, this should be thought of before you start the research and the participants you choose need to be secured as available for the two interviews.

Remember that initial questions only provide a surface response to most issues and these responses are often not sufficient in themselves for you to gain insights into the deeper thought processes and reasoning behind the responses. There can be no such thing as a scientific 'neutral' or purely 'objective' interview. Initial responses, therefore, need probing by follow-up questions. This can be done skilfully after the initial prompt questions at the time of the interview or you may prefer to first analyse the responses you have – especially if you have interviewed several people. You can then look for patterns in the responses that can then be followed up by further questioning in interviews with the same participants.

Another way to proceed, if doing this individually could be as follows.

1. Begin with one interview.
2. See what this tells you and where it leads you.
3. Investigate further with another interview with someone else, and so on.

This type of open-ended exploration could also involve use of other research tools such as looking at documents (for example, things people write) or observing behaviour and appearance (for example, how people stand around with each other, what people wear). You may also decide to turn the interview into a conversation, which may be less daunting and 'formal' for the participant. Seeing the interview as a conversation may also help you to learn something more about yourself, through your own role in the process.

 Task C1.1.2 The interpersonal factor

➤ Reflect upon the interpersonal factor in researching people. Do you think that you, as the interviewer interviewing a set of people, uncover the same data as another interviewer interviewing another set of people? What factors may affect the answers your respondents make to your questions? How relevant are the following factors?

- Who you are and your relationship to the interviewee.
- The issue of whether people are able to distance themselves from their own cultural formation.
- The actual knowledge base of the respondents – the knowledge base upon which they claim to know what they state?
- The mood the person is in at the time of the interview.
- The degree to which the respondent may feel there is a boundary to what can be disclosed, i.e. talked about. This involves the socially learnt concept of taboo and the notion of what degree of intimacy is acceptable for disclosure to others.

■ The issue of whether people want to appear likeable and 'nice' when talking to other people (maintain their positive face).

Hopefully you will agree that trying to uncover 'the truth' is a sensitive task. Would you agree that what one uncovers in interviews is rather 'versions of the truth' than 'the truth'? In this particular type of research – social research – you should not conclude, therefore, that such a feeling means what you are doing is flawed research. It is rather to understand a vital point about social reality. In research project C1.1.1 it is not so much the quest to find out if the interviewees really are different from each other that is of interest, but rather to find out if the interviewees feel that they are different from other people from other generations. It is what people choose to assert that is interesting. The 'story of the self', i.e. one's identity, and it is told by the self to the self and to others, is the focus of this research exercise. This story is important because it exerts a powerful influence on people's actions and behaviours. It is important for intercultural communicators to be aware of this story and the influence it exerts on identity and therefore communicative styles.

Now we can conclude this unit with an intercultural communication research task. This follows logically from the previous task in that it should now be evident that interviewing people from age groups other than your own is in fact an example of intercultural communication. Hence, use Figure C0.1.1 to help complete Task C1.1.3.

Task C1.1.3 Interview as cultural interaction

➤ Event: retrospective.

➤ Actors: you and a person you have interviewed.

➤ Setting: as Task C1.1.1.

➤ Cultural circumstances: age difference.

➤ Angle: understanding self by finding out about others.

➤ Observation: reconstruct what happened. Your research diary (see Task C0.1.1) should be a useful resource here.

➤ Disciplines: 5, 7, 8.

➤ Outcome: draw conclusions about how the interviewee appeared to feel about her/his cultural identity from the way in which she/he behaved and told her/his story. Look into how your own behaviour might have contributed to what happened.

UNIT C1.2   BECOMING THE SELF BY DEFINING THE OTHER

As you may have found in Task C1.1.1, culture is very pervasive – something that individuals seem to absorb from their environment. The formation of a person's identity can, therefore, be seen, at least partly, to be shaped by external circumstances. It may also be apparent, from Task C1.1.3, that for the 'self' to be defined – to take shape – there is use made of 'contrastive others'. As is argued in the theory of deconstruction, things are often what they are in terms of what they are not. In this sense cultural identity is inevitably somewhat exclusive. You are something because you are not something else. You are Peruvian because you are not Chilean, you are an American Democrat because you are not a Republican, in other words you are X because you are not Y. In Text B0.2.1, Fay attacks a view of culture – the 'standard view' – which sees culture as a force that penetrates its members mentally and that leads to socially and physically conditioned behaviour. He questions this 'standard' view which holds that members are seen to have absorbed the culture that surrounds them, thus becoming part of that culture themselves, with 'distinctive capacities and characteristics'.

> **Stop and think:** What do you think Fay may have against this view of culture? Does his perspective coincide with your findings from your research and thought to this point?

Fay's main criticism of this view of culture is that it is overly deterministic. It is for this reason that we state that identity is only *partly* shaped by external circumstance, not that it is *completely*.

Determinism is the view that we are completely formed by our environment and thus we are in a sense victims of circumstances. The problem with this view is that it ignores the fact that people, given the possibility of circumstance, are potentially able to become critical over this process and able to exert choice over how they source their identities. The determinist argument may therefore be criticised for viewing people as lacking agency, i.e. the ability to critically reflect upon and distance themselves from their environment and their own formation and act upon it to change it.

> **Stop and think**: How far do you think people are able to critically reflect upon their identity formation? See Holmes in Text B3.6.1 and consider the concepts of Avowed Identity versus Prescribed Identity. What conditions do you think are necessary for people to be able to question these two identities and make choices? What barriers are there that may stop people exercising a critical reflection on their identity and putting this into action?

Some things to consider may be: access to education and the concepts of 'criticality' and 'plurality'; overcoming the fear of being different and the danger of not following a prescribed mode of cultural behaviour; fear of change and its possible consequences; the exercise of group and ideological pressure.

The determinism/voluntarism perspectives form an argument that runs throughout Cultural Studies and you will have to have taken a position on this when you read the various arguments presented in Section B. It is probably true to state here that although the various authors have differing views and positions on the nature and extent of influence of 'culture' upon individual actions – and no doubt you will also develop different insights from undertaking the tasks in this book and through reflection upon the results – they are, however, linked by the common theme that the more critical we can be about the process of how we construct ourselves and others in intercultural encounters, the better. In other words, we are aware of the danger inherent in the process of 'Othering' and the goal-directed (political) and mediated (through third parties) nature of representation of others that we are exposed to. The more we can develop our own critical understanding of this, the more we will be in control of our intercultural communication.

It is against the danger of this Othering and 'stagnant' view of others (i.e. cultural essentialism) that the concept of culture as fixed and an internally absorbed force that people then carry around with them is questioned in this book.

In Task C1.2.1 you will investigate the degree to which people use contrasts (the 'contrastive Other') as a way of arriving at an understanding of who they are. It is important that you as researchers do not fall into this potential essentialist trap yourselves. Some of our international research students at Canterbury Christ Church University have tended to present findings when researching British culture in contrastive terms: one group looking at personal interaction between strangers came to the conclusion from their research that 'the British are much politer than the Swedish. Because they always say "sorry" and "please"'. Another group concluded from observation of female dress codes in Britain that 'young British women are not as independent from men as young German women because they have to dress to sexually please men by showing a lot of bare flesh – even when it is very cold'.

Note: The etic and emic levels of cultural analysis

It is easy to fall into the 'contrastive trap' of 'they are . . .' therefore 'we are . . .'. But this is problematic because different cultural groups operate with different norms that only make sense *within* the groups, not necessarily *between* the groups. In other words, the politeness demonstrated in Britain or the dress codes and their messages can only be properly interpreted ('read') from a perspective from within the cultural group being analysed itself. It cannot be understood from without as an outsider does not have the 'language', that is, the semiotic codes, with which to read the culture and the signs. The signs operate within a culture and are designed to be invested with meanings by those who also share the code. This is what is encompassed by the terms 'etic' and 'emic' levels of analysis. The terms come from linguistics. Very crudely, phonetics is the study of all possible meaningful sounds used by all people across the world in the construction of languages. The study of phonemics is the study of a specific set of sounds used by a particular language group: Spanish has 24, Japanese 21 and Arabic 28. In other words, phonemics is a subset of phonetics.

If we take a generally applicable human concept such as 'clothing' or 'interaction' we can take this as a generic 'etic' level concept; after all, all people, whatever cultural groups they belong to, 'interact'. In Culture X they do A; in Culture Y they do B. So far so good, but this is the limit of our understanding. As soon as you compare behaviour in Culture X with Culture Y because you are assuming that Behaviour A is in some way exclusively relatable to Behaviour B you fall into the danger of drawing false conclusions. The two behaviours are not comparable because they only have contrastive meaning within their own cultural and semiotic systems, that is, when they are studied from within each culture.

Note: Semiotics

Semiotics is the study of signs. It looks at how meaning and signification are transmitted – through construction by the sender and interpretation by the reader, within a cultural group. In semiotics, signs are believed to have denotative and connotative meanings. In Arabic 'khobz' is the word for 'bread' and refers to a food type usually made from wheat – this is the denotation indexed by these two random signs (words). This is the literal denotation. However, this khobz or bread may have religious or other meanings associated with it (perhaps in one culture it has associations of poverty, in another wealth): these are the connotations of the sign khobz/bread. Connotations are obviously influenced by the cultural context in which the sign operates. In the above example of the way some English girls dress when going out in the evening, 'clothing' has a denotative meaning – which is along the lines of 'material you cover your body with': however, it is the connotations with regard to the type of clothing, the amount of clothing and the location and time of day of wearing such clothing (or lack of it!) that give the clothing its connotations for those 'reading' it, and these readings are undertaken using culturally acquired schemata (rules). Schemata for reading a sign in one culture may not be useful in reading the same sign in another culture. Not to realise this can lead to various outcomes, from comic to tragic! Consider the use of the veil and the covering of the body in one culture and the associated connotative meanings derived when convention is not followed in that culture and contrast this with the example of the English girls going out on a Saturday night. It is easy to see how both groups may read each others' clothing signs using their own schemata. People misread signs when they cross cultural borders and make errors of interpretation because they use their own cultural semiotics for this.

This study of cultural systems of meaning from within that system is referred to as the emic level of analysis. Because you, as a researcher, are also a cultural being, operating with certain cultural norms that are no doubt distinct from those you may be researching, you are in danger of interpreting them falsely if you use your own norms of reference. It may be that British people are not actually politer than Swedish people but that 'sorry' and 'please' are simply used in different ways from their 'linguistic or other equivalents' in Swedish. They may be necessary systemic tags in one culture but not in another. To compare cultures as if they were operating from the same meaning template as one's own is to commit the 'emic fallacy'. It is a very common error to make.

Task C1.2.1 Contrasting yourself with others

➤ Decide on a particular cultural group that you see as distinct from yourselves. Try and define what it is about the group that signals it as different.

➤ If you are in a business context and wish to think of this issue in relation to your company, think of the particular department or business unit you work in and another business unit or department of the company, for example, R and D, Finance or HR.

➤ You can approach this by doing the following:

- They are . . . whereas we are . . .
- They do . . . whereas we do . . .

Or

- We are . . . whereas they are . . .
- We do . . . whereas they do . . .

➤ Now work out what the effect of this Othering impulse is when you contrast 'us' with 'them' when you assume that you are operating to the same system of norms and interpretative values.

➤ Devise a strategy for how you might be able to approach researching the other group at an emic level. What procedures, techniques and guidelines could you use? In the case of the group of Swedish students mentioned earlier, the following guidelines were drawn up. How do they compare to yours?

- You have to get some 'insider' interpretation of data, not just rely on your own 'outsider' interpretation.
- You need to develop trusting relationships with 'insiders'.
- You need to look for examples of behaviour that don't fit with your first conclusions and thus resist closing your eyes and ears to new possible meanings.

- You must be aware of how easy it is to draw on stereotypes rather than to learn to see what is actually there.
- Can you add any more to the list? In a business what about shadowing a person from another department?

➤ Once you have done this go and research the group in question following the procedures, techniques and guidelines you have drawn up. Then look back at the list of differences you drew up previously. Are the differences still clear? If differences do exist, do you understand them better? Do you feel that the group you have researched are 'like that' by nature, or do you think that they are simply operating in a different cultural environment and would change if the environment changed?

Note: Being critical

At this point it is important to explain what is meant by the term 'critical'. It is a term that is used a lot in social science and has a precise meaning in that context. In many respects the key objective of this section of the book is to develop your critical thinking about culture and interaction. It does not mean that one holds a negative view of something – that is the more current, everyday meaning of the word. Being critical is seen as a good thing to be in that it shows a person has developed the ability to analyse something employing criteria they have developed for that purpose. It means a person is not simply accepting something as true because it is said to be so. Being critical, therefore, takes independence of thought and a certain degree of intellectual courage, as you may find that you are not in agreement with the way you are expected or supposed to think about something. This is a necessary ingredient of Discipline 2 (Table A3.4.1), in which we must often try very hard to resist what our conditioning presents as 'obvious'. Being critical, however, needs to be based upon evidence and justification: in other words a vague feeling that something is not right needs to be refined into the ability to begin to understand the basis as to why it is felt that something is not right and the ability to com-municate this in a convincing fashion. Critical thinking can be seen to be a desirable achievement at the end of much reflection and analysis. Without reflection and analysis, thoughts are likely to remain vague and difficult to communicate in a convincing fashion to others.

Note: Othering

Othering is the process that we undertake in ascribing identity to the 'self' through the often negative attribution of characteristics to the 'other'. (See the definition and discussion in Unit A2.1.) We may attribute these characteristics to other people so that their willingness or agreement to be understood in terms of these characteristics is overlooked and often negated. In other words, Othering can be seen as a 'culture first view of individuals'. In this book this is seen to be problematic in that this does not allow for the agency of other people to be a factor in their identity construction. It does not permit the *negotiation* of identity between people, but is about the imposition of crude, second-hand (off-the-peg) and often reductive identities, on others.

Othering may be undertaken by the self upon the self too. If a prescribed view of the self, set by dominant others becomes internalised as valid, then the self may 'other' the self. As Guo and Harlow (Text B2.2.2) show, a persistent stereotype of Latinos may be 'laziness'. Self Othering may arise if the ascribed or avowed self-view becomes 'I'm Latino, therefore I'm lazy' or 'I'm lazy because I'm Latin.' What dangers do you feel may be inherent in such self-Othering? How can this be avoided?

Having stated the case against over-hasty imposition of traits to others, this is not to say that the issue of cultural difference can be hypothesised away. People, as we all know, are different from each other and people do affiliate themselves to distinct cultural groups which promote 'distinctive capacities and characteristics'. If this were not a reality then there would be no such thing as culture and there would be no need to study 'intercultural communication' but just interpersonal communication. The point is that in intercultural communication it is wise not to impose categories to which you ascribe a person as belonging to when you have minimal evidence for this, that is, not to assume that a person can be understood firstly as a member of a certain cultural group. It is more felicitous to allow for negotiated identity in interaction.

➤ Look at Holliday (Text B3.6.2). What is his proposal for how this may happen? What do you understand by his terms 'block' and 'thread' in relation to this approach?

Indeed, categories or 'invoked templates' are often mythical in nature – they may serve to trap people within 'imposed webs of belonging'. Resisting the temptation to undertake Othering may result in you wondering if any defined culture, as you experience it, does in fact present the characteristics that its members profess it has or that other cultures profess that that culture has. In a sense this is not important as much as the fact that you are aware of the danger of these constructed images for your intercultural communication. It may perhaps be the case that genuinely successful communication relies upon trust developing between interactants from professedly distinct cultures and that this involves a process whereby the larger cultural templates (stereotypes) are gradually debunked in favour of a more dynamic and creative construction of identities between interactants. This does not occur in the examples in Units A2.2, A2.3 and A3.1, where the outcomes are unsuccessful.

Stop and think: Look at these examples and try to pinpoint where you think they 'go wrong'.

Task C1.2.2 'Signalling my characteristics'

➤ Determine the distinctive capacities and characteristics that you feel you can draw on for your cultural identity. To what aspects of your identity do they refer? How much do you draw on these and perhaps manipulate or negotiate them according to who you are communicating with and where you are communicating?

You may find Table C1.2.1 useful as a starting point for self-reflection. You will find that in this task you are dealing with large-scale social understandings of how these particular aspects of identity are signalled and 'read'. These are what Gee refers to as Discourses with a capital 'D' (Text B1.3.2). They are the socially sanctioned ways that a group of people orientate themselves towards representing and interpreting 'objects', i.e. the thing that is constructed. In this task the objects in each case are the various components of identity you have identified in Table C1.2.1. While these constructed understandings may not necessarily be accurate, or you may not agree with them in essence, they can be argued to exist in the collective consciousness of a cultural group (and the media that is read by that group) and therefore exert a powerful influence upon members of that cultural group. Because of this they need to be negotiated by individuals interacting in that group, particularly by those who may not conform to them.

People respond to the signals you send out. One particular signal that people read is your language: the accent, the register, the vocabulary selected. See Holmes in Text B3.6.1 for a discussion of the use of English in a work setting. What effect does the lack of 'insider' expertise in the use of language code have on the interactants and their views of each other? Another may be your attire: the formality or otherwise of this according to context.

> **Stop and think:** Think about yours and other people's dress codes and a) the message you are sending out b) the messages you are picking up. If you work in a company/organisation, what regulations a) official b) unofficial are there about dress codes? What corporate image does the dress code try to project? Can you think of instances where individuals break the code? What effect does this have and what consequences arise?

Pick one of the categories in Table C1.1.2 to focus on. Over a period of time decide to note down how people respond to the signals you send out with regard to this component, and also note your own responses to these responses. You are best doing this by using your diary and making notes after each 'event'. Once you have collected a range of instances in different contexts, try to determine any underlying patterns. Do different people in different contexts respond to your identity signal in different ways? How? Why do you think this is? You will need in each instance to consider your role, your relationship to any interactant, the time and place of each event, and your feelings (affective reaction). Figure C0.1.1 will help you with this. One way of organising this is to devise a chart to fill in after each 'event'. You

Table C1.2.1 Self-reflection chart

Identity component	Capacity/characteristic	Variety according to context of communication (give two examples of each)
Nationality		
Region		
Ethnicity		
Social class		
Gender		
Age		
Religion		
Social role (e.g. 'mother')		
Employment role		

will probably find that the categories you finally use to analyse and collect the data develop as you undertake the research.

Alternatively, and this may be of particularly interest to you if you are in a corporate cultural environment, you may wish to change a signal you send out and note its effects and your responses to these. This may be as simple as wearing a suit and tie when normally you do not wear one or vice versa, sitting in a different place to normal or it may be some action such as sending congratulatory emails for anything others achieve when you may normally not do this – the choice is yours. You will need to note any differences in response to you because of these signals, including any opposition to this slight upsetting of the status quo. Reflect upon how powerful the force is for keeping things as they are – for 'maintaining homeostasis' in your company and how this is signalled. What does this say about the corporate culture you are working in and what lessons may there be there for you and the company? Many companies employ multicultural workforces and indeed may internationalise their operations. What are the implications of this for institutional/corporate culture and for its maintenance?

Task C1.2.3 How you manage your identity

➤ Keep a record of how you actually manage your identity according to the above identity components over the next week with people that you encounter.

➤ Once you have done this, consider the following questions.

- Do you catch yourself representing different versions of yourself and struggling against other people's perceptions of you?
- Are you aware of how you manipulate the possibilities available to you at the time?
- Do you meet occasions where you are unable to do this because your interlocutor(s) have already decided who you are – i.e. Othered you?
- How does this make you feel?
- What do you do if this is the case?
- What are your findings?

Identity is ideally a negotiated feature between interactants. However, you may discover that in many instances this is not possible because in interaction people may be assuming who the other person is without the willingness to enter into more fluid negotiation and time-consuming research of the other person. An interesting comment made by one student studying cultural identity is: 'It is much easier to hold and use undifferentiated categories about others than not to.'

➤ Discussion point: Consider the following and then either with a partner or as a group discuss the issues raised.

A concept relating to one's self-view is that of perceived powerfulness (how culturally powerful or lacking in power you may feel you are when engaged in interaction in relation to your perception of the cultural other). It is worth considering how this self-view may influence one's willingness or ability to engage in cultural negotiation with the other. Consider this point in relation to the notion of the 'cosmopolitan ideal' in Sobré-Denton and Bardham (Text B1.2.2). Is this an ideal you think you yourself a) should achieve b) can achieve?

We can complete this unit with a further intercultural communication research task. Use Figure C0.1.1 to help with this.

 Task C1.2.4 Watching yourself

➤ Events: which take place normally within your own milieu.

➤ Actors: same each time.

➤ Setting: your choice.

➤ Cultural circumstances: same each time.

➤ Angle: how your image of yourself influences your interaction.

➤ Observation: monitor yourself, describe carefully and deconstruct.

➤ Discipline: 8.

➤ Outcome: as you become more aware of yourself, how do your perceptions of the Other people improve? In what ways are you more likely to avoid the traps into which Agnes, François and Jeremy fall in Units A2.2 and A2.3?

When to take notes

It is clearly impossible to describe what is happening *during* the process of communication events. Once you get into the habit of keeping your research diary regularly, you will also develop your ability to recall. You should then be able to make fairly detailed notes of what has happened at the earliest convenient private time after the event has happened, even if this is the following day. Also, there is no need to audio-record and transcribe events in order to collect useful data. Indeed, it is advisable not to with this type of informal research. Behavioural descriptions of what has happened, with the occasional note of what was said, can be very rich. Transcribing is very time-consuming and, unless your study is specifically a linguistic discourse analysis, may mean you are using up your limited time on this rather than developing your research.

UNIT C1.3   UNDOING CULTURAL FUNDAMENTALISM

If we believe or subscribe to a view that people have innate cultural traits – i.e. that they carry within them certain essential characteristics that belong to them and the larger group of which they are seen to form a part, rather as we carry genetic information within us (information that leads to different skin colour etc.) – then this, we argue, is to hold of a view that can be termed 'cultural fundamentalism' or 'culturism' (see Unit A2.1).

While it is true that we are socialised into certain ways of interpreting the context of our existence – i.e. we are 'trained in expectation', ('programmed' to expect certain behaviours of others and to have certain behaviours expected of us by others) – it is important to remember two factors that tend to override cultural uniformity:

■ For each individual each context is unique and these contexts may vary considerably between members of what may ostensibly be the same culture; this is true even within the same family. This means that it is illusory to hold a generalised notion that people are uniform within cultures.
■ Contexts are interactive. People are not powerless to create new contexts. People can adapt to new influences and learn new ways of being. It is therefore problematic to think of the self as unchanging, readily describable and definable. It is hard to define something that has the potential to, and does, change.

So while there may be certain commonalities between two people from the same cultural context (from the same temporal and geographical location) and a general notion of 'typicality' held between them (i.e. an understanding of expected behaviour or the norm for behaviour in various contexts), it is risky to assume that the contextual influences they have been exposed to result in two people having the same outlook, i.e. 'culture'.

Stop and think: If we kick a stone with a certain force in a certain location we can measure what will happen. We will be able to then predict how far such a stone will move according to the force applied. If, on the other hand, we kick a particular dog (I am not suggesting we do this!) we cannot use this as a fool-proof guide as to what will happen if we kick another dog in the same way. This is because living things learn from experience, have different histories, have different psychologies and, therefore, different reactions. The external environment impacts in different ways on the individual because of this.

Note: introspection and subjectivity

In Task C1.3.1, as indeed in Task C1.2.2, you are required to be introspective, that is, to collect not only external data through observation, but also to become aware of your own subjectivity. Each person interprets the external world from their own experience and it is an awareness of this subjectivity that allows us to accept and recognise plurality and interpersonal difference. This awareness is very necessary for effective intercultural communication. It is the recognition of difference and then the negotiation of various subjectivities to achieve shared understanding that is central to skilled intercultural communication. Intercultural communication can be described, therefore, as a process of 'intersubjectivity'.

 ### Task C1.3.1 Drawing a culture star

➤ Compare yourself with another person in your study group to see what cultural influences there are upon both of you and how these:

- may vary from each other, and
- may be interpreted differently by you both.

➤ To do this you will need to draw a 'culture star'.

The idea of a culture star comes from Singer (1998) who considers the various cultural contexts in which individuals exist and which they may use to 'source' their identities. A person's culture is seen here to be the result of belonging to a myriad of 'small cultures' each of which demands a certain normativeness. These small

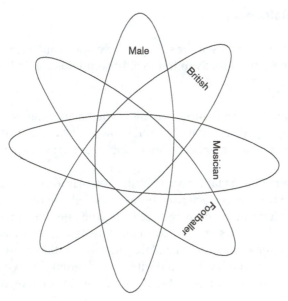

Figure C1.3.1 Culture star

groupings are inherently unstable in that they come and go – as individuals enter and leave them – and they change according to the influence of their members. Some are more enduring than others.

Figure C1.3.1 is an example of one such culture star. Each band in the star is one in which the individual is potentially recognised by others, and recognised by themselves as a competent member of a group, that is, one in which there are perceived norms of behaviour and values and beliefs that the individual recognises and uses as a member of the group. The choice over which groups you think are of influence, or of significance, is up to you.

➤ Once you have drawn a star you need to compare it with someone else's.

➤ When you have done this, consider how much variety there is between the two stars. You may then like to discuss what influences each cultural group has over you in terms of your personal identity and look at how this identity changes according to each cultural group to which you are affiliated (done by oneself to oneself) and ascribed (done by others to oneself).

Considering these multiple belongings, can you actually choose one influence, or cultural group, for example, 'nationality' or 'ethnicity', as one that successfully serves to describe both you and the person who has done the other star? Doing this must inevitably result from a process of 'cultural reductionism', i.e. a negation of the true complexity of each of you. Indeed, is there any way in which you can actually say that you and the other person are the same or is it that all you can perhaps say is that there are similarities in certain areas between you?

Task C1.3.2 Belonging

➤ Look again at the bands of the stars you have drawn and identified. What are the key expectations that you feel each band proposes as cultural norms for members to subscribe to?

➤ In other words, consider how you know you belong, and how others in the particular group identified in the band know you belong to that small culture. What is it that holds members of each 'club' together as different from others?

This may be a very difficult task to accomplish – you may feel that while superficially there are key values and characteristic behaviours that you can identify, the more you think about it the more complex it becomes to be sure about these. This may be because the small cultures are in a constant state of shift and change. You may therefore like to think of what the standard image is that the group promotes or is seen to have by others, both within and without each group. From the fictional star this may be as follows. (This is a worked example, you do not have to agree with it!)

- Male: does not show emotions too openly.
- British: is proud of things British; appreciates humour – i.e. is able to 'take a joke'.
- Yorkshireman: is proud of things from Yorkshire and dislikes Lancashire; is not 'fancy' and 'Southern', but blunt and to the point – i.e. 'calls a spade a spade'.
- Musician: has things in common with other musicians, such as knowledge of various pieces of music; likes to feel he is more expressive than an engineer.
- Football player: feels loyalty to others in the same football team; participates in 'male bonding' behaviour.
- Son in the Cole family: understands the rules of participation and the responsibilities of being a son in the family.
- Garage mechanic: has an understanding of car engines; is not scared of getting hands dirty.
- Motorcycle rider: has a knowledge and interest in motorcycles and things to do with motorcycles; has a special bond with other motorcyclists as opposed to car drivers.
- Regular pub goer: has an understanding of pub etiquette; is knowledgeable about the different kinds of beers available.
- London resident: has a knowledge of the city; subscribes to the unwritten rules of living in that city.

Note: Discourse – a definition for use in intercultural communication

From a sociological IC perspective, discourse analysis is used here to look at how commonly held frameworks for shaping reality interact with individual expression. This may be in language use but can also relate to ideology (thought patterns), and to non-linguistic aspects of expression (dress codes, fashion).

Of course, how you negotiate your membership in each membership group, or small culture, is up to you, but in order to 'negotiate' you obviously need to know certain basic features of each of these (see Gee's large 'Discourses' written with a big 'D' described in Text B1.3.2). Your individual negotiation within these Discourses can be seen to be your small 'discourses', written with a small 'd'. Another possible set of terminology for the same thing is to see the larger frameworks as discourse types (DTs) and your own negotiating with these as your discourse actions (DAs). The DTs can be seen to be large cognitive schemas (see Gandy, Task B3.1.4), and the DAs can be seen to be your personal relationship to the DTs. The Discourse Types are communally held, whereas Discourse Actions are personal instances of interaction. DTs exist because, for communication to occur, it is necessary for groups of people (within the same culture) to have norms by which they can communicate. From a discourse analysis point of view one could argue, therefore, that a culture is a set of DTs which members draw on to create their own DAs. Without the DTs there could be no DAs. It is also the DAs that constantly reconfirm the existence of the DTs.

From a look at your culture star you will notice that the small cultures that you belong to vary in the degree of autonomy they allow you membership of each of them or not. This is not to say that you have to be an uncritical member of any of them, but that they vary in the degree of choice you have – to decide to be a member or not. You cannot, for example, choose the ethnicity you have or the place you are born or the family you are born into, but you can choose whether or not you will join a karate club or go to university or join a reading circle. To build on a concept presented in Unit A1.3 you may consider the experience of negotiating identity from a 'games perspective', with the following cards metaphor: you can see yourself as having been dealt a set of cards by your life circumstances – 'culture cards'. Some of these cards you cannot change but others you can gain, get rid of, or change, and indeed play. Of course, some of the inherited cards you may choose to downplay or attempt to change: one thinks of people who actually attempt to change their gender through sex change operations; of the plastic surgery that Michael Jackson had to change his features, or of a migrant who changes national cultures and languages (see Ribeyro, Text B1.1.1, and his description of someone attempting to change his cultural cards).

These changes are not, however, purely under the individual's control in that, as the large DTs that one may be opposing are not individually held but communally held, it may be that the community does not accept the new cards that an individual tries to play the culture game with. Remember that it is large and often stereotypically crude DTs (ideological structures) that others may invoke when interacting with you (see Unit A1.1 and Parisa's struggle in Example A1.1.1 to be understood for what she is). You may therefore find that, frustratingly, identity is not a negotiated entity between interactants; rather, it is like a game of cards with rules as to how you can play. Interacting may be seen as a game which you play with the cards at your disposal. Some of these cards may be powerful, socially advantageous ones, whereas others may be less so. This depends on the power structure represented by the dominance of certain DTs in the society in which you are using your DAs, i.e. playing the culture game. The word 'game' does not imply that the stakes are not high or that this activity is frivolous. It is also possible that what may be a weak card in one particular context may be a strong one in another. It may also seem obvious that the more cards you can play the wider the possibility of having useful cards for more situations. The more cards you have, the more membership possibilities you have. At certain times you may emphasise the cards you feel you have in common with the other people you're interacting with; at other times you may downplay or play up a culture card that you feel is opposed to or promotes your interests and goals in the communicative context in which you find yourself. Which cards you play thus depends upon a strategic consideration of which ones you can draw on and which ones you want to draw on in a particular context and upon the goals you have. The same, of course, is true of the people you interact with. As mentioned before, the more cards you can draw on the more possibilities you have in playing the culture card game. A person who has an Indian mother, an English father, who was born in France and who was educated in the USA, evidently has many cards to potentially draw on. This does not necessarily make interaction with this person easier, however. People may like to play the culture card game with people who use a reduced set of cards and thus not risk being trumped by the other person, who may be playing the game with a set of powerful cards up their sleeve. It is perhaps uncomfortable for people to play the culture card game with a cultural chameleon. It's easier to play the game with a person who has their cards visibly on the table. For this reason it may be tactical for people to choose to deliberately hide their complexity in certain interactions. Again such a decision is strategic and up to the individual – it is a weighing-up of the benefits and losses that the playing of each card may bring within each context of interaction.

★ Task C1.3.3

➤ Think of a culture card you hold. Think of how you use it or maybe hide it. Analyse why you do this.

➤ Discuss your views on the cards metaphor as an explanation of intercultural interaction.

★ Task C1.3.4

➤ Prepare either a presentation or an assignment with the title 'An analysis of my own cultural formation'.

★ Task C1.3.5

➤ Read the following anecdote, and try to explain it in terms of Discourse Types, Discourse Actions and the strategic use of 'culture cards':

An Englishman who is the director of a private company in Spain addresses his workforce one day in Spanish, but with a slightly detectable non-Spanish accent. In his speech he uses the following term: '*Nosotros, los españoles, somos una gente muy orgullosa*' (translated: 'We Spanish are a very proud people'). A certain number of the Spanish workers exchange looks with each other upon hearing this that seem to express a mixture of discomfort and mirth.

Now it is time to convert the observations in this unit into observation of intercultural communication, with reference to Figure C0.1.1.

Task C1.3.6 Culture cards and stars

➤ Event: your choice, but it might take a series of events, with the same people, to find out what you need to know, especially if the other people come from small groups or societies which you know little about.

➤ Actors: you and two other people.

➤ Setting: within your milieu.

➤ Cultural circumstances: your choice.

➤ Angle: use of 'culture cards', the complexity of the culture star.

➤ Observation: use Table C1.3.1 and record as much detail as you can about the culture cards that are played by you and by each of the other two people. More rows can be added for other people.

➤ Disciplines: 2 and 3. You are focusing here on the complexity, but you will need to try hard to put aside what you *imagine* about the other people and to base your investigation on what you *observe*.

➤ Outcome: analysis of the effectiveness of each interaction. Also, what you can learn about the complexity which the other person is bringing with them.

UNIT C1.4 INVESTIGATING DISCOURSE AND POWER

As has been suggested so far in Section C, particularly with the concept of culture cards, communication does not take place in a power void. As Bourdieu suggests with his notion of Cultural Capital, because of the power structure of a society at a certain instance, some cards will have greater social currency and value than others. Power is manifest within all communication because the culture cards that one draws on are valued differently within different social structures. Certain images that are in circulation in a social group about other social groups may be

Table C1.3.1 Record of playing culture cards

Description of the context	*Analysis of the cards you felt were at your disposal (a), that you played and their effectiveness (b), that you felt your interactants had at their disposal (c), and that they played and their effectiveness (d)*
Person 1	(a)
	(b)
Setting 1	(c)
	(d)

drawn upon or countered by interactants. The result of this may be that interactants may insist on playing with these dominant discourses or images and thus not allow other interactants the individual freedom to create and present themselves as they wish. To thus attempt to curb someone's autonomy for intersubjectivity is to attempt to exercise power.

Note

The issue of brain-washing and 'radicalisation' and 'grooming' are given concepts very much in the media currently. One way of approaching these phenomena may be to consider them as a result of the conflation of a 'prescribed identity' and resultant behaviour with an individual's 'avowed identity' and behaviour. The mechanism by which this is achieved may be through coercion and reward or/and through the controlled internalisation of a hegemonic discourse operating in a particular environment.

Stop and think: Look at the cards you potentially hold. Which of these have you inherited from the Dominant Discourses around you and which have you managed to create yourself?

In each interactive context you basically have two strategies for action. First, you may choose to show 'solidarity' – that is, play the cards that bind you to the person you are interacting with (for example, draw upon a shared belongingness or identity).

Second, you may choose to use a distancing strategy, whereby you play cards that emphasise the difference in status between you. The decision about which strategy to use may vary according to context. The wrong use of the wrong strategy may have a detrimental effect in terms of an interactant's communicative goals. If you use distancing strategies when solidarity strategies may be felt by your interlocutor to be more appropriate, then you will appear to be cold and unfriendly – possibly snobbish. If, on the other hand, an interactant uses a bonding, solidarity strategy with someone who evidently feels of a different status, or from a distinct identity group, or is in an official role that would be compromised by solidarity, then the interactant may be rebuffed for using such a 'levelling' strategy. (Think of Jeremy's misuse of such a bonding strategy in his dealings with Jabu in Example A2.3.1, Unit A2.3.) In certain languages of the world, the actual degree of solidarity or distance is encoded in the personal pronouns chosen for use between two forms of 'you'. In French there is '*tu*' or '*vous*'. The use of these pronouns is by no means straightforward as '*vous*' can imply coldness and distance, but it can also be used to show respect, which is not the same as coldness. The way '*vous*' is interpreted depends very much on the context of its use. In non-Latin based languages such as English and Japanese, solidarity and social distance are encoded in other ways – through the forms of address people choose to use with each other and through politeness strategies, which includes the degree of directness or indirectness in language use.

Another example of the marking of solidarity or social distance in language use is the form of greeting employed in Latin American Spanish. The term '*compadre*', for example, is a marker of equality. However, if it is used with someone who feels of higher status and thus deserving of respect, the use of the term may be interpreted as cheeky and an attempt to belittle that person's status. In this sense the use of term '*compadre*' can be a power strategy through its potential to 'level out' difference. It has a pragmatic force equal to saying: 'I do not consider you to be any better than me or in any position of authority over me in any way.'

> **Stop and think:** In British English the same can be said of the term 'mate' (although this also acts as a social class marker) or in US English the term 'buddy'. In Moroccan Arabic the term '*khoya*' (my brother) is used for solidarity. Think about your own language group. What words are used to indicate solidarity or social distance? How do they work to do this?

Task C1.4.1 Trying to gain solidarity

➤ Analyse the following dialogue and decide whether a solidarity strategy or a distancing strategy is being employed, and which possible culture cards are being played. Also consider their effectiveness.

■ **Those involved in the dialogue:** A Spanish woman (Pilar) – a secondary school teacher working for the Instituto Cervantes in an Arabic country.

A local Arabic woman (Amina) who has become a friend of the teacher through both of them having met on the roof terrace of the same block of flats they share.

■ **The situation:** Amina decides to invite Pilar into her flat for a cup of tea. Both sit on a couch and Pilar looks around the room. She spots a painting on the wall opposite (it is of mediocre quality, but of the local countryside). As in her culture it is customary to compliment people on their house, she says:

> Pilar: That's a lovely painting, where is it of?
>
> [Amina looks slightly regretful, and gets up and goes over to the painting . . .]
>
> Amina: It's of the countryside in my home village. It was painted by my brother.
>
> [She takes the painting off the wall.]
>
> Amina: Here please have it.
>
> [Pilar feels bad as she does not want to take the painting which is obviously of value to Amina and she doesn't even really like the picture so would not display it herself in her home.]

This example leads us to consider how we may be constrained in our interactive behaviour not only by contextual cultural factors but also by the self-view one has and the identity which that reinforces.

In many interactions we are perhaps constrained by notions of typicality and expectation fulfilment. Although it may be a rule that to stick to what is most expected, or in other words 'appropriate', is the safest way to communicate – especially with strangers – this is only so providing, of course, that the two interactants are plugged into similar notions of what is typical in those contexts.

➤ How may the interaction described have been more successful? What is required of the interactants for this?

➤ Looking at Holmes (Text B3.6.1), find examples of where praise in a multi-cultural company setting does not work as intended. Analyse the underlying reason for discomfort on the part of the recipient of the praise. How may this interaction be made more successful do you think?

 Task C1.4.2 Manipulating discourse

➤ Reread Example A1.3.1 ('Girl on the bus'). What have the schoolgirls done to subvert the original power to wound of certain words traditionally used by men to negatively type women? Try to explain this in terms of Discourse Types, the use of culture cards and solidarity strategies. To what extent does your explanation coincide with the one following?

Possible explanation

The girls are appropriating a sexist and misogynistic Discourse Type, traditionally belonging to a male domain. They thus use terms of abuse from this DT: derogatory terms that equate females with animals and sexual licentiousness (the former suggesting inferiority to men, the second perhaps hinting at a fear that females whose libido cannot be controlled by social propriety are dangerous). The fact that it is girls using these terms to bond with each other rather than men – the girls would seem to demand of each other the use of insulting words from a particular type of 'male speak' as a form of greeting – would seem to subvert the words' original wounding power and intent. In a sense these words are disarmed by this female strategy. They lose their original meaning through being appropriated in this particular way. The girls are thus using a culture card from the male pack and playing with it themselves. The scene is shocking because it is normally only a DT within the male domain of possibilities to which this belongs. It is not a DT used by women – not women about women – and then not in such a public manner. Girls, traditionally, are not supposed to swear or use 'rough and rude' language in public either; this is not considered to be traditionally 'feminine'. The exchange in the bus, intended for the public at large, is thus part of a power strategy of the colonisation and neutralisation of a male space.

➤ Do some research on the various terms that the girls use and determine the significance of them.

Task C1.4.3 Analysing discourse

➤ Choose a section of interactive text to analyse. (a) Choose the text carefully so that it involves people in social interaction, perhaps discussing or arguing points. (b) Transcribe the text by writing it out. (c) Avoid the use of punctuation or capital letters and leave gaps between words to reflect pauses in speech; also use double lines with parallel texts when two people are talking at the same time. (d) Analyse the text by referring to DTs and DAs and to the use of various 'culture cards'. Prepare a presentation of the text explaining your analysis.

Example of transcribed text

Interactant A:	in Albania we say what we mean, not like here!
Interactant B:	yes but ok but you won't get far in interviews like that
Interactant A:	why not?
Interactant B:	they'll think you are rude and not able to deal with British customers

Now see if you can apply this type of analysis to other examples of intercultural communication in your own milieu, with reference to Figure C0.1.1.

Task C1.4.4 How close or far apart do we signal we may be?

➤ Events: of your choice, but where you can hear people talking, preferably on several occasions so that you can begin to see patterns of discourse emerging, and (see following) develop relations which allow you to interview.

➤ Actors: of your choice, but always the same small group.

➤ Setting: of your choice.

➤ Cultural circumstances: of your choice, but where the interaction is marked by some form of cultural difference.

➤ Angle: success and failure in using solidarity or distancing strategies. Look again at Jeremy's failure in trying to achieve solidarity with Jabu in Example A2.3.1. Notice particularly that Jeremy does in fact have good intentions, but in a sense chooses the wrong content.

➤ Observation: use your research diary to note down as much detail as possible. If it is appropriate you might also interview the interactants to see how they feel about what is happening.

➤ Disciplines: 2, 13 and 14. Although you are not one of the interactants, you need to employ these disciplines as though you were, so that you put aside your own preoccupations and presumptions about what might bring solidarity or distance, so that you can try and see things in the terms of the actors.

➤ Outcome: experience for your own interactions.

This is a complex and difficult research task. You will need to discuss this with others to explore the best way to proceed as delicately as possible.

UNIT C1.5   LOCALITY AND TRANSCENDENCE OF LOCALITY: FACTORS IN IDENTITY FORMATION

When analysing the way people read texts, Barthes sees the reader as potentially engaged in two acts: that of '*plaisir*' and that of '*jouissance*'. These psychological needs that the reader has are in fact contradictory tendencies. Barthes' terminology is sexual, suggesting that he approaches individual psychology from a Freudian perspective. '*Plaisir*' is the need the reader has to feel a sense of belonging. It is the reconfirmation of the world as one expects and feels it is. '*Jouissance*', on the other hand, is the opposite tendency: the urge to break out and transcend. It is the excitement (the word means 'orgasmic' pleasure) generated from transgressing the boundary of the accepted and the known.

If we relate this idea to that of individual identity generally, we may argue that these two tendencies are inherent in individual identity construction. To be part of the society you are in one needs to be familiar with the 'text' of that society – the rituals and the accepted modes of being and the values you are expected to uphold. This sense of belonging is a source of pleasure ('*plaisir*'). It is the sense of not being alone but of belonging to a group. This offers comfort and security. On the other hand there is potentially excitement and invention to be found through the breaking of this 'order'. Crossing the boundary of the accepted and experimenting with new forms can be invigorating and on an individual may be felt to be liberating. The contradiction is that you can only achieve this transcendence if at one and the same time you are beholden to the values you are transcending – in other words, both aspects of cultural belonging and transcendence are forces (in many ways contradictory) that work together within individuals.

Task C1.5.1 Sources of '*plaisir*' or '*jouissance*'

➤ Look at the following list and decide how each one may be a source of '*plaisir*' or '*jouissance*'.

- Feeling patriotic, for example, supporting your national football team along with others from your nation.
- Going on an exotic holiday alone.
- Learning and speaking a foreign language.
- Breaking established taboos (e.g. cross-dressing, experimenting with banned drugs).
- Using language at variance with the expected and established norms of the society you are in (e.g. schoolgirls swearing on a bus).
- Using slang, or a local dialect, with your friends.
- Swapping jokes with friends and finding the same things funny.
- Smoking a cigarette with friends as a teenager behind the bike shed at school.

Note: using dichotomous model

The dichotomy (the two possible options) used for analysis of '*plaisir*' and '*jouissance*' proves a useful heuristic device (a tool for analysis), but becomes more complicated to maintain as an either/or option the more you dig into the examples. It would appear that the essence of '*plaisir*' is an indulgence in normativeness, that is, in the psychological benefit of sharing. The essence of '*jouissance*', on the other hand, would appear to be the personal transcendence from the established cultural norms that surround the individual. In other words '*jouissance*' is not a cultural construct as '*plaisir*' is, but a psychological, personal one – it is about transcending the cultural formations that surround one. However, transcendence may also become normative and hence a 'subculture' of people may together be transcending the more established norms of the wider culture; this may mean that the subgroup is enjoying '*jouissance*' together. If this is the case, then is this not in actual fact also '*plaisir*'? After all, it is a shared and normative transcendence. This initial transcendence on a group level can indeed lead to very rigid forms of '*plaisir*' as in the phenomenon of cult membership. It would appear that an initial act of '*jouissance*' can become a form of '*plaisir*' once it becomes shared and hence normative. Thus an act of rebellion – be it a liberation movement, a terrorist organisation or as, say, that of punk rock in the 1970s – soon becomes a form of '*plaisir*' for its adherents as it becomes an established mode of rebellion, including dress code, language and behaviour.

It is worth noting that the pursuit of '*jouissance*' brings risks and sanctions from the cultural group being transcended (rejected) by the individual. Members of a culture work hard to protect their culture from being under-mined, by re-establishing, on a daily basis, the norms by which the group in question operates (see Anderson 1983). This may mean attacking anything that is 'heretical' to those norms. Members have a duty to protect the norms the group lives by and the '*plaisir*' that this sources. Transgressors of these norms may be feared and suffer social ostracism (exclusion) and demonis-ation (see Unit B3.5). Indeed, any cultural group would seem to need to have a serviceable 'Other' – a thing against which the group finds its own identity. A punk in the 1970s was a punk because he/she was not symbolically a member of the 'dominant' society against which punks were rebelling. Unfortunately, the consequences of this process can often lead to violence. People are not seen as complex and variegated and changing but as service-able objects for use in establishing a group's identity – even if this is at times a counter-identity. History and current world events are full of such examples. Think of the fate of 'witches' in medieval Europe, for example.

Note: heuristic devices

This analysis starts with the use of a dichotomy – the use of two different extremes. These extremes thus serve to question and probe a phenomenon. It may be that these extremes in themselves are too crude to be useful as explanations in themselves. They may, however, prove a useful tool for analysis. This is what is meant by stating that they are 'heuristic devices'. You are free to use any such dichotomies as tools for your own analyses, always, of course, bearing in mind that they are tools for use that you have created and are not necessarily true reflections of an external reality in themselves.

 Task C1.5.2 In- and out-groups

➤ Interview groups of young people about their musical tastes and the clothes they wear. Note how they thus create identities based on their professed musical tastes and the fashion they follow. Note if they associate and identify with certain groups and how the borders between them as members of such a group and others are drawn. Interviewing small groups instead of individuals should help the members of the group being interviewed show you how they help each other to create borders.

➤ Also use observation to look at the activities that certain groups of youths engage in and their attire, thus noting to what extent activity type is also part of the overall image a group has and uses to define itself.

➤ When you have collected your data, see if you find any common themes. What can you apply from your findings to yourself as an individual and to your own identity formation?

Application to industry

If you are in a corporate setting you can apply this study to the effort that is made to develop a corporate image and culture among the company's members. Analyse how the use of any competitor company is used for this. What is it that we as a company have that others do not have?

The same can be applied to company products. After all, what is branding, if not the successful contrastive image the company's product(s) obtains in the minds of the consumers compared to its rivals and their products? If you are working in a manufacturing or service delivery industry, how is your product differentiated in the market? Does the process make use of a 'contrastive other' for this?

Toyota, for example, developed an image for reliability and cost effectiveness with its cards, which contrasted with cars manufactured in the West. It borrowed from Sony and the reputation Japanese products have gained for sophisticated miniaturisation. As Bourdieu controversially states, when we drink a French wine, we do not drink a French wine, we drink our image of a French wine. If this is true it puts cultural understanding at the heart of image construction and manipulation for the marketing of products.

What is it that creates an in-group member (consumer) and what is it that creates an out-group member? Now think about yourself. In what ways do you balance '*plaisir*' with '*jouissance*'? Do you feel you belong to any oppositional counter-cultures that through group '*jouissance*' offer a different version of '*plaisir*' from the wider culture against which it is rebelling? Can you describe how this works?

Note: national identity

If we look at the world's cultural groups, caught between tradition and modernity, between established agricultural communities tied to the land and city dwellers, freed from their link to the land through the use of technological invention, then we may see the world as divided between this fundamental tension of tradition and modernity. In the search for a collective identity and the fear that modernity may be undermining this identity, people may psychologically return to, or try to retain a sense of local cultural identity. City dwellers may indulge in a comforting nostalgia for the traditional food, costumes, language and dialects, dances and songs of their forbears – often a highly romanticised view. In the centre of Osaka, a modern metropolis in Japan, there is in the city centre, next to the Umeda Sky building, a reconstructed peasant paddy field. It helps the city dwellers link with their past. The discourse of national identity may manifest itself in a pride in local cuisine, in claims about the beauty and good nature of the women, in the bravery of the men, and there may be a mystical attachment to a romanticized countryside. In Hungary people may claim and feel a profound link with the Puszta – the Hungarian Plain. Argentinians may similarly refer to the Pampas. The myth of national identity based on a rural idyll may become the stuff of tourism. It is noticeable that romantic pictures of gauchos, the Pampas cowboys, adorn upmarket restaurant walls in Buenos Aires. North Americans may conduct a similar romantic affair with the Wild West, which becomes emblematic not only of a geography but also of a way of life that projects the self-view of the pioneering spirit and toughness in the face of adversity, however mythical this may be.

 Task C1.5.3 Artefacts and identity

➤ Interview members of your study group and use Table C1.5.1 to make a record. When doing this consider your nation's or region's use of these cultural artefacts and factors in the creation of a national/regional identity and a sense of traditional belonging.

Nationalism or regionalism is perhaps one of the most powerful sources of identity in modern society. More and more the world is divided into states with frontiers; the people within these states are encouraged to see themselves as belonging to these particular groupings and as being distinct from those in other states. In many cases these boundaries have been historically forged through war and political negotiation.

It is usual for all regions or nations and inhabitants thereof, to define themselves by contrasting themselves with their neighbours (think of how you as a national experience this or do this). Having briefly mentioned this powerful and emotive use of culture within and between nation states – a use of culture that is very politicised, and indeed a force which a lot of us are perhaps seduced by to some extent – it is also worth looking at another aspect of modernity that influences us in how we understand who we are. This is again represented as a dichotomy: the rural and the urban. Industrialisation has led people away from the land and into

Table C1.5.1   Cultural artefacts

Artefact/factor	Description	Function in terms of identity formation
Costumes/dress		
Dances		
Songs/music		
Language and dialect		
Cuisine		
Nature – landscape		
Fauna		
Flora		
Sports and sporting events		
Festivals and holidays		
Physical appearance of people		
Qualities of people		

metropolitan centres. The growth of cities is a key feature of life today, along with the increased use of technology within our lives, from fridges to cars to computers. We may also take pride in the way we see ourselves and the way we present ourselves to others through 'conspicuous consumption' – arguably a key characteristic of urban modernity. A person polishing a new car in the street on Sunday morning, or ostentatiously using the latest mobile phone, the newly married couple dedicating a year's wages and thought into getting the most up-to-date kitchen installed in their new home; these are people who help to define their existence and sense of who they are, at least in part, by these modern artefacts that act as indexes of success and status. The seeking of power through consumption is the bedrock of capitalism whereby consumer objects become symbols of success. While this may be joked about – 'I have just indulged in some retail therapy', 'I shop therefore I am' – there is also a reality that underlies these phrases.

We will briefly explore two aspects of this phenomenon in relation to culture and individual identity: first, the relative value of the rural and the urban in your context; and secondly, the commodification of cultural goods for consumption within the capitalist system and how this may impinge upon you. (See the discussion of globalisation and identity in Unit B1.2 in relation to this.) The relationship between city and country is a complex one in many countries. The rural may be seen as the backyard of the city – a place for sports and relaxation by the city people, or a place to stay away from – a place of backwardness and poverty, or it may be mythologised and be romanticised as the location of the true soul of the nation. The urban may be seen as a place of wealth and possibility, invigorating and exciting, or may be seen as degenerate, dangerous and polluted, and a place to move away from.

 ### Task C1.5.4 Rural and urban images

➤ Look at the following terms from British and American English to describe people and homes. What do they suggest about the urban and the rural? What perspective is behind each word?

Yokel   oik   hick   country-retreat   yob

mugger   city-slicker   man-about-town/city girl

peasant   yuppie   cottage   tenement

hillbilly   high-rise   flat   suburbia   the hood

➤ How does each term fit into the general picture of the urban and the rural and the relationship between them? If you are from a non-English language background, do you have similar terms associated with the urban and the rural in your culture and language?

➤ Find out the relative conceptions of the rural and the urban in the society that surrounds you.

➤ You can collect data through interviewing people by asking them for key words (such as those shown) and/or you can analyse the representation of the urban and the rural in advertising by deciding what key words you would use to describe the image of each.

Cultural objects may be made into saleable products: the country cottage may be sold as a second home to the urban rich and thus marketed as a form of Arcadia; clean air and flowers can become selling points or indeed commodities that can thus be bought and sold, and so cultural products from other places can be marketed in the 'global supermarket'; this may include holidays abroad, foods, drinks, martial arts, dances, music, sport – indeed anything and everything. For the English it may be that a bottle of wine becomes the consumption of France and things French, to dance a tango is to imbibe a little 'Argentinianness', eating a Chinese meal is to have a mini-voyage into the exotic, walking through the Amazon rainforest on an eco-holiday is to buy into a small chunk of pristine purity, and so on.

Stop and think: How much are these cultural promises mediated, made appetising, by an image of the thing you are consuming? In other words, how much are you influenced by this when buying and consuming the commodity?

Task C1.5.5 Cultural knowledge, manipulation and advertising

➤ In Moloney, Text B3.3.3, the way readers are directed to respond to media images is analysed. Re-read this article before undertaking this exercise. For this task you need to collect three advertisements and then undertake the following six step analysis. When you have done this, choose one of them and prepare it as a presentation. To help you with this an example analysis is presented below. This is taken from an Hispanic island in the Caribbean in the late 1980s.

Example:

Step 1: There is an image of two white people: A young and attractive mother who is looking straight out of the ad at the observer. A baby is playing happily at her feet. Beneath these is an image of a tinned milk product with its brand name on it.

Table C1.5.2 Analysis of adverts

	1. Who are the subjects?	2. What is the context?	3. How are the people represented?	4. What is the effect of this?	5. What is the possible purpose of this?	6. Provide a 'considered' response
Advert 1						
Advert 2						
Advert 3						

Step 2: The ad is on the roadside in a poor rural setting just outside a village. The local people are predominantly black. Lighter skinned people tend, as a rule, to be more urban and economically well-off than these village people.

Step 3: The mother and baby are depicted as happy, healthy and confident. The mother is well dressed which suggests she is of the professional middle class. There are white goods in the background that also suggest this. The baby is chubby. The overall impression is that of successfulness.

Step 4: These people, who happen to be white people in a predominantly non-white island, are healthy, confident and successful people. Such people use tinned milk for their babies. The message would seem to be that it must be part of being successful to have tinned milk in your lifestyle.

Step 5: Poorer black people may be encourage to aspire towards the successful lifestyle represented in the ad. They may thus be encouraged to purchase the tinned milk with its connotations of success.

Step 6: The image uses race and historical context. The island's history has led to economic inequality along racial lines existing on the island today. The ad plays upon rural fears of ill health, lack of education and class aspirations. It also plays upon the maternal urge to try and do what is best for one's child and improve its life chances. The product itself, as a Peace Corps worker informed me, was in fact detrimental to babies' health in the countryside because the water used to dilute the tinned milk was not always clean and breast milk is known to be good for babies. He was leading workshops in the countryside to persuade mothers not to use tinned milk for this reason. The mothers however had identified with using tinned milk as part of being modern and successful. The message in the ad is therefore, from this perspective, morally suspect.

 ### Task C1.5.5 Buying cultural promise

➤ Before undertaking the following task, it is suggested you read the article below entitled 'The tourist gaze: a visit to Magome'.

The tourist gaze: a visit to Magome

Magome is a touristic village in Japan – a 'post station' on the historic Nakasendo pathway that linked Edo (Tokyo) with Kyoto. The next post station, Tsumago, is 7.5 kilometres away. The walk along the pathway through the hills has been reconstructed and is popular with Japanese and foreign tourists.

On a visit to Japan I decided to visit Magome, run the pathway to Tsumago and back and spend the night in a local guesthouse. The following is taken from an account of my visit as a foreign tourist that I wrote up soon after the visit. I speak no Japanese.

I arrived by taxi from the local railway station and headed for the tourist office, where luckily there was a young member of staff who spoke some English and was able to book me into and direct me to a local guesthouse. After a little discussion I agreed that the efficient member of staff also book supper at the guesthouse for me. On entering the entrance hall of the guesthouse I took off my shoes (I have been told this is very important in Japan) and pushed a button (the English word 'ring' was under it). That seemed to connect to a mobile phone. A voice answered in Japanese. I simply said 'Hello'. Soon afterwards an elderly Japanese woman appeared. She spoke no English and indicated for me to follow her. I did – to a traditional room with sliding doors. I asked her what time supper was – miming eating food and pointing to my watch. She held up her right hand – five fingers stretched out with the first finger of the left hand also pointing upwards and resting against the base of the palm of the right hand and she pointed across the street to a restaurant. I guessed 6:00 pm – or could it be 5:30? She then turned and disappeared along the corridor – it was the last time I saw her. I laid out the futon on the floor and changed into my running gear. There was no key for the room as there was no locking device for the room. The idea of theft and locking things up was evidently an alien one but I felt concerned having to leave certain 'valuable' objects behind as I was going for a run.

On the run through the forest I passed occasional wooden houses with old women undertaking various chores in their yards – they didn't even raise their heads to look at me the passer-by. After a while I chanced upon a group of European female hikers at one little hamlet. As I approached them I noticed that one of them had caught the eye of one of the old Japanese women who was wearing traditional country dress. She was spreading out various seeds to dry on a cloth in front of her house. The middle-aged European woman bowed and smiling said 'Conichiwa'. The Japanese woman looked up and moved her head ever so slightly in response. The European smiled broadly – perhaps enjoying this encounter in a foreign culture with a local and being able to use Japanese successfully *in situ*. As I approached the group I was wondering whether to acknowledge them or run past in silence. It was a beautiful day and I decided to offer a greeting. I smiled and said 'hello' as I proceeded past them. However, my salutation was met with stares and silence. I had the impression I had transgressed something. As I continued on my run I surmised that perhaps the answer was the following: the fantasy of rural Japan – of getting away from industrial commercial Europe, of having the authentic experience of trying out a word or two of Japanese – of managing to communicate across the cultural, social and age divides – perhaps also of experiencing female-to-female communication across all these potential divides – that joy of communion had, I surmised, been rudely shattered by a European male in modern jogging gear, addressing them in the international and most commercial of languages – English. As I carried on I was glad to get out of their sight, I felt vaguely guilty that I had maybe shattered a certain magic of the moment.

My conjecture continued: so it must be that tourism, like this, the more sophisticated kind, is about a search for something constructed as 'authentic' and more genuine than what is to hand on a daily basis. It is about satisfying a need to meet and interact with a constructed other: a Latin lover, an African Maasai warrior, an old Japanese peasant lady . . . It is somehow about forgetting that in fact we are all the same – and is perhaps based on a fantasy of difference.

Back in Magome at the guesthouse I got ready for supper (I hung about outside the restaurant from 5:30 pm onwards). There seemed to be no action inside. At 6:00 pm I went in and sat at a table. I then heard a noise within the kitchen area. An old couple also entered the restaurant and sat at the table next to me. They both looked at me and smiled and bowed – I did the same back. Shortly after, a young man brought various dishes of food to our tables. I carefully copied what my co-eaters did as I didn't know in what order, or how to eat the dishes presented to me.

In the morning I got up and packed my things. My bus was going to leave in twenty minutes. I wondered how I could pay for the room and the supper. No-one had taken any details from me – no-one knew who I was – I could have simply walked off without paying. Evidently the idea that people do this had not occurred to the owners and so no system was in place to cover this eventuality. I went to the restaurant and there was the young man with an extensive breakfast laid out for me. I hadn't, I thought, ordered breakfast at the Tourist Office – because of the early bus, so I pointed at the food and indicated 'no' by waving my hand – I pointed at my watch and said 'bus now'. He seemed to understand. I then had a change of mind – my thoughts were 'Oh well, I have ten minutes and the young man had spent the morning cooking for me'. It seemed churlish not to eat and pay for it – so I smiled, sat down and started to eat. The young man then came to my table and picked up the invoice that was waiting for me on a clip on my table – I had only just noticed it. He got a pen out of his pocket and did something to the invoice and put it back in the clip. I took the invoice and noticed he had crossed out the third item and readjusted the total downwards (obviously the breakfast). I took out money for the full previous amount and gave it to him. He went into the kitchen – I heard the clinking of a till – and he then reappeared with the money for the breakfast on a plate. I said 'no', smiled and offered the money back, but he too smiled and waving his hand refused to take it. I decided I had to accept the money. He had worked out, no doubt, that I had not thought I had ordered breakfast and so decided I could not be charged for it. Later, on reflection, I realised that no doubt the Tourist Office had ordered breakfast and that they had thought that I had agreed to a 'food' package of breakfast and supper, not only supper. Why would anyone not want breakfast anyway?

Once on the bus the system seemed to be that it is the responsibility of the passenger to work out, from the timetable what the fares are and then put the necessary money into the 'slot machine' near the driver for the trip. There seemed to be no system of control for ensuring that people were putting in the correct amount.

At the railway station I had a couple of coffees in the bar. Instead of asking in English how much it was – English was beginning to feel to me like a particularly blunt and intrusive instrument – I simply went up to the counter and pulled out a handful of coins and held them up for the serving woman to pick out the amount I owed. She smiled at this and picked away at the coins, laying out the amount for me to check on the counter. I noticed that the other Japanese customers in the café had been watching this interaction with interest and made efforts to catch my eye and smile and nod at me. Maybe the thought processes were: 'A foreigner who trusts us.' Whatever, there was no doubt that as an action it had been the opposite of the faux pas of the day before with the Europeans.

➤ What is the cultural promise that the author suggests the European tourists were searching for? Can you understand this urge? Why do you think it exists (if it does) and what do you think about it?

➤ What aspects to the visit did the author of the piece perhaps feel surprised or even delighted by? Would you have had the same reaction? Why/Why not?

➤ What products do you buy that are packaged and are aimed at making you feel that you are transcending the confines of the local for you? Look at the things you have bought or the experiences you have paid money for recently. How does marketing perhaps take advantage of this urge?

➤ Use Table C1.5.3 to list the products you buy and explain the cultural promise that each one offers.

For example, you may be influenced by the promise of science and the accomplishments of modernity when you decide to take some industrially produced medicine, or on the other hand you may be influenced by an image of natural healthiness and folk wisdom and decide to take a herbal remedy sold by an alternative health practitioner. Both forms of treatment are wrapped in cultural

Table C1.5.3 Commodities as cultural promise

Commodity	Cultural promise of the commodity

representation. It is easy to see how desire can thus be created and sold through the advertising of cultural products. Our urges for '*plaisir*' and '*jouissance*' can be taken advantage of.

Group discussion point

➤ To what extent are we involved and perhaps manipulated in this cultural consumption?

Note: text

The word 'text' traditionally refers to a sample of writing. However, the word can be extended to mean anything that can be read – in this sense we can 'read' architectural styles, as well as visual images such as adverts and films. Indeed, there is an argument that can be made that we are thus 'readers' of the multitude of texts that surround us and it is the way we 'read' these texts that is how we make sense of the world.

Task C1.5.6 The use of words

➤ Through an examination of texts within your everyday milieu, collect examples of the use of the following words and their derivations: 'modern', 'new', 'natural'

Table C1.5.4 Words and social images

Word: 'modern'	
Context 1: E.g. 'Spacious, *modern* apartment in city centre location' from estate agent blurb in shop window, UK.	Intended effect/reading of the word, e.g. the apartment symbolises what wealthy people aspire to – perhaps there is more than one bathroom and a fully-fitted kitchen

and 'alternative'. Table C1.5.4 is an example of how to keep a record of each instance for each word. In the left column explain where the word comes from; in the right column tease out what you feel is the intended effect of the word and the connotations it carries in the context from which it is taken. You can then do the same for other words with other rows.

➤ Compare your findings and assessment of the effects of the use of the words with your study peers. You may like to do this task with other words that you feel are in some way significant today as indicators of the cultural clash produced by modernity and tradition.

➤ Now refer to Figure C0.1.1 before completing Task C1.5.7.

Task C1.5.7 Diverse identities

➤ Event: of your choice.

➤ Actors: where there is evidence that different people who you presume come from the same cultural group tell different stories about their culture. There is an example of this in Unit A1.2, where Ming and Zhang give different impressions of their 'national culture'.

➤ Setting: of your choice.

➤ Cultural circumstances: of your choice.

➤ Angle: images of modernity, tradition and the alternative in people's accounts of who they are.

➤ Observation: listen to the way in which people characterise their cultural backgrounds. Find opportunities to talk to them about who they say they are and to find the deeper meanings behind their perceptions. Also try to find out how far the way in which the actors project themselves has to do with their reactions to new cultural circumstances, whether it is a new country or a new office. You may find Figure C1.3.1 useful.

➤ Disciplines: 4, 5, 6 and 12. Figure A1.1.1 may be a useful guide to untangling what may seem conflicting perceptions as you try to build a thick description of what the actors are actually trying to project. By deconstructing the way in which you project onto them you can imagine what they may be reacting to. You must also be careful not to generalise what you hear beyond the person who tells you.

➤ Outcome: an understanding of the complexity that people bring with them, and an ability to see other people's thinking in the same way as you see your own.

Theme 2
Othering

UNIT C2.1   OTHERING

Othering has been presented to you already in this book (it was introduced in Unit A2.1). However, it is helpful to analyse the term again. 'Othering' is used to describe the process that we undertake in ascribing identity to the Self through the often negative attribution of characteristics to the Other. Othering is a 'culture first' view of individuals. It is seen to be problematic by the authors of this book in that it restricts the agency of other persons as a factor in their identity construction. It reduces the possibility of negotiation of identity between people. As such it is crudely reductive, and so it is typical of unskilled intercultural communication. As it does not allow for the true complexity of other people to be considered, it is fundamentally a dehumanising process. It is most obviously evident in the discourse of war, where the enemy is reduced to something uncomplicatedly and irredeemably evil, non-human and therefore not worthy of compassion. To illustrate this, the following piece of text comes from the British *The War Illustrated*, 19th May, 1917 published in the middle of the First World War. It is from an article written by a Mr. Frederic William Wile 'Ten Years Berlin Correspondent of the *Daily Mail*: '. . . the German Armies in the Field maintain Corpse Utilisation Establishments (Kadaver-Verwertungs-Anstalten), where soldiers dead are rendered down for lubricating oils, fats, and pig food.' Another example is the Nationalist propaganda in the Spanish Civil War, which depicted in posters Republicans as having red tails. Current similar examples are all too easy to find.

Stop and think: With reference to the previous units in this section think about the following questions:

- Who controls the way you want to be understood or viewed?
- Is it you or are you involved in a struggle to assert this?
- Have you ever felt at times that you are being 'read' in ways contrary to the one you wish to be?
- Why do you think this struggle arises?
- What can you do about this?

Within all societies there are dominant ways of constructing the cultural Self and cultural Other, that is, the accepted and promoted view from the culture(s) you are affiliated and ascribed to. In other words the cultures you belong to tell you who you are – or should be – as a member of those cultures. Examples of this can often be heard, for example, 'Us Mexicans are . . .' or 'It's not British to . . .'. There are also, conversely, dominant ways of constructing the cultural Other: the cultures to which you belong tell you how those in different cultures (i.e. outsiders from your culture) are to be read and understood – for example, 'The British are a cold people', 'Well what do you expect from the French?', 'How Italian of you!' If these modes of understanding the Self and the Other become part of the daily currency by which individuals make sense of the world around them, then these can be seen to represent the dominant constructions that have become internalised within the individuals of a particular society.

It is evident that to control these dominant ways of understanding the Self and the Other within a society is to exercise power. For this reason these representations are not immobile but are open to change: they change as members of the society in question struggle with each other over the power to control these representations. Re-read Guo and Harlow, Text B2.2.2, and consider how different ethnic groups have been successful or otherwise in this struggle. A society is thus a set of competing modes of construction of the Self and of Others. You may find, therefore, that your particular construction of your Self and of Others may run up against some of these competing constructions and this may be a reason why you feel misread at times. Because these constructions of who you are and who others are constitute a power struggle, there may be deliberate readings of you to the one you attempt to assert. In other words, you may be deliberately Othered by others for their own 'political' motives.

 Task C2.1.1 Othering and power

➤ Work on the following three examples. Discuss with your study peers how an Othering impulse is perhaps being used as part of a power strategy.

Example C2.1.1

Sheena is a college secretary, in her early twenties and unqualified beyond school-leaving certification. She earns a salary of around £18,000 per year. Michael is a lecturer in the college; he has several post-graduate qualifications and earns about £35,000 per year. Collin, another lecturer, similar to Michael, decides to try and use the new photocopier machine for back to back scanning of documents. He does not wish to disturb the secretary, Sheena, who is on the computer, writing. Once at the machine he realises he doesn't know the sequence in which he needs to press buttons to operate it, so he appeals to Sheena for help. Sheena then remarks loudly: 'Michael asked me the same question the other day. Honestly, you men!'

Example C2.1.2

Ian and Peter are two brothers, in their mid-thirties. Ian studied civil engineering at university and Peter studied fine art. Ian studied engineering mainly to do something different from his older brother Peter, but also because he felt it would lead to a more secure job. Peter developed his artistic inclinations mainly because of family praise about his early efforts at drawing and because he had often been told that his Uncle Reginald was a good painter and that there was a strong artistic streak in the family that he had inherited. Although he studied art, Peter is actually very practical with his hands and methodical. He likes working out how things work mechanically; he used to take his motorcycle engine apart and reassemble it just for fun as a teenager. Although Ian studied engineering he is not very good with his hands and as a student he played the bass guitar in a rock band.

When at home visiting their parents, their mother would make the following type of comments: 'Peter, as the artist in the family, what colour should we paint the kitchen?' and 'Ian, where should we best put our savings?' or 'How best should we design the living room extension?' Being typed as an artist was something Peter found very annoying and something he found difficult to get away from. He remembered the joke a friend, who studied maths at university, made at his expense when he introduced him to a girl: 'This is Peter. He studies art with a capital "F".' Everyone laughed, including Peter, but it annoyed him deeply. From his point of view, the fact that people could label him an artist was a way of trivialising him and making him seem peripheral to 'important' things. Ian, as it happened, had the opposite problem: he felt people saw him as boring and not worth talking to as an engineer. At university he would pretend he was studying an arts subject when at parties for this reason.

Example C2.1.3

(Extracts from Barroso, M. and Reyes-Ortis, I. (1996). 'Caribbean Chronicles' [translated by M. P. Hyde], *El País Aguilar*, pp. 65–70)

Extract 1

When in Europe a person talks about a 'multiethnic society', the term refers to Africans cleaning the Paris metro or picking apples in Lerida, Spain, or to Turks tightening bolts in Mercedes Factories. In Trinidad and Tobago, the term 'multiethnic society' means that there are various nations treading the same soil, who struggle over the same jobs and who eye each other warily in the street.

Extract 2

The further you descend the social hierarchy, the more the divisions of labour are evident. The sale of ice and everything to do with it has traditionally been the domain of the Negro, just as the sale of bread has been the domain of the Hindu. A Negro would have problems if he tried to open a bakery, and even more problems if he opened a cleaner's because Trinidadians believe that the hands that knead their bread and wash their clothes should be white or yellow. In the same way they believe that Negroes are not good at making money because they like to talk too much.

Extract 3

The law is ignored and there exist no clear models of conduct. 'You can't talk of Trinidad and Tobago as a society,' says Abu Bakr. 'The only dynamic is race. Our society has no shared goals. There exist separate groups and each group has its leaders. The whites control everything and are fearful of the Hindus; that's why they place the Negroes in positions of administrative power in the State because Negroes have no economic power and are not a threat to them.'

Analysis

➤ Read the following analyses and then offer your interpretations. You may not agree with them. Indeed, if you do not, the reasons you may not do so could provide a useful starting point for your discussions.

In Example C2.1.1 there is an appeal to male and female stereotypes. The men, who are in higher positions in terms of status and salary in the work environment, are typed as being impractical and dependent on women – in this case by a woman who is on a lower salary and has a lower-status job. The implication is that as men they do not really deserve to have this higher status. Of course, the reason that the men may not be able to operate the scan facility on the new machine is that in their work routine this is not normally something they do. Their being male may have very little to do with their inability to operate the machine. The underlying questioning of their status within the working context as being a consequence of their gender and not perhaps merit based on ability is, however, implicit in the secretary's 'joke'.

In Example C2.1.2 the pinning of qualities and abilities onto individuals and stereotyping them as either 'artistic and expressive' or 'practical and sensible' may run deep within certain societies. It would seem that a person needs to be one or the other – obviously not the case in this example of the two brothers. To be categorised as an artist would seem to disenfranchise one from being serious about 'more important' issues in life, whereas to be categorised as a scientist or 'non-artist' is to mean that one is perhaps not capable of being a colourful and interesting person.

In Example C2.1.3 we are given an account of Trinidad and Tobago, where it is suggested that race has a strong determining factor on who one can be in terms of the job one has and the economic position one has on the island. This division of labour, which fits with the power structure on the island, means that according to race, people are thought of as capable of, and deemed to rightly undertake certain functions. It would seem that a belief develops that race leads to occupation and that this becomes mythologised as a natural state of affairs. On a much larger scale than in the first two examples, people are reduced in their potential according to a crude label that is seen to explain them. In Example C2.1.1, technological incompetence is explained as a factor of academic maleness. In Example C2.1.2, the legitimisation of opinions and outlooks is attributed to whether a person is artistic or not. In Example C2.1.3, race would seem to be a determinant of social function and potential. In all three examples, however, the reducing of the other to these characteristics and potentials is a form of power wielding. By reducing the other, certain advantages can be accrued to the person or those within a system that encourages this. How may this be resisted?

Now we can connect this with our ongoing investigation of intercultural communication, with reference to Figure C1.3.1.

Task C2.1.2 Trap avoidance

➤ Events: of your choosing, ongoing.

➤ Actors: of your choosing.

➤ Setting: within your milieu.

➤ Cultural circumstances: personal.

➤ Angle: the way we reduce the foreign Other to sexist, racist or culturist stereotypes.

➤ Observation: deconstruct the thoughts you have when you interact with people who are culturally different. Begin by noting these thoughts in your research diary, until eventually you begin to analyse them at the point where you are actually interacting.

➤ Disciplines: 10.

➤ Outcome: culturist trap avoidance – being able to see the traps coming and changing the trajectory of your interaction.

UNIT C2.2 'AS YOU SPEAK THEREFORE YOU ARE'

Before continuing re-read Text B1.5.1 by Pellegrino on 'language use in social context'. Language is a bridge between people, but it is also a wall that divides people. Perhaps as noticeable as the colour of one's skin, the noises one makes to communicate with other human beings is an obvious indicator of 'difference'. Language, apart from allowing for the transmission of culture from one generation to the next, serves to identify its users as belonging to particular cultural groups.

Indeed, to the extant that a language is only intelligible to those who use it, language is exclusive. Language is thus a great divider of people. As soon as people use language they are judged by the people who hear them as belonging to certain social groups, and the images and stereotypes that are attached to these groups may be invoked and applied to them. Indeed, a branch of linguistics, called sociolinguistics, is concerned less with the transactional content of language itself than with talk as being the assertion of belonging and identity.

There is, it may be argued, no such thing as neutral transaction in communication. All communication, apart from being about the 'what' that is said, is also about the negotiation of interpersonal relationships; of the signalling of the status of each interactant, of the power relationship between the interactants, of the social distance between them or the solidarity they may offer each other. This is deducible through the use of politeness strategies, of honorifics (terms of address) and other communicative devices. These devices obviously differ according to the language group and cultural background of the users, which in turn depends on the histories and evolution of the societies of the language users. Some societies may be more divided than others and hierarchical in terms of social class; some may be more homogenous than others. In a more divided society, politeness and the showing of deference may be very important for communicative success. Members of societies that are not, perhaps, so divided may have less need for politeness strategies and the demonstration of relative rank during their interactions with each other. There is a multiplicity of factors that lead to the particular way people orientate themselves to each other in various locations and these ways inevitably vary from location to location and from context to context within these locations. In Text B3.5.2 Triandis discusses culture specific ways of talking and looks at ways of possibly linking this to differences in cultural value systems that, he hypothesises, exist in the world between different cultures.

 Task C2.2.1 Accent and stereotyping

It has been said that an Englishman only has to open his mouth for half the population to despise and the other half to admire him. The point being that people jump to conclusions about a person's worthiness and character simply from the accent that person has when speaking a language. Pellegrino makes the point that this typing also happens to foreign users of a code who will be ascribed the characteristics of being intellectually diminished, immature and lacking a sense of humour.

All of us can signal our identity through our accent. Accents can indicate belonging to certain regional, class, ethnic and gender groups. Accents therefore produce affective responses in the listener, according to his or her view of the characteristics of the group that is invoked in this way – the speaker can try to control their accent (some can use various registers and accents – while others may be less skilled at this) but speakers cannot control the prejudices that such accents may invoke in the minds of hearers. The speaker, however, may be able to second guess these prejudices and therefore change the way he or she speaks to different people accordingly. This pragmatic, goal-oriented use of language may be considered to be a communicative skill. People who have communicated a lot with non-native speakers of a language may also be skilled at adjusting their own language to a standard variety that avoids the use of localisms and idiomatic phrases, to help their foreign listener understand their message clearly. This exercise is about being aware of your own language use and about being able to therefore grade your language. This is a key intercultural skill. You need to become aware of your language use.

➤ In Part A you will focus on your use of accent during a usual day's interaction; in Part B you focus on your own reactions to accents you hear. You may find the best way to do this is by copying this chart into your diary.

Part A

The register and accent you used.	*Context (person/people you interact with, place, event, etc.).*	*Purpose of interaction and assessment of success of interaction. Explanation of your motives for using the particular register and accent you chose to.*

Part B

The register and accent you hear.	*Context (person/people you interact with, place, event, etc.).*	*Purpose of interaction and assessment of success of interaction. Explanation of your reaction to the particular register and accent you heard.*

Task C2.2.2 Language of address

➤ Think of all the different ways people may address each other in a language. Make a list of them with examples from the language group(s) you are familiar with. Table C2.2.1 may be of use. Continue the table for as many items you can think of.

➤ Discuss any similarities and differences with your study peers. To help you make comparisons you might like to think when, in English, the following terms may be used, that is, between which people and in what contexts?

First name   Family name   Mr/Mrs/Miss/Ms plus family name

Sir/Madam   Dr   Lord/Lady   The Right Honourable Gentleman/Lady

Hey, you!   Oi, you!   Father/Mother (and other family role titles)

Darling/sugar/honey (and other terms of endearment)

Familiar shortened version of name, e.g. Mick for Michael   Nickname

Duck/love

➤ Why do these terms vary and what factors do you take into account when using these forms of address?

Table C2.2.1   Cultural use of language

Language item	Interactants who use the item	Context of interaction

Note: Revisiting the etic and emic levels of analysis

We all use the communicative systems we have been socialised into. Because in one cultural group's language use there are a lot of politeness markers, such as 'please' and 'thank you', it does not necessarily follow that the people who use these are politer and respect each other more than those who do not use them habitually. It is just that in one group this is expected out of force of habit and in the other group it is not. It is very risky to judge other people by one's own linguistic habits and derive conclusions in this way. One has to understand other groups and the language use within other groups from a perspective from within those groups. When one moves from one linguistic and cultural group to another it is also risky to assume that the other group will use language in the same way. One needs to observe how language is used in the other group and not assume that one's primary group is the norm against which other groups' language use can be judged. We also need to be aware of the fact that when someone moves into our primary language use group that that person is probably not expert in the language use patterns of our group. In other words, we need to be wary of interpreting a person's personality or intentions through the linguistic behaviour of that person, as we would a person who has been socialised from birth into that pattern of language use. A person from a language group that uses fewer 'pleases' for requests may be seen as rude by a group that expects the more ubiquitous use of 'please'. However, rudeness may well not be intended at all.

'Languacism' could perhaps serve as a neologism to stand for the stereotyping of people according to their language use, as racism stands for stereotyping people according to race. The way language is used by groups of people may become connected with a judgement about the people of that group and certain values and characteristics may be ascribed to people in that group because of their language use. In British English people who drop the 'h' at the beginning of such words as 'home' and substitute 'f' for the 'th' sound in 'think' – that is, 'fink' – may be considered uneducated or less intelligent than those who do not do this, merely because of the way they speak. We tend to other each other very readily from very minimal audial clues.

Discussion point

➤ Think of how in your cultural context you may place people in boxes according to the way they speak. Think how you also respond to people speaking your language when it is not their first language and how you may also be tempted to judge them as having certain characteristics because of the way they use the language. Look at the following and try to explain them in terms of the above.

- A Swedish female states: 'The English are not honest because they are always saying "please" and "thank you" even when they don't mean it.'
- The word 'barbarian' derives from the Ancient Greeks, who typed those who couldn't speak Greek as uttering meaningless noise like the sound 'babababa'.
- A Spanish man, talking about the rise of Spanish in the USA, states that Spanish will never rival English because it is the language of the poor.
- A Moroccan teenager enquires of a British tourist who is speaking Arabic to him, why he is speaking Arabic if he is not a Muslim.
- Sarah, a working-class British girl from the County of Essex, who has a good job in the City of London, is paying for elocution lessons because she wants people to treat her as 'herself'.

➤ You can now continue your ongoing investigation of intercultural communication in your own milieu, with reference to Figure C0.1.1.

 Task C2.2.3 Langua–culture

➤ Re-read Holmes 'The cultural stuff around how to talk to people' (Text B3.6.1). Complete the following chart that identifies pragmatic and cultural aspects of language (langua–culture) as variables in intercultural communication. Decide a) if the aspect is discussed or not and note the examples mentioned and b) if you have experience from your own life of these and can supply examples of the importance of these.

Langua–culture aspect	Example in text	Example in your own life experience
Honorifics		
Indirectness/Directness		
Field dependence/independence		
Silence		
Intonation and volume		
Politeness norms		
Body language		
Proxemics		
Eye contact		

Langua–culture aspect	Example in text	Example in your own life experience
Turn taking norms		
Backchannelling		
Topic choice		
Disclosure		
Touch (haptics)		
Other		

Task C2.2.4 Exploring language

➤ Events: conversations between people, conversations *with* people *about* culture.

➤ Actors: of your choice.

➤ Setting: of your choice.

➤ Cultural circumstances: of your choice.

➤ Angle: cultural use of language.

➤ Observation: note down the different ways people from different cultural groups, whether national or other, greet each other. Also, have conversations with people about how they feel about the way they are addressed by their culturally different interactants.

➤ Disciplines: 4. You will need to create a thick description by piecing together different fragments of evidence, both about how to collect the data and about how to communicate with your informants.

➤ Outcome: awareness of how to tune your language to the languages of others.

Note: Conversations

Having conversations with informants is an alternative to the more formal interview. It enables you to search out meanings and ideas in dialogue with your informant. The development of your own thoughts also helps to build the thick description.

UNIT C2.3 THE 'LOCATED' SELF

This unit looks at the issue of the degree to which we are shaped in our outlook by our environment. It raises issues about the extent to which we can be truly considered individuals and also the range of possible selves we can be according to circumstances. It therefore suggests that we need to be very careful about making judgements about others if we are not aware of the context in which others live or have lived and not aware that we too could equally well hold different values and have different outlooks were we in different circumstances.

Discussion point

➤ In groups consider the following questions.

1a If you live in a place in the world or in a time where there is a high level of infant mortality, how may this be reflected in parent–child emotional attachment?

1b If you live in a place in the world or in a time where there is a low level of infant mortality, how may this be reflected in parent–child emotional attachment?

2a If you live in a place in the world or in a time where there is a high level of sexually transmitted disease, some of it fatal and with no known cure, how may this affect the sexual mores of the society experiencing this situation?

2b If you live in a place in the world or in a time where there is effective and readily available contraception and treatment of sexually transmitted disease, how may this affect the sexual mores of the society experiencing this situation?

3a If you live in a period of history in a society where there are food shortages, or recent experience of food shortage, how may this influence the view that that society has of eating and desirable body shape?

3b If you live in a period of history in a society where there is an overabundance of food, how may this influence the view that that society has of eating and desirable body shape?

➤ What possible social mores, values and beliefs may emerge as normal, do you think, in each of the circumstances described in questions 1 to 3? Figure C2.3.1 may help you.

After looking at Figure C2.3.1 decide in what way the circumstances described may be reflected in the cognitive, affective and behavioural domains of individuals.

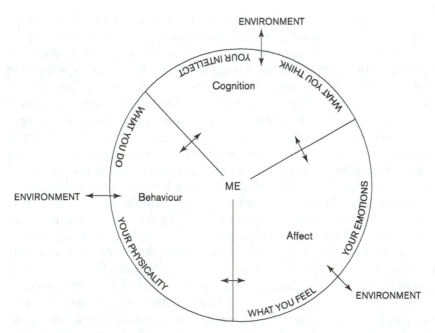

Figure C2.3.1 Three spheres of human experience

Task C2.3.1 Exploring language

➤ Refer to Figure C0.1.1.

- ■ Events: conversations *between* people, conversations *with* people, observations of people's behaviour.
- ■ Actors: of your choice.
- ■ Setting: of your choice.
- ■ Cultural circumstances: of your choice.
- ■ Angle: observation of how people behave and what values they state they have concerning selected issues.
- ■ Observation: think of some social phenomena that you have noticed and that you feel give rise to certain cognitive, affective and behavioural expression. Decide how you may organise the collection of data to test this.
- ■ Disciplines: 3 and 11.
- ■ Outcome: awareness of how circumstance influences all of us in the affective, cognitive and behavioural domains.

UNIT C2.4   INTEGRATING THE OTHER

Often when we consider what we may term 'other cultures' we compare them to what we see as our own. Because we know, have an insider perspective on, and understand 'our own culture' better than the 'foreign' one. For this reason we tend to feel that the foreign one is strange. We have been taught since birth to interpret and understand one another in certain ways, and when we meet a different system of interpretation we may feel that it is therefore not the 'right' way to do things. If we have become accustomed to sleeping from 11 pm to 7 am, we might think that people who have a siesta are odd or characterise them as lazy. Similarly, we may feel that people who eat other foods to us are strange, or family structures that are different to ours are unnatural. In other words, we tend to defend our cultural inheritance as the norm and see other modes of existence as mistaken. This perhaps natural reaction to difference is something we need to be wary of and try to overcome, for, in effect, there is no blueprint or copyright to existence and there are always interesting things to be found and learnt in the ways other communities manage their existence. Different communities have come up with different solutions to the challenges of communal existence within the environments in which they exist. Your cultural milieu – the one that you feel you belong to – is but one attempted solution. The problem is that there may be those within various communities who profess that their vision of how life is to be lived is the only true and correct way and that other ways are aberrations. This 'voice' may be powerful and exercised by politicians, religious leader and the media. This promotes intolerance and conflict. Rather than reject the way other communities live and the values they have learnt to subscribe to, another way forward is to try to understand and learn what one can from these different cultural outlooks.

It is of course imperative to maintain a moral sense of what one believes is right and wrong – in other words, openness to other cultures does not imply an abstention from judgement but rather an abstention from *prejudgement* based on ignorance. Openness implies the willingness to learn through researching other cultures and this aids in the development of one's own moral sense. This is useful in a world in which we are increasingly exposed to and required to engage with a myriad of different cultural perspectives.

In the next task you will be asked to find a positive aspect to behaviour that may initially appear negative. It is perhaps a natural reaction to find different behaviour threatening or disconcerting, and we may indeed judge such behaviour as rude or negative. However, if we train ourselves not to jump to such hasty conclusions, we may be able to reassess difference in less negative terms.

 Task C2.4.1 Turning thinking around

➤ Look at the following example. It is based on a true event. Try to transfer it from a negative experience to a positive one – in other words, do not prejudge it but work with it to see if there are any positive lessons to be learnt from it.

Example C2.4.1

When Peter, an Englishman, had been working for about a month in a town in the north of Morocco as a teacher he decided to try and further a friendship he was developing with several local Moroccan teachers in his school. He decided to invite them for supper to his apartment. This they readily accepted and agreed to turn up at 8 pm that evening. He prepared a meal. By 9 pm he began to realise that his guests were not coming and cleared away the food. The next day he went into school wondering what excuse they would have. He entered the staffroom and met his two friends. They smiled and offered him mint tea. Instead of showing any embarrassment they seemed to regard their relationship as not soured in any way. He enquired what had happened the night before and why they had not turned up. One of them then explained that they had been on their way to his flat, but on passing a café they noticed that there was an interesting football match on, so they sat down and watched it. As far as he could glean, that was the extent of the 'excuse'. In fact, it was not an excuse at all but a statement of what happened, pure and simple. He went off to his class feeling confused.

As he lived in this new environment he began to adapt to it. He would at times be invited for mint tea to the homes of people who, frankly, he had little interest in. This could use up a whole evening as one was expected to remain chatting for hours, not just drink the tea and leave as is the custom in England ('to pop in for a quick cuppa'). He therefore developed the tactic of accepting an invitation to avoid the discomfort and rudeness of refusing it to someone's face, and thus keep his options open for the evening: if nothing better presented itself, he would go; if something more interesting turned up, he wouldn't. The next day he would just smilingly explain that something else cropped up.

Peter was brought up in a system in which the demands of politeness and 'face' require either that one goes against one's real wishes and accepts invitations that one would really prefer not to accept, or that one finds elaborate excuses (an ill child is a very useful one) to avoid commitment. What may be the possible benefits of this alternative system?

Note: face

This is a concept that refers to a person's self-image and to how a person's self-esteem and sense of identity are related to the degree to which that person's self-image is supported in encounters with others. A threat to a person's face is therefore a threat to a person's self-concept – to how that person prefers to see himself or herself and to be seen, or at least regarded, by others.

To try and combat the tendency to see difference in negative terms, we need to look at how we can see the positive aspects that other perspectives and modes of existence can offer us and how we can appreciate these and even work them into our own way of being.

Othering is based on the assumption that the cultural Other is not as complex or as sophisticated as the cultural Self, and that the Other can therefore be reduced to essential and often negative characteristics. This rendering of the Other as inferior or bad may be a psychological prop to make the Self seem superior. In Mark Twain's *Huckleberry Finn* there is an obvious example of this with Huck's drunken and dangerous father – who has obviously got few redeeming characteristics – holding a view of 'Negroes' as inferior, when in fact we are presented with the noble and compassionate figure of the runaway slave Jim. His Othering is thus shown by Twain to be a baseless psychological prop based on self-delusion. It is a device designed to preserve his own face.

★ Task C2.4.2 Liberation into the Other

➤ Make a list of experiences you had when you entered another cultural milieu by concentrating on the things you have found liberating in this experience. By filling in Table C2.4.1 try to assess what it is in your own cultural milieu that you find repressive. Use the table to record your experience. One example is given. Add more rows if you need to.

Table C2.4.1 Cultural preferences

Description of different cultural experiences and aspects that you found liberating	*Analysis of own cultural milieu and aspects of it that you find repressive*
Example Working with agricultural workers from my village as a student – picking apples. The ease with which everyone made jokes about each other – the enjoyment of this.	The fact that in more professional circles people tend to take themselves rather seriously and forget that they have foibles and that these can be a healthy source of amusement.

★ Task C2.4.3 Stages for appreciation

➤ Consider this list of stages that could be used as a guide to overcoming Othering when confronted with difference. Put these stages in the order you feel they should be in. Then think about whether there are any stages missing and to what extent you agree with this or not as a model.

1. Reappraisal of own norms of behaviour.
2. Integration of new norms into one's own cultural system.
3. Making sense of new norms (assessing the validity of the new norms and rejecting or accepting them).
4. Investigation of new phenomena – information-seeking stage.
5. Shock and possible anger at difference.

6. Adaptation and adoption of new norms through practice into own cultural system.
7. Assumption that difference doesn't really exist.

(The intended stages are as follows: 7, 5, 4, 3, 1, 6, 2.)

➤ Now continue your investigation of your own milieu, with reference to Figure C0.1.1.

Task C2.4.4 Being positive about the Other

➤ Events: of your choice, ongoing.

➤ Actors: you and others of your choice.

➤ Setting: of your choice.

➤ Cultural circumstances: of your choice.

➤ Angle: trying to be positive about the Other.

➤ Observation: continue your observation of your own thinking while taking part in intercultural communication. Reassess the list in Task C2.4.3 against your own lived experience of working out how to communicate. Integrate notes about this into your research diary. Observe and note the ways in which your interactants do the same.

➤ Disciplines: 4 and 9.

➤ Outcome: developing experience of how to communicate.

UNIT C2.5 'ARE YOU WHAT YOU ARE SUPPOSED TO BE?'

Task C2.5.1 Are you saying what you are supposed to?

➤ Look at the following quote that the author of Section C collected one evening.

When I was at school in the Republic of Ireland I had to learn Gaelic. I was forced to spend 30 per cent of my time, not learning something useful like maths or science, which would serve me in life. I was a victim of a nostalgic, misguided and retrograde Irish nationalism that the politicians of the day decided to inflict upon us school kids to make themselves feel better.

In order to do this task you need to have a rudimentary knowledge of the historical and political context of the Republic of Ireland. Ireland was colonised for hundreds of years by the English (and British) with the English language displacing the native language. The Celtic Irish have also remained predominantly Catholic, while the English and British have been predominantly Protestant. The Republic of Ireland achieved independence this century after a long and bitter struggle. Eire (the Republic of Ireland) is now about 95 per cent Catholic and 5 per cent Protestant.

When we receive statements from people we need to know who the person is that makes the statement in order to be able to process the statement and make a judgement about it. Who do you think the person is who made this statement? What identity tags would you find useful for further placing and understanding this statement?

The following are tags that we may tend to use for interpreting what is said:

- nationality
- gender
- age
- ethnicity
- religious affiliation
- social background
- current life context (married or single or divorced, father or mother, job, etc.)
- sexual identity

➤ Re-read the quote. Then look at the possible authors of the quote and make notes on your reaction in each case.

Person: with minimal descriptors (basic typology)	*Your reaction: explain why*
A middle-aged, Protestant Irish woman	
A middle-aged, Catholic Irish man	
An English person who attended school in Ireland due to the fact that their parents worked there for a period of time	
An immigrant Ugandan Asian who arrived in Ireland as a child in the 1970s	

➤ Who of the above do you think it was most likely to be and why?

➤ Are you surprised to learn that it was the second person in the list? Why?

Due to 'tags' and our interpretation of them we bring expectations about what we think people must believe and may tend to interpret the Other accordingly. This is dangerous, as it may override individual difference and we need to be on our guard against it. Sometimes the context of a person's discourse can become so oppressive that it is not possible for the person to speak freely.

The following task is designed to illustrate the fact that it is not just what is said that is important but who says what is said. The social and political context in which that person says what is said is also important for our interpretation and understanding of what is said. Are people limited in what they can therefore say by the fact of who they are and the context of their speaking? Is it perhaps the case that certain people can say certain things and certain people cannot because of who they are supposed to be? Do you feel this pressure? Are there certain things that you refrain from stating because of who you are deemed to be?

Task C2.5.2 What we can say

➤ Can you give examples and explain why it is difficult to perhaps say certain things?

Thing that should not be said	Social and political reason

Tasks C2.5.1 and C2.5.2 are designed to raise awareness as to how we may other people through what we expect them to say. We may do this by imposing stereotypical notions onto people based on vague notions we carry as to 'who' they are. Thus an Irish Catholic may be expected to be nationalistic and pro the cultural 'Irishification' of Ireland. We may think that such a person should naturally be in favour of this and be disconcerted if he or she is not. We must also be careful of assuming that what people say is in any case what they actually think and believe, as the context of utterances may be a factor in allowing what can be said by certain people according to their 'typography'. Unit B2.1 is relevant to this point with texts by Sugimoto on the fabrication of national identity in Japan (Text B2.1.3) and Boye Lafayette de Mente on the public face (*tatamae*) versus private thought (*honne*) that is argued to exist in Japanese society (Text B2.1.2).

As well as Othering the people we communicate with we may also other ourselves through our own self-conceptions. We may do this through using the following mechanism: to say that one is something is to thus say that one is not something else. To be Canadian or to be Turkish Cypriot is not to be American or not to be mainland Turkish.

We perhaps use our neighbours more for this process of self-definition as they are the ones we encounter more frequently. As discussed earlier, we tend to represent these others in more negative terms than the self (see Unit B2.1). Said (1978) argues that the historical imperialism of Europe in the rest of the world has meant that Europeans constructed the colonised Other based on the repressions that the colonisers held themselves. Thus the colonised have been depicted as emotional and non-rational, as potentially immoral and degenerate and therefore in need of firm guidance. This argument is also one found in feminist literature, which argues that women have been Othered in this manner and typed with having these same characteristics – ones that a repressed male psyche has projected onto them. In this way colonised subjects and women are argued to have become 'serviceable others' used for the construction of the identity and self-view of the dominant – in Said's argument for an imperialist Western male.

In the next task you are asked to look at your own potential use of this potential 'serviceable Other' in the construction of your 'Self'. The question you are asked to investigate here is that of what boundary lines you draw in the process of self-definition.

 Task C2.5.3 Using the Other to define the Self

➤ Events: of your choice.

➤ Actors: yourself and others of your choice.

➤ Setting: of your choice.

➤ Cultural circumstances: of your choice.

➤ Angle: analysing how we use a contrastive Other to define the identity of the Self.

➤ Observation: Collect either introspective data about how you psychologically contrast yourself with others (use your journal), or interview people to see what they say about others and the implications this has for their self-view.

➤ Disciplines: 10, 12, 13 and 14.

➤ Outcome: developing an understanding and a sensitivity of how stereotypes may be used in everyday discourse and thought to establish the Self. Learning to be on guard against this.

If we become aware of this function – this basic binary division and dichotomisation process that we employ and that sets up a Self versus an Other – we can at least be on our guard against this tendency. There is a need to take people you meet 'as they are' and not to impose a stereotype used for one's own purpose of self-definition. This is difficult because, as we will see in Theme 3, our images and stereotypes of Others are mediated by the societies we are in and by the media itself, which tend to reinforce stereotypical images of Others.

➤ Re-read Text B3.6.2, Holliday's article. What disciplines is the author using to avoid falling into the 'Othering' trap? What approach does he adopt and what is your view of this?

Theme 3
Representation

UNIT C3.1   'YOU ARE, THEREFORE I AM'

There can be no doubt that we absorb the messages around us about 'the Other' that the media and the culture we are in project. There is also no doubt that today the media is a very powerful tool for those who want both to control society and to sell ideas and products to its members. For this reason we have included a section in this book on 'representation', which is the way the world is presented to us. Representation and Othering are similar processes. One could argue that Othering is a form of representation that projects the Other but in a negative 'inferior' manner. However, a subtle difference that we feel exists is that whereas Othering is a natural consequence of dichotomisation and the affirmation of the Self – and is therefore something we have to be wary of as individuals – representation is more political in that it is controlled by external bodies that offer images and understandings of 'the Other' for us to consume. It is often guided by political purpose. Theme 3 of Section C concentrates on looking at how our understanding of the world and the people in it may be mediated.

> **Stop and think**: Think of the inherited stereotypes and images of others that you have been exposed to in your cultural milieu. Use the table below to list them. With your study peers, discuss where you think these images have come from and the purposes you think they serve. Who gains and who loses by them?

Stereotype and example of phrases used to convey this stereotype in the media	Examples of contexts in which you have come across this stereotype

A further problem with being programmed to associate certain peoples with certain characteristics is that certain characteristics become looked for in certain groups, and even though other groups of people may exhibit the same characteristics in equal measure, this can be overlooked. One may well approach other people looking for confirmation of the characteristics they are supposed to exhibit and may thus also overlook other characteristics that may disconfirm the stereotype. It would seem that once cognitive schemas (mental frames of reference) are in place they become the lenses through which the world is observed and it is difficult to change them. In a sense, experience of the world can become contaminated by the glasses that you have been handed to look at it through (this is what we mean by 'mediated' experience).

Task C3.1.1 Familiarity breeds illusion

➤ Investigate how an object is represented through either the media or in discourse (the way people talk about something) in the cultural context you are currently in.

First, you need to decide what the object is that you are to investigate and collect data on. Will it be a material object such as a car or an item of food, or will it be a less consumable object such as a group of people, for example, travellers, asylum seekers, Americans, or indeed the British countryside or the Hungarian Plain? You need to consider both the visual and the non-visual in this project. Both are semiotic systems that work to represent objects.

Once you have decided on the object, you need to devise a work plan for data collection. Will you be collecting images and text together? What sites will you go to to collect data? How much data will you collect and how will you record and later analyse the data? You also, therefore, need to devise a timescale for data collection and analysis.

In the analysis phase it is important to move beyond description of the data you have collected to suggest how the object the data refers to is represented and how this is achieved. This means analysing the data and linking it to a theoretical system of interpretation. As an example of this, one group of students in a class decided to analyse the use of nature as a backdrop to products being sold in TV advertisements. The theoretical approach was a psychological one that suggested there is an urge in industrial society for escapism from the urban and congested. This desire to escape to a pure, natural Arcadia is manipulated to promote products through association with this urge. Thus a soap is advertised in association with a pristine, tropical waterfall. This theory about the psychological desire for escapism from modern society for something pure and elementary was the basis upon which the ads were analysed and gave the data analysis a theoretical coherence it would have otherwise lacked. The advertisement for tinned milk discussed in C1.5.5 works in the opposite way, by playing on the rural poor's dream of urban sophistication and wealth.

➤ Once you have collected your data and analysed it, prepare a presentation of your findings.

It is useful to combine images in your presentation of your findings. These can either be taken with a digital camera and used in a PowerPoint presentation or you may prefer to circulate the images to the audience in hand-outs. In the latter case it is wise to label each image and direct the audience's attention to each image at the apposite moment in the presentation.

While it is important to develop a theory as to how the data works, it is also important to remain open to new interpretations offered by others which may further develop your understanding of the data. For this reason allowing time for responses from an audience to your presentation is a vital part of the process. The presentation is not the end point of your exploration.

UNIT C3.2 'SCHEMAS': FIXED OR FLEXIBLE?

It may, at this point, be useful to look at what the difference is between a stereotype and a type. It is inevitable that we carry around with us mental structures which we impose on the world in an attempt to make sense of it. These cognitive structures, or schemas, are essential for us to navigate our way through life and are the building blocks of learning. The first time we encounter something new we form a mental schema of that event and then the next time we encounter a similar event we use the schema from the first encounter to help us navigate and understand the event the next time. It is, however, unwise to let a mental schema become hardened, so that it no longer takes account of new data. Schemas, while psychologically inevitable, need to be constantly updated and seen as imperfectly constructed models, not absolute replacements for reality.

 Task C3.2.1 Navigating the world

➤ Write down the schema you have for a typical event – for example, a wedding, or going out for a meal. Break it down into expected stages. The expected (or 'ideal') model – that is, template. This is sometimes called the 'prototype', and even if this is not followed to the letter, it is the model we have by which we can then judge 'deviancy', and thus know if something is unusual or significant.

Knowing the cultural schema of events, such as dancing a salsa or ordering a meal in McDonald's, is derived from empirical experience of that 'event'. It is reinforced each time that it serves as a useful guide for behaviour in that particular context or 'genre'. Of course the schemas of these different genres can be very different in different countries. When we are faced with a new genre, even within our own culture, we may be nervous and find the event tiring because we have to watch others and learn how to do it. For example, the author of Section C recently attended a funeral – the burial of a friend's husband – and as he had never been to a burial before he found himself anxious not to do the wrong thing. He was quiet and followed the others. He noticed he was one of the few without a black tie; he felt self-conscious about this, hoping it wouldn't be seen as disrespectful by the family of the deceased. He now has a schema for burials, which hopefully he won't have to employ too often! Schemas are therefore used to reduce anxiety and to reduce the amount of thought we need to employ in different cultural events. This is natural. I would suggest that when we experience an event such as 'visiting a friend's house' or 'going to a wedding', or 'eating a meal in a restaurant', or 'meeting the parents of a girl/boyfriend for the first time' or 'visiting the doctor' in a different culture from the one you are generally acclimatised to, it is best to learn the event as if it were the first time and to tentatively feel one's way. It is very useful to have a cultural informer – someone on the inside who can help guide you. 'Don't forget to wear a black tie' would have been useful information in the author's case. The problem is that if we have a schema for an event already established in our national, regional or ethnic cultural milieu, we are likely to make the error of thinking that the event in the other culture will be the same – or similar.

> Marisa, a Spanish lady married to a British man, was shocked that at the funeral of a relative of the British man, the family and guests held what she thought was a party, with people eating food and having drinks. She felt this was wrong and that people should be focussing on the memory of the deceased in a more sombre and sober manner.

When expectations are upset one may experience a certain degree of shock that can perhaps translate into resentment, anger and perhaps negative judgement of the other culture. Marisa felt the British family were unfeeling and somewhat heartless, for example. This is because expectations have not been fulfilled and one may therefore feel vulnerable and 'adrift'. To further illustrate problems that may occur when one imports a schema from one cultural context into another let's look at the author's 'drinking in the pub in Britain' schema compared to his learnt schema for the same ostensible event in Spain.

In a particular region of Spain the schema may be: enter the bar and greet the people there with a general '*Buenos dias*'; go to the bar; see if there are any friends around; offer to get them drinks; order the drinks at the bar; drink and accept any offers of other drinks from others; when you want to go ask how much you owe, often clarifying with the barman/woman which drinks you are responsible for; make sure you say goodbye to everyone you know and to those you don't with a general '*Hasta luego*'.

A Spaniard used to this schema, greeting strangers in a bar in England would probably be disappointed by the lack of reciprocity of his greeting. The locals would be suspicious or amused; the Spaniard would feel the locals are perhaps unfriendly. He may be seen as dishonest or evasive if he doesn't offer to pay for the first drink he asks for upon being served that drink. An Englishman entering a

Spanish bar may be seen as a little odd or ungenuine if he uses 'please' and 'thank you' all the time. These terms tend to be reserved for asking favours and for having rendered a favour, and are thus not used so 'lightly'. The Englishman would also be seen to be a little over-zealous or ill at ease if he attempts to pay for his drink immediately – as if he automatically felt the barman or woman was someone who would not place trust in him. In both instances the transgressor of norms would seem to reinforce larger suspicions and negative traits that may be attributed to non-locals of various origins. This example is designed simply to show how we need to rebuild our schemas when in different cultures and not feel that we can 'get by' with our previous ones. There is a schema for 'visiting a Spanish bar' that is distinct from the schema 'visiting an English pub'. This is a schema that needs to be learnt in order to navigate one's way successfully through the new cultural situation.

Task C3.2.2 Sketching a map

➤ Research a cultural schema. This is different from Task C3.2.1, in which you were asked to note down the components of a schema you felt you were familiar with. To do this task you need either to attend an event that you are not familiar with or to attend an event you are familiar with but look at it through 'ethnographic eyes'.

Note: ethnographic observation

The term 'ethnographic eyes' means that you should strive to make the familiar 'strange'. You need to act against the taken-for-grantedness that familiarity brings and try to see the event from the perspective of a cultural debutant – an outsider. One way to do this is to imagine you are watching the event and then going to explain it to a child who has not experienced that event before. To do this mini-ethnography it is useful to develop 'ways of seeing'. You need to start from the point that nothing that you see is normal or self-explanatory – everything you see is meaningful and tells you something about the society you are in. Look for the details and note them down. You may like to look at the spatial distribution of participants and objects in the event you have chosen to analyse – where are objects and where are people in relation to each other? What kind of people are where? You may ask whether females position themselves differently to males – that is, is there a difference in distribution of people according to gender? What may this suggest about the relations of the sexes in that society and about the relative power of each group? Is age a factor? How are people dressed, and what are the semiotics of this? Do people show their belonging to different cultural groups within the event you have selected? You may like to look at speech – who talks to who and when? Who holds the floor (i.e. speaks) most? Do people touch at all, and again what are seen to be the conditions governing this – the unwritten rules by which the people in the event seem to be guiding themselves? The questions you can ask are many and they are for you, the ethnographer, to decide. It is useful to have questions that you want to find answers to but you may want to enter the event initially without any precise questions to answer and wait and see if anything suggests itself as worthy of further investigation.

This stage of ethnography is very descriptive – you observe what is occurring, note it down and try to see patterns of behaviour. This means revisiting the event (does the time of day change the pattern of behaviour?). However, the exciting part of the project is the next stage, which is, having noted the patterns you have seen – i.e. gathered 'empirical' evidence – you try to understand the 'why'. What are the possible reasons for the patterns of behaviour you have observed? There are two paths to follow at this juncture: that of interviewing participants, or indeed analysing your own motives if you are a participant observer (i.e. an acculturated participant in the event under study). One tactic you may use for further development of understanding is to present people from the group under study with the 'evidence' you have collected and then ask them why they think such patterns seem to operate. Again, you will then need to find patterns in the responses you collect. Another path is to read literature on cultural analysis and on other ethnographic studies of a similar nature to develop theoretical perspectives with which to interpret your data. Does a feminist account of the events make sense? Does it partly or completely explain what you have observed? Does a Marxist account shed light on it, or does transactional analysis help? Is a Freudian or Jungian interpretation useful? Of course it takes many years to build up a knowledge of such theories! Remember, however, that it is the ability to coherently argue an interpretation that is important and that all theories are, after all, simply coherent arguments.

Once you have undertaken this study in your groups, present it to colleagues and be ready to defend your interpretation from their questions and to listen to new insights they may offer after having listened to your presentation.

Note: the mediated nature of schemas

The fact that we have mental schemas about what we expect in certain events raises the question about how we develop these schemas, that is, where they come from. While many of them come from our own experience, it is also probably true that many of them are mediated, i.e. that we are offered the schemas for interpretation before we experience situations and that we thus enter these situations, not finding our own way, but imitating and copying a blueprint that has been offered to us. This mediation may be through what other people tell us, through TV and film or via the printed word. At times this may be like following a script that someone else has written and that we are actors in, trying to get it right. This may be particularly true of events that one does not do very often, such as getting married. Again the cultural power invested in the control of schema formation is obvious and the media can be seen to have a pivotal role in this.

Note: the need for flexibility in schemas

A type is therefore a schema; it is a pattern of typicality that helps us to organise the world around us so that events can have meaning. It can also, however, become something of a straitjacket and may degenerate from something potentially helpful into something less helpful. If a schema does not become modified each time a person experiences a certain event then it can be argued to have become hardened and can help less and less with describing and offering a path through the reality of the changing world around us. The hardening of schemas could be argued to suggest a sloppiness of thought when this happens; a schema may become a stereotype when this occurs (see Gandy's quote in Task B3.1.4). A stereotype is thus the point at which a schema becomes rigid and no longer capable of, or indeed a genuine attempt at, describing or understanding the object it is focused on in a full and non-reductive manner. In a sense it is the giving up of investigation and becomes simply the promotion of a certain characteristic of the object it is focused on beyond its real occurrence in nature. Again the media can encourage us in this sloppiness of thought by repeatedly portraying objects in reduced and inaccurate ways. This may often of course serve certain political purposes.

Task C3.2.3 Exploring media representations of the Other

➤ Events: of your choice.

➤ Actors: of your choice.

➤ Setting: of your choice.

➤ Cultural circumstances: the media operating in a setting of your choice.

➤ Angle: discourse analysis.

➤ Observation and strategy: collect instances of representations of a chosen object/group of people. Analyse how this is undertaken and achieved. Look at how messages about this object are communicated to the 'reader'. Think about who this advantages and disadvantages.

➤ Disciplines: 15, 16 and 19.

➤ Outcome: awareness of how we as individuals may be susceptible to the manipulations of the media or popular discourse in our interpretation of objects or other people.

UNIT C3.3 'WHAT'S UNDERNEATH?'

In this unit we will look at how stereotypes and the reinforcement of what are seen to be 'intrinsic' values and ways of being, exist in much popular humour. In the British media the Germans may often be represented as being 'mechanical' and the Swedes are seen as 'emotionless' – think of the way in which the tennis champion Björn Borg became named the 'Ice-Borg'. Think of the traits that are attached to various others from your cultural context. One way of doing this is to analyse the source of the 'humour' of jokes about others. If stereotyping is about not allowing the 'object' the freedom to be what it may be or what it may want to be, but is rather the imposition upon that object of a certain way of interpreting that object, then certain jokes can be seen to be part of this reinforcement process – which is inevitably a power strategy in that it restricts the freedom of the object it 'describes'. It is a power strategy because stereotyping is about shutting down the possibilities and potentialities of the Other and is thus used to disempower and consequently disadvantage certain people. Jokes are a common cultural phenomenon that involve representation on a grand scale, and for this reason it is felt they form an important part of the analysis of popular discourse and representation and are looked at here.

Task C3.3.1 What's so funny about it?

➤ Read the following joke and 'unpack' it in terms of the stereotyping that it may reveal.

Mexican joke about Galicians

A Galician pilot brings his plane to land in Mexico. Upon touching down on the runway he has to slam the brakes on so that the plane screeches to a halt and even then it is right at the end of the runway when it stops. The pilot remarks to the co-pilot, 'These stupid Mexicans. Look at how short they build their runways.' The co-pilot replies, 'Yes, but look at how wide they build them too!'

The joke may be considered to be amusing in that it is the Galician who is deemed to be 'stupid', not the Mexican: he lands his plane across the runway, not using it as he should, yet he insists it is his view that is right. We may laugh at the stupidity of this Galician pilot and his inability to see his own 'stupidity' and 'obstinacy'. Of course, the pilot is designed to represent all Galicians – this is the nature of jokes – it is not just a joke about one foolish person who happens to be Galician. The joke is a 'jibe' at Galicians.

Galicians are people of Celtic origin from the north-west corner of the Iberian Peninsula – they are part of Spain. Spain was the colonising power in Mexico and so the joke has a strong political edge to it. What is more, Galicia has traditionally been a poor and backward part of Spain, and so many immigrants to the Americas (Spanish America) have been Galicians ('Gallegos' in Spanish). Being poor and 'uneducated' yet at the same time being 'colonisers' from Spain, they form the butt of this Mexican joke. This is the political context in which the joke operates.

 ### Task C3.3.2 Stereotypes in jokes

➤ Events: group joke-telling.

➤ Actors: of your choice.

➤ Setting: of your choice.

➤ Cultural circumstances: people bonding by joke-telling.

➤ Angle: cultural use of stereotypes in jokes.

➤ Observation: note down examples of different jokes you encounter. Describe the cultural setting very carefully. Interview people about what it is in the 'joke' that they see as the main point of the joke and their attitudes towards this point.

➤ Disciplines: 17 and 18.

➤ Outcome: awareness of how jokes may operate to perpetuate stereotypes against groups of people, operate politically against certain people, and reinforce prejudices against and promote disadvantage for those people in society.

Note: politics with a small 'p'

Politics with a small 'p' refers to the daily jockeying for position and advantage that individuals may indulge in as part of the everyday struggle of existence and the search for advantage. It is thus political to present oneself in a certain way to certain people so that one may achieve one's aims. This is not the same as whole-scale ideological subscription that politics of the left-wing or right-wing variety refers to.

UNIT C3.4 'MANUFACTURING THE SELF'

In Unit C3.3 we looked at how jokes may be used to stereotype others and to gain a certain advantage over those others which may psychologically satisfy the teller. Jokes are thus, to a certain extent, exercises in the domination of others. Of course not all humour is negative. In a play entitled *Comedians*, the writer Trevor Griffiths talks of humour that is based on fear and increases negative feeling towards others and humour that is liberating in that it teaches us something about ourselves and how we may be using stereotypes. An example of this may be the tongue-in-cheek comment the author of this section heard a black British comedian make when in front of an all-white audience in a working men's club in northern England. Upon being heckled he enquired: 'Could the person who made the comment please stand up. I'm sorry, but you all look the same to me!' The joke provoked laughter as it inverted the usual 'racist' comment by certain white people that 'they [black people] all look the same to me' – a comment which de-individualises and hence dehumanises the people at whom it is aimed.

In this unit we will look at how we may indeed stereotype ourselves as well as others – how we may be encouraged to see ourselves in certain ways, perhaps in ways that others have maybe told us we 'are'. This may be to make us feel 'good' and 'important' or it may result in us having a negative image of ourselves.

The cultural context we exist in offers us models as to how we should see ourselves and the values and beliefs we should ascribe to. The media also promotes images of what it is to be a member of the nation state one is in. Of course this is not uniform, and there are often competing images available to us.

Discussion point

➤ What are the values and beliefs that you feel are promoted in your cultural milieu and where is this promotion undertaken?

I recall, from my childhood, at breakfast, looking at the image on the back of the cornflakes box. It depicted an 'ideal family' – all white, one boy, one girl, blond-haired, healthy-looking, a domesticated mother and a strong-jawed father, both in their early thirties, middle-class, all enjoying being together as a unit, flying a kite in a meadow. Of course this image may not sell well in the more multicultural population that Britain has become over the last thirty years, not to mention the fact that the number of single-parent families has increased substantially. This image was promoting the ideal of the nuclear family – the family as an independent, compact economic and emotional unit – and presumably the basis as to the way society should be structured. The family should be aspiring to middle-classdom and this is to be achieved through attachment to the Protestant work ethic and conscious self-control, part of the ideology of which, through family planning, is to have a small number of children (the ideal being one boy and one girl). The strong jaw of the father suggests unswerving devotion to work, the aim of which is to provide for one's family. The wife behind him enjoys (signalled by the smile) being a 'homemaker' – her reward being clean, healthy children and a happy husband. Nature is also seen as 'man's' backyard – a place in which to enjoy leisure time – a conquered and tamed space. The white skin colour of this ideal family acts as an unmarked default norm – see Guo and Harlow in Text B2.2.2.

There is thus often a gap between the promoted ideal and what you feel you are. This can be a pressure not only from the media, but also from your peers who have imbibed certain ideals from certain sources and thus attempt to reproduce these ideals. This pressure is particularly acute among teenagers and can be a source of much unhappiness for those who do not fit in. It can also be used by marketing companies as a pressure that helps sell certain products aimed at the teenage market. An advertisement in Britain in the early 1990s featured a cream that was supposed to clear up facial spots. A teenage girl who had such a spot was seen wearing a bucket over her head at a party. Once she used the cream she could take the bucket off. The message is clear: if you are a girl and have spots on your face you are so ugly it's better to wear a bucket over your head than to openly accept the 'blemish'. You should be so worried of what people think of you physically that wearing a bucket is a solution. The message also suggested that continuing to have a spot is antisocial and a sign of slovenliness as the solution is within reach – it just requires you to go out and buy the cream. Remaining spotty is thus an active choice and becomes your fault.

Note: Digital communication and possibility for dis-embodied 'play'

One of the key differences today between face-to-face and digital communication is that face-to-face is 'embodied', i.e. the producer of the text can be readily linked to the text. Markers of identity: gender, age, nationality, ethnicity, social class etc. are detectable and present in such communication. The internet, on the other hand, can allow for disembodied communication. What challenges does this present for inter-cultural communication? What contextualisation clues do you use to overcome these difficulties?

 Task C3.4.1 Creating the need

➤ From an analysis of the advertisements that you are subjected to in your particular cultural context and the intended pressure they exert, complete the table on p. 295.

Task C3.4.1 may illustrate how much we are influenced in our conceptions of ourselves through the media and how this may lead to certain outcomes in our behaviour and help to shape our beliefs. Of course, consumerism, and the advertising industry that promotes it, may not be the only force that shapes our behaviour; it may be religious doctrine or political ideology, or indeed it may be a collection of beliefs that we have amassed that make us into what we feel we are. The fact that many of these beliefs are contradictory is something that we have noted before in this section. Trying to overcome these inherent contradictions may lead to certain insecurities – it may be hard to reconcile certain religious doctrines and beliefs with materialism and consumerism, and this may lead to a retreat away from one or the other in an attempt to maintain a unified 'Self'. This may partly explain the move by certain people towards fundamentalist notions of explaining our existence and our purpose on earth. It is one way of trying to reconcile the abundance of contradictory choice that exists in an increasingly interconnected world. Burkhalter's article (Text B3.4.1) looks at how on the Web we can actually now play at being different people. It is as if the Self can be 'invented'.

The retreat from such a potentially bewildering world, where the traditional tags we have employed to 'locate' people and ourselves as 'beings' that we can thus 'read' and 'understand' may also be a consequence of a globalisation, which may be seen to be imposing a uniform 'cultureless' pattern on the world. International tourism, more and more, seems to offer a similar formula wherever it occurs, with local culture only intruding to the extent that it is colourful and an entertaining sideshow.

A dervish may twirl for tourists in Turkey, a demonstration paella may be prepared for tourists in southern Spain, Brazilian dancers may do a samba for you and Cypriots may offer a rendition of 'Zorba the Greek' on a bouzouki, all within a uniform 'international' space of the resort hotel. Culture is thus commodified and reduced in its impact to entertainment, amusement and pleasure. The same may be said of food. International chains offering a standard fast food meal, such as MacDonald's, can be found all over the globe; Coca-Cola has penetrated the earth and crossed boundaries that religious and political ideals have not been able to. There is a retreat away from this perceived 'deculturing', felt as cultural imperialism by certain groups of people and this may partly explain the move towards cultural and religious fundamentalism as an alternative. It may be the psychological reaction to what is be seen as an assault on one's identity. It is perhaps not too risky to assert that people thus seek the familiar wherever they are and that familiarity is a useful psychological prop that keeps more worrying issues as to who one may be – the other possible modalities of existence that are potentially available to us – at bay. This may explain the way expatriates root each other out in overseas settings, or why immigrants prefer to congregate in certain areas of their new countries of abode. They are thus able to return to the familiar.

Advert 1 Brief description of advert:		
Promoted values	Antithesis of the values promoted and from which you may be 'suffering'	Plugging the gap – what action you are expected to undertake and the ideal result of that action
Advert 2		
Advert 3		
Advert 4		

Task C3.4.2 How do I come out of this?

➤ Revisit the jokes collected in Task C3.3.2. However, this time you are required to look not at the image of the Other that is promoted by the jokes, but at the image of the Self that is promoted. The following table is designed to help you in this.

Joke number and image of the Self	Analysis as to how this is achieved

★ Task C3.4.3 What's this really saying?

➤ Read the following newspaper article, which is from the *Houston Chronicle* dated Friday, 5 July 2002. Once you have read it, analyse the potential messages that the article contains in terms of the assumed roles and values that one may take from it about what it means to be male or female in the society the article is aimed at.

Male teachers are odd men out in female dominated profession

By Greg Toppo

Associated Press

Zach Galvin teaches English, drama and public speaking in Natick, Mass. But high living costs make it hard to make ends meet in the Boston suburb.

'I'm earning a salary in a town that I'll never be able to afford to live in,' he said.

Galvin, 32, said he makes more than $50,000 a year, but can't afford to buy a down payment on a house. Other guys his age often make $70,000 to $80,000.

'They say, "You're doing great work, but you're a fool to be doing that job",' Galvin said. 'It's tongue-in-cheek, but there's some truth in it.'

Gathered at their annual meeting this week in Dallas, members of the National Education Association talked about why so few men go into teaching – statistics show that only one in four public school teachers is male.

'It's not macho – it's not cool,' said Ned Good, a middle school teacher in Burr Oak, Mich. Good, the only male out of 12 teachers in his tiny school district, echoed the comments of many who said teaching still carried little prestige for men. 'Your job as a male is to provide for your family – it's not to be a nice guy and do what you can to help others,' he said.

UNIT C3.5   'MINIMAL CLUES LEAD TO BIG CONCLUSIONS'

This final unit will look at how we may attribute personality, and hence a theoretical notion as to 'who' other people are, their entire value system and beliefs, from often 'minimal clues'. We may in this way tend to 'idealise' and 'demonise' others accordingly. This unit begins with the questioning of the notion that people, anyway, hold stable personalities and coherent sets of beliefs, but that we are in fact perhaps more contextual and consist of a range of selves. We may think we are consistent in different situations, but how far is this empirically the case? While it is the case that not to hold any central value system and notion of who one is would lead to having no clear sense of identity and would also be a problem for ourselves and those around us – in that we would be untrustworthy or at best seen as hypocritical – it is worth looking at how we may present different aspects of our Self according to the situations we are in, or how different aspects of our Self may come to the fore in different circumstances. How else can the process of 'brain-washing' be understood?

Task C3.5.1 Am I really like that?

➤ Note down how you see yourself, that is, the qualities that you feel you hold to and present – for example, 'calm', 'open', 'outgoing', 'shy', 'sensitive'. Enquire of people you know how they see themselves – this can be done by presenting them with a tick list and asking them to tick the five qualities that best sum themselves up. Leave a blank for them to fill in and answer the question 'How easy was this for you to do and why?' Look at the self-descriptions – how close are they to the descriptions you would have assigned to these people? How close do you think the view you have of yourself is that which others have of you? Do different people who know you in different contexts see you in different ways? How can you gauge this?

When we meet people we tend to make judgements as to their personalities; we may be led to do this by generalised stereotypes that we have inherited previously. In other words our judgement can be a result of mediation. We may carry a prejudice against certain people in this way. We may assign qualities to people according to certain 'minimal clues'. One that comes to mind is when someone says they are vegetarian and British; this may also mean that the following is attributed to that person: they are an animal lover and have 'alternative' and certainly not 'conservative' political views. If the person is female, she is feminist; if male, he is likely to be highly strung, etc. We tend to ignore or not look for further contextualisation before casting judgement on someone. Someone may be a vegetarian for a number of reasons, including health-motivated and religious reasons, or simply from not liking the taste of meat.

Task C3.5.2 So that's why I treat you as I do!

➤ Collect, throughout a day, information on how you respond to other people and how you attribute qualities to them. (Use the table below to help you.) Do this with people who are relatively new to you, or strangers. In each case you need to think about the minimal clues (signs) that you use in each case to do this.

Person and context	Minimal signs that lead to attribution	Attribution

Obviously if we feel that people are attributing large-scale theories about who we are and the value and belief systems that we have according to minimal clues, then this may become a frustrating barrier for us in our communication with people. Look at the problem Parisa has with this in Example A1.1.1. When we enter different cultural contexts this procedure may be even less useful than it is in what we feel is a context in which we feel these signs can be more 'justifiably' read and interpreted. In the following part of this unit we will look at the way 'hair' may be interpreted. Hair – be it facial, the stuff we have on the top of our head (or lack of it) and other body hair – is a good example of the facility we have for building up large assumptions about people based on minimal clues. In England blonde girls may be the subject of such typing – of being stupid and promiscuous. The expressions 'dumb blonde' and 'bimbo' attribute these qualities to blonde-haired girls.

As for men and hair, I will limit an example to interpretations of beards. Traditionally the right wing press in the UK stereotyped left wing press readers as being bearded. The beard helps to symbolise a certain middle class, mildly left wing person: someone who is typed as being somewhat ineffectual and woolly in their thinking. Since 9/11 the beard has taken on more menacing symbolic value – representing fundamentalist terrorist threat. The beard has also re-surfaced as a symbol of the beatnik 'hipster' among young men, thus recasting the way beards may be interpreted and their associated connotations.

Task C3.5.3 Why do they behave like that to me?

➤ What about you? What, do you think, are the signals that your dress and appearance give out? How much do these potential signals control your appearance?

➤ What about you and the way you type others according to the style of their hair? The following table may be of use for analysing this.

Person and context	Description of hair	Interpretation given (you believe)

We need to recall that this use of minimal clues is reductive and that it is also a mediated interpretation in that the image of blondes, say, or men with beards, is brought to us through the discourse of others. In a sense we are told how to interpret these signs. We may forget that there are a number of ways of interpreting signs and that to look for other interpretations rather than to opt for one interpretation is a useful way to try to counter this reductive practice.

Task C3.5.4 It depends how you look at it

➤ Look at the following examples and decide how there may be different interpretations of each event according to which perspective – that is, through which eyes – you view the events. What may these interpretations be?

Example C3.5.1

I was dressed up in a graduation gown and waiting in a queue with others to receive my master's award from my university. In front of me was a student from Mauritania called Djack. As one's name was read out one went forward to the podium, shook the proffered hands of various deans and dignitaries, and then returned to the aisle. As the student's name was read out and the award given, the audience would clap. When Djack's name was read, he muttered to me, 'Just you wait and see the claps I get – "He got a master's and he's black!"' Indeed, I noted that the claps he received were louder and more effusive than they had been previously.

Example C3.5.1 boils down to different interpretations and intentions. What do you suppose the intentions of the audience were? Why did the black student see this as an example of racism?

> **Example C3.5.2**
>
> Mike and Jane, agronomists, had moved to the Dominican Republic to work in a large tropical fruit producing company. They were housed in a company apartment, like many other company employees. Soon they were asked by a local woman if they wanted to employ a maid. Everyone seemed to have a maid and Mike thus felt that it would be mean not to have one – it gave a job to someone, after all. The maid – Josefina – also worked for some of the local Dominican families. When Mike discovered what a small amount the maids were paid he and Jane decided to double Josefina's wage when she worked for them.

➤ How may this action be viewed in different ways by the different participants? Try to get inside the minds of the following participants and see how the same act may be interpreted in distinct ways – not always favourably: from Mike's perspective, from Josefina's perspective, from the perspective of Señora Sanchez, one of the local company employees who hires Josefina as a maid.

When a person's intentions are read in a way other than they are intended to be read, then we may talk about this as being an instance of 'mis-communication' (MC). It is much easier for this to occur if one is ignorant of how the other person or people you are with is/are likely to read events. The more sensitive one can become to this multiple reading of events, the better. Literature is of course one of the key ways of gaining insights from other perspectives. In this sense the more we read the accounts of others the less trapped in our own solipsistic outlook we may be. Conversely the less we read about or have the opportunity to think about and investigate others, the more likely we are to misunderstand them.

> **Stop and think**: What other means do we have that can enable us to break out of our solipsistic world view and to gain 'multiple perspectives'?

 Task C3.5.5 Exploring miscommunication

➤ Events: of your choice, from your own experience.

➤ Actors: yourself in interaction with others.

➤ Setting: of your choice.

➤ Cultural circumstances: of your choice.

➤ Angle: how your intentions from the language you use to the semiotics of your clothes or hairstyle, etc. have been misread.

➤ Observation: note down the different ways people from different cultural groups, whether national or other, have, in your view, misread you. You need to note the clues that you read that may indicate this too. Try to analyse how it is that this has happened – what are the cognitive steps these people may have taken to do this misreading?

➤ Disciplines: 17 and 19.

➤ Outcome: awareness of how you may be misread through a dominant reading of you and of how you in turn may be doing the same thing to another person.

References

Agha, A. (2009) *Language and Social Relations*. Cambridge: Cambridge University Press.

Alaasutari, P. (1995) *Researching Culture: Qualitative Method and Cultural Studies*. London: Sage.

Anderson, B. (1983) *Imagined Communities*. London: Verso.

Apple, M. W. (1996) 'Power, meaning and identity: critical sociology of education in the United States'. *British Journal of Sociology of Education* 17/2, pp. 125–44.

Augoustinos, M. (1998) 'Social representations and ideology: towards the study of ideological representations', in Flick, U. (ed.) *The Psychology of the Social*. Cambridge: Cambridge University Press, pp. 156–69.

Bakhtin, M. M. (1984) *Problems of Dostoevsky's Poetics* (Trans. by Emerson, C.) Austin, Texas: University of Texas Press.

Bakhtin, M. M. and Medvedev, P. N. (1978) *The Formal Method in Literary Scholarship: A Critical Introduction to Sociological Poetics* (Trans. by A. J. Wehrle). Baltimore: Hopkins University Press.

Barroso, M. and Reyes-Ortiz, I. (1996) 'Caribbean chronicles' (Trans. by M. R. Hyde) from *El País-Aguilar*. Madrid: El País-Aguilar, pp. 65–70.

Barthes, R. (1973) *Mythologies*. London: Granada.

Bauman, Z. (1990) *Thinking Sociologically*. Oxford: Blackwell.

Baynham, M. (2015) 'Identity brought about or brought along? Narrative as a privileged site for researching intercultural identities', in Dervin, F. and Risager, K. (eds.) *Researching Identity and Interculturality*. Abingdon: Routledge, pp. 67–85.

Beck, U. and Sznaider, N. (2006). 'Unpacking cosmopolitanism for the social sciences: a research agenda'. *British Journal of Sociology* 57(1), pp. 1–23.

Benson, P., Barkhuisen G. P., Bodycott P. and Brown, J. (2013) *Narratives of Identity in Study Abroad*. Basingstoke: Palgrave Macmillan.

Berg, D. N. and Smith, K. K. (1985) *The Self in Social Inquiry: Researching Methods*. Newbury Park, California: Sage.

Bhabha, H. (1994) *The Location of Culture*. London: Routledge.

Billig, M., Condor, S., Edwards, D., Gane, M., Middleton, D. and Radley, A. (1988) *Ideological Dilemmas*. London: Sage.

Bouvier, G (2015) 'What is a discourse approach to Twitter, Facebook, YouTube and other social media: connecting with other academic fields? *Journal of Multicultural Discourses* 10/2, pp. 149–62.

Brown, S., Hayashi, B. and Yamamoto, K. (2014) 'Japan/Anglo-American cross-cultural communication', in Paulston, C. B., Kiesling, S. F. and Rangel, E. S. (eds) *The Handbook of Intercultural Discourse and Communication*. Chichester: Wiley Blackwell, pp. 252–71.

Canagarajah, A. S. (1999) 'On EFL teachers, awareness and agency'. *ELT Journal* 53(3), pp. 207–14.

Cardon, P. W. (2008) 'A critique of Hall's contexting model: a meat-analysis of literature on international business and technical communication'. *Journal of Technical and Business Communication* 22/4, pp. 399–428.

Chassy, P. (2015) 'How language shapes social perceptions', in D Evans (ed.) *Language and Identity: Discourse in the World*, London: Bloomsbury, pp. 36–50.

Chiarenza, A. (2012) 'Developments in the concept of "cultural competence"', in Ingleby D. *et al.* (eds) *Inequalities in Health Care for Migrants and Ethnic Minorities.* Antwerp: Garant, pp. 66–81.

Chiawei O'Hearn, C. (ed.) (1998) *Half and Half: Writers on Growing Up Biracial and Bicultural.* New York: Pantheon Books.

Clausen, L. (2010) 'Moving beyond stereotypes in managing cultural difference: communication in Danish–Japanese corporate relationships'. *Scandinavian Journal of Management* 26, pp. 57–66.

Coffey, A. (1999) *Ethnographic Self.* London: Sage.

Cohen, A. P. (1985) *The Symbolic Construction of Community.* London: Routledge.

Collier, M. J. (2015) 'Intercultural communication competence: continuing challenges and critical directions'. *International Journal of Intercultural Relations* 48, pp. 9–11.

Collins, H. (2016) 'The emergence and intitutionalisation of the intercultural: navigating uneven discourses in a British university' (PhD Thesis), Canterbury Christ Church University, Canterbury.

De Fina, A. (2015) 'Enregistered and emergent identities', in Dervin, F. and Risager, K. (eds) *Researching Identity and Interculturality.* Abingdon: Routledge, pp. 46–66.

D'Hondt, S. (2009) 'Others on trial: the construction of cultural otherness in Belgian first instance criminal hearings'. *Journal of Pragmatics* 41/4, pp. 806–28.

Delanty, G. (2006). 'The cosmopolitan imagination: critical cosmopolitanism and social theory'. *British Journal of Sociology* 57(1), pp. 25–47.

Delanty, G., Wodak, R. and Jones, P. (2008). Introduction: migration, discrimination and belonging in Europe, in Delanty, G., Wodak, R. and Jones, P. (eds) *Identity, Belonging and Migration* (pp. 1–20). Liverpool: Liverpool University Press.

Denzin, N. K. (1997) *Interpretive Ethnography: Ethnographic Practices for the 21st Century.* Thousand Oaks, California: Sage.

Denzin, N. K. (1994) 'Postmodernism and deconstruction' in Dickens, D. R. and Fontana, A. (eds) (1994) *Postmodernism and Social Inquiry.* London: University College London Press, pp. 182–202.

Derrida, J. (1982) *Margins of Philosophy* (Trans. by A. Bass) Chicago: University of Chicago Press.

Dervin, F. (2011) 'A plea for change in research on intercultural discourses: a "liquid" approach to the study of the acculturation of Chinese students'. *Journal of Multicultural Discourses* 6(1), pp. 37–52.

Dobbin, F. R. (1994) 'Cultural models of organisation: the social construction of rational organising principles', in Crane D. (ed.) *The Sociology of Culture* (pp. 117–41). Oxford: Blackwell.

Eades, D. (2005) 'Applied linguistics and language analysis in asylum seeker cases'. *Applied Linguistics* 26/4, pp. 503–26.

Eades, D. (2008a) *Courtroom Talk and Neocolonial Control.* Berlin: Mouton de Gruyter.

Eades, D. (2008b) 'Telling and retelling your story in court: questions, assumptions, and intercultural implications'. *Current Issues in Criminal Justice* 20/2, pp. 209–30.

Edgar, A. and Sedgwick, P. (1999) *Key Concepts in Cultural Theory.* London: Routledge.

Fairclough, N. (1995) *Critical Discourse Analysis: The Critical Study of Language.* London: Addison Wesley Longman.

Fairclough, N. (2001) 'The discourse of New Labour: critical discourse analysis' in Wetherell, M., Taylor, S. and Yates, S. J. (eds) *Discourse as Data: A Guide for Analysis*. London: Sage/Open University, pp. 229–66.

Fairclough, N. (2006) *Language and Globalization*. London: Routledge

Featherstone, M. (2002) 'Cosmopolis: an introduction'. *Theory, Culture & Society* 19/1–2: 1–16.

Fleming, M. (2009) 'Introduction' in Feng, A., Byram, M. and Fleming, M. (eds) *Becoming Interculturally Competent through Education and Training*. Bristol: Multilingual Matters.

Foucault, M. (1980) *Power/Knowledge: Selected Interviews and Other Writings 1972–77*. Brighton: Harvester Press.

Gabriel, Y. and Lang, T. (1995) *The Unmanageable Consumer: Contemporary Consumption and Its Fragmentations*. London: Sage.

Gandy, O. H. (1998) *Communication and Race: A Structural Perspective*. London: Arnold.

Gee, J. P. (1990) *Social Linguistics and Literacies: Ideology in Discourses*. London: Falmer Press.

Geertz, C. (1973) *The Interpretation of Cultures*. New York: Basic Books.

Geok-Lin Lim, S. (1996) *Among the White Moonfaces*. Singapore: Time Books International.

Gergen, K. J. (1996) 'Technology and the self: from the essential to the sublime', in Grodin, D. and Lindlof, T. R. (eds) (1996) *Constructing the Self in a Mediated World*. London: Sage, pp. 127–40.

Gergen, K. J. (1999) *An Invitation to Social Construction*. London: Sage.

Goodman, S. (1996) 'Visual English' in Goodman, S. and Graddol, D. (eds) *Redesigning English: New Texts, New Identities*. Open University/Routledge, pp. 38–72.

Grande, E. (2006) 'Cosmopolitan political science'. *British Journal of Sociology* 57(1), pp. 87–111.

Gumperz, J. J. (1996) 'The linguistic and cultural relativity of conversational inference', in Gumperz, J. J. and Levinson, S. C. (eds) *Rethinking Linguistic Relativity*. Cambridge: Cambridge University Press, pp. 374–406.

Hall, S. (1997) 'The spectacle of the "Other"' in Hall, S. (ed.) *Representation: Cultural Representations and Signifying Practices*. London: Sage/Open University, pp. 223–90.

Halualani, R. T. (2011) 'In/visible dimensions: framing the intercultural communication course through a critical intercultural communication framework'. *Intercultural Education* 22/1, pp. 43–54.

Hammersley, M. and Atkinson, P. (1995) *Ethnography: Principles in Practice*. London: Routledge.

Hannerz, U. (1991) 'Scenarios of peripheral cultures', in King, A. D. (ed.) *Culture, Globalization and the World-System* (pp. 107–28). New York: Palgrave.

Hargie, O., Saunders, C. and Dickson, D. (1994, third edition) *Social Skills in Interpersonal Communication*. London: Routledge

Health Council of Canada (2012) 'Empathy, dignity, and respect: creating cultural safety for Aboriginal people in urban health care'. http://www.naccho.org.au/download/aboriginal-health/Canda%20Aboriginal_Report-Cultural%20safety.pdf.

Hewstone, M. and Augoustinos, M. (1998) 'Social attributions and social representations', in Flick, U. (ed.) *The Psychology of the Social*. Cambridge: Cambridge University Press, pp. 60–76.

Hoffman, E. (1989) *Lost in Translation*. London: Verso.

Hofstede, G. (1991) *Culture and Organizations: Software of the Mind*. London: McGraw-Hill.

Holliday, A. R. (2011) *Intercultural Communication and Ideology*. London: Sage.

Holliday, A. R. (2013) *Understanding Intercultural Communication: Negotiating a Grammar of Culture*. London: Routledge.

Holliday, A. R. (2016) *Doing and Writing Qualitative Research* (3rd ed.). London: Sage.

Humphrey, D. (2007) *Intercultural Communication Competence: The State of Knowledge*. London: CILT.

Hyland, K. (2000) *Disciplinary Discourses: Social Interactions in Academic Writing*. Harlow: Longman Pearson.

Jaworski, A. and Coupland, N. (1999) 'Introduction', in Jaworski, A. and Coupland, N. (eds) *The Discourse Reader*. London: Routledge, pp. 1–44.

Jaworski, A., Ylanne-McEwen, V., Thurlow, C. and S. Lawson (2003) 'Social roles and negotiation of status in host–tourist interaction: a view from British television holiday programmes'. *Journal of Sociolinguistics* 7/2, pp. 135–63.

Jensen, I. (2006) 'The practice of intercultural communication: reflections for professionals in cultural meetings', in Samovar, L. A. and Porter, R. E. (eds) *Intercultural Communication: A Reader* (pp. 39–48). Belmont, Ca: Wadsworth.

Keesing, R. M. (1994) 'Theories of culture revisited', in Borofsky, R. (ed.) *Assessing Cultural Anthropology*. New York: McGraw-Hill.

Kellner, D. and Kim, G. (2010) 'YouTube, critical pedagogy, and media activism'. *The Review of Education, Pedagogy, and Cultural Studies* 32, pp. 3–36.

Kimmel, P. R. (2006) 'Culture and conflict', in Deutsch, M., Coleman, P. T. and Marcus, E. C. (eds: 2nd edn) *The Handbook of Conflict Resolution: Theory and Practice*. San Francisco: Jossey-Bass, pp. 625–48.

Kress, G. and van Leeuwen, T. (2001) *Multimodal Discourse: The Modes and Media of Contemporary Communication*. London: Arnold.

Kumaravadivelu, B. (2007) *Cultural Globalization and Language Education*. Yale: Yale University Press.

Kumaravadivelu, B. (2012) 'Individual identity, cultural globalisation, and teaching English as an international language: the case for an epistemic break'. In Alsagoff, L., Renandya, W., Hu, G., and McKay, S. (eds) *Principles and Practices for Teaching English as an International Language* (pp. 9–27). New York: Routledge.

Kurasawa, F. (2011) cited in Sobré-Denton, M. and Bardhan, N. (2013) *Cultivating Cosmopolitanism for Intercultural Communication: Communicating as Global Citizens*. London: Routledge.

Leech, G. N. (1983) *Principles of Pragmatics*. London: Longman.

Lynn, N. and Lea, S. (2003) 'A phantom menace and the new Apartheid: the social construction of asylum-seekers in the United Kingdom'. *Discourse and Society* 14/4, pp. 425–52.

Marcoccia, M. (2012) 'The internet, intercultural communication and cultural variation'. *Language and Intercultural Communication* 12/4, pp. 353–68.

Moeran, B. (1996) 'The Orient strikes back: advertising and imagining in Japan'. *Theory, Culture and Society* 13(3), pp. 77–112.

Moscovici, S. (1976) *Social Influence and Social Change* (Trans. C. Sherrard and G. Heinz) London: Academic Press.

Moscovici, S. (1998) 'The history and actuality of social representations', in Flick, U. (ed.) *The Psychology of the Social*. Cambridge: Cambridge University Press, pp. 209–47.

Muspratt, S., Luke, A., and Freebody, P. (1997) *Constructing Critical Literacies*. Cresskills, NJ: Hampton.

Norton, B. and Toohey, K. (2011) 'Identity, language learning, and social change'. *Language Teaching*, 44, pp. 412–46. doi:10.1017/S0261444811000309.

Nzimiro, I. (1979) 'Anthropologists and their terminologies: a critical review', in Huizer, G. and Mannheim, B. (eds), *Politics of Anthropology: From Colonialism and Sexism Towards a View from Below* (pp. 67–83). The Hague: Mouton.

Oyserman, D. and Markus, H. R. (1998) 'Self as social representation', in Flick, U. (ed.) *The Psychology of the Social*. Cambridge: Cambridge University Press, pp. 107–25.

Punch, M. (1994) 'Politics and ethics in qualitative research', in Denzin, N. K. and Lincoln, Y. S. (eds) *The Handbook of Qualitative Research*. London: Sage, pp. 83–97.

Risager, K. (2015) 'Linguaculture: the language-culture nexus in transnational perspective', in Sharifian, F. (ed.) *The Routledge Handbook of Language and Culture*. London: Routledge, pp. 87–99.

Razak Gurnah, A. (2001) *By the Sea*. London: Bloomsbury.

Rosenberg, E., Richard, C., Lussier, M.-T. and Abdool, S. N. (2006) 'Intercultural communication competence in family medicine: lessons from the field'. *Patient Education and Counseling* 61, pp. 236–45.

Said, E. (1978) *Orientalism*. London: Routledge and Kegan Paul.

Said, E. (1993) *Culture and Imperialism*. London: Chatto and Windus.

Sealey, A. and Carter, B. (2004) *Applied Linguistics as Social Science*. London: Continuum.

Shuter, R. (2012) 'Intercultural new media studies: the next frontier in intercultural communication'. *Journal of Intercultural Communication Research* 41/3, pp. 219–37.

Singer, M. R. (1998) *Perception and Identity in Intercultural Communication*. Yarmouth, Maine: International Press, Inc.

Sorrells, K. (2011) 'Re-imagining intercultural communication in the context of globalization', in Nakayama, T. K. and Halualani, R. T. (eds) *The Handbook of Critical Intercultural Communication*. Hoboken, NJ: John Wiley & Sons, pp. 171–89.

Sorrells, K. (2013) *Intercultural Communication: Globalization and Social Justice*. Los Angeles: Sage.

Spears, A. K. (1999). 'Race and ideology: an introduction', in Spears, A. K. (ed.) *Race and Ideology: Language, Symbolism, and Popular Culture* (pp. 11–58). Detroit: Wayne State University Press.

Spencer-Oatey, H. (2008) 'Face, (im)politeness and rapport' in Spencer-Oatey, H. (ed.) *Culturally Speaking: Culture, Communication and Politeness Theory*. London: Continuum pp. 11–47.

Spencer-Oatey, H. and Franklin, P. (2009) *Intercultural Interaction: A Multidisciplinary Approach to Intercultural Communication*. Basingstoke: Palgrave

Spradley, J. P. (1980) *Participant Observation*. New York: Holt Rinehart and Winston.

Street, B. (1991) 'Culture is a verb'. Plenary Lecture at the BAAL Conference, Sussex University, 1991.

Strinati, D. (1997) 'Postmodernism and modern culture', in O'Sullivan, T. and Jewkes, Y. (eds) *The Media Studies Reader*. London: Arnold, pp. 421–33.

Strongman, K. T. (1996) *The Psychology of Emotion* (4th edn). Chichester: Wiley.

Suurmond, J. and Seeleman, C. (2006) 'Shared decision-making in an intercultural context: barriers in the interaction between physicians and immigrant patients'. *Patient Education and Counseling* 60, pp. 253–59.

Thompson, J. B. (1995) *The Media and Modernity: A Social History of The Media*. Cambridge: Polity Press.

Trompenaars, F. (1993) *Riding the Waves of Culture*. Burr Ridge, Ill.: Irwin Professional.

Tylor, E. (1871) *Primitive Culture*. London: John Murray.

Urry, J. (2002) *The Tourist Gaze* (2nd edn). London: Sage.

van de Vijver, F. J. R., Blommaert, J., Gkoumasi, G. and Stogianni, M. (2015) 'On the need to broaden the concept of ethnic identity'. *International Journal of Intercultural Relations* 46, pp. 36–46.

Van Dijk, T. A. (1998) *Ideology*. London: Sage.

van Ginneken, J. (1998) *Understanding Global News*. London: Sage

Vygotsky, L. S. (1986) *Thought and Language* (Trans. by A. Kozulin). Cambridge, Mass: MIT Press.

Wagner, R. (1981) *The Inventions of Culture*. Chicago: University of Chicago Press.

Watson, R. (1997) 'Ethnomethodology and textual analysis', in Silverman, D. (ed.) *Qualitative Research: Theory Method and Practice*. London: Sage, pp. 80–98.

Weenink, D. (2008) 'Cosmopolitanism as a form of capital: parents preparing their children for a globalizing world'. *Sociology* 42(6), pp. 1072–88.

Wetherell, M. and Maybin, J. (1996) 'The distributed self: a social constructionist perspective', in Stevens, R. (ed.) *Understanding the Self*. London: Sage/Open University, pp. 219–79.

Whorf, B. L. (1956) *Language, Thought and Reality*. New York: Wiley.

Wierzbicka, A. (1994) 'Emotion, language and cultural scripts', in Kitayama, S. and Markus, S. R. (1994) *Emotion and Culture: Empirical Studies of Mutual Influence*. Washington, D.C.: American Psychological Association, pp. 133–96.

Wodak, R. (1996) *Disorders of Discourse*. Harlow: Longman.

Wodak, R. (2008) 'Us and them: inclusion and exclusion', in Delanty, G., Wodak, R. and Jones, P. (eds), *Identity, Belonging and Migration* (pp. 54–77). Liverpool: Liverpool University Press.

Wodak, R., De Cillia, R., Reisigl, M. and Liebhart, K. (1999) *The Discursive Construction of National Identity*. Edinburgh: University of Edinburgh Press.

Ylanne-McEwen, V. and Coupland, N. (2000) 'Accommodation theory: a conceptual resource for intercultural sociolinguistics' in Spencer-Oatey, H. (ed.) *Culturally Speaking: Managing Rapport through Talk across Cultures*. London: Continuum, pp. 191–214.

Further reading

Suggestions are included below for further reading on issues raised in the book. Where appropriate, suggestions are made for accessible introduction to the issue(s) for the reader, for more in-depth and specialised reading, and for books which collect together key papers and book extracts previously published elsewhere.

INTERCULTURAL COMMUNICATION

Accessible introductions to intercultural communication include:

Bowe, H. J., Martin, K. and Manns, H. (2014) *Communication Across Cultures: Mutual Understanding in a Global World.* Cambridge: Cambridge University Press.
Holliday, A. R. (2013*) Understanding Intercultural Communication: Negotiating a Grammar of Culture.* London: Sage.
Hua, Z. (2014) *Exploring Intercultural Communication: Language in Action.* Abingdon: Routledge.
Jackson, J. (2014) *Introducing Language and Intercultural Communication.* Abingdon: Routledge.
Martin, J. N. and Nakayama, T. K. (2011: 4th edn) *Experiencing Intercultural Communication: An Introduction.* New York: McGraw-Hill.
Spencer-Oatey, H. and Franklin, P. (2009) *Intercultural Interaction: A Multidisciplinary Approach to Intercultural Communication.* Basingstoke: Palgrave Macmillan.

Books on critical approaches to intercultural communication include:

Holliday, A. R. (2011) *Intercultural Communication and Ideology.* London: Sage.
Piller, I. (2001) *Intercultural Communication: A Critical Introduction.* Edinburgh: Edinburgh University Press.
Sorells, K. (2013) *Intercultural Communication: Globalization and Social Justice.* Los Angeles: Sage.

Edited collections of papers and book extracts on intercultural communication include:

Asante, M. K., Miike, Y. and Yin. J. (eds) (2008) *The Global Intercultural Communication Reader.* Abingdon: Routledge.
Hua, Z. (ed.) (2014) *The Language and Intercultural Communication Reader.* Abingdon: Routledge.
Jackson, J. (ed.) (2012) *Routledge Handbook of Intercultural Communication.* Abingdon: Routledge.

Kiesling, S. F. and Bratt Paulston, C. (eds) (2005) *Intercultural Discourse and Communication: The Essential Readings.* Oxford: Blackwell.

Kotthoff, H. and Spencer-Oatey, H. (eds) (2009) *Handbook of Intercultural Communication.* Berlin: Mouton de Gruyter.

Monaghan, L. and Goodman, J. E. (eds) (2007) *A Cultural Approach to Interpersonal Communication: Essential Readings.* Oxford: Blackwell.

Nakayama, T.K. and Halualani, R. T. (eds) (2010) *The Handbook of Critical Intercultural Communication.* Hoboken, NJ: John Wiley & Sons.

Paulston, C. B., Kiesling, S. F. and Rangel, E.S. (eds) (2014) *The Handbook of Intercultural Discourse and Communication.* Chichester: Wiley Blackwell.

Sharifian, F. and Jamarani, M. (eds) (2012) *Language and Communication in the New Era.* Abingdon: Routledge.

Spencer-Oatey, H. (ed.) (2000) *Culturally Speaking: Managing Rapport through Talk across Cultures.* London: Continuum.

Spencer-Oatey, H. (ed.) (2008) *Culturally Speaking: Culture, Communication and Politeness Theory.* London: Continuum.

IDENTITY

Accessible introductions to identity include:

du Gay, P., Evans, J. and Redman, P. (eds) (2000) *Identity: A Reader.* London: Sage/Open University.

Gergen, K. J. (2000: 2nd edn) *The Saturated Self: Dilemmas of Identity in Contemporary Life.* New York: Basic Books.

Hall, S. and du Gay, P. (eds) (1996) *Questions of Cultural Identity.* London: Sage.

Stevens, R. (ed.) (1996) *Understanding the Self.* London: Sage/Open University.

Wetherell, M. (ed.) (1996) *Identities, Groups and Social Issues.* London: Sage/Open University.

Woodward, K. (1997) *Identity and Difference.* London: Sage/Open University.

If you are interested in doing further reading on cultural aspects of identity the following titles are recommended:

Delanty, G., Wodak, R., and Jones, P. (eds) (2008) *Identity, Belonging and Migration.* Liverpool: Liverpool University Press.

Dervin, F. and Risager, K. (eds) (2015) *Researching Identity and Interculturality.* Abingdon: Routledge.

Sarup, M. (1996) *Identity, Culture and the Postmodern World.* Edinburgh: Edinburgh University Press.

Scott, S. (2015) *Negotiating Identity: Symbolic Interactionist Approaches to Social Identity.* Malden, MA: Polity Press.

Weedon, C. (2004) *Identity and Culture: Narratives of Difference and Belonging.* Maidenhead: Open University Press.

CULTURE, IDENTITY, LANGUAGE AND COMMUNICATION

If you are interested in doing further reading on the relationships between culture, identity, language and communication the following titles are recommended:

Burke, L, Crowley, T. and Girvin, A. (eds) (2000) *The Routledge Language and Cultural Theory Reader*. London: Routledge.

Duranti, A. (2009: 2nd. ed.) *Linguistic Anthropology*. Cambridge: Cambridge University Press.

Evans, D. (ed.) (2015) *Language and Identity*. London: Bloomsbury.

Gumperz, J. J. and Levinson, S. C. (eds) (1996) *Rethinking Linguistic Relativity*. Cambridge: Cambridge University Press.

Holmes, P. and F. Dervin (2016) *The Cultural and Intercultural Dimensions of English as a Lingua Franca*. Clevedon: Multilingual Matters.

Riley, P. (2007) *Language, Culture and Identity*. London: Continuum.

Schieffelin, B. B. and Ochs, E. (eds) (1987) *Language Socialization Across Cultures*. Cambridge: Cambridge University Press.

Sharifian, F. (ed.) (2015) *The Routledge Handbook of Language and Culture*. Abingdon: Routledge.

Watt, D. and C. Llamas (2014) *Language, Borders and Identity*. Edinburgh: Edinburgh University Press.

If you are interested in doing further reading on pragmatics in intercultural communication the following titles are recommended:

Alcón Soler, E. and Martínez-Flor, A. (2008) *Investigating Pragmatics in Foreign Language Learning, Teaching and Testing*. Clevedon: Multilingual Matters.

Archer, D. and P. Grundy (eds) (2011) *The Pragmatics Reader*. Abingdon: Routledge.

Bardovi-Harlig, K. and Hartford, B. S. (eds) (2008) *Interlanguage Pragmatics*. New York: Routledge.

Brown, P. and Levinson, S. C. (1987: 2nd edn) *Politeness: Some Universals in Language Usage*. Cambridge: Cambridge University Press.

Goddard, C. (2006) *Ethnopragmatics: Understanding Discourse in Cultural Context*. Berlin: Mouton de Gruyter.

Kádár D.Z. and Haugh, M. (2013) *Understanding Politeness*. Cambridge: Cambridge University Press.

Kasper, G. and Blum-Kulka, S. (1993) *Interlanguage Pragmatics*. New York: Oxford University Press.

Kasper, G. and Rose, K. (2002) *Pragmatic Development in a Second Language*. Oxford: Blackwell.

Keckes, I. (2014) *Intercultural Pragmatics*. Oxford: Oxford University Press.

Rose, K. and Kasper, G. (eds) (2001) *Pragmatics in Language Teaching*. Cambridge: Cambridge University Press.

Watts, R. (2003) *Politeness*. Cambridge: Cambridge University Press.

Watts, R., Ide, S. and Ehlich, K. (eds) (2005) *Politeness in Language*. Berlin: Mouton de Gruyter.

Wierzbicka, A. (1991) *Cross-Cultural Pragmatics: The Semantics of Human Interaction*. New York: Mouton de Gruyter.

DISCOURSE AND DISCOURSE ANALYSIS

Gee's Introduction to Discourse Analysis is now in its 4th edition:

Gee, J. P. (2014: 4th edn), *An Introduction to Discourse Analysis*. Abingdon: Routledge.

Other accessible introductions to discourse and discourses analysis are:

Gee, J. P. (2014: 2nd edn) *How To Do Discourse Analysis*. Abingdon: Routledge.

Scollon, R. S. W., Wong Scollon, S. D. and Jones, R. H. (2012: 3rd ed.) *Intercultural Communication: A Discourse Approach*. Oxford: Blackwell.

De Fina, A., Schiffrin, D. and Bamberg, M. (eds) (2006) *Discourse and Identity*. Cambridge: Cambridge University Press.

Fairclough, N. (2003) *Analysing Discourse: Textual Analysis for Social Research*. London: Routledge.

Wetherell, M., Taylor, S. and Yates, S. J. (eds) (2001) *Discourse as Data: A Guide for Analysis*. London: Sage/Open University.

If you are interested in doing further reading on approaches to discourse and discourse analysis, the following titles are recommended:

Barker, C. and Galasinski, D. (2001) *Cultural Studies and Discourse Analysis*. London: Sage.

Benwell, B. and Stokoe, E. (2006) *Discourse and Identity*. Edinburgh: University of Edinburgh Press.

Caldas-Coulthard, C. and M. Coulthard (eds) (1996). *Texts and Practices: Readings in Critical Discourse Analysis*. Abingdon: Routledge.

Fairclough, N. (1992) *Discourse and Social Change*. Cambridge: Polity Press.

Fairclough, N. (1995) *Critical Discourse Analysis: The Critical Study of Language*. Harlow: Longman.

Potter, J. and Wetherell, M. (1987) *Discourse and Social Psychology: Beyond Attitudes and Behaviour*. London: Sage.

Wodak, R. (1996) *Disorders of Discourse*. Harlow: Longman.

Wodak, R., De Cillia, R., Reisigl, M. and Liebhart, K. (1999) *The Discursive Construction of National Identity*. Edinburgh: University of Edinburgh Press.

Wodak, R. and Reisigl, M. (2001) *Discourse and Discrimination*. Harlow: Longman.

Collections of published papers and chapters on discourse and discourse analysis include:

Gee, J.P. and Handford, M. (eds) (2013) *The Routledge Handbook of Discourse Analysis*. Abingdon: Routledge.

Hyland, K. (ed.) (2013) *Discourse Studies Reader*. London: Bloomsbury.

Jaworski, A. and Coupland, N. (eds) (1999) *The Discourse Reader*. London: Routledge.

Sarangi, S. and Coulthard, M. (eds) (2000) *Discourse and Social Life*. Oxford: Oxford University Press.

Schiffrin, D., Tannen, D. and Hamilton, H. E. (eds) (2001) *The Handbook of Discourse Analysis*. Oxford: Blackwell.

Van Dijk, T. A. (ed.) (1997) *Discourse as Social Interaction*. London: Sage.

Van Dijk, T. A. (ed.) (1997) *Discourse as Structure and Process*. London: Sage.

Willig, C. (ed.) (1999) *Applied Discourse Analysis: Social and Psychological Interventions*. Buckingham: Open University.

Wodak, R. and Meyer, M. (eds) (2001) *Methods of Critical Discourse Analysis*. London: Sage.

CULTURE, IDENTITY, AND LANGUAGE LEARNING AND TEACHING

If you are interested in doing further reading on issues of culture and identity in language teaching and learning the following titles are recommended:

Benson, P., Barkhuisen, G. P., Bodycott, P. and Brown, J. (2013) *Narratives of Identity in Study Abroad*. Basingstoke: Palgrave Macmillan.

Block, D. (2007) *Second Language Identities*. London: Continuum.

Block, D. and Cameron, D. (eds) (2002) *Globalization and Language Teaching*. London: Routledge.

Byram, M., Morgan, C. *et al.* (1994) *Teaching-and-Learning Language-and-Culture*. Clevedon: Multilingual Matters.

Canagarajah, A. S. (1999) *Resisting Linguistic Imperialism in English Language Teaching*. Oxford: Oxford University Press.

Corbett, J. (2003) *An Intercultural Approach to English Language Teaching*. Clevedon: Multilingual Matters.

Cortazzi, M. and Jin, L. (eds) (2013) *Researching Intercultural Learning*. Basingstoke: Palgrave Macmillan.

Gray, J. (2010) *The Construction of English: Culture, Consumerism and Promotion in the ELT Global Coursebook*. Basingstoke: Palgrave Macmillan.

Guilherme, M. (2002) *Critical Citizens for an Intercultural World: Foreign Language Education as Cultural Politics*. Clevedon: Multilingual Matters.

Hinkel, E. (ed.) (1999) *Culture in Second Language Teaching and Learning*. Cambridge: Cambridge University Press.

Holliday, A. R. (1994) *Appropriate Methodology and Social Context*. Cambridge: Cambridge University Press.

Holliday, A. R. (2005) *The Struggle to Teach English as an International Language*. Oxford: Oxford University Press.

Jackson, J. (2007) *Language, Identity and Study Abroad*. London: Equinox.

Jin, L. and Cortazzi, M. (eds) (2013) *Researching Cultures of Learning*. Basingstoke: Palgrave Macmillan.

Kramsch, C. (1993) *Context and Culture in Language Teaching*. Oxford: Oxford University Press.

Kubota, R., and Lin, A. M. Y. (eds) (2009) *Race, Culture, and Identities in Second Language Education: Exploring Critically Engaged Practice*. New York: Routledge.

Kullman, J. P. (2013) 'Telling tales: changing discourses of identity in the contemporary "global" English language coursebook' in Gray, J. (ed.) *Critical Perspectives on Language Teaching Materials*. Basingstoke: Palgrave Macmillan, pp. 17–39.

Kumaravadivelu, B. (2008) *Cultural Globalization in Language Education*. Yale: Yale University Press.

Lantolf, J. P. (ed.) (2000) *Sociocultural Theory and Second Language Learning*. Oxford: Oxford University Press.

Lantolf, J. P. and M.E. Poehner (2014) *Sociocultural Theory and the Pedagogical Imperative: Vygotskian Praxis and the Research/Practice Divide*. Abingdon: Routledge.

Liddicoat, A. J. and A. Scarino (2013) *Intercultural Language Teaching and Learning*. Chichester: Wiley-Blackwell.

McKay, S. L. and Wong, S.-L. C. (eds) (2000) *New Immigrants in the United States: Readings for Second Language Educators*. Cambridge: Cambridge University Press.

Norton, B. (2000) *Identity and Language Learning: Gender, Ethnicity, and Educational Change*. Harlow: Pearson Education.

Pellegrino Aveni, V. (2005) *Study Abroad and Second Language Use*. Cambridge: Cambridge University Press.

Tsui, B.M. and Tollefson, J.W. (eds) (2006) *Language Policy, Culture and Identity in Asian Contexts*. Mahwah, N.J.: Lawrence Erlbaum.

RESEARCHING CULTURE, IDENTITY, LANGUAGE AND COMMUNICATION

If you are interested in doing further reading on approaches to researching culture, identity, language and communication the following titles are recommended:

Alasuutari, P. (1995) *Researching Culture: Qualitative Method and Cultural Studies*. London: Sage.

Atkinson, P., Coffey, A., Delamont, S., Lofland, J. and Lofland, L. (eds) (2001) *Handbook of Ethnography*. London: Sage.

Brewer, J. D. (2000) *Ethnography*. Buckingham: Open University.

Byrd Clark, J. S. and Dervin, F. (eds) (2014) *Reflexivity in Language and Intercultural Education*. Abingdon: Routledge.

Coffey, A. (1999) *The Ethnographic Self: Fieldwork and the Representation of Identity*. London: Sage.

De Walt, K. M. and De Walt, B. R. (2002) *Participant Observation: A Guide for Fieldworkers*. Walnut Creek, Ca: AltaMira Press.

Flick, U. (2006: 3rd edn) *An Introduction to Qualitative Research*. London: Sage.

Gray, A. (2003) *Research Practice for Cultural Studies: Ethnographic Methods and Lived Cultures*. London: Sage.

Holliday, A. R. (2007: 2nd edn) *Doing and Writing Qualitative Research*. London: Sage.

Kaplan-Wenger, J. and Ullman, C. (2015) *Methods for the Ethnography of Communication: Language in Use in Schools and Communities*. Abingdon: Routledge.

Lindlof, T. R. and Taylor, B. C. (2011: 3rd edn) *Qualitative Communication Research Methods*. London: Sage.

Pickering, M. (2008) *Research Methods for Cultural Studies*. Edinburgh: Edinburgh University Press.

Roberts, C., Byram, M., Barro, A., Jordon, S. and Street, B. (2001) *Language Learners as Ethnographers*. Clevedon: Multilingual Matters.

Taylor, S. (ed.) (2002) *Ethnographic Research: A Reader*. London: Sage/Open University.

INFORMATION TECHNOLOGY, CULTURE, REPRESENTATION AND COMMUNICATION

If you are interested in doing further reading on the impact of information technology on 'culture', representation and communication the following titles are recommended:

Jenks, C. (2014) *Social Interaction in Second Language Chatrooms*. Edinburgh: Edinburgh University Press.

Jones, A. (2006) *Self/Image: Technology, Representation and the Contemporary Subject*. London: Routledge.

Lewis, T. and O'Dowd, R. (2016) *Online Intercultural Exchange: Policy, Pedagogy, Practice*. Abingdon: Routledge.

Wood, A. F. and Smith, M. J. (2005: 2nd edn) *Online Communication: Linking Technology, Culture and Identity*. Mahwah, N.J.: Lawrence Erlbaum.

GLOBALISATION, CULTURE, AND IDENTITY

If you are interested in doing further reading on globalisation, culture and identity, the following titles are recommended:

Beck, U. (2000) *What is Globalization?* Cambridge: Polity Press.
Featherstone, M. (1995) *Undoing Culture: Globalization, Postmodernism, and Identity.* London: Sage.
Friedman, J. (1994) *Culture, Identity and Global Process.* London: Sage.
Held, D. (ed.) (2000) *A Globalizing World?* Abingdon: Routledge.
King, A. D. (ed.) (1991) *Culture, Globalization and the World-system.* New York: Palgrave.
Tomlinson, J. (1999) *Globalization and Culture.* Cambridge: Polity Press.

If you are interested in doing further reading on consumption and identity, the following titles are recommended:

Bourdieu, P. (1984) *Distinction: A Social Critique of the Judgement of Taste.* London: Routledge and Kegan Paul.
Gabriel, Y. and T. Lang (1995) *The Unmanageable Consumer: Contemporary Consumption and Its Fragmentations.* London: Sage.

'CULTURE' IN THE SOCIAL SCIENCES

If you are interested in doing further reading on the concept of 'culture' in the social sciences, the following titles are recommended:

Baldwin, J. R., Faulkner, S. L., Hecht, M. L. and Lindsley, S.L. (eds) (2006) *Redefining Culture: Perspectives Across the Disciplines.* Mahwah, N.J.: Lawrence Erlbaum.
Clifford, J. and Marcus, G. E. (1986) *Writing Culture: The Poetics and Politics of Ethnography.* Berkeley, California: University of California Press.
Fay, B. (1996) *A Contemporary Philosophy of Social Science.* Oxford: Blackwell.
Geertz, C. (1973) *The Interpretation of Cultures.* New York: Basic Books.
Smith, M. J. (1998) *Culture: Reinventing the Social Sciences.* London: Sage/Open University.

OTHERING

An accessible introduction to othering is:

Pickering, M. (2001) *Stereotyping: The Politics of Representation.* Basingstoke: Palgrave.

Key texts on notions of 'the Other' and othering are as follows:

Bhabha, H. K. (1994) *The Location of Culture.* London: Routledge.
Fanon, F. (1967) *Black Skin, White Mask.* London: Pluto Press.
Hallam, E. and Street, B. (eds) (2000) *Cultural Encounters: Representing 'Otherness'.* London: Routledge.

Law, I. (2010) *Racism and Ethnicity: Global Debates, Dilemmas, Directions.* Harlow: Longman Pearson.

Mernissi, F. (2001) *Scheherazade goes West: Different Cultures, Different Harems.* New York: Washington Square Press.

Jervis, J. (1999) *Transgressing the Modern: Explorations in the Western Experience of Otherness.* Oxford: Blackwell.

Said, E. (1978) *Orientalism.* New York: Random House.

Said, E. (1993) *Culture and Imperialism.* London: Vintage.

Wetherell, M. and Potter, J. (1992) *Mapping the Language of Racism: Discourse and the Legitimation of Exploitation* London: Harvester Wheatsheaf.

Notions of 'the Other' and othering are also central in literature on postcolonialism. Accessible introductions to postcolonialism include:

Loomba, A. (1997) *Colonialism/Postcolonialism.* London: Routledge.

Young, R. C. (2002) *Postcolonialism: A Very Short Introduction.* Oxford: Oxford University Press.

Other recommended books on postcolonialism include the following.

Ansell-Pearson, K. Parry, B. and Squires, J. (eds) (1997) *Cultural Readings of Imperialism: Edward Said and the Gravity of History.* London: Lawrence and Wishart.

hooks, b. (1992) *Black Looks: Race and Representation.* Boston, Mass.: South End Press.

Moore-Gilbert, B. (1997) *Postcolonial Theory: Contexts, Practices, Politics.* London: Verso.

Pennycook, A. (1998) *English and the Discourse of Colonialism.* London: Routledge.

Williams, P. and Chrisman, L. (eds) (1993) *Colonial Discourse and Post-Colonial Theory.* London: Routledge.

Discussions of Othering are also to be found in texts on race and racism. Collections of previously published papers and book extracts on race and racism include the following:

Back, L. and Solomos, J. (eds) (2000) *Theories of Race and Racism.* London: Routledge.

Cashmore, E. and Jennings, J. (eds) (2001) *Racism: Essential Readings.* London: Sage.

Fine, M. et al. (1997) *Off White: Readings on Race, Power and Society.* London: Routledge.

A book that focuses specifically on this role of discourse in othering is:

Wetherell, M. and Potter, J. (1992) *Discourse and the Legitimation of Exploitation.* New York: Columbia University Press.

Processes of Othering in the mass media are discussed in the following:

Cottle, S. (ed.) (2000) *Ethnic Minorities and the Media.* Buckingham: Open University Press.

Spears, A. K. (ed.) (1999) *Race and Ideology; Language, Symbolism, and Popular Culture.* Detroit: Wayne State University Press.

Van Dijk, T. A. (1991) *Racism and the Press.* London: Routledge.

REPRESENTATION

Accessible introductions to representation are:

Hall, S. (ed.) (1997) *Representation: Cultural Representations and Signifying Practices*. London: Sage/Open University.
Spencer, S. (2014: 2nd edn) *Race and Ethnicity: Culture, Identity and Representation*. Abingdon: Routledge.

If you are interested in doing further reading on representation in the mass media, the following are recommended:

Allan, S. (1999) *News Culture*. Milton Keynes: Open University.
Bell, A. and Garrett, P. (eds) (1998) *Approaches to Media Discourse*. Oxford: Blackwell.
Bignell, M. (1997) *Media Semiotics*. Manchester: University of Manchester Press.
Fairclough, N. (1995) *Media Discourse*. London: Edward Arnold.
Van Ginneken, J. (1998) *Understanding Global News*. London: Sage.

Collections of previously published papers and book extracts on representation in the mass media include the following:

Boyd-Barrett, O. and Newbold, C. (eds) (1995) *Approaches to Media: A Reader*. London: Arnold.
Marris, P. and Thornham, S. (eds) (1996) *Media Studies: A Reader*. Edinburgh: University of Edinburgh Press.
O'Sullivan, T. and Jewkes, Y. (eds) (1997) *The Media Studies Reader*. London: Arnold.

If you are interested in reading more about visual representation, the following are recommended:

Kress, G. and Van Leeuwen, T. (1996) *Reading Images: The Grammar of Visual Design*. London: Routledge.
Kress, G. and Van Leeuwen, T. (2001) *Multimodal Discourse: The Modes and Media of Contemporary Communication*. London: Arnold.
Mirzoeff, N. (ed.) (1998) *The Visual Culture Reader*. London: Routledge.
Pink, S. (2000) *Doing Visual Ethnography: Images, Media, and Representation in Research*. London: Sage.
Rose, G. (2001) *Visual Methodologies: An Introduction to the Interpretation of Visual Materials*. London: Sage.

If you are interested in representation in advertising, the following are recommended:

Goffman, E. (1979) *Gender Advertisements*. Basingstoke: Macmillan.
Messaris, P. (1997) *Visual Persuasion: The Role of Images in Advertising*. London: Sage.
Williamson, J. (1978) *Decoding Advertisements: Ideology and Meaning in Advertising*. London: Marion Boyars.

If you are interested in issues of culture, representation and Othering in travel and tourism, the following are recommended:

Pickard, D. and di Giovone, M.A. (2014) *Tourism and the Power of Otherness: Seductions of Difference*. Bristol: Channel View Publications.

Selwyn, T. (1996) *The Tourist Image*. Chichester: John Wiley.

Urry, J. (1990) *The Tourist Gaze*. London: Sage.

SOCIAL CONSTRUCTIONISM

In addition to Burr (1996), an accessible introduction to social constructionism is:

Gergen, K. J. (1999) *An Invitation to Social Construction*. London: Sage.

If you are interested in doing further reading on social constructionism, the following are recommended:

Berger, P. L. and Luckmann, T. (1966*) The Social Construction of Knowledge: A Treatise in the Sociology of Knowledge*. Harmondsworth: Penguin.

Gergen, K. J. (2001) *Social Constructionism in Context*. London: Sage.

Potter, J. (1996) *Representing Reality: Discourse, Rhetoric and Social Construction*. London: Sage.

If you are interested in reading further on social representations, the following are recommended:

Flick, U. (ed.) (1998) *The Psychology of the Social*. Cambridge: Cambridge University Press.

Moloney, G. and Walker, I. (eds) (2007) *Social Representations and Identity: Content, Process and Power*. New York: Palgrave Macmillan.

Moscovici, S. (2000) *Social Representations: Explorations in Social Psychology*. London: Sage.

INTERCULTURAL EDUCATION AND TRAINING

If you are interested in doing further reading on intercultural education and training, the following titles are recommended:

Alred, G., Byram, M. and Fleming, M. (eds) (2003) *Intercultural Experience and Education*. Clevedon: Multilingual Matters.

Berardo, K and D.K. Deardorff (eds) (2012) *Building Cultural Competence*. Sterling, Virginia: Stylus.

Boyacigiller, N. A, Goodman, R. A. and Phillips, M. E. (2004) *Crossing Cultures: Insights from Master Teachers*. London: Routledge.

Byram, M. (1997) *Teaching and Assessing Intercultural Communicative Competence*. Clevedon: Multilingual Matters.

Byram, M., Nichols, A. and Stevens, D. (eds) (2001) *Developing Intercultural Competence in Practice* Clevedon: Multilingual Matters.

Deardoff, D. K. (ed.) (2009) *The Sage Handbook of Intercultural Competence*. London: Sage.

Dervin, F. and Liddicoat, A. (2013) *Linguistics for Intercultural Education*. Amsterdam: John Benjamins.

Earley P. C., Ang, S. and Tan, J.-S. (2006) *CQ: Developing Cultural Intelligence at Work*. Stanford: Stanford University Press.

Feng, A., Byram, M. and Fleming, M. (eds) (2009) *Becoming Interculturally Competent through Education and Training*. Clevedon: Multilingual Matters.

Fowler, S. and Mumford, M. (eds) (1995) *Intercultural Sourcebook Vol. 1*. Boston: Intercultural Press.

Fowler, S. and Mumford, M. (eds) (1999) *Intercultural Sourcebook Vol. 2*. Boston: Intercultural Press.

Hogan, C. (2007) *Facilitating Multicultural Groups: A Practical Guide*. London: Kogan Page.

Landis, D., Bennett, J. M. and Bennett, M. J. (eds) (2004) *Handbook of Intercultural Training*. London: Sage.

Marginson, S. and Sawir, E. (2011) *Ideas for Intercultural Education*. Basingstoke: Palgrave Macmillan.

Ting-Toomey, S. and Oetzel, J. (2001) *Managing Intercultural Conflict Effectively*. London: Sage.

Index